Contents

JOURNALS AND ABBREVIATIONS   vii

INTRODUCTION   1

Part I: Social Science Perspectives

1. Who Are Basic Writers?
   Andrea Lunsford and Patricia A. Sullivan   17

2. Developmental Psychology and Basic Writers
   Donna Haisty Winchell   31

3. Literacy Theory and Basic Writing
   Mariolina Salvatori and Glynda Hull   49

Part II: Linguistic Perspectives

4. Modern Grammar and Basic Writers
   Ronald F. Lunsford   77

5. Dialects and Basic Writers
   Michael Montgomery   95

6. TESL Research and Basic Writing
   Sue Render   117

Part III: Pedagogical Perspectives

7. Basic Writing Courses and Programs
   Michael D. Hood   143

8. Computers and Writing Instruction
   Stephen A. Bernhardt and Patricia G. Wojahn   165

9. Writing Laboratories and Basic Writing
   Donna Beth Nelson   191

10. Preparing Teachers of Basic Writing
    Richard A. Filloy   207

   APPENDIX: Selective Bibliography of Basic Writing Textbooks
   Mary Sue Ply   221

   NAME INDEX   239

   SUBJECT INDEX   249

   ABOUT THE CONTRIBUTORS   257

Journals and Abbreviations

ADE Bul	Association of Departments of English Bulletin
Adult Ed Q	Adult Education Quarterly
AEB	Arizona English Bulletin
Africa	Africa
Am Schol	The American Scholar
Anthro Ed Q	Anthropology and Education Quarterly
CCC	College Composition and Communication
CE	College English
Change Mag	Change Magazine
Chron Higher Ed	Chronicle of Higher Education
CLAJ	College Language Association Journal
Class Comp L	Classroom Computer Learning
Coll Micro	Collegiate Microcomputer
Comm Ed	Communication Education
Comp Comp	Computers and Composition
Comp Hum	Computers and the Humanities
Compute	Compute!
Conn Eng J	Connecticut English Journal
Cur Inq	Curriculum Inquiry
Dev Psych	Developmental Psychology
Educ Eval Pol Anal	Educational Evaluation and Policy Analysis
Educ Tech	Educational Technology

EE	English Education
EJ	English Journal
Engl Lang Teach J	English Language Teaching Journal
FEN	Freshman English News
Flor For L Rep	Florida Foreign Language Reporter
Focus	Focus: Teaching English Language Arts
Harvard Engl Stud	Harvard English Studies
HER	Harvard Educational Review
Human Dev	Human Development
Info Tech Ed	Information Technology and Education
Int J Instr Med	International Journal of Instructional Media
IRAL	International Review of Applied Linguistics in Language Teaching
JBW	Journal of Basic Writing
J Ed Tech S	Journal of Educational Technology Systems
J Educ	Journal of Education
J Exp Educ	Journal of Experimental Education
J Inst Psych	Journal of Instructional Psychology
J Negro Ed	Journal of Negro Education
J Psychol	Journal of Psychology
J Res Dev Ed	Journal of Research and Development in Education
J Teach Writ	Journal of Teaching Writing
JTWC	Journal of Technical Writing and Communication
J Youth Ado	Journal of Youth and Adolescence
Lang Arts	Language Arts
Lang L	Language Learning
Lit Disc	Literacy Discussion
Mod Lang J	Modern Language Journal
New Dir Comm Coll	New Directions for Community Colleges
New Inter	New Internationalist
P/T	PRE/TEXT
Prospects	Prospects
Rev Ed Res	Review of Educational Research
RR	Rhetoric Review
RTE	Research in the Teaching of English
Sat Rev	Saturday Review
Science	Science
Soc Pol	Social Policy

Stud Lang L	Studies in Language Learning
TESOL Q	Teachers of English to Speakers of Other Languages Quarterly
TETYC	Teaching English in the Two Year College
WCJ	The Writing Center Journal
WI	The Writing Instructor
W J Bl Studies	Western Journal of Black Studies
WCJ	The Writing Center Journal
WLN	Writing Lab Newsletter

RESEARCH IN BASIC WRITING

Introduction

That basic writing is now an important subdiscipline within the larger area of rhetoric and composition cannot be denied. What is surprising is that it took so many years for scholars to turn their attention to the problem of extremely weak student writers. This fact is particularly surprising when we consider that, as the professional literature suggests, teachers had long recognized the existence of students unprepared or unable to write effectively enough to complete high school and college work successfully. Too often, however, these students were dismissed as lazy, nonverbal, slow, or even retarded and were given little attention beyond a grammar-based "bonehead" English course designed to teach them to produce grammatically correct sentences and structurally competent paragraphs. In the 1940s and 1950s, it became common to call the students in such bonehead courses "subfreshmen," a term that paralleled, we assume, "subhuman."

Attitudes toward these students changed during the 1960s and 1970s. The egalitarian spirit of equal opportunity brought many so-called nontraditional students to American colleges and universities. Because of affirmative action and other such government programs, schools began actively to recruit minorities, many of whom came from rich oral traditions that did not emphasize the written word. At the same time, American secondary education, due to a variety of influences, began graduating students of all races and backgrounds less prepared for advanced academic work than students of previous generations had been. Colleges, which had once admitted only a select and homogeneous group of reasonably well-prepared students, found themselves forced to address the needs of the unprepared and the disadvantaged. If these students were to have any chance of graduating, they would need intensive training in areas such as mathematics, reading, and writing before they could successfully take college-level courses. Responsible universities met their obligations to such students by developing precollege programs. One school that did so was the City College of New York, which in the early 1970s developed its SEEK program to develop in its nontraditional students the skills needed to complete college work. To head up the writing segment of SEEK, it hired Mina Shaughnessy, who became and in many ways remains the central figure in basic writing, the field that she did much to define and legitimate. The current volume of bibliographical essays is a direct outgrowth of her work because it attempts to outline some of the central issues associated with teaching the unprepared writer.

Since Shaughnessy's pioneering work in the early to mid–1970s, there has developed a body of seminal texts that provide teachers of basic writers more support than they have had in the past. While these books are largely on the level of anecdote and description, and hence do not qualify as research in the empirical sense of that term, they do address many of the practical and some of the philosophical questions that teachers should consider when planning and teaching basic writing courses. We would like to begin by discussing some of the key texts within this canon to suggest its wealth as well as its limitations.

THE DEVELOPING CANON

Mina Shaughnessy had much to do with encouraging the acceptance of basic writing as a distinct area of teaching and research. She named the field and founded in 1975 the *Journal of Basic Writing*, which continues as one of the most important vehicles for the dissemination of research articles. In 1977, she published one of the most important scholarly books on the subject, *Errors and Expectations*, a book that remains the most important single study of basic writers and their prose. The book is important for many reasons, but we will point out three central ones. First, it is the first long study to look sympathetically at basic writers and their problems. Rather than viewing them as immature, unsuccessful, inarticulate failures, Shaughnessy recognized them as adults who possessed an impressive command of at least some forms of language and who were often successful in other parts of their lives. Many were masters of the spoken word who had not yet developed matching skills in the written. Second, Shaughnessy took these students' writing problems seriously enough to examine carefully the kinds of errors they made in their papers in order to discover underlying patterns and powerful explanations for these errors. Using the new methodologies of error analysis being developed in applied linguistics, she argued that teachers could examine errors in order to discover how writers misunderstood and therefore misapplied the rules of written discourse. In other words, one of the values of her book is that she showed teachers how they could, by viewing errors as linguistic misconceptions, determine the causes of writing problems that on the surface might appear confusing and unconnected. Third, *Errors and Expectations* advances many pedagogical strategies that teachers can apply in the classroom to help basic writers recognize their linguistic misconceptions and to learn to apply linguistic and rhetorical principles to write more effectively.

Since Shaughnessy's untimely death in 1978, a number of book-length studies have appeared that contribute to the definition and development of the field. One of the first of these was *Basic Writing* (1980), a collection of essays edited by Lawrence N. Kasden and Daniel R. Hoeber. This volume addressed a diverse group of educators concerned with basic writing instruction: trainers of teachers, curriculum planners, program administrators, and researchers. To meet these diverse needs, the book falls into five sections. The first, called "The Basic Writer," contains Sondra Perl's important essay entitled "A Look at Basic Writers in the Process of Composing" (13–32), which argues that these students spend little time prewriting and begin editing too soon. The second section examines four successful basic writing programs. Section 3 discusses the question of developing placement tests for these students, and section 4 presents essays concerned with training teachers of basic writing and with staffing and operating writing centers using peer tutors. The final section addresses questions of interest to the researcher and contains an extensive but unannotated bibliography (164–73). If the volume now appears a little thin, we should remember that only ten or so years ago basic writing was still in its initial stages of definition and that this volume helped define it more clearly.

A second important early book was Harvey S. Wiener's *The Writing Room* (1981), which is a practical, hands-on discussion of teaching basic writers. As Wiener states in his introduction, the book addresses the needs of the beginning teacher placed in the basic writing classroom; consequently, its advice might seem obvious to experienced teachers. The book's strength, however, is that it offers workable, practical strategies for dealing with some of the problems basic writers and their teachers face. For instance, in his first chapter he addresses questions about what to do the first day, how to set up the physical environment of the room, how to walk students through the writing process, what comments to write on finished papers, and what to do in class when returning papers. The book also contains chapters on teaching the paragraph, diction, spelling, grammar, and sentence manipulation; on support services such as writing centers and student-teacher conferences; on ways to test writing abilities; and on the relationship between basic writing and other parts of the curriculum. If this book at times appears rigid—emphasizing form over matter, for instance—it makes up for this weakness in the specificity of advice and the years of experience condensed within its covers.

A more recent book providing an excellent introduction to the teaching of basic writing is Marcia Farr and Harvey Daniels's *Language Diversity and Writing Instruction* (1986). Though short, this volume provides an accessible overview of research from linguistics and contemporary composition theory and pedagogy as they relate to basic writing instruction.

By reviewing modern linguistic theory, the authors establish some principles of language with which basic writing teachers should be familiar. Like all humans, basic writers possess linguistic competence because they know how to speak and have internalized the complex system of rules of their native language. Many such students, however, speak a particular dialect that is similar to (in many respects) but distinct from standard English, the form of the language used in most reading and writing done in school. Farr and Daniels note, however, that there is substantial variation with dialects; consequently, teachers must be careful to recognize that no student will use a nonstandard dialect with perfect consistency. Furthermore, students will vary their dialects according to situational contexts, speaking more or less formally depending on audience and place. Even though such students might occasionally use the rules of standard English, this does not mean that they know them. Therefore, one of the teachers' primary duties when working with writers of nonstandard dialects is to help such students undergo "a substantial shift, or change in one's 'home' linguistic system, toward the features of standard English" (35). The authors thereby reject the arguments for bidialectalism, the view that students can and should be encouraged to master two dialects, their own and standard English. This shift that Farr and Daniels advocate does not come easily because dialects are deeply embedded systems that resist change due to linguistic and cultural factors.

While Farr and Daniels spend the first half of their book discussing linguistic theory, they do not advocate the use of traditional workbook instruction in grammar and mechanics to help basic writers master standard English. Instead, in the second half they review contemporary research to develop fifteen principles of successful writing instruction. Their approach is largely rhetorical rather than grammatical because they assume that basic writers, like all students learning to write, must learn first to create meaning before turning to matters of correctness. Teachers should begin by helping them develop fluency by allowing them to write often and to write to significant audiences. Grammar and mechanics are best taught by means of sentence combining and within the context of actual compositions. Students should learn to revise essays, and teachers should offer comments to facilitate the development of abilities in this area. While teachers familiar with recent research in composition and rhetoric will find these fifteen principles familiar, Farr and Daniels make an important contribution to basic writing instruction by emphasizing that these students too must be encouraged to write meaningful discourse.

Another new study that develops a rhetorical approach to teaching basic writers is Donald L. Rubin and William M. Dodd's *Talking into Writing* (1987). This volume develops its approach from two major assumptions. First, basic writers have trouble writing not because they are linguistically naive but because they are unfamiliar with the conventions of written discourse. Coming from oral-based cultures, many of these writers often have had little experience reading and writing; therefore, they have not internalized the conventions of the written code. Second, many of these writers have not developed the rhetorical skills needed to write well. They lack the experience and abilities to decenter from their own points of view in order to understand the views of others, and they lack the skills necessary to focus, develop, and expand their ideas in writing. Given these difficulties, Rubin and Dodd develop a series of exercises that are rhetorically sound and that draw on basic writers' command of oral communication. Their series includes (1) role-switching activities that require students to play four different roles and to assume four different perspectives on a controversial topic; (2) peer-questioning activities that require students to pair up and assist each other in planning their papers; (3) topic-sculpting activities that require students to personalize and focus a supplied topic in an impromptu speech before intimate and larger groups; and (4) forensic-discussion activities that divide the class into two groups to debate policy or situational issues. All four activities draw on the students' oral communication skills and help them develop rhetorical skills within social contexts. The volume is particularly useful because it provides a bibliography and sample exercises as well as advice on using the activities.

These first four books are marked by a concern for defining a new field and for developing methods for teaching basic writers to write apart from mastering other skills. Recently, the field has shifted its emphasis away from viewing writing as an isolated act; the field has become more interested in the relationship between reading and writing. One of the first books to recognize this change is Marie Ponsot and Rosemary Deen's *Beat Not the Poor Desk* (1982), which is one of the most thoroughly realized approaches to basic writing developed to date. Like most of the best work being done in the field, this book argues that these students should not spend their valuable class time completing contextless grammar and mechanical exercises; instead, students should spend their time mastering the ''elemental'' skills of rhetoric that they can develop through reading and writing. Ponsot and Deen consider their teaching method inductive because they develop assignments designed to help students master these elemental writing skills through direct engagement with the reading and writing processes. To accomplish this goal, they advocate the development of five particular skills: the abilities to write prolifically; to use whole structures (many of them abstracted from traditional literary types); to make direct observations distinct from forming inferences or conclusions; to write both concretely and abstractly while being able to move back and forth between these two perceptual planes; and to rewrite and edit drafts.

One of the elemental skills that the authors emphasize most consistently is the structural one, and they develop numerous assignments that help basic writers gain a sense of structure. For instance, they borrow from the *progymnasmata* of ancient Greece models such as the fable and the parable in order to teach basic writers to move from concrete narratives to abstract maxims or morals. Such models, which in part continue the rich oral traditions many students enjoy, not only help basic writers distinguish between details and abstractions, but also encourage them to draw on their oral repertoires and linguistic strengths. The authors also develop simple expository structures that are tied closely to student experience. For instance, they use what they call structures of coordination and subordination to teach exposition. An example of a coordinate structure would be set up by the following kernel sentence that would give rise to a bipartite essay: "Once I was _____ ; now I am _____ " (71). A sample structure of subordination would be the "Essay of Hindsight," set up by the following kernel: "When I saw the fork in the road just ahead in my life, I chose this _____ instead of that _____ " (93). Each kernel sentence contains within it an implied structure, an intellectual and organizational strategy for exploring a personal topic. While some teachers might object to their clichéd nature, these sentences and the topics residing in them engage students' interests by tapping into what appear to be cultural and literary structures familiar to many basic writers. Such models, the authors claim, program the students to success rather than failure.

Another book that emphasizes the reading-writing connection is *Facts, Artifacts and Counterfacts* (1986) by David Bartholomae and Anthony Petrosky. By emphasizing this connection, the authors point to new ways of teaching beginning writers to use language. Unlike Ponsot and Deen, however, who emphasize for the most part personal writing, Bartholomae and Petrosky teach students to use the language of the university. To be able to read and write this language, they argue, students must be empowered to construct the kinds of meanings appropriate to the academic world. When students begin to understand this world and assume necessary authority over their reading and writing, they will be able to participate in the kind of academic discourse that instructors expect of them. To help them develop this kind of authority, Bartholomae and Petrosky offer a series of reading and writing assignments on the subject of growth and change in adolescence that students write on all semester. One of the important contributions of the book is the elaborate set of course materials—readings, assignments, journal entries, and so forth—that they use in Basic Reading and Writing, the basic studies seminar they have been offering at the University of Pittsburgh for over a decade.

Facts, Artifacts and Counterfacts is important for three reasons, First, it questions the traditional assumptions of basic writing pedagogy that view reading and writing as separate activities to be taught in different departments on the remedial level. In order to write academic prose, students must learn to read and interact with reading in the sophisticated ways the academy demands. Reductionist approaches that teach students to find topic sentences and examine connecting words do not teach the sophisticated reading skills students need to master in college. Second, the book also questions the common assumption that basic writers learn to read and write by completing exercises and drills. As do most of the books in the basic writing canon, this one rejects the skills model, replacing it with an approach that requires students to learn to read and write by doing so under the guidance of an experienced academician. Third, the book argues for an integrated curriculum, set up as a small seminar, that encourages basic studies students to participate in the give and take of academic dialectic. By experiencing the discussions, the readings, and the writings associated with academic life, the authors assume, students will become fuller participants in the learned community and master its conventions. While Bartholomae and Petrosky offer little evidence beyond the anecdotal that their methods achieve these goals, the goals themselves are laudable, and the book offers a significant contribution to the debate about teaching basic writers.

Because basic writers often have idiosyncratic problems in their writing, the individual tutorial has always been an important pedagogical tool when working with them. Several books have appeared recently that discuss the conference and small group work, including Muriel Harris's *Teaching One-to-One* (1986) and Anne Ruggles Gere's *Writing Groups* (1987), but the best book for basic writing instructors is Emily Meyer and Louise Z. Smith's *The Practical Tutor* (1987). This volume contains the most detailed discussions of running tutorials we have found. It is particularly strong on demonstrating ways that tutors, even peer tutors, can ask questions to help writers develop fluency and analytical skills. It also has excellent chapters on tutoring basic skills, including sentence-level, punctuation, spelling, and vocabulary problems, and it contains a very strong chapter on tutoring students with dialect problems. The book is notable because it integrates the practical with the theoretical, rooting its practical advice in the current research in composition and rhetoric. While some of the sample tutorial dialogues appear to be idealizations of actual tutorials, many of them are masterful examples of tutors leading writers toward self-consciousness about their writing and its effect on an experienced reader.

One of the most elegant arguments for the individualized approach is Mike Rose's new book, *Lives on the Boundary* (1989). Part autobiography about Rose's own intellectual development, part attack on traditional notions of remediation, this book argues that teaching beginning readers and writers requires a mentoring process in which the teacher-tutor connects personally with the students. Using this personal connection as a base, the instructor can help students enter the world of academic discourse. Rose offers numerous case studies to demonstrate the power of his approach, while at the same time he warns that progress is often slow and fitful. Because of the humanistic assumptions of his approach, he argues against reductionist methods that emphasize correctness alone, calling instead, as do Bartholomae and Petrosky, for engaging students in academic discourse and discourse about that discourse. The book is particularly powerful because Rose draws on his own experiences as a poor child growing up in Los Angeles and being misdiagnosed as a slow student when entering secondary school. He understands basic writers from the inside.

We will end this part of our discussion by citing the single most important collection of essays in the field, *A Sourcebook for Basic Writing Teachers* (1987), which is edited by Theresa Enos with help from Lynn Quitman Troyka, David Bartholomae, and Andrea A. Lunsford. This impressive collection of essays, many of them reprinted from scholarly journals, some others written especially for this volume, addresses the most important issues of interest to both teachers and researchers. Although we might quibble with essays not included—for instance, David Bartholomae's classic ''The Study of Error'' appears only in the bibliography, the book defines basic writing as it is conceived by many of the best scholars and teachers now working in the field. Because many of these essays are discussed in the bibliographical essays to follow, we will not discuss them in detail here.

BIBLIOGRAPHIES

Most of the books we have surveyed contain excellent bibliographies, but these bibliographies are usually either annotated lightly or not at all. Some of the most useful of these are Sally Harrold's bibliographies appended to Enos's *Sourcebook* (1987). While the bibliographies of books and monographs (594–602) and of dissertations (603–11) are unannotated and therefore difficult to use, the third listing, "Annotated Bibliography of Articles on Basic Writing" (612), includes brief annotations of important articles published in the field. Similarly, Erika Lindemann's *The Longman Bibliography of Composition and Rhetoric* (1984–85; 1986), which promises to be a yearly listing of publications in composition and rhetoric, contains a section on basic writing with lightly annotated citations.

The first significant bibliography devoted to basic writing was Mina Shaughnessy's "Basic Writing," an essay published in Gary Tate's *Teaching Composition* (1976) and reprinted in the revised and enlarged edition in 1987 (177–206) with Andrea Lunsford's "An Update of the Bibliography on Basic Writing" (207–26). While Shaughnessy's essay is important because it defines basic writing and analyzes the state of scholarship at the time, it also demonstrates that little important work had as yet been completed. Lunsford's update is far richer in terms of material available to cite, and this change indicates the increasing amount of research now being conducted in the field.

A second and more extensive bibliography concerned largely with the teaching of basic writing appears in *Research in Composition and Rhetoric* (1984) edited by Michael G. Moran and Ronald F. Lunsford. Entitled "The Basics" (266–450), the third section of the book contains seven extensive bibliographic essays devoted to topics of interest to basic writing teachers and researchers, beginning with Glynda A. Hull and David J. Bartholomae's "Basic Writing" (265–302). This essay is followed by reviews of the research on the sentence, on spelling, on vocabulary development, on punctuation, on usage, and on the paragraph.

THE PRESENT VOLUME

The present volume continues the work of "The Basics" section of Moran and Lunsford's *Research in Composition and Rhetoric* (1984). Unlike the earlier volume, which concentrates for the most part on specific pedagogical issues associated with basic writing, this one examines the field of basic writing from three general theoretical perspectives.

The first of these views basic writing through the lens of the social sciences, concentrating on social, psychological and political perspectives on the field. In the first chapter in this section, "Who Are Basic Writers?" Andrea Lunsford and Patricia A. Sullivan reject the notion that basic writers are those students whom we place in basic writing classes. However, the research does not support the view that basic writers come from any single social class or discourse community, nor does it support the notion that basic writers lack cognitive development. Their backgrounds are too complex and rich to support simple generalizations about class and psychology to be particularly useful in helping us understand these students. A third approach to define basic writers, Lunsford and Sullivan argue, is the research growing out of Shaughnessy's seminal work that has examined basic writers' prose, but even this work has led to contradictory results. Errors in basic writers' prose cannot easily be analyzed because it, like the students themselves, manifests a "rich diversity" that defies pigeonholing.

In the second chapter in the first part, Donna Haisty Winchell examines the research in developmental psychology to determine what insights this field offers to our understanding of basic writers and how we might best teach them. Reviewing the research using a Piagetian frame, Winchell concludes that, though we lack a "systematic delineation" of what cognitive psychology can teach us about the writing process in general and about teaching basic writers in particular, there has been a considerable amount of interest in the application of psychological research in cognition and problem solving to the field of basic writing.

In the third chapter in this section, Mariolina Salvatori and Glynda Hull review the research on literacy theory and basic writing. They reject the notion that literacy is value free, arguing instead that literacy and its development are deeply rooted within political institutions and cultural assumptions. Literacy campaigns are always political, and these campaigns, the authors argue, are often designed to achieve social control over classes and groups. Therefore, Salvatori and Hull question the belief that making basic writers literate will offer them social mobility and access to the benefits of class. The authors also argue that basic writers suffer from restrictive definitions of literacy that emphasize literacy as a series of skills, the learning of the mechanics of reading and writing, for instance. In place of such restrictive definitions, they suggest that we recognize that literacy is a way to view ourselves, our experiences, and our languages. It is more a way of being than a mechanics of processing and communicating information.

The second major part of the book views basic writing from linguistic perspectives. In the first chapter under this division, Ronald F. Lunsford examines the contributions of modern grammar to our understanding of basic writers and their prose, arguing that grammar is central to an effective approach to basic writing. Whether that grammar should be traditional grammar has been debated for many years, with the bulk of the empirical evidence suggesting that teaching students traditional grammar probably does not improve writing skills. Even tagmemics, the form of structural grammar that has been most influential in recent composition theory, has not been used much with basic writers. However, generative-transformational grammar, with its emphasis on the competence-per-formance distinction, has proven itself far more fruitful, especially in the form of sentence combining; furthermore, the relatively new field of discourse analysis has helped teachers and researchers develop new ways to analyze student texts. Both of these systems, Lunsford argues, are helping to contribute to an evolving definition of basic writing.

In the next chapter, "Dialects and Basic Writers," Michael Montgomery addresses the various meanings scholars have given to the term "dialect" as well as the various degrees of importance the study of dialects has received in the field of basic writing. Montgomery argues that although the number of writing problems caused by dialect interference is small, the attention given to them is well deserved for these three reasons: dialect forms stigmatize the user as a "non-standard" speaker and writer; an emphasis on dialect forms tends to produce basic writing classes made up mainly of minority students; and the errors attributable to dialects seem resistant to traditional means of error correction. Regarding the first reason, Montgomery reports that, since "no one writes the way he or she speaks," we must be careful in our predictions of how a person will write on the basis of how the person speaks. Regarding the second reason, Montgomery reports on the political repercussions of bidialectalism, particularly James Sledd's concerns about racial and political repression and Thomas Farrell's responses to Sledd. Regarding the pedagogical reason, Montgomery encourages using advances in ESL (English as a second language) instruction and redirecting attention from mechanics to theme development and overall coherence.

The third chapter on linguistics and basic writing is Sue Render's "TESL Research and Basic Writing," which argues that research on English as a second language is useful to basic writing teachers because learning academic English is similar in many ways to learning a new dialect. Render discusses concepts such as contrastive analysis and error analysis that, after being developed by ESL specialists, have become important in basic writing research. She also discusses concepts such as interlanguage and contrastive rhetoric that have not yet been widely used in basic writing research. Because basic writing teachers and teachers of ESL face many of the same problems, Render's essay is a rich source of approaches developed by applied linguists that might prove useful to basic writing researchers and specialists.

The final section of the volume addresses four loosely related but important issues in basic writing from the pedagogical perspective. In the first of these, "Basic Writing Courses and Programs," Michael D. Hood explores the issues associated with designing, developing, administering, and evaluating basic writing courses and programs. The research on assessing students suggests that they can be tested before entering the program (placement), at the beginning of the course (diagnosis), and at the end of the course (proficiency). He also distinguishes between two kinds of basic writing courses, the analytic and the synthetic or holistic. Analytic courses assume that students must be taught discrete skills while the newer, holistic courses engage students in issues of substance through reading and discussion. The holistic approach assumes that students learn the conventions of academic language not by completing exercises or writing assignments alone but by reading widely in academic prose. Such approaches also teach students to function within a social context so that they experience how academic writers actually function. The trend, Hood concludes, is toward holistic approaches.

In the second chapter in this section, "Computers and Writing Instruction," Stephen A. Bernhardt and Patricia G. Wojahn review the research on using computers in the basic writing classroom. The authors discuss developments in using computers to tutor students, a use that Bernhardt and Wojahn see as an adjunct to, not a replacement for, traditional instruction. They also review research that evaluates computers as a writing aid. Such uses include interactive programs that assist students in inventing, organizing, drafting, revising, and editing their papers. While such functions are becoming more widely used in college writing classrooms, the use of computers as word processors continues to be the most common application. The growing use of computers and the rapid development of computer technology, the authors conclude, are changing the classroom environment by making it less teacher centered.

Donna Beth Nelson in "Writing Laboratories and Basic Writing" also discusses student-centered instruction. With the development of writing laboratories or centers across the country, scholars of basic writing have conducted research on topics such as conference methodology. Of particular interest is the process-oriented writing lab in which students master strategies of the writing process. Other kinds of labs exist, however, and these include the autotutorial lab in which students work with self-teaching materials to master the conventions of written English. Nelson also discusses the research on how to analyze and eliminate errors and how to address the psychological problems that basic writers often suffer.

The last chapter in this section, by Richard A. Filloy, examines the research on preparing basic writing teachers. Although little research has been done in this area, researchers have articulated clear goals for teacher training programs for basic writing teachers. Such teachers must understand diverse fields such as grammar, dialectology, and reading theory as well as pedagogical principles such as methods of setting goals, evaluating papers, and developing effective courses and programs. While few such programs exist in the country, basic writing teachers also need professional training in the form of degree programs that specialize in basic writing theory and pedagogy. Because such degree programs are rare, Filloy argues that some of the best training takes place within institutions that develop more informal in-house training programs for faculty and graduate students. Finally, he reviews the research on training basic writing tutors, whether they be faculty specializing in operating writing centers, graduate students put in such centers as part of their assignments, or undergraduate peer tutors paid to work with basic writers.

The book ends with Mary Sue Ply's appendix that reviews basic writing textbooks.

We hope that this collection proves useful to those students and teachers entering the field of basic writing and to those scholars doing research in this field. We would also like to thank our contributors and Marilyn Brownstein, Acquisitions Editor for Greenwood Press. We especially hope the volume will have an indirect effect on the many basic writing students who work hard to develop the writing and thinking skills they need to participate fully in the academic life that American colleges and universities, unlike those of many other countries, offer them.

REFERENCES

Bartholomae, David, and Anthony Petrosky. *Facts, Artifacts and Counterfacts: Theory and Method for a Reading and Writing Course*. Upper Montclair, N.J.: Boynton/ Cook, 1986.

Enos, Theresa, ed. *A Sourcebook for Basic Writing Teachers*. New York: Random House, 1987.

Farr, Marcia, and Harvey Daniels. *Language Diversity and Writing Instruction*. New York: ERIC, 1986.

Gere, Anne Ruggles. *Writing Groups: History, Theory, and Implications*. Carbondale: Southern Illinois University Press, 1987.

Harris, Muriel. *Teaching One-to-One: The Writing Conference*. Urbana, Ill.: NCTE, 1986.

Hull, Glynda A., and David Bartholomae. "Basic Writing." *Research in Composition and Rhetoric: A Bibliographic Sourcebook*. Ed. Michael G. Moran and Ronald F. Lunsford. Westport, Conn.: Greenwood Press, 1984, pp. 265–302.

Kasden, Lawrence, N., and Daniel R. Hoeber, eds. *Basic Writing: Essays for Teachers, Researchers, and Administrators*. Urbana, Ill.: NCTE, 1980.

Lindemann, Erika, ed. *Longman Bibliography of Composition and Rhetoric*. New York: Longman, 1984–85, 1986.

Lunsford, Andrea. "An Update of the Bibliography on Basic Writing." *Teaching Composition: Twelve Bibliographical Essays*. Ed. Gary Tate. Fort Worth: Texas Christian University Press, 1987, pp. 207–26.

Meyer, Emily, and Louise Z. Smith. *The Practical Tutor*. New York: Oxford University Press, 1987.

Moran, Michael G., and Ronald F. Lunsford, eds. *Research in Composition and Rhetoric: A Bibliographic Sourcebook*. Westport, Conn.: Greenwood Press, 1984.

Ponsot, Marie, and Rosemary Deen. *Beat Not the Poor Desk: Writing: What to Teach, How to Teach It and Why*. Upper Montclair, N.J.: Boynton/Cook, 1982.

Rose, Mike. *Lives on the Boundary: The Struggles and Achievements of America's Underprepared*. New York: Free Press, 1989.

Rubin, Donald L., and William M. Dodd. *Talking into Writing: Exercises for Basic Writers*. Urbana, Ill.: ERIC, 1987.

Shaughnessy, Mina P. "Basic Writing." *Teaching Composition: Twelve Bibliographic Essays.* Ed. Gary Tate. Fort Worth: Texas Christian University Press, 1987, pp. 177–206.

————. *Errors and Expectations: A Guide for the Teachers of Basic Writing.* New York: Oxford University Press, 1977.

Wiener, Harvey S. *The Writing Room: A Resource Book for Teachers of English.* New York: Oxford University Press, 1981.

PART I

Social Science Perspectives

1

Who Are Basic Writers?

Andrea Lunsford and Patricia A. Sullivan

A dozen or so years ago, as she was charting in *Errors and Expectations* (1977) the unknown territory we now call basic writing, Mina Shaughnessy noted with alarm how little we know about the students identified as, among other things, "remedial," "developmental," "non-traditional," "new," or even "handi-capped." In her bibliographical essay, "Basic Writing" (1976), she demon-strated that we know little about what we mean by such metaphoric labels or about the students they purportedly describe; know little about their writing or about what constitutes development in their writing; and know even less about what strategies and practices might foster such development.

In the early pages of her bibliographical essay, Shaughnessy draws on the influential work of K. Patricia Cross to sketch a very tentative answer to our title question:

First, [basic writers] tend to produce, whether in impromptu or home assignments, small numbers of words with large numbers of errors (roughly from 15 to 35 errors per 300 words) that puzzle and alarm college teachers when they see them for the first time, errors with the so-called regular features of standard English (the past tense of regular verbs, for example, or the plural inflections of nouns), misspellings that appear highly idiosyncratic, syntactic snarls that often seem to defy analysis, and punctuation errors that reflect an unstable understanding of the conventions for marking off the boundaries of sentences and little or no acquaintance with the uses of colons, semi-colons, par-antheses, or quotation marks. Second, they seem to be restricted as writers, but not necessarily as speakers, to a very narrow range of syntactic, semantic, and rhetorical options, which forces them into either a rudimentary style of discourse that belies their real maturity or a dense and tangled prose with which neither they nor their readers can cope.

From these features alone we can infer much about their backgrounds. We can infer that they have never written much, in school or out, that they have come from families and neighborhoods where people speak other languages or variant, non-prestigious forms of English and that, while they have doubtless been sensitive to the differences between their ways of speaking and their teachers', they have never been able to sort out or develop attitudes toward the differences that did not put them in conflict, one way or another, with the key academic tasks of learning to read and write and talk in standard English. (139)

Shaughnessy was writing out of her own extensive experience with the students in the City University of New York (CUNY) system, and her generalized description indeed fits large numbers of her students. Yet as the decade wore on, basic writing classes grew larger and larger, their ranks swelling under the impact of open admissions in particular and broader access to higher education in general. This latter move brought into basic writing classes not just students from clearly defined social or economic groups but from every avenue of American public education: students in basic writing classes, depending on the college or university, were almost as likely to have graduated from an elite private school as from a large urban ghetto school. Thus we came to see that notwithstanding the groundbreaking attempts of Cross and Shaughnessy at definition and taxonomy, we still knew very, very little about basic writers.

In practical terms, this lack of knowledge—lack even of a basic agreed-upon definition—did little to hinder or bother us bureaucratically. We simply held to a convenient if indefensible circular definition: basic writers are those whom we place in basic writing classes. But this facile answer has never set well with scholars of basic writing, whose work over the last dozen years has consistently attempted more complete and richer definitions and answers to our title question. In the space allotted us here, we will review basic writing scholarship as it has addressed four subquestions: From what backgrounds do basic writers enter the academy? What characterizes the strategies and processes of basic writers? What characterizes the prose of basic writers? And how are basic writers situated in the academy?

FROM WHAT BACKGROUNDS DO BASIC WRITERS ENTER THE ACADEMY?

Research on the backgrounds of basic writers has tended to focus on the larger population of "nontraditional" or "underprepared" students rather than on those students specifically enrolled in basic writing courses. In the main, such studies have attempted to define nontraditional students in terms of a common socioeconomic background and shared educational experiences. Drawing on the early work of K. Patricia Cross (*Beyond the Open Door* [1971]) and John Roueche (*A Modest Proposal* [1972]), for example, William Moore, Jr., writes in *Community College Response to the High-Risk Student* (1976) that underprepared or "high risk" students are "first generation college enrollees, have few if any intellectual contacts, are likely to need remedial work, are the sons and daughters of lower-class workers, and are represented by a disproportionately high percentage of minority group students" (6). Moore maintains that such characteristics, while widely agreed upon by educators, are as yet hypotheses in need of further research.

Lynn Quitman Troyka refines the portrait sketched by Shaughnessy and Moore in "Perspectives on Legacies and Literacy in the 1980's" (1982). Asking what are the "major characteristics" of the growing population of nontraditional students attending two- and four-year colleges, Troyka answers:

Generally, they are older. In the last decade, the number of college students over twenty-five years of age doubled, so that as of today one-third of America's college student body is over twenty-five. Non-traditional students usually represent the first generation in their families to go to college. Non-traditional students are often parents, some married and some single. Most non-traditional students have jobs which often demand twenty to forty hours a week. They work on construction crews, in restaurants, as practical nurses, on the police force; some are on welfare. Many non-traditional students barely finished high school and have been admitted to college on waivers. Others dropped out of high school but later decided to earn an equivalency diploma. Many non-traditional students are women, some of them returning to school after having started a family. Indeed, women became the new majority in the nation's college student body in 1980. Not a few of the non-traditional students are foreign born: currently 300,000 foreign students attend America's college and universities; by the early 1990s, at least 1,000,000 such students are expected. (17)

In a more recent essay, "Defining Basic Writers in Context" (1987), however, Troyka cautions that we might be "building generalizations about basic writers on local evidence" (3). Reporting her findings from a national study of what typifies basic writing, Troyka concludes that the term "basic writing" as found in the professional literature does not cover the enormous diversity among basic writers: not only do no clear patterns emerge with respect to demographic data, but there is little agreement about what typifies levels of basic writing itself. Troyka's research indicates that basic writers differ from college to college and may even differ from year to year within a single academic setting. This national study holds important implications for future efforts to define basic writers in context because it shifts the thrust of such research from an attempt to analyze these students' "common" cultural heritage to an exploration of their social and linguistic diversity.

Like Troyka, George H. Jensen emphasizes the diversity among the basic writers in our classrooms in his essay, "The Reification of the Basic Writer" (1986). "Within one program," he says, "students will differ from class to class, and the composition of students in different programs will vary with admission and placement policies" (63). Jensen argues that past attempts to characterize basic writers form "too much of a portrait in broad strokes," and he warns that characterization may lead to "reification," to political and social buttonholing. Notwithstanding Jensen's frequent reference to "the Georgia State basic writer," somewhat ironic in context, his conclusion that we should "not believe that there is any one way to define, signify, label, identify, or teach those students who are called basic, remedial, or developmental writers" (63) accords with Troyka's findings.

In "Conflict and Power in the Reader-Responses of Adult Basic Writers" (1987), Nicholas Coles and Susan V. Wall discover common socioeconomic patterns among the adult basic writers who are the subjects of their study at the University of Pittsburgh: they are all first-generation students whose parents did not attend college; all are workers, employed or unemployed, mostly in working-class jobs; the majority are black; and most are female. But Coles and Wall emphasize the "particular histories" each of these students brings to the academic community. From analyses of their students' written responses to various books about what it means to work in American society, Coles and Wall conclude that "it is a simplification . . . to represent our students as coming from one distinct discourse community, that of their own culture, and entering another, that of the university" (313). Rather, adult basic writers bring "the cultural forms of each with them as they move back and forth, transforming both worlds in the process" (313).

Mina Shaughnessy would likely laud the basic writing course that Coles and Wall describe, for in their classroom the teacher listens carefully as the students tell about themselves. Shaughnessy noted a decade ago that "statistics tell us little directly about the students as writers or even as learners. Surprisingly little effort has been made to analyze the content of their essays . . . " ("Basic Writing" 142). Shaughnessy's message is clear: to understand where our basic writers are coming from, to understand their backgrounds and personal histories, we must consult not statistics or demographic data but our students' own writing.

Shaughnessy observed that basic writers "have written of themselves, often in powerful, generous ways in the transient anthologies that writing classes generate" (143). A number of colleges and universities are now compiling permanent anthologies and producing in-house publications of student-authored stories and essays. Martin M. McKoski and Lynne C. Hahn have collected successful essays from basic writers across the nation for a basic writing anthology and textbook, *Developing Writers: Prize-Winning Essays* (1988). Such local and national publications of the students' own writing should prove a rich source of information about the particular histories basic writers bring to our classrooms. They thus offer us an opportunity to learn more about a population whose diversity and complexity we are only beginning to appreciate.

WHAT CHARACTERIZES THE STRATEGIES AND PROCESSES OF BASIC WRITERS?

Attempts to answer this second question also lead into complex diversities. Early on, it seemed at least possible that we might be able to map strategies and processes, yielding a clear psychological profile of the typical basic writer. One of the earliest attempts to illuminate the psychology of basic writers is Marie Jean Lederman's "A Comparison of Student Projections" (1973). After reading 1,500 placement essays responding to the prompt "You will be reborn again tomorrow morning. You may come back as anything you choose—except yourself. What would you like to come back as?" Lederman pinpointed some disturbing tendencies. The basic writers in the sample (231 students) chose to "come back" as something smaller and less powerful than a person (e.g., a bird, mouse, dog, flower, tree), and their writing reflected a desire to escape, a sense of oppression, and poor self-concept.

Very little has been done to follow up on Lederman's evocative and powerful essay (see Andrea A. Lunsford, "The Content of Basic Writers' Essays" [1980] on self-concepts of basic writers, and Patricia Bizzell's call for more information on basic writers' worldviews in "What Happens When Basic Writers Come to College?" [1986]). Instead, perhaps in response to the growing influence of cognitive science on composition studies, attempts have focused on trying to characterize basic writers in terms of cognitive developmental theory. Two early works attempting such a characterization are Barry Kroll's "Cognitive Egocentrism and the Problem of Audience Awareness in Written Discourse" (1978) and Lunsford's "Cognitive Development and the Basic Writer" (1979). Drawing on Piagetian psychology, Kroll identifies "de-centering" as a goal in helping writers mature. Lunsford reviews work by Jean Piaget, Lev Vygotsky, and Michael Polanyi and finds that basic writers, in general, can be characterized as having great difficulty using formal operational procedures in academic tasks (449). Also looking at basic writers through the lens of cognitive theory, Linda Flower, in a series of perceptive and influential articles, identifies and describes egocentric or what she calls "writer-based" prose (see "Writer-Based Prose" [1979] and "Revising Writer-Based Prose" [1981]).

Following these works are a number of attempts to use one developmental model or another to describe basic writers. Most often cited, as we might expect, is the powerful but flawed and limited Piagetian model. Among others who use this model as a basis for discussing maturation in basic writers, see Marilyn K. Goldberg's "Overfamiliarity" (1985); Annette N. Bradford's "Cognitive Immaturity and Remedial College Writers" (1983); and John C. Bean's "Involving Non-English Faculty in the Teaching of Writing and Thinking Skills" (1981–82). Other writers draw on Benjamin S. Bloom's taxonomy of cognitive skills (Karen I. Spear, "Building Cognitive Skills in Basic Writers" [1983]), on William Perry's model of intellectual development or Lawrence Kohlberg's model of moral development (Janice N. Hays, "The Development of Discursive Maturity in College Writers" [1983]; Karen Spear, "Promoting Cognitive Development in the Writing Center" [1984]). Still others concentrate on cognitive processes that *inhibit* composing (see especially Mike Rose, "Rigid Rules, Inflexible Plans, and the Stifling of Language" [1980]).

The dangers of using developmental models devised to describe children or particular subgroups of college students (Perry's subjects were Harvard males, for instance) are obvious, and have been pointed out both by researchers using them in analogical or metaphorical ways and by scholars such as David Bartholomae, who asks basic writing teachers and researchers to stop concentrating so extensively on finding one and only one model of basic writing cognition ("Inventing the University" [1985]). Particularly informative is Mike Rose's "Narrowing the Mind and Page" (1988), which argues that we'd be more vigilant in interrogating any system of intellect for its unspoken assumptions, biases, and constraints.

If available cognitive-developmental models do not adequately describe basic writers, then why not? Continued exploration again reveals the diversity and depth of experience in basic writers, making them simply too protean to be captured by any single psychological model. In fact, drawing hard and fast conclusions of any kind about the psychology of basic writers seems increasingly reductive and unhelpful. Tantalizing glimpses of these writers, however, continue to appear. In addition to the work of Mike Rose (whose "Remedial Writing Courses" [1983] places the basic writer within the academic context and argues, among other things, that the cognitive developmental models have been misused), the research of Sondra Perl and Nancy Sommers has been of great interest. In a series of articles, Perl challenges yet another tacit assumption—that basic writers have no consistent strategies or processes that they use in composing. On the contrary, Perl's case studies of basic writers reveal consistent and stable— though often unhelpful—processes at work ("Five Writers Writing" [1978]; "The Composing Processes of Unskilled College Writers" [1979]). Perl's case studies also reveal the diversity among individual composing processes, and her later work, "Understanding Composing" [1980], in fact indicates ways in which recursivity, a "felt sense" of topic and purpose, and what she calls "retrospective" and "projective" structuring are characteristic of basic writers as well as their more skillful peers.

Focusing on one particular aspect of the composing process, revision, Nancy Sommers again challenges received wisdom about basic writers, demonstrating that basic writers do indeed have a concept, albeit a limited one, of revising. Her studies reveal that basic writers make strong attempts to revise but use a rigid and narrow concept of revision as rewording ("Revision Strategies of Student Writers and Experienced Adult Writers" [1980]; "Intentions and Revisions" [1981]). The insights such research offers into the psychology and cognitive processes of basic writers reveal not a single profile, what Jensen calls a "gross . . . composite characterization" (53), but a rich, complex, and intriguing mix of worldviews, personalities, and processes. Certainly researchers are continuing to describe this complexity. But rather than aiming for a monolithic description, basic writing research seems bent on being ready, in Troyka's words, to "meet the diversity" ("Defining" [1986] 2).

WHAT CHARACTERIZES THE PROSE OF BASIC WRITERS?

If the possibility of creating a representative sketch of basic writers' processes seemed difficult and remote, scholars in the field had reason to believe that describing texts would be much more straightforward. After all, we have been carefully trained in textual analysis of various sorts, and the text can be made to stand still for examination in a way that students and their multivarious processes cannot. As researchers and scholars turned their attention to the texts of basic writers, they naturally tended to focus on the most immediately conspicuous feature of those texts—errors. Indeed, early studies managed to describe such errors fairly well. Most important, of course, is Shaughnessy's taxonomy of error sources in *Errors and Expectations* (1977). As she explains in the introduction, "I have divided this territory of difficulty into familiar teaching categories . . . : 'Handwriting and Punctuation, Syntax, Common Errors, Spelling, Vocabulary, and Beyond the Sentence. In each . . . I have tried . . . first, to give examples of the range of problems that occur under each category of difficulty . . .' " (4). Like Shaughnessy, other researchers have worked to identify error patterns in basic writing. Some have focused on particular types of error, such as fragments or run-on sentences (Dona M. Kagan, "Run on and Fragment Sentences" [1980]); others have focused on broader concepts such as syntax in an attempt to map basic writing errors (David A. Carkeet, "Understanding Syntactic Errors in Remedial Writing" [1977]; Valerie Krishna, "The Syntax of Error" [1975]). Some have devised specific exercises to eliminate errors (Donna Gorrell, "Controlled Composition" [1980]; Sarah D'Eloia, "The Uses—and Limits—of Grammar" [1977]). And a number of dissertations have attempted to describe the errors typical of basic writing, in particular those by Marilyn Sternglass ("Similarities and Differences" [1973]), Andrea A. Lunsford ("An Historical, Descriptive, and Evaluative Study of Remedial English" [1977]), and Daniel R. Steinberg ("A Comparison of Errors" [1979]).

Again building on Shaughnessy's remarkable insights, basic writing scholars began to understand that a "typical" error profile would be about as hard to develop as would a psychological or cognitive profile. And, of course, such profiles may not be at all desirable insofar as they direct our attention in certain ways, some not necessarily beneficial to our students. As always, a "typical" profile can quickly harden into a stereotype or a self-fulfilling prophecy.

The attempts to sort out basic writers' errors and to describe their prose in terms of those errors were, however, necessary and beneficial because they led to a growing awareness of how various and complex such patterns of error are. Even more importantly, such studies demand that we view error and its relation to an emerging text in an entirely new way. The patterns of error that appear in a student's prose become not offenses to be plucked out or illness to be cured but, in Gilbert Ryle's telling phrase in *The Concept of Mind* (1949), "exercises of competences" (60).

As a result of this shift, researchers began to focus on the prose of basic writers anew, intent not on counting errors but on uncovering the logic and nature of error. Shaughnessy makes the most comprehensive and eloquent case, echoed by a number of other influential scholars. Patricia Laurence's 1975 essay, "Error's Endless Train," was followed by Barry M. Kroll and John C. Schafer's "Error Analysis and the Teaching of Composition" (1978), which advocates a careful analysis of the strategies that underlie errors. David Bartholomae's sensitive reading of basic writers in "The Study of Error" (1980) also recommends error analysis and sets the entire question of error in a philosophical context, relating error, choice, strategy, and process of thought. Joseph Williams continues the contextualization of error in "Re-evaluating Evaluating" (1978) and "The Phenomenology of Error" (1981), urging us to see error in relationship to readers responding to a text and suggesting that our judgments about "errors are much more complex than we might have expected." In another important study, Colette Daiute situates error within a larger and richer semantic field ("Performance Limits of Writers" [1984]).

Related to the attempts to describe basic writing in terms of errors has been the effort to describe that writing as heavily influenced by oral culture or by dialect. The controversy engendered in this discussion makes the others pale in comparison. The question is deceptively simple: Are basic writers relying on oral speech and dialect patterns in their attempts to produce written discourse? Those examining the transition from spoken to written discourse and the influence of the former on the latter include Roger L. Cayer and Renee K. Sacks ("Oral and Written Discourse" [1979]), Mary Epes ("Tracing Errors to Their Sources" [1985]), and especially Thomas J. Farrell ("Open Admissions, Orality, and Literacy" [1974]; "Literacy, Basics, and All That Jazz" [1977] "IQ and Standard English" [1983]). But those voices are strongly countered by a number of others, such as James L. Collins and M. N. Williamson ("Spoken Language and Semantic Abbreviation in Writing" [1981]), Karen L. Greenberg ("Research on Basic Writers" [1987]), and Patrick Hartwell ("Responses to Thomas J. Farrell" [1984]), who argue that we have no evidence to indicate that dialect interferes with acquisition of writing skills and that basic writers' difficulties come instead from "orthographic, pragmatic, and rhetorical constraints and conventions of different writing tasks" (Greenberg, "Research on Basic Writers" [1987] 196).

In spite of the tentativeness, contentiousness, and even contradictoriness, one result of this research has been a general enrichment of our understanding of basic writers' prose. We are now less sanguine about assuming that the products of basic writers can be any more pigeonholed or described or taxonomized than the processes of such writers. Those products, in fact, may vary as much among basic writers as they might among other groups of students, a point Lynn Troyka makes in the opening of "Defining Basic Writing in Context" (1986)(2). After studying 109 basic writing essays from all areas of the country, Troyka reports that her efforts at general descriptive labels would not fit her data, that the "complexities of [textual] differences within and among the [papers] is fascinating, but not given to facile rubric. . . . the message," she concludes, "is clear: Basic writers are a diverse group" (11–12). In spite of this diversity, there is some evidence that teachers may tend to stereotype basic writers in detrimental ways (Richard H. Haswell, "Dark Shadows, [1988]).

HOW ARE BASIC WRITERS SITUATED IN THE ACADEMY?

This question presupposes, of course, that institutions of higher education have found a place for basic writers; it thus conceals the fact that very much at issue today is whether basic writers *should* have access to higher education. In a 1973 essay, K. Patricia Cross addresses the question of egalitarian versus elitist higher education and argues that "the way to raise the standard of living for everyone is no longer to train leaders but rather to educate the masses to their full humanity" ("The New Learners" 31). Many universities take an opposite view, however, and are unwilling to allocate funds for "remedial" courses, including basic writing. Historical and philosophical precedents of the academy's current resistance to basic writing courses (and by extension to basic writers) have been traced in three recent essays. In "Toward an Ethnohistory of Writing in American Education" (1981), Shirley Brice Heath points out that during the last three decades of the nineteenth century, standards in writing became increasingly associated with normative judgments about the individual creators of language. "The strong implication was that those who wrote and criticized well had more intelligence, morality, and industry than did their fellow students" (35). Stephen Witte and his colleagues also trace the historical association of intelligence with literacy in "Literacy and the Direct Assessment of Writing" (1986). They focus on Hillegas's 1912 "Scale for the Measurement or Quality in English Composition by Young People," noting that it valorized "literary writing" about works in the accepted literary canon and thus equated literacy with intelligence and illiteracy with "low" topics and low intelligence. Andrea Lunsford's "Politics and Practices in Basic Writing" (1986) documents the historical resistance to basic writing and argues that an understanding of this history should inform our classroom practices because these practices "reflect our own definitions of literacy and our response to the debates over access to higher education" (253). A comprehensive treatment of literacy theory and basic writers appears in the third chapter of this volume.

In "The Language of Exclusion" (1985) Mike Rose addresses the modern equivalent of the academy's historical resistance to basic writers by analyzing current institutional language about writing instruction that excludes basic writers

from full participation in the university. In doing so, he deconstructs some of
the terms that surround basic writing, including "remediation" and what he
calls "the myth of transcience"—the belief that the need for preparatory instruction is only a recent phenomenon, one that will be "cured" in the foreseeable
future. Rose argues that we need to define our work as "initiatory, orienting,
or socializing . . . to the academic discourse community"; such a redefinition
requires us "to reject a medical-deficit model of language, to acknowledge the
rightful place of all freshmen in the academy, and once and for all to replace
loose talk about illiteracy with more precise and pedagogically fruitful analysis"
(358).

The equation of literacy and intelligence and the notion that basic writers are
cognitively deficient have come under attack in recent years by scholars who
have argued that access to higher education and academic success are matters
of acculturation rather than "innate" propensities or intellect. They argue, in
essence, that basic writers' difficulties stem from their unfamiliarity with the
linguistic and social conventions of academic discourse. Patricia Bizzell had
criticized cognitive-based pedagogical models because they obscure the political
agenda operating in basic writing classrooms. In a series of essays, she has
argued that such models "prejudge those unequally prepared for school as un-
equal in mental development" ("College Composition" [1982] 196); that writing
teachers need to instruct their students in the rhetoric of the academy to ensure
their students' full participation ("Ethos" 1978); and that instruction in the
conventions of academic discourse must complement "inner-directed" pedagogies ("Cognition" 1982). Like Bizzell, Myra Kogen maintains that it is "all
too easy to conclude that those who do not do, or who do not wish to do, what
we seem to be able to do are deficient and underdeveloped." From her analysis
of student writing samples, Kogen concludes that "students are not inept thinkers
but simply insufficiently familiar with the conventions of expository discourse"
("The Conventions of Expository Writing" [1986] 25). In a 1979 essay, Sandra
Stotsky urges basic writing teachers to instruct their students in the vocabulary
of academic discourse ("Teaching the Vocabulary of Academic Discourse").
And David Bartholomae writes that beginning students need to learn to "extend
themselves into the commonplaces . . . that constitute knowledge within the various branches of our academic community" ("Inventing the University" [1985]
11). Bartholomae maintains that basic writers' problems are the fault of our own
curricula, which "fail to involve students in scholarly projects that would allow
them to act as though they were colleagues in an academic enterprise" (11).
Like Rose and Bizzell, Bartholomae urges us to dispense with traditional concepts
and practices that locate basic writers outside the academic community.

Not all theorists agree that basic writers need to be initiated into the academic
discourse community, however. Richard Ohmann argues that the academic code
reflects the military-industrialist ideology of capitalist society; rather than in-
doctrinating students in an academic language that reproduces the "power re-
lations of society," teachers must help students see language as a means of

achieving their own political and personal aims ("Reflections on Class and Language" [1982]). James Sledd also examines the social-political nature of the academy to argue on behalf of the NCTE document, "Students' Right to Their Own Language" ("In Defense of the *Students' Right*" [1983]). And John Rouse's controversial essay "The Politics of Composition" (1979) attacks Mina Shaughnessy's "formalistic" and "authoritative" approach to basic writing instruction because it "processes" rather than educates students. Rouse argues for a pedagogy that emphasizes the student's personal judgments. (See also "Feeling Our Way Along" [1980], in which Rouse responds to criticism of his earlier essay.)

How basic writers are, and ought to be, situated in the academy will likely be matters of ongoing controversy and debate. Although basic writing scholars generally agree that these students have a rightful place in the university, questions remain as to their institutional roles and thus their status. The diversity among basic writers complicates the issue, for the policies and practices of teachers and administrators are contingent on the kinds of students they serve. But the population of basic writers, as we have seen, continues to resist our best attempts at description and definition.

CONCLUSION

The questions we have posed admit of no easy answers. We began hopefully enough, submerging our own experiences and our reading of and conversations with basic writing researchers and teachers into our mental developing solution, waiting for a photograph to emerge and smile up at us from the darkroom table. What emerged, however, was no clear, well-defined photograph but a shifting, protean image that finally interested us much more. Trying to answer these questions, in other words, only led us to new ways of asking the questions and even to questions about questions. We came to see the value of examining these questions from what Kenneth Burke calls "perspective by incongruity," that is, by looking at them in different linguistic, institutional, and social contexts in an attempt to explore the rich complexities of the questions rather than to search for certain or simple answers.

Perhaps that is just as well. As Burke continually reminds us, our drive for order, closure, clarity—our obsession with simple taxonomies—often assures that we will miss the forest for the trees. Making matters more complex rather than more simple, Burke insists, may lead to greater understanding.

And so we will close with a question, one Burke often asks his exhausted and frustrated readers: where are we now? From our basic writing students, whose rich diversity continues to resist our greatest taxonomic efforts, we have learned much. Perhaps most important, we have learned that we have no pat answers, that in a very real sense, we do not know. But in that realization, as Socrates often said, lie the seeds of wisdom. The articles that follow all attempt to nurture those seeds.

REFERENCES

Bartholomae, David. "Inventing the University." *When a Writer Can't Write: Studies in Writer's Block and Other Composing-Process Problems*. Ed. Mike Rose. New York: Guilford, 1985, pp. 134–65.

———. "The Study of Error." *CCC* 31 (1980): 253–69.

———. "Teaching Basic Writing: An Alternative to Basic Skills." *JBW* 2.2 (1979): 85–109.

Bean, John C. "Involving Non-English Faculty in the Teaching of Writing and Thinking Skills." *Int J. Instr Med* 9.1 (1981–82): 51–69.

Bizzell, Patricia. "Cognition, Convention and Certainty: What We Need to Know About Writing." *P/T* 3 (1982): 213–43.

———. "College Composition: Initiation into the Academic Discourse Community." *Cur Inq* 12 (1982): 191–207.

———. "The Ethos of Academic Discourse." *CCC* 29 (1978): 351–55.

———. "What Happens When Basic Writers Come to College." *CCC* 37 (1986): 294–301.

Bradford, Annette N. "Cognitive Immaturity and Remedial College Writers." *The Writer's Mind: Writing as a Mode of Thinking*. Ed. Janice N. Hays et al. Urbana, Ill.: NCTE, 1983, pp. 15–24.

Carkeet, David. "Understanding Syntactic Errors in Remedial Writing." *CE* 38 (1977): 682–95.

Cayer, Roger L., and Renee K. Sacks. "Oral and Written Discourse of Basic Writers: Similarities and Differences." *RTE* 13 (1979): 121–28.

Coles, Nicholas, and Susan V. Wall. "Conflict and Power in the Reader-Responses of Adult Basic Writers." *CE* 49 (1987): 298–314.

Collins, James L., and M. N. Williamson. "Spoken Language an Semantic Abbreviation in Writing." *RTE* 15 (1981): 23–26.

Crew, Louie. "The New Alchemy." *CE* 38 (1977): 707–11.

Cross, K. Patricia. "The New Learners." *Change Mag* (February 1973): 30–34.

———. *Beyond the Open Door*. San Francisco: Jossey-Bass, 1971.

Daiute, Colette. "Performance Limits of Writers." *New Directions for Composition Research*. Ed. Richard Beach and Lillian Bridwell. New York: Guilford, 1984, pp. 205–24.

D'Eloia, Sarah. "The Uses—and Limits—of Grammar." *JBW* 1.3 (1977): 1–48.

Epes, Mary. "Tracing Errors to Their Sources: A Study of the Encoding Process of Adult Basic Writers." *JBW* 4.1 (1985): 4–33.

Farrell, Thomas J. "IQ and Standard English." *CCC* 34 (1983): 470–84.

———. "Literacy, the Basics and All That Jazz." *CE* 38 (1977): 443–59.

———. "Open Admissions, Orality, and Literacy." *J Youth Ado* 3 (1974): 247–60.

Flower, Linda. "Revising Writer-Based Prose." *JBW* 3.3 (1981): 62–74.

———. "Writer-Based Prose: A Cognitive Basis for Problems in Writing." *CE* 41 (1979): 19–37.

Goldberg, Marilyn K. "Overfamiliarity: A Cognitive Barrier in Teaching Composition." *JBW* 4.1 (1985): 34–43.

Gorrell, Donna. "Controlled Composition for Teaching Basic Writing to College Freshmen." Diss. Illinois State University, 1980.

Greenberg, Karen L. "Research on Basic Writers: Theoretical and Methodological Issues." *A Sourcebook for Basic Writing Teachers*. Ed. Theresa Enos. New York: Random House, 1987, pp. 187–207.

———. "Response to Thomas J. Farrell, 'IQ and Standard English,' *CCC* 34 (1983): 470–84." *CCC* 35 (1984): 455–60.

Hartwell, Patrick. "Grammar, Grammars, and the Teaching of Grammar." *CE* 47 (1985): 105–27.

———. "Response to Thomas J. Farrell. 'IQ and Standard English' [*CCC* 34 (1983): 470–84]." *CCC* 35 (1984): 461–65.

Haswell, Richard H. "Dark Shadows: The Fate of Writers at the Bottom." *CCC* 39 (1988): 303–15.

Hays, Janice N. "The Development of Discursive Maturity in College Writers." *The Writer's Mind*. Ed. Janice N. Hays et al. Urbana, Ill.: NCTE, 1983, pp. 127–44.

Heath, Shirley B. "Toward an Ethnohistory of Writing in American Education." *Writing: The Nature, Development, and Teaching of Written Communication*. Ed. Marcia Farr Whiteman. Hillsdale, N.J.: Lawrence Erlbaum Associates, 1981, pp. 25–45.

Jensen, George H. "The Reification of the Basic Writer." *JBW* 5.1 (1986): 52–64.

Kagan, Dona M. "Run on and Fragment Sentences: An Error Analysis." *RTE* 14 (1980): 127–38.

Kogen, Myra. "The Conventions of Expository Writing." *JBW* 5.1 (1986): 24–37.

Krishna, Valerie. "The Syntax of Error." *JBW* 1.1 (1975): 43–49.

Kroll, Barry M. "Cognitive Egocentrism and the Problem of Audience Awareness in Written Discourse." *RTE* 12 (1978): 267–81.

Kroll, Barry M., and John C. Schafer. "Error-Analysis and the Teaching of Composition." *CCC* 29 (1978): 243–48.

Laurence, Patricia. "Error's Endless Train: Why Students Don't Perceive Errors." *JBW* 1.1 (1975): 23–42.

Lederman, Marie Jean. "A Comparison of Student Projections: Magic and the Teaching of Writing." *CE* 34 (1973): 674–89.

Lunsford, Andrea A. "An Update of the Bibliography on Basic Writing." *Teaching Composition: Twelve Bibliographical Essays*. Ed. Gary Tate. Fort Worth: Texas Christian University Press, 1987, pp. 207–26.

———. "Cognitive Development and the Basic Writer." *CE* 41 (1979): 38–46.

———. "The Content of Basic Writers' Essays." *CCC* 31 (1980): 278–90.

———. "An Historical, Descriptive, and Evaluative Study of Remedial English in American Colleges-Universities." Diss. Ohio State University, 1977.

———. "Politics and Practices in Basic Writing." *A Sourcebook for Basic Writing Teachers*. Ed. Theresa Enos. New York: Random House, 1986, pp. 246–58.

McKoski, Martin M. and Lynne C. Hahn, eds. *Developing Writers: Prize-Winning Essays*. Chicago: Scott, Foresman, 1988.

Moore, William, Jr. *Community College Response to the High-Risk Student: A Critical Reappraisal*. ERIC/AACJC Monographs, 1976.

Ohmann, Richard. "Reflections on Class and Language." *CE* 44 (1982): 1–17.

Perl, Sondra. "The Composing Processes of Unskilled College Writers." *RTE* 13 (1979): 317–36.

———. "Five Writers Writing: Case Studies of the Composing Process of Unskilled College Writers." Diss. New York University, 1978.

————. "A Look at Basic Writers in the Process of Composing." *Basic Writing*. Ed. Lawrence N. Kasden and Daniel R. Hoeber. Urbana, Ill.: NCTE, 1980, pp. 13–34.

————. "Understanding Composing." *CCC* 31 (1980): 363–69.

Rose, Mike. "The Language of Exclusion: Writing Instruction at the University." *CE* 47 (1985): 341–59.

————. "Narrowing the Mind and Page: Remedial Writers and Cognitive Reductionism." *CCC* 39 (1988): 267–302.

————. "Remedial Writing Courses: A Critique and a Proposal." *CE* 45 (1983): 109–28.

————. "Rigid Rules, Inflexible Plans, and the Stifling of Language: A Cognitivist Analysis of Writer's Block." *CCC* 31 (1980): 389–401.

Roueche, John E. *A Modest Proposal*. San Francisco: Jossey-Bass, 1972.

Rouse, John. "Feeling Our Way Along." *CE* 41 (1980): 868–75.

————. "The Politics of Composition." *CE* 41 (1979): 1–12.

Ryle, Gilbert. *The Concept of Mind*. New York: Barnes and Noble, 1949.

Shaughnessy, Mina P. "Basic Writing." *Teaching Composition: Ten Bibliographical Essays*. Ed. Gary Tate. Fort Worth: Texas Christian University Press, 1976, pp. 137–68.

————. *Errors and Expectations: A Guide for the Teacher of Basic Writing*. New York: Oxford University Press, 1977.

Sledd, James. "In Defense of the *Students' Right*." *CE* 45 (1983): 667–75.

Sommers, Nancy. "Intentions and Revisions." *JBW* 3.3 (1981): 41–49.

————. "Revision Strategies of Student Writers and Experienced Adult Writers." *CCC* 31 (1980): 378–88.

Spear, Karen I. "Building Cognitive Skills in Basic Writers." *TETYC* 9 (1983): 91–98.

————. "Promoting Cognitive Development in the Writing Center." *Writing Centers: Theory and Administration*. Ed. Gary A. Olson. Urbana, Ill.: NCTE, 1984, pp. 62–76.

Steinberg, Daniel R. "A Comparison of Errors Made on a WEEPT and Those Found in Student Writing Samples as Basis for Placement in Freshman Composition." Diss. Indiana University, 1979.

Sternglass, Marilyn. "Similarities and Differences in Nonstandard Syntactic Features in the Composition of Black and White College Students in Remedial Writing Classes." Diss. University of Pittsburgh, 1973.

Stotsky, Sandra L. "Teaching the Vocabulary of Academic Discourse." *JBW* 2.3 (1979): 15–39.

Troyka, Lynn Quitman. "Defining Basic Writing in Context." *A Sourcebook for Basic Writing Teachers*. Ed. Theresa Enos. New York: Random House, 1987, pp. 2–15.

————. "Perspectives on Legacies and Literacy in the 1980's." *CCC* 33 (1982): 252–61.

Williams, Joseph M. "The Phenomenology of Error." *CCC* 32 (1981): 152–68.

————. "Re-Evaluating Evaluating." *JBW* 1.4 (1978): 7–17.

Witte, Stephen et al. "Literacy and the Direct Assessment of Writing: A Diachronic Perspective." *Current Issues in the Assessment of Writing*. Ed. Richard Donovan, Karen Greenberg, and Barbara Schier-Peleg. New York: Longmans, 1986, pp. 13–34.

2

Developmental Psychology and Basic Writers

Donna Haisty Winchell

Development as a writer is inextricably bound to general intellectual development, whether approached, as by Jerome Bruner (*Toward a Theory of Instruction* [1966]), with the assumption that language facilitates general intellectual development or, as by Albert Kitzhaber (*Themes, Theories, and Therapy* [1963]), with the assumption that general intellectual development facilitates improvement in writing. Composition theorists, researchers, and teachers in the last third of the twentieth century have increasingly drawn on the work of cognitive developmental psychologists in an attempt to understand the deficiencies of basic writers and to reevaluate composition instruction in light of what is known about developmental changes in writers' perceptions of their world.

Loren S. Barritt and Barry M. Kroll, in "Some Implications of Cognitive-Developmental Psychology for Research in Composing" (1978), argue that cognitive-developmental psychology is replacing the psychology of behaviorism as the basis of communication research. Barritt and Kroll point out that the two parts of the compound designation *cognitive-developmental* accurately describe the two bases of the approach, with its emphasis on mind rather than on behavior and on sequential stages rather than immediate response to environmental stimuli: "The cognitive-developmentalist posits underlying cognitive structures to explain observable actions. Thus, in research on composing, the cognitive-developmental approach shifts the emphasis from the *what* of composing (the product) to the *how* of composing (the process). The theory leads one to ask how a composing skill develops and how a person is able to accomplish certain cognitive tasks" (50–51).

By 1978 the developmental theories of Swiss psychologist Jean Piaget had already become influential in the realm of psychology, but Barritt and Kroll note the lack of any "systematic delineation" (50) of the implications of Piaget's theory for research in written composition. Their article suggests four specific areas of composition research in which the cognitive-developmental approach has particular relevance: speaking-writing differences, the concept of error, ego-centrism and audience awareness, and writing and social-emotional development. On a more general level, they see cognitive-developmental psychology offering composition researchers a theoretical base, a research direction, and a methodology.

We still lack a "systematic delineation" of what cognitive-developmental psychology has taught and can teach us about the composing process, but the 1970s and 1980s have produced a number of individual and group attempts to explain the links between cognitive development and the development of writing ability. Piaget's theory is where most attempts begin.

DEVELOPMENTAL LEVELS

One frustration in dealing with Piagetian theory is the amount of attention devoted in Piaget's works to cognitive development in early childhood and the disappointing lack of attention devoted to adolescence and beyond. The formal operational stage, the stage of concern to those dealing with adolescents and adults, is introduced in Bärbel Inhelder and Piaget's *The Growth of Logical Thinking from Childhood to Adolescence* (1958). A much more accessible version of Piaget's stages of development exists, however, in his "Piaget's Theory" (1970). Excerpts from key primary sources are collected in *A Piaget Sampler*, edited by Sarah Campbell (1976); more discussion of his key ideas appears, in his own words, in Jean-Claude Bringuier's *Conversations with Jean Piaget* (1980); and an excellent secondary source is John H. Flavell's *The Developmental Psychology of Jean Piaget* (1963).

A key question for those interested in written composition is whether students have attained the level of development that would enable them to perform the writing tasks assigned them. In *The Growth of Logical Thinking* Inhelder and Piaget proposed the years from eleven to fifteen as the period when an individual develops formal operational thought. Piaget revised that view rather drastically, however, in 1972 in "Intellectual Evolution from Adolescence to Adulthood." There he acknowledged that some students may not achieve equilibrium at the level of formal thought until sometime between the ages of fifteen and twenty, and that in some severe cases, formal thought may never develop. This revision in Piaget's thinking has profound consequences for those who teach writing to students at the end of their secondary career and at the beginning of the college years.

Most researchers who have sought to test Piaget's developmental theories have done so not on the basis of the subjects' ability to write, but on their ability to reason about the same mechanical tasks on which Piaget based his original research with Swiss children, a method that has led Mike Rose ("Narrowing the Mind and Page'' [1988]) to question their relevance to the field of composition studies.

Researchers at the University of Oklahoma have been responsible for some of the most carefully conducted studies of cognitive development based on Piaget's experiments. Two of them, John W. Renner and Donald G. Stafford, set out in 1970–71 to determine if Piaget's age ranges apply to students in American secondary schools. The results of their study are reported in ''The Operational Levels of Secondary Students'' (*Research, Teaching, and Learning with the Piaget Model* [1976]): Of the 588 students sampled, only 2.4 percent were fully formal operational; 22.3 percent were transitional into formal operations. Robert J. Ross's ''The Empirical Status of Formal Operations'' (1974) summarizes a variety of similar studies, most of which report 50 percent or fewer of the secondary school subjects operating at the level of formal thought.

Studies involving college age and adult subjects indicate that formal thought can by no means be assumed simply because those tested have reached adolescence. Everett Dulit (''Adolescent Thinking à la Piaget'' [1972]) reports finding formal-stage thinking to be fully developed in only 20 to 35 percent of average older adolescents. Joe W. McKinnon (''The College Student and Formal Operations'' [1976]) reports on two studies in which 51 percent of the students tested were still operating at the level of concrete-operational rather than formal-operational thought. The ''average older adolescents'' studied in Dulit's case were sixteen and seventeen years of age, and McKinnon's subjects were college freshmen. Also see Milton Schwebel's ''Formal Operations in First-Year College Students'' (1975).

Other studies, however, have shown that over 50 percent of a group sampled may be functioning at the fully formal operational level if the group represents ''a cognitively superior adolescent sample or a college sample presumably somewhat above average in intelligence'' (Ross, ''Some Empirical Parameters of Formal Thinking'' [1973]). In fact, such groups may reach the 75 percent mark that Piaget used to determine that an age group had reached a particular stage of development. Even the most optimistic estimates of cognitive maturity, however, make it impossible to *assume* that beginning college students, especially basic writers, are fully formal operational. Dulit concludes that ''formal-stage thinking does *not* appear to be 'characteristic' of adolescence in the sense of being routine, expected, or highly likely. By contrast, the earlier Piagetian stages *are* characteristic or typical at their age ranges in *all* the usual senses of those words. Thus for adolescents the formal stage is more of a *characteristic potentiality* only sometimes becoming an actuality'' (298).

A number of composition specialists have tried to explain the problems that basic writers face in terms of the lack of formal operational thought. In fact, Robert M. Holland in ''Piagetian Theory and the Design of Composing Assignments'' (1976) concludes that composing itself ''may be usefully defined as Piaget's Formal Operational Thought represented in tangible symbolic form'' (22). Karen I. Spear's ''Promoting Cognitive Development in the Writing Center'' (1984) includes a useful summary of the primary characteristics of formal operational thought and links them to specific problems faced by basic writers. Her generalizations are based on basic students in the writing center, but apply equally well to basic writers in other contexts. (See also Karen I. Spear's "Building Cognitive Skills in Basic Writers" [1983]). Peggy Jolly, in "Meeting the Challenge of Developmental Writers" (1987), also clearly analyzes the problems student writers face because of the lack of formal operational thought.

On the other hand, Myra Kogen, in "The Conventions of Expository Writing" (1986), questions composition researchers' assumptions that the abstract and analytical thought necessary for academic discourse is beyond many of our students. She argues rather that perceived deficiencies are attributable not to the inability for analytic thought but to a lack of familiarity with the conventional modes of expository writing expected by the academic world. Joseph G. R. Martinez and Nancy C. Martinez, in "Reconsidering Cognition and the Basic Writer" (1987), join her in warning against too hastily assuming cognitive immaturity on the part of college students:

Specifically, some researchers mistakenly assume that stages describing patterns of physiological and cognitive development in children must also describe the cognition of adults. Other researchers confuse cognitive development with the acquisition of specific types of knowledge or a particular world view. In addition, the common method of analyzing essays as though they provided a direct measure of cognitive processes ignores the myriad affective and situational factors which can influence learning outcomes. (79)

In "Remedial Writing Courses: A Critique and a Proposal" (1983), Mike Rose contends that our attempts to foster growth in college remedial writers may be ineffective and even counterproductive:

we must . . . question our assumptions about our students' abilities and the pedagogies we have built on these assumptions. All too often these days we hear that remedial writers are "cognitively deficient," locked, for example, at the Piagetian level of concrete (vs. formal) operations. These judgments are unwarranted extrapolations from a misuse (or overuse) of the developmental psychologist's diagnostic instruments, for as Jean Piaget himself reminded us in one of his final articles, if we are not seeing evidence of formal operations in young adults, then we should either better acquaint them with our diagnostics or find more appropriate ones. (27)

Most of the theoretical assumptions about the link between developmental level and writing ability have been tied to two cognitive-developmental assumptions that have their roots in Piagetian theory. (1) Since intelligence is, by definition, adaptation to new situations, there is a continual building up of mental structures, structures linked to a need for internal consistency and organization. As they confront new experiences, individuals must constantly seek to regain a sense of equilibrium by either assimilating new information into their existing mental structures or adapting their existing structures to accommodate that new information. (2) At each level of cognitive development individuals go through a period of egocentrism before some source of conflict forces them to adjust their way of thinking to regain equilibrium. This repeated decentering out of egocentrism is necessary if they are ever to get to the level of formal thought, at which they can see simultaneously their own and their audience's point of view.

ACCOMMODATION AND ASSIMILATION

Charles Stallard, in "Composing" (1976), notes that research into the mental activities of composing has been conspicuous by its absence and goes on to describe the composing process in terms of the related changes in the writer's existing cognitive structures. A more detailed account of the cognitive aspects of the composing process is Robert J. Bracewell's "Writing as a Cognitive Activity" (1980), and a discussion of the cognitive aspects of the writing of poor writers in particular appears in "Problems and Difficulties" by Margaret Martlew (1983). Chris Anson et al. ("From Schemes to Themes" [1983]) apply schema theory to the teaching of writing, and Vincent Puma et al., in "Cognitive Approaches to Writing" (1983), provide an annotated bibliography of works on the application of psychological methodologies to the composing process.

Others have tried to link mental structures and formal rhetorical structures. The point of view taken in Frank D'Angelo's *A Conceptual Theory of Rhetoric* (1975) is that topical categories such as definition, classification, exemplification, comparison, contrast, and the like "may be considered as formal patterns of arrangement for organizing discourse on almost any level of structure" (57). They serve a heuristic function, but they are also to be considered "dynamic organizational processes, symbolic manifestations of underlying mental processes, and not merely conventional, static patterns" (57). In "Evidence for a Conceptual Theory of Rhetoric" (1977), David E. Jones summarizes the studies that support his contention that there is an essential continuity of natural thought processes and formal rhetorical structures. Karl K. Taylor's "DOORS English" (1979) is a report on a core of six courses at Illinois Central College that were a coordinated effort to introduce the same rhetorical types (comparison/contrast, classification, etc.) in all of the content areas at the same point in the term in an attempt to move students from the concrete into the formal operational stage. Anna Berg and Gerald Coleman report on a remedial curriculum at Passaic County Community College, the "Cognitive Project," that makes the development of identifiable cognitive structures the explicit rather than the implicit goal of remedial instruction ("A Cognitive Approach to Teaching the Developmental Student" [1985]).

Marilyn K. Goldberg's "Overfamiliarity" (1985) does an excellent job of applying Piaget's theories of accommodation and assimilation to the teaching of basic writing. If a student lacks a conceptual structure—the concept of "thesis statement," for example—it is impossible to assimilate new experiences related to the concept simply because of the lack of an existing structure into which to assimilate them. Goldberg contends that the mental structures are so familiar, unconsciously, that they have to be brought to the foreground. Andrea Lunsford, on the other hand, in the oft-cited "Cognitive Development and the Basic Writer" (1979), argues that basic writers "have not yet attained the level of cognitive development which would allow them to form abstractions or conceptions" (38). Goldberg advocates an inductive approach to make students aware of the ability to generalize that they already possess; Lunsford's goal is for her students to arrive at the ability that Goldberg presupposes: "The best way to move students into conceptualization and analytic and synthetic modes of thought is to create assignments and activities which allow students to practice or exercise themselves in these modes continuously" (41). In the article, she presents a sampling of such assignments and activities, which range from recognizing verbs to writing essays in analytical modes.

Lunsford turns for theoretical support to James Britton, who in a major work, *Language and Learning* (1970), traces the development of cognitive processes and the role that language plays in children's development. As Lunsford points out, Britton has based an educational model on the theory that "students learn by doing and *then* by extrapolating principles from their activities" ("Cognitive Development and the Basic Writer" 40). The theory upon which *Language and Learning* is based, Britton writes, is "the theory that we use language as a means of organizing a representation of the world" (7). In the participant role as language users, we interact via language. In the spectator role, we are able to step back and contemplate what has happened.

Britton provides valuable insight into Piaget's contribution to the theory of language learning and an excellent introduction to the work of Lev Vygotsky, a Soviet psychologist whose theories of concept formation and the relationship between speech and writing have increasingly drawn the attention of the composition community. In *Thought and Language* (1962), Vygotsky sets up three stages of concept formation. Only in the third stage, the true-concept formation stage, do individuals become aware of the thought processes that they are using. It is this final stage of conceptual ability that Lunsford feels her basic writers have not yet attained and it is this attainment that her activities are designed to foster by engaging the students in inferential reasoning.

Induction is not the end of the developmental progression, however. Goldberg, Lunsford, Britton, and others advocate an inductive approach to teaching students how to discover, for themselves, the unifying principles behind a mass of empirical data. Once they are aware that these unifying principles exist—once their mental structures have developed to the point that they begin to mesh into more general operational groupings that will apply to a broader range of situations— they are able to approach problems deductively. Piaget termed the formal operational stage "hypothetico-deductive." Because hypothetical and deductive reasoning are advanced reasoning skills that have long been viewed as coming late in the developmental progression, writing assignments that require such skills have been largely absent from the basic writing curriculum. Basic writers are often limited to narrative and descriptive writing and are not even encouraged to undertake the sorts of abstracting and synthesizing activities that Lunsford sees as critical for academic survival: "The basic writing course that works exclusively on narration and description will probably fail to build the cognitive skills its students will need to perform well in other college courses" ("Cognitive Development and the Basic Writer" 45). (See also Mike Rose's "Remedial Writing Courses" [1983]). Argumentative assignments that require hypothesis or deductive reasoning are generally considered even further beyond their reach. Both James Moffett, in *Teaching the Universe of Discourse* (1968), and James Britton et al., in *The Development of Writing Abilities (11–18)* (1975), however, argue convincingly that students' failure to write in the argumentative mode is due more to the ineffectiveness of present schooling than to developmental limitations. Moffett arranges types of writing on a spectrum of discourse based on increasing levels of abstraction that parallel Piaget's developmental stages. With increased cognitive maturity comes increased ability to escape the limitations of time and space—to write about the possible as well as the real, the future as well as the present and the past.

The cognitive structures that give shape to students' perception of their world have also attracted the attention of those who seek to understand the logic behind the errors made by basic writers. The success of Mina Shaughnessy's *Errors and Expectations* (1977) was due in part to her ability to see past the sometimes overwhelming number of errors in the work of basic writers to see a pattern in those errors. Her belief was that the systematic nature of the majority of basic writers' errors indicates a logic behind them that differs from the logic of conventional grammar, but that can be put to use in helping students overcome their errors. She agreed with Lunsford that basic writers need to see beyond the surface jumble of errors to perceive unifying principles at work and that they can be led inductively to discover those principles for themselves. In an even more recent article, "The Study of Error" (1980), David Bartholomae presents errors as necessary stages of individual development but goes beyond Shaughnessy to make a distinction between individual systems of errors and general systems: "If [errors] are systematic in the writing of an individual writer, then they are evidence of some idiosyncratic rule system—an idiosyncratic grammar or rhetoric, an 'interlanguage' or 'approximate system.' If the errors are systematic across all basic writers, then they would be evidence of generalized stages in the acquisition of fluent writing for beginning adult writers" (256). Also see Barry Kroll and John C. Schafer ("Error-Analysis and the Teaching of Composition" [1978]) for further discussion of how errors can help teachers to identify the cognitive strategies that learners are using to process information and Patricia Laurence ("Error's Endless Train" [1975]) for a discussion of how basic writers may have trouble with words because of interference from mental structures derived from a second language or a dialect variation.

AUDIENCE AWARENESS

A larger body of work is based on the second of the cognitive-developmental assumptions—the assumption that the individual must decenter out of a basic egocentrism in order to achieve equilibrium at the level of formal thought. Piaget has termed egocentrism "the undifferentiated state prior to multiple perspectives" (Inhelder and Piaget, *Growth of Logical Thinking* 345). For a writer to communicate with an audience outside of himself, he must be able to view his subject from perspectives other than his own. He has to be aware of an audience and must be able to "get outside of himself" to the extent that he can look at his subject from someone else's point of view.

An excellent general introduction to the cognitive aspects of audience awareness is Barry Kroll's "Cognitive Egocentrism and the Problem of Audience Awareness in Written Discourse" (1978). He focuses on two crucial concerns that should guide an investigation of audience awareness: "First, it is important to understand how people go about constructing mental representations of others. . . . We need a cognitive theory that will specify what a speaker does in being aware of an audience. Second, we need to chart how this awareness develops, since it is obvious that mature audience awareness does not emerge full-blown" (271). Kroll continues,

The cognitive-developmental orientation calls attention to the dependency of audience awareness on specific cognitive functions in a speaker or writer. Writers who can decenter their perspective, taking the view of a hypothetical readership, are more likely to display audience awareness than writers who are embedded in their personal view of reality. Hence, the crucial factors in an investigation of audience awareness are not salient characteristics of audiences, but the constructive processes operative in the mind of the writer. We need research efforts aimed at identifying the specific cognitive correlates of audience awareness. (279)

Lisa Ede's "Audience" (1984) includes a summary of recent cognitively based empirical research on audience.

Piaget's primary concern was with the development of cognitive skills that allow the individual to manipulate the world of objects and ultimately the world of ideas. A number of researchers have now sought to discover if there are parallel stages in the development of perception of other persons. The concept of role taking has been the subject of research since the 1930s. One of the most complete treatments of the subject is John H. Flavell's *The Development of Role-Taking and Communication Skills in Children* (1968). Robert Selman ("Social-Cognitive Understanding" [1976]) presents one of the most extensive models of role taking or interpersonal inference yet developed. He explains the purpose of his research thus: "In my research, I have used structural analysis to describe developmental transformations (or stages) in order to describe the development of role-taking ability. Therefore, instead of viewing progression in role taking simply as the result of quantitative accumulation of social knowledge, I have viewed it in terms of qualitative changes in the child's structuring of his understanding of the relation between the perspectives of self and others'' (301). He goes on to relate his role-taking stages to Piaget's cognitive ones. Selman's stages of role taking closely parallel Lawrence Kohlberg's of moral development (''Moral Stages and Moralization'' [1976]). Kohlberg's extension of his own theory of moral development into the college years plus Diane Byrne's extension of Selman's stages of role taking beyond adolescence (''The Development of Role-Taking in Adolescence'' [1973]) provide significant insight into the advanced stages of both social and moral development.

Andrea Lunsford deals in two articles (''Cognitive Development and the Basic Writer'' [1979] and ''The Content of Basic Writers' Essays'' [1980]) with the problems that basic writers face because of their difficulty in decentering. Moffett sees ''differentiating among modes of discourse, registers of speech, kinds of audiences'' as ''essentially a matter of decentering, of seeing alternatives, of standing in others' shoes, of knowing that one has a private or local point of view and knowledge structure'' (*Teaching the Universe of Discourse* [1968] 57). The further removed a writer or speaker is from his audience, the more communication depends on shared mental structures, a point well made by Heinz Werner and Bernard Kaplan in ''General Nature of Developmental Changes in the Symbolic Process'' (1978).

The ability to ''get outside of themselves,'' or decenter, is crucial for young children making the transition from speech to writing. Piaget differentiates children's early egocentric speech from the socialized speech toward which they move in the course of the preoperational stage. Vygotsky (*Thought and Language* [1962]) seems to have been one of the first, however, to point out that the development of writing does not repeat the development of speaking, because writing requires a level of abstraction not required by speech. If the purpose in writing is for the writer to communicate to an audience exterior to himself, the writing may demand abstractive skills that have only begun to emerge at the time that writing instruction usually begins (*Thought and Language* 142).

Moffett's curriculum for K–13 (*Student-Centered Language Arts and Reading, K–13* [1976]) is based on a list of continuities that are variations on the theme of decentering. One movement in his series of assignments is from those that ask the students to address small, known audiences like themselves to those that ask them to address distant, unknown, and different audiences. Moffett writes, ''The primary dimension of growth seems to be a movement from the center of the self outward'' (59). Peter Elbow in ''Closing My Eyes as I Speak'' (1987) has more recently argued, however, that it is also important to invoke the opposite model: ''According to this model, we *start out* social and plugged into others and only gradually, through learning and development, come to 'unplug' to any significant degree so as to function in a more private, individual and differentiated fashion'' (56). Writers of all ages must develop audience awareness, but must also develop the ability to *turn off* audience awareness, "especially when it confuses thinking or blocks discourse'' (56).

One developmental dimension measured by James Britton and his colleagues in the British Schools Counsel Project (*The Development of Writing Abilities* [1975]) is the students' growing sense of audience. The researchers are realistic, however, as they appraise the extent to which students are affected by the fact that their audience is usually a teacher, and, more often than not, a teacher in the role of examiner. The project in this sense becomes as much an evaluation of the British examination system as of the developmental levels of the students involved.

Researchers have recently begun to investigate how awareness of audience affects writing strategies. In a small-scale study reported in "Revision Strategies of Basic and Competent Writers As They Write for Different Audiences'' (1984), Brian Monahan investigated the revisions made by the two categories of writers as they revised for audiences of teachers and of peers. Monahan's subjects were twelfth graders. Gary Schumacher and his colleagues asked beginning and advanced college writers to explain the cognitive and grammatical activities that went on during pauses in their writing ("Cognitive Activities of Beginning and Advanced College Writers'' [1984]). An empirical study conducted by Donald Rubin and Gene Piche ("Development in Syntactic and Strategic Aspects of Audience Adaptation Skills'' [1979]) "investigated audience adaptation in persuasive writing as a function of age and of measured social cognitive ability. It examined use of both syntactic complexity and persuasive strategies in messages addressed to targets varying in degree of intimacy to the writer'' (293).

PROBLEM SOLVING, PERRY, AND THE PROBLEM OF DICTATING VALUES

Linda Flower and John Hayes are well known for their studies of the problem-solving strategies of writers. Two assumptions on which their research and the resulting problem-solving strategies are based are the same assumptions that have generally been used to link composition theory with cognitive developmental theory. In "Problem-Solving Strategies and the Writing Process'' (1977), Flower and Hayes present an overview of the heuristics that they have learned by means of protocol analysis. A heuristic is defined as "simply the codification of a useful technique or cognitive skill'' (450): "Because the heuristics are a kind of shorthand for cognitive operations, they give the writer self-conscious access to some of the thinking techniques that normally constitute 'inspiration.' '' A second advantage of the heuristics is that they focus on the need to construct ideas in language in such a way that the ideas are adapted to both the goals of the writer and the needs of a reader (452).

Flower and Hayes have made use of recorded "thinking-aloud'' protocols to study just what it is that "good'' writers do when they write and just what it is that makes the problem-solving strategies of "poor" writers less successful. In "The Cognition of Discovery" (1980), they report that one of the hallmarks of good writers is the time they spend thinking about how to affect a reader. Flower and Hayes are concerned with the way that writers interpret the problem that a writing task presents and the goals that they set for themselves as they go about solving that problem. The most striking difference that the researchers found was in the differing goals for dealing with audience that novice and expert writers set for themselves.

Patricia Bizzell, however, in reviewing Hayes and Flower's "Identifying the Organization of Writing Processes" and other articles in *Cognitive Processes in Writing* (1980), argues that Hayes and Flower are insensitive to the problems of basic writers and indeed misinterpret basic writers' difficulties ("Cognition, Convention, and Certainty" [1982]). She raises significant questions not simply about the goals of writing, but about the goals of writing instruction. Here and elsewhere ("What Happens When Basic Writers Come to College?" [1986] and "William Perry and Liberal Education" [1984]), Bizzell asks her readers to stop and consider the extent to which development is measured in terms of the values of a fairly limited discourse community. Of Hayes and Flower's chapter in *Cognitive Process in Writing* Bizzell writes:

The implication here seems to be that cognitive deficiency keeps poor writers from forming their own goals, keeps them locked in the myopia of goals appropriate to a much earlier stage of cognitive development. . . . I think these students' difficulties with goal-setting are better understood in terms of their unfamiliarity with the academic discourse community, combined, perhaps, with such limited experience outside their native discourse communities that they are unaware that there is such a thing as a discourse community with conventions to be mastered. (230)

Bizzell is one of a number of composition theorists who have looked to William Perry and his colleagues at the Harvard Bureau of Study Counsel for what their work can contribute to the understanding of students' developing perceptions of their world and of knowledge. Where Piaget devotes relatively little attention to development during the college years, the whole purpose of Perry's report *Forms of Intellectual and Ethical Development in the College Years* (1968; rpt. 1970) is to describe a series of nine positions that the majority of college-aged individuals go through as they mature. The report is based on interviews conducted with Harvard students during the 1950s and 1960s. Interviews with each student at the end of each of his or her four years of college led Perry to believe that there is a general movement in college students from a basic dualism to an awareness of relativism to an evolution of commitment.

Perry has a great deal to offer those who teach writing because of what his scheme reveals about students' developing awareness of multiple perspectives. Where Piaget concerns himself more with the abilities that develop with maturation, the later positions of what has come to be called the Perry Scheme describe what students do with their newfound mental abilities. Thus the emphasis in the title of Perry's major work is on forms of both intellectual and ethical development.

While Bizzell acknowledges that the Perry Scheme has value for the teacher of writing, she also cautions against using it as a blueprint for writing curricula ("William Perry and Liberal Education" 451). A major distinction that she sees between Piaget and Perry is that Perry traces the development of philosophical assumptions rather than cognitive stages. Just as Dulit points out that the level of formal thought is a potential rather than a necessary stage of development, a relativistic worldview is one developmental goal, not the only conceivable one. What Perry describes does not necessarily happen to all cognitively normal eighteen to twenty-one-year olds. What he describes happens *when* they receive an education. (See Martinez and Martinez, "Reconsidering Cognition and the Basic Writer" [1987].) He focuses particularly on liberal arts education and the worldview it inculcates. He tries to show that undergraduates in a liberal arts college *do* pass through these developmental stages but also that such development is desirable.

A number of researchers and educators have tried to replicate Perry's study or to apply its findings to the classroom. In "Cognitive and Ethical Growth" (1981) Perry himself sums up the research that had been done through 1981. So many researchers from such a variety of disciplines have been attracted to the Perry Scheme that a newsletter regularly updates a Perry Scheme bibliography. (Contact Larry Copes, ISEM, 10429 Barnes Way, St. Paul, MN 55075.)

Among those who have related the Perry Scheme specifically to the teaching of writing are Christopher C. Burnham in "The Perry Scheme and the Teaching of Writing" (1986), Janice N. Hays in "The Development of Discursive Maturity in College Writers" (1983), Donna Haisty in "The Developmental Theories of Jean Piaget and William Perry" (1983), Jack Orr in "Communication, Relativism, and Student Development" (1978), Joanne Kurfiss in *Development in College* (1983), and Susan Beers in *An Analysis of the Interaction between Students' Epistemological Assumptions and the Composing Process* (1984). Myra Kogen in "The Conventions of Expository Writing" (1986) and Martinez and Martinez in "Reconsidering Cognition and the Basic Writer" (1987) respond to what they consider to be Hays's faulty Perry-based assumptions about student writers and their developmental levels. Hays herself calls Ann Berthoff's article "Is Teaching Still Possible?" (1984) "the most emphatic published statement challenging developmental perspectives" (11). However, Hays's own response to Kogen and others, "Models of Intellectual Development and Writing" (1987), remains to date the most complete clarification of common misconceptions about intellectual development and its relevance to writing.

Where Janice Hays is among the leading defenders of the application of developmental psychology to the basic writing classroom, Mike Rose sounds an equally strong cautionary note. In "Narrowing the Mind and Page" (1988), he warns against what he calls "cognitive reductionism"—the tendency "to seek singular, unitary cognitive explanations for broad ranges of poor school performance'' (267). Piaget's work on the development of logical thought is one of four theories he examines in terms of the claims about writers they have been used to support. (The other three are field dependence-independence, hemisphericity, and orality-literacy theories.) He writes:

I think we need to look closely at these claims and at the theories used to support them, for both the theories and the claims lead to social distinctions that have important consequences, political as well as educational. . . . Consideration of the theories leads us naturally to consideration of their applicability to areas beyond their original domain. Such application often overgeneralizes the theory. . . . A further problem—sometimes inherent in the theories themselves, sometimes as a result of reductive application—is the tendency to diminish cognitive complexity and rely on simplified cognitive oppositions: independence vs. dependent, literate vs. oral, verbal vs. spatial, concrete vs. logical. These oppositions are textbook-neat, but, as much recent cognitive research demonstrates, they are narrow and misleading. Yet another problem is this: these distinctions are usually used in a way meant to be value-free (that is, they highlight differences rather than deficits in thinking), but, given our culture, they are anything but neutral. Social and political hierarchies end up encoded in sweeping cognitive dichotomies. (268)

When teachers attempt to accelerate their students' cognitive development, they must be aware that they are dealing with far more than the surface features of written discourse. They are asking their students to accept a value system in which communication is important enough to make valuable, in and of itself, the acquisition of the formal operational structures that make cooperation in its literal sense both possible and desirable. They are also asking their students to accept a relativistic worldview as the desirable end goal of education. To the extent that success in college and beyond is bound up in the ability to achieve these developmental goals, a background in developmental psychology is an essential part of the training of teachers of basic writers.

REFERENCES

Anson, Chris M., et al. "From Schemes to Themes: Implications of Schema Theory for Teaching Writing." *J Teach Writ* 2 (1983): 193–211.

Barritt, Loren S., and Barry M. Kroll. "Some Implications of Cognitive-Developmental Psychology for Research in Composing." *Research on Composing: Points of Departure.* Ed. Charles R. Cooper and Lee Odell. Urbana, Ill.: NCTE, 1978, pp. 49–57.

Bartholomae, David. "The Study of Error." *CCC* 31 (1980): 253–69.

Beers, Susan E. *An Analysis of the Interaction between Students' Epistemological Assumptions and the Composing Process.* 1984. ERIC ED 249 503.

Bereiter, Carl. "Development in Writing." *Cognitive Processes in Writing.* Ed. Lee W. Gregg and Erwin R. Steinberg. Hillsdale, N.J.: Erlbaum, 1980, pp. 73–93.

Berg, Anna, and Gerald Coleman. "A Cognitive Approach to Teaching the Developmental Student." *JBW* 4.2 (1985): 4–23.

Berthoff, Ann E. "Is Teaching Still Possible? Writing, Meaning, and Higher Order Reasoning." *CE* 46 (1984): 743–55.

———. "Tolstoy, Vygotsky, and the Making of Meaning." *CCC* 29 (1978): 249–55.

Bizzell, Patricia. "Cognition, Convention, and Certainty: What We Need to Know about Writing." *P/T* 3 (1982): 213–43.

———. "What Happens When Basic Writers Come to College?" *CCC* 37 (1986): 294–301.

———. "William Perry and Liberal Education." *CE* 46 (1984): 447–54.

Bracewell, Robert J. "Writing as a Cognitive Activity." *Visible Language* 14 (1980): 400–422.

Bradford, Annette N. "Cognitive Immaturity and Remedial College Writers." *The Writer's Mind: Writing as a Mode of Thinking.* Ed. Janice Hays et al. Urbana, Ill.: NCTE, 1983, pp. 15–24.

Bringuier, Jean-Claude. *Conversations with Jean Piaget.* Trans. Basia Miller Gulati. Chicago: University of Chicago Press, 1980.

Britton, James. *Language and Learning.* Harmondsworth, Eng.: Penguin, 1970.

———, et al. *The Development of Writing Abilities (11–18).* London: Macmillan Education, 1975.

Bruner, Jerome S. *Toward a Theory of Instruction.* Cambridge, Mass.: Harvard University Press, 1966.

Burnham, Christopher C. "The Perry Scheme and the Teaching of Writing." *RR* 4 (1986): 152–58.

Byrne, Diane Friedman. "The Development of Role-Taking in Adolescence." Diss. Harvard University, 1973.

D'Angelo, Frank. *A Conceptual Theory of Rhetoric.* Cambridge, Mass.: Winthrop, 1975.

Dulit, Everett. "Adolescent Thinking à la Piaget: The Formal Stage." *J Youth Ado* 1 (1972): 281–301.

Ede, Lisa. "Audience: An Introduction to Research." *CCC* 35 (1984): 140–54.

Elbow, Peter. "Closing My Eyes As I Speak: An Argument for Ignoring Audience." *CE* 49 (1987): 50–69.

Elifson, Joan M., and Katharine R. Stone. "Integrating Social, Moral, and Cognitive Developmental Theory: Implications of James Fowler's Epistemological Paradigm for Basic Writers." *JBW* 4 (1985): 24–37.

Elsasser, Nan, and Vera P. John-Steiner. "An Interactionist Approach to Advancing Literacy." *Harvard Educ Rev* 47 (1977): 355–69.

Flavell, John H. *The Development of Role-Taking and Communication Skills in Children.* New York: Wiley, 1968.

———. *The Developmental Psychology of Jean Piaget.* Princeton: D. Van Nostrand, 1963.

Flower, Linda, and John R. Hayes. "The Cognition of Discovery: Defining a Rhetorical Problem." *CCC* 31 (1980): 21–32.

———. "A Cognitive Process Theory of Writing." *CCC* 32 (1981): 365–87.

———. "Problem-Solving Strategies and the Writing Process." *CE* 39 (1977): 449–61.

Goldberg, Marilyn K. "Overfamiliarity: A Cognitive Barrier in Teaching Composition." *JBW* 4.1 (1985): 34–43.

Haisty, Donna B. "The Developmental Theories of Jean Piaget and William Perry: An Application to the Teaching of Writing." Diss. Texas Christian University, 1983.

Hayes, John R., and Linda S. Flower. "Identifying the Organization of Writing Processes." *Cognitive Processes in Writing*. Ed. Lee W. Gregg and Erwin R. Steinberg. Hillsdale, N.J.: Erlbaum, 1980.

Hays, Janice N. "The Development of Discursive Maturity in College Writers." *The Writer's Mind*. Ed. Janice N. Hays et al. Urbana, Ill.: NCTE, 1983, pp. 127–44.

———. "Models of Intellectual Development and Writing: A Response to Myra Kogen." *JBW* 6.1 (1987): 11–27.

Holland, Robert M. "Piagetian Theory and the Design of Composing Assignments." *AEB* 19 (October 1976): 17–22.

Hull, Glynda A., and David J. Bartholomae. "Basic Writing." *Research in Composition and Rhetoric: A Bibliographic Sourcebook*. Ed. Michael G. Moran and Ronald F. Lunsford. Westport, Conn.: Greenwood Press, 1984, pp. 265–302.

Inhelder, Bärbel, and Jean Piaget. *The Growth of Logical Thinking from Childhood to Adolescence*. Trans. Anne Parsons and Stanley Milgram. New York: Basic Books, 1958.

Johnson, Melanie, and William G. Perry, Jr. "Some New Thoughts on the Perry Scheme." *Perry Developmental Scheme Newsletter* 3 (1981): 3–6.

Jolly, Peggy. "Meeting the Challenge of Developmental Writers." *TETYC* 14 (1987): 32–40.

Jones, David E. "Evidence for a Conceptual Theory of Rhetoric." *CCC* 28 (1977): 333–37.

King, Patricia M. "William Perry's Theory of Intellectual and Ethical Development." *New Directions for Student Services* 4 (1978): 35–52.

Kitchener, K. S. "Cognition, Metacognition, and Epistemic Cognition: A Three-Level Model of Cognitive Processing." *Human Dev* 26 (1983): 222–32.

Kitzhaber, Albert R. *Themes, Theories, and Therapy*. New York: McGraw-Hill, 1963.

Kogen, Myra. "The Conventions of Expository Writing." *JBW* 5.1 (1986): 24–37.

Kohlberg, Lawrence. "Moral Stages and Moralization." *Moral Development and Behavior: Theory, Research, and Social Issues*. Ed. Thomas Lickona. New York: Holt, Rinehart and Winston, 1976, pp. 31–53.

Kroll, Barry. "A Cognitive-Developmental Approach to the Teaching of Composition." *TETYC* 7 (1980): 17–21.

———. "Cognitive Egocentrism and the Problem of Audience Awareness in Written Discourse." *RTE* 12 (1978): 269–81.

Kroll, Barry, and John C. Schafer. "Error-Analysis and the Teaching of Composition." *CCC* 29 (1978): 243–48.

Kurfiss, Joanne. *Development in College: Perspectives, Processes, and Reflections on the Role of Writing*. 1983. ERIC ED 254 145.

———. "Sequentiality and Structure in a Cognitive Model of College Student Development." *Dev Psychol* 13 (1977): 565–71.

Laurence, Patricia. "Error's Endless Train: Why Students Don't Perceive Errors." *JBW* 1.1 (1975): 23–42.

Lunsford, Andrea. "Cognitive Development and the Basic Writer." *CE* 41 (1979): 38–46.

——— "The Content of Basic Writers' Essays." *CCC* 31 (1980): 278–90.

McKinnon, Joe W. "The College Student and Formal Operations." *Research, Teaching, and Learning with the Piaget Model*. Ed. John W. Renner and Donald G. Stafford. Norman: University of Oklahoma Press, 1976, pp. 110–29.

Martinez, Joseph G. R., and Nancy C. Martinez. "Reconsidering Cognition and the Basic Writer: A Response to Myra Kogen." *JBW* 6 (1987): 79–82.

Martlew, Margaret. "Problems and Difficulties: Cognitive and Communicative Aspects of Writing Development." *The Psychology of Written Language: Developmental and Educational Perspectives*. New York: Wiley, 1983.

Milner, Joseph O. *Writing Stages: A Developmental Hierarchy*. 1983. ERIC ED 249 496.

Moffett, James. *Student-Centered Language Arts and Reading, K–13: A Handbook for Teachers*, 2nd ed. Boston: Houghton Mifflin, 1976.

———. *Teaching the Universe of Discourse*. Boston: Houghton Mifflin, 1968.

Monahan, Brian D. "Revision Strategies of Basic and Competent Writers as They Write for Different Audiences." *RTE* 18 (1984): 288–304.

Orr, Jack. "Communication, Relativisim, and Student Development." *Comm Ed* 27 (1978): 83–98.

Perry, William G., Jr. "Cognitive and Ethical Growth: The Making of Meaning." *The Modern American College*. Ed. A. Chickering. San Francisco: Jossey-Bass, 1981, pp. 76–116.

———. *Forms of Intellectual and Ethical Developmental in the College Years: A Scheme*. 1968. New York: Holt, Rinehart and Winston, 1970.

Phillips, John L., Jr. *The Origins of Intellect: Piaget's Theory*, 2nd ed. San Francisco: W. H. Freeman, 1975.

Piaget, Jean. "Intellectual Evolution from Adolescence to Adulthood." *Human Dev* 15 (1972): 1–12.

———. *A Piaget Sampler: An Introduction to Jean Piaget Through His Own Words*. Ed. Sarah Campbell. New York: Wiley, 1976.

———. "Piaget's Theory." Trans. Guy Gellerier and Jonas Langer. *Carmichael's Manual of Child Psychology*, 3rd ed., 2 vols. Ed. Paul H. Mussen. New York: Wiley, 1970. 1:729–32.

Puma, Vincent, et al. "Cognitive Approaches to Writing: An Introductory Annotated Bibliography." 1983. ERIC ED 233 375.

Renner, John W., and Donald G. Stafford. "The Operational Levels of Secondary Students." *Research, Teaching, and Learning with the Piaget Model*. Ed. John W. Renner and Donald G. Stafford. Norman: University of Oklahoma Press, 1976, pp. 90–109.

Rose, Mike. "Narrowing the Mind and Page: Remedial Writers and Cognitive Reductionism." *CCC* 39 (1988): 267–302.

———. "Remedial Writing Courses: A Critique and a Proposal." *CE* 45 (1983): 109–28.

———. "Rigid Rules, Inflexible Plans, and the Stifling of Language: A Cognitive Analysis of Writer's Block." *CCC* 31 (1980): 389–401.

———. *Writer's Block: The Cognitive Dimension*. Carbondale: Southern Illinois University Press, 1984.

Ross, Robert J. "The Empirical Status of Formal Operations." *Adolescence* 9 (1974): 413–20.

———. "Some Empirical Parameters of Formal Thinking." *J Youth Ado* 2 (1973): 167–77.

Rubin, Donald L., and Gene L. Piche. "Development in Syntactic and Strategic Aspects of Audience Adaptation Skills in Written Persuasive Communication." *RTE* 13 (1979): 293–316.

Schumacher, Gary M., et al. "Cognitive Activities of Beginning and Advanced College Writers: A Pausal Analysis." *RTE* 18 (1984): 169–87.

Schwebel, Milton. "Formal Operations in First-Year College Students." *J Psychol* 91 (1975): 133–41.

Selman, Robert. "Social-Cognitive Understanding." *Moral Development and Behavior: Theory, Research, and Social Issues*. Ed. Thomas Lickona. New York: Holt, Rinehart and Winston, 1976, pp. 299–316.

Shapiro, Nancy S. *Finding a Frame of Reference: Toward an Analysis of Contextual Elaboration in College Writing*. 1986. ERIC ED 270 753.

Shaughnessy, Mina. *Errors and Expectations: A Guide for the Teacher of Basic Writing*. New York: Oxford University Press, 1977.

Smith, Myrna J. "Bruner on Writing." *CCC* 27 (1977): 129–33.

Spear, Karen I. "Building Cognitive Skills in Basic Writers." *TETYC* 9 (1983): 91–98.

———. "Promoting Cognitive Development in the Writing Center." *Writing Centers: Theory and Administration*. Ed. Gary A. Olson. Urbana, Ill.: NCTE, 1984, pp. 62–76.

Stallard, Charles. "Composing: A Cognitive Process Theory." *CCC* 27 (1976): 181–84.

Taylor, Karl K. "DOORS English—The Cognitive Basis of Rhetorical Models." *JBW* 2 (1979): 52–66.

Vygotsky, Lev S. *Thought and Language*. Ed. and trans. Eugenia Hanfmann and Gertrude Vakar. Cambridge, Mass.: MIT Press, 1962.

Werner, Heinz, and Bernard Kaplan. "General Nature of Developmental Changes in the Symbolic Process." *Developmental Processes: Heinz Werner's Selected Writings*, 2 vols. Ed. Sybil S. Barten and Margery B. Franklin. New York: International Universities Press, 1978. 1:487–98.

3

Literacy Theory and Basic Writing

Mariolina Salvatori and Glynda Hull

In *Literacy in Theory and Practice* (1984) Brian Street argues, as many others have recently done (Resnick and Resnick, [1977]; Scribner and Cole [1981]; Pattison [1982]; Heath [1983]; Rose [1985]; Bartholomae [1986]; Cook-Gumperz [1986]; Lunsford [1987]), that while literacy is often viewed as a technology, a set of tools, becoming literate is not a neutral process. That is to say, literacy is not politically separate or culture-free. Rather, it is embedded within society and depends for its meaning and its practice upon social institutions and conditions. It is permanently and deeply ideological, and teaching it necessarily means inculcating and reproducing a specific set of values and evaluations.

Because we agree with this way of thinking about literacy, we are utterly skeptical about the possibility of anyone's writing a "neutral" bibliographical essay on it, even less so an essay on literacy *and* basic writing, the kind of writing that, within certain views of literacy, can be read as cognitively deficient, illiterate, oral, or primitive. Our experience as teachers, and particularly as teachers of basic writing, has unequivocally taught us that some views of literacy foster a productive, helpful, and respectful pedagogy, while others are more likely to produce a pedagogy that is not only unhelpful but also damaging and oppressive. In addition, we don't believe it is possible for us to write a neutral essay, because as much as we are aware of the intellectual and social traditions that shape and filter our ways of viewing literacy theory and practice, we also know that some of the implications that these traditions have for our way of thinking might escape us. For these reasons, in our survey of the rich and diverse literature on literacy, we have made a point of reminding ourselves of the title of this essay—"Literacy Theory and Basic Writing." On the one hand, we have chosen to read "and" as "in the service of"; in other words, the guiding principle for our selections has been the extent to which a given definition of literacy can help teachers to understand and to devise an effective pedagogy for basic writing. On the other hand, we have chosen to read "and" as "seen from the perspective of"; that is, we have relied on our theoretical and practical understanding of "basic writers" in order to assess and to test the adequacy of various definitions of literacy.

For other, more comprehensive bibliographies on literacy, see Harvey Graff's citations in the notes to his *The Legacies of Literacy* (1987), as well as Robert Pattison's notes to *On Literacy* (1982); Harvey Graff's *Literacy in History* (1981); Carmen St. John Hunter and David Harman's *Adult Illiteracy in the United States* (1979); and Ron Scollon's "Language, Literacy, and Learning" (1985).

We began with a flexible definition of basic writers drawn from recent literature: writers unfamiliar with the conventions of academic discourse (see Patricia Bizzell, "The Ethos of Academic Discourse" [1978]; David J. Bartholomae, "The Study of Error" [1980]; Glynda Hull, "Constructing Taxonomies for Error" [1987]); "outsiders" who do not quite know that and why they are outsiders (Edwin J. Delattre, "The Insiders" [1983, 1987]); writers "who simply have not had enough experience writing in a variety of roles and registers for a variety of concerned readers" (quote by Karen Greenberg in Theresa Enos's "Preface" to *A Sourcebook for Basic Writers Teachers* [1987] v); writers whose unconventional readings threaten the literacy status quo (Robert Connors, Enos's "Preface" [1987]); writers who sometimes (but do not necessarily) make a lot of mistakes, but whose errors can be read as systematic and understandable attempts to appropriate the conventions of written language (David Bartholomae, "Inventing the University" [1985]; Mina Shaughnessy, *Errors and Expectations* [1977]). (*A Sourcebook for Basic Writing Teachers*, edited by Theresa Enos [1987], offers an excellent selection on scholarship on basic writing and basic writers' literacies.)

Implicit in our definition of basic writers is the recognition that reading and writing are "unnatural" acts, acquired technologies that, as the phenomenon of basic writing suggests, are not by themselves factors of change—cognitive, social economic, political—but can contribute to some or all of these changes. Far from occurring automatically, however, these changes are fostered by that complex web of factors that constitute the ecological environment in which literacy itself is conceptualized, valued, evaluated, transmitted, acquired.

Our reading of the research on literacy informed by the available research on basic writing confirms what Harvey Graff says in *The Legacies of Literacy* (1987): "Literacy is *profoundly misunderstood*. That is as true for the past as for the present. The misconstrual of the meanings and contributions of literacy, with the revealing contradictions that result, is not only a problem of evidence of data but also a failure in conceptualization and, even more, epistemology" (3). The main reasons that discussions of literacy flounder, he argues, are that researchers, theorists, and critics "slight efforts to formulate consistent and realistic *definitions of literacy*, have little appreciation of the *conceptual complications* that the subject presents, and ignore the vital role of *sociohistorical* context" (3).

Graff's historical bias, one he openly acknowledges, leads him to emphasize the role of sociohistorical context. Other scholars, researchers, and theorists emphasize different roles; and in so doing, they not only construct different meanings for and assess different contributions of literacy, but they also denounce different misunderstandings. Because these differences in the assessment of literacy's functions, consequences, and implications can cause considerable confusions, we want to stress the necessity of keeping in mind the extent to which the theorist's, researcher's, or scholar's bias determines his or her methodology and consequently his or her reading of the phenomenon. (See Frank Smith's "Introduction to Hillel Goelman, Antoinette Oberg, and Frank Smith's *Awakening to Literacy* [1984].)

The definition of "functional literacy" is a case in point. According to certain definitions, basic writers are "functionally literate" (see Harman [1970]; Resnick and Resnick [1977]; Corbett [1982]; Pattison [1982]); and yet, when basic writers are confronted with specific academic tasks that require reflexivity about "the uses and problems of language" that they are expected to express "in the ways evolved and sanctioned by" the particular academic context (Pattison 6), their literacy is clearly not "functional." Consequently, in the academy, basic writers are often labeled "illiterate" (see Mike Rose's discussion in "The Language of Exclusion" [1985]) or with a euphemism that is still an indictment of their not measuring up to certain standards—"nonliterate." In "Writing on the Margins" (1987), David Bartholomae addresses the problem of how the profession has defined basic writing and basic writers. He forcefully argues that the definition begins with an abstraction and turns students into an abstraction. A similar problem, we believe, haunts most discussions of literacy. The danger, then, when we address the issue of basic writing and literacy, is that of compounding two sets of abstractions.

We have divided the material surveyed into two broad categories. In the first we treat the work of theorists and researchers who are situated within different disciplines, but who nevertheless seem to share the belief that literacy *causes* important changes—cognitive, economic, social, political. We titled this category: "The *Causal* Perspective: The *Consequences* of Literacy"; in it we first examine the literature on literacy as a causal agent in cognitive development; we next look at works that treat literacy as a prerequisite for social, economic, and political change. Next, in the section we call "The *Enabling* Perspective: The *Implications* of Literacy," we survey the work of those who call into question the teleological interpretation of literacy, and who focus rather on the various, complex forces that either can foster or hinder literacy's *potentiality* to bring about changes.[1] This latter perspective, it will become clear, is the one that is most in tune with our own pedagogy and politics.

We have set up this division as a heuristic for uncovering, for making manifest, "the significant lines of cleavage in the field of literacy studies" (Brian Street, *Literacy in Theory and Practice* [1984] 3), but above all, for exposing the assumptions about learning that different views of literacy originate from and reproduce. It is important that this division not be reified into a dichotomy, but that it be conceptualized, rather, as an enabling and necessary fiction—a way to set up a context where theory and practice interrogate, test, and monitor each other, where different theories and practices read their own and each other's differences critically, where researchers, theorists, and teachers create for themselves and measure up to the responsibility that literacy thrusts upon them.

THE *CAUSAL* PERSPECTIVE: THE *CONSEQUENCES* OF LITERACY

Some view literacy, not just as a positive force promoting an individual's intellectual growth by facilitating particular modes of thought, but as an essential stage, one that is required if a person is to attain full cognitive development. The work of L. S. Vygotsky and his friend and colleague A. R. Luria has been appropriated and, we suggest, reduced to support this view. (For different approaches to research on cognitive development, see Barbara Rogoff and Jean Lave, *Everyday Cognition* [1984].)

In the 1930s, Vygotsky and Luria conducted a set of studies in Soviet Central Asia that revealed considerable differences in the ways in which literate and nonliterate subjects performed on abstract reasoning tasks, such as categorizing familiar objects and deducting conclusions from syllogistic premises. The studies showed that nonliterate subjects tended to rely on practical experience in their reasoning, whereas literate subjects were able or willing to use language to move to higher levels of abstraction. These particular studies, which were part of Vygotsky's investigation of the *interconnections* between sociocultural history and the development of mental functions, tend to be interpreted more frequently as an indication that literacy is a *prerequisite* for abstract reasoning, rather than, for example, as a demonstration of the effects that (even minimal) schooling can have.

Although American psychology has been hospitable to Vygotsky's ideas since the 1962 publication of his monograph, *Thought and Language*, the complexity of his theories began to be fully appreciated only with the publication of *Mind in Society* (1978) (a collection of essays edited, at the urging of Luria, by Michael Cole, Vera John-Steiner, Sylvia Scribner, and Ellen Souberman) and with Alex Kozulin's fuller version of *Thought and Language* (1986). Vygotsky's brilliant insights into the dialectical and reciprocal interaction of mind and society have led to the current exciting and more detailed explorations of how changes in cultural conditions—for example, the introduction of schooling and literacy—affect cognition. Scribner and Cole's assessment of Vygotsky's work points out the reductive ways in which it has been understood and used (*The Psychology of Literacy* [1981] 8–13) and the necessity of studying the process of ''litericization'' (13) more accurately and responsibly. At the same time, their application and amplification of Vygotsky's insights confirm the extraordinary perceptiveness of his theory and research. (We recommend James V. Wertsch's highly informative study of Vygotsky, *Vygotsky and the Social Formation of Mind* [1985]; Kozulin's "Vygotsky in Context" [*Thought and Language* (1986)] for its useful analysis of the split between naturalistic scientific psychology and philosophical descriptive psychology; Susan Wells's stimulating reading, "Vygotsky Reads *Capital*" [*Correspondences Two*]; and James Thomas Zebroski's response to Wells's article, "Tropes and Zones" [*Correspondences Four*].)

Proponents of what is referred to as the Great Divide theory use Vygotsky's work as evidence for their claim that *only* through the acquisition of literacy do humans acquire the ability to manipulate language in ways that advance higher mental functioning. They also enlist, as support, Eric Havelock's early learned study (*Preface to Plato* [1963]) on the differences between the language of Homeric epics—mnemonic, concrete, imagistic—and the language of Platonic dialogues—analytic, conceptual, reflexive—and his analysis of the remarkably different modes of thought that such languages seem to have embodied and made possible. (See also Havelock's *Origins of Western Literacy* [1976] and *The Greek Concept of Justice* [1978].) Scholars who see in literature the documentation of mankind's progressive intellectual and artistic development find this view of literacy particularly meaningful. And we too see it as an appropriate and justifiable use of a particular understanding of literacy. There is a problem, however, when Vygotsky's or Havelock's observations about the correlation between literacy and the development of higher psychological processes are generalized out of context into the claim that there exists a cause-effect relationship between writing and advanced cognitive skills. These inferential leaps lead to unwarranted conclusions about there being a fundamental difference in modes of thought between literate and nonliterate societies. Since this difference has traditionally valorized the "literate," when these conclusions are extended to characterize basic writers vis-à-vis mainstream students, teaching can become a practice of exclusion. If, on the other hand, as Scribner and Cole seem to suggest (*The Psychology of Literacy* 7), the problem has to do with the fact that certain methods of inquiry are adequate for and certain conclusions are pertinent to particular disciplines, then we need to research more seriously the knowledge produced by these disciplines and to test it rigorously in terms of the extent to which it enhances our productive understanding of basic writing. (For a critique of the Great Divide theory, see Ruth Finnegan's "Literacy versus Non-Literacy" [1973] and Arthur W. H. Adkins's "Orality and Philosophy" [1983]. For a balanced assessment of the strengths and the shortcomings in the work of its major proponents, see Harvey Graff's *Legacies of Literacy* [1987] and *The Literacy Myth* [1979] and Robert Pattison's *On Literacy* [1982].)

In their early work on literacy ("The Consequences of Literacy" [1968]), Jack Goody and Ian Watt adapted Havelock's classic approach to the framework of social sciences. They explicitly linked the formation of the disciplines of logic and history with the rise of alphabetic literacy without which, they claim, the development of analytical and syllogistic reasoning and of the concepts of space and time would have not been possible. In "Literacy in Culture and Cognition"

(1987), an article we recommend as a valuable guide to a critical reading of the vast body of material on literacy, Patricia Bizzell points out that Goody's early work with Watt helped to advance the Great Divide theory, but that in his more recent work, Goody "qualifies his position because he questions the identification of illiterates as cognitively deficient" (129). Scribner and Cole suggest that the shift in Goody's work is manifested in a subtle and important change in terminology; his later work, they argue, "emphasized that what had previously been termed the *consequences* of literacy ought really to be considered literacy's *implications*, implications that might, or might not, come to fruition in any particular cultural/historical circumstances" (*Psychology of Literacy* [1981], emphasis added, 7). Like Harvey Graff, Scribner and Cole call for more responsible methods of research, and for greater attention to the implications of the very language used to set up the study of literacy and to communicate the results of that study. (For an additional critical reading of Goody and Watt's work, see Arthur Applebee, "Writing and Reasoning" [1984]. But see also Jack Goody's own reflections on the dangers of the language of dichotomy in *The Domestication of the Savage Mind* [1977] 36. Also, for a persuasive argument about the ways in which metaphorical frameworks "can limit what inquiry will consider" [195], see Frank Smith, "A Metaphor for Literacy" [1985].)

While Walter Ong's research into literacy and his application of this research to the teaching of writing reaffirms Havelock's theory about the cognitive advantages of literacy over orality, his celebration of orality (which he differentiates into "primary orality"—"the pristine orality of mankind untouched by writing or print which remains still more or less operative in areas sheltered to a greater or lesser degree from the full impact of literacy and which is vestigial to some degree in us all"—and "secondary orality"—"the orality induced by radio and television . . . by no means independent of writing and print but totally dependent on them") may suggest ways for teachers to use and to interpret their students' orality constructively ("Literacy and Orality in Our Times" [1978] 3). As James Raymond points outs, Ong's work "has encouraged contemporary writing teachers to view their beginning students as nonliterate rather than illiterate, and to understand the cultural and psychological chasm they must cross if they are to participate in the consciousness of literate communities" (*Literacy as a Human Problem* [1982] 170).

It may be argued, however, that the very use of terms like "nonliterate" and "chasm" calls attention to the basic writer's condition of separateness from the rest of the academic culture. In "Literacy, the Basics, and All That Jazz" (1977), Thomas J. Farrell claims that "Ong's observations can be helpful to us in understanding the effects of the shift from orality to literacy in [basic writing] students" (30), and calls for a teacher's sensitivity to the complexity of that shift. Stressing the interdependence of innate cognitive structures and learned structures, Farrell emphasizes the potentiality for reading and writing to "add yet another dimension to the interactive unfolding of thinking capacities" (35), and consequently for literacy to increase "human awareness of and control of self, others, and the surrounding world in a variety of ways'' (36). As one acknowledges Farrell's pedagogical commitment, one nevertheless wonders whether the dichotomy that is at the basis of his approach can actually ever be resolved. (See Farrell's use of Ong's and Havelock's research in ''IQ and Standard English'' [1983], but see also the responses to his article by Karen L. Greenberg, Patrick Hartwell, Margaret Himley, and R. E. Stratton [*College Composition and Communication*, 1984], and Scribner and Cole's critique of his method in ''Unpackaging Literacy'' [1981].)

In ''Cultural Literacy'' (1983), as in the various subsequent articles in which he advocates his project, E. D. Hirsch claims that ''we can only raise our reading and writing skills significantly by consciously redefining and extending our cultural literacy'' (169). For Hirsch, linguistic literacy depends on a certain amount of canonical information, the sharing of which makes understanding possible. For this reason, he advocates curricular reforms that make the administering of this information possible. Basic writing teachers who are concerned about their students' ''orality'' need to question the ''noetic operations'' (see Ong, *Orality and Literacy* [1982]) that Hirsch's literacy would enable their students to engage in so as to assess whether they are adequate to their students' academic needs. For critical readings of the concept of ''cultural literacy'' and its efficacy in fostering literacy, see John Warnock, ''Cultural Literacy'' (1985); Mariolina Salvatori, '' 'Cultural Literacy' '' (*Correspondences Four*); and Hephzibah Roskelly, ''Redeeming 'Cultural Literacy' '' (*Correspondences Four*). See also E. D. Hirsch's reply to Warnock, ''Cultural Literacy Does Not Mean a List of Works'' (1986) and Warnock's reply to Hirsch, ''Reply to Hirsch's Comment on 'Cultural Literacy' '' (1986).

The belief that literacy radically restructures a person's perception of reality is at the center of Frank D'Angelo's work on literacy. In ''Luria on Literacy'' (1982), he argues that the thinking of nonliterate people is concrete, specific, embedded in a particular situation, that it is sensorimotor and perceptual rather than conceptual. He agrees with Jean Piaget (whose work Vygotsky had criticized because he thought it relied too heavily on ''maturation'' and did not sufficiently take into account sociocultural influences) that ''the thinking of nonliterate people . . . does not advance beyond the level of . . . the stage of concrete operations'' (155). In support of Luria's theory, D'Angelo mentions Bruner's more recent claim (Luria's studies were conducted fifty years ago) that literacy fosters metalinguistic '' 'analytic competence' '' (164). (See also Frank D'Angelo's ''Literacy and Cognition'' [1983].)

One of the dangerous inferences that can be made (and we believe is often made) from an uncritical adoption of both ''neutral'' classic studies of literacy and ''objective'' scientific ones is that nonliterate people are childlike, insufficiently developed, or defective in some way. Perhaps aware that his reading of Luria's study might lend itself to such reductive interpretations and applications, D'Angelo acknowledges David Olson's, William Labov's, and Scribner and Cole's objections to Luria's findings, and he concludes his essay by reminding us that "nonliterate and illiterate people have considerable intelligence, and many can outperform their literate counterparts in a variety of practical and cognitive tasks" (168). The fact that this clarification is necessary is worth reflecting on.

An additional, related body of work on literacy, work with a different and ultimately equally problematical causal focus, puts great stock in the social, economic, and political effects of literacy. This work documents the goals and efforts and chronicles the achievements and failures of adult literacy campaigns in the Third World and in the United States and other "developed" nations. Most of this work has been propelled by the belief that literacy both marks and determines a Great Divide—in this case, a social, economic, and political one. Though well intentioned and undoubtedly praiseworthy for its social commitment, most of this work has been less effective than it could and should have been. Its most apparent weakness has been the simplistic understanding of literacy that has shaped it—a simplistic understanding clearly manifested in the top-down model of teaching and learning it has generally enforced. At the same time, however, this work exposes the expediency of explaining the occurrence and resiliency of educational problems solely in terms of the nature and the complexity of what is being taught, i.e., literacy. A more accurate and authentic explanation of why literacy does not merge in certain contexts, this body of work demonstrates, must take into account the fundamental social and political problems that both shape educational policy and limit what people can accomplish with or without literacy. We suggest that our review of this material be read as a cautionary tale: insofar as this body of work exposes the consequences of facile assumptions about both the acquisition of literacy and its consequences, it has, in fact, some important implications for basic writing pedagogy, for it urges teachers to reexamine, redefine, and reassess both what they can be responsible for and what they can make possible.

There are some extreme examples of faith in literacy as a direct agent for social and economic change, such as UNESCO's adult literacy campaigns for the Third World. These campaigns started in the 1960s and took as their ambitious aim overcoming illiteracy in countries like Algeria, Iran, Ecuador, and Ethiopia—but overcoming it in order to achieve certain economic and social returns. The assumption was that education, and literacy education in particular, were necessary prerequisites for economic growth and development. There was a widely cited estimate, a threshold figure, that 40 percent of any given population needed to be literate in order for economic development to commence (Arnold Anderson "Literacy and Schooling on the Development Threshold" [1965]). Thus, the focus of the campaigns seemed to be the individual's literacy insofar as it advanced society's gains.

The UNESCO campaigns prided themselves on progressing beyond the traditional concept of literacy, wherein the aim of training was simply to teach the "mechanisms" of reading and writing, to the goal of functional literacy, wherein instruction on reading and writing was integrated with other sorts of occupational training. (Note the different meaning that "functional" assumes in this context.)

For example, one functional literacy project in the Sudan situated its instruction on reading and writing within training on how to grow cotton. One of its training objectives was "to encourage favorable attitudes towards manual labor," particularly as such attitudes pertained to cotton growing. Another was "to provide learners with the ability to (a) read and write some of the words relevant to cotton-picking operations, and (b) acquire the ability to read and understand sentences related to these operations" (UNESCO, *The Experimental World Literacy Programme* [1976] 62). These and other examples all seem to be offered nonreflexively, without apparent acknowledgement of the limited and limiting conception of literacy that the projects embody, or of the political and economic agendas hidden beneath the teaching of a literacy that is "functional." This or any literacy is functional, we need to ask, for whom and for whose benefit? (The most complete description of UNESCO's literacy theory and practice is *The Experimental World Literacy Programme Practical Guide to Functional Literacy* [1973]. *The World of Literacy* [1979] provides further discussion of Third World adult literacy theory and practice from the perspective of UNESCO.)

By all estimates, the Experimental World Literacy Campaign was unsuccessful. Jonathan Kozol claimed that UNESCO, in its own assessment of the effort, "virtually conceded that it had just wasted thirty-two million dollars" (*Children of the Revolution* [1978] 74). In *The Experimental World Literacy Programme* (1976), UNESCO writers explored the failure of the campaigns and speculated about the validity of their original notion of functional literacy. And out of their self-analysis, there emerged a more complex understanding and definition of literacy, one that is more in tune with recent scholarship on literacy (see our next section). They concluded that literacy is not solely a technical problem, just as the lack of development in a country is not just the result of an uneducated, illiterate work force. In order for literacy programs to be fully functional, UNESCO writers said, those programs must "accord importance to social, *cultural* and political change as well as economic growth" (emphasis added, 122). For critiques of the assumptions that inform literacy campaigns whose main aim is national economic development, see Brian Street, *Literacy in Theory and Practice* (1984), and Ruth Finnegan, "Literacy versus Non-literacy" (1973).

For a collection of viewpoints that illustrate the tension in UNESCO literacy campaigns over the functionality principle, we recommend Leon Bataille's *A Turning Point for Literacy* (1976). This book grew out of an international symposium on literacy held in Persepolis, Iran, in 1975, to assess the evolution of literacy theory and practice since a similar 1965 conference held in Teheran. Its final report on the conference distinguished two kinds of literacy functions, economic and cultural, and noted that some conference participants were alert to the fact that "narrowly economic functions were liable to shore-up the established order in a social system founded on injustice and inequality" (249). (For a similar argument, see also Robert F. Arnove and Jairo Arboleda, "Literacy" [1973].)

Such acknowledgments echo through most recent literature on adult literacy campaigns and powerfully contribute to problematizing facile concepts of literacy and to exposing pernicious ideologies. For example, Carman St. John Hunter and David Harman, in their thorough evaluation, *Adult Illiteracy in the United States* (1979), list several oversimplified assumptions about literacy, including the "assertion that economic development, increased gross national product, and modernization automatically follow or are contingent upon literacy" and "the parallel claim that anyone who becomes literate is automatically better off economically, better able to find employment, and becomes a better citizen" (14–15). Hunter and Harman also expose the myth that equates adult illiteracy with ignorance and cultural deprivation (as does Arlene Fingeret in "Social Networks" [1983]). If you are illiterate, Hunter and Harman argue, your problem isn't just that you cannot read and write, but that you are oppressed by race, class, and power structure.

Part of the empirical base for such arguments comes from recent historical treatments of literacy. Harvey Graff, for example, investigated literacy in nineteenth-century Ontario, and thereby exploded a lot of received wisdom about the effects of literacy. In the case that Graff documents, literacy didn't necessarily lead to social mobility or economic growth; social class did. The main correlate of poverty was not the inability to read or write, but ethnic origin. (See Graff's *The Literacy Myth* [1979] for his own study of Canada, and his edited *Literacy and Social Development in the West* [1981] for other examples of revisionist thinking about the benefits of literacy. We also recommend Kenneth Lockridge's *Literacy in Colonial New England* [1974] and Michael Clanchy's *From Memory to Written Record* [1979] as other historical works that question what can and cannot be considered a by-product of literacy. For a contemporary example of how social and institutional forces can determine literacy practices among the economically poor, see Alonzo B. Anderson and Shelley J. Stokes, "Social and Institutional Influences on the Development and Practice of Literacy" [1984].)

Reading and writing can be useful tools, then, only for "those who are in all other respects full members of the society" (Hunter and Harman 109). Like literacy campaigns in the Sudan, literacy campaigns in this country that claim to be offering people a means of improving their economic situations risk offering a sham, unless those campaigns are also accompanied by changes in social structure. David Harman believes that the only literacy program that will work is one that is "allied with something else"—"the promise of a better life for every man and woman in the land" (quoted in Kozol, *Children of the Revolution* [1978] 77). See as well Michael Holzman's related argument in "Teaching Is Remembering" (1984). Although we agree with Harman, we also want to register our skepticism about literacy campaigns, or educational programs for that matter, that promise a "something else" that they are not designed to provide, or that use the rhetoric of "something else" to divert attention from the limitedness of their goals.

The campaigns in Cuba and Nicaragua can be cited as examples of recent Third World literacy programs that are allied with something else. An engaging account of the Cuban campaign is Jonathan Kozol's record of his visit to Cuba in 1976, taken to learn about the great literacy campaign that took place there in 1961, shortly after Fidel Castro came to power. Kozol recreates the events that followed Castro's announcement at the United Nations assembly that, during the next year, Cuba would teach every citizen to read and write. He describes the training of thousands of young *brigadistas* and their crusades to the remotest areas of Cuba, where, armed with a lantern and a book, they would make a country literate. See Kozol's *Children of the Revolution* (1978) and "A New Look at the Literacy Campaign in Cuba" (1978). Nicaragua's Literacy Crusade followed upon the heels of the overthrow of the Somoza regime in 1979; the Sandinista government declared 1980 as their "year of literacy." After much thoughtful and vigorous preparation—a census to locate illiterates and teachers, the construction and revision of literacy materials, the training of volunteers, fund-raising, and publicity—the campaign began, and between March and August of 1980, 400,000 people are reported to have completed the basic program. For accounts of the Nicaraguan campaign, see Valerie Miller's *Between Struggle and Hope* (1985) and Fernando Cardenal and Valerie Miller's "Nicaragua 1980" (1981).

By most assessments, the campaigns in Cuba and Nicaragua were successful, for they did reach a great proportion of their populations and these people did learn rudimentary reading and writing skills. Most commentators attribute the success the campaigns were able to achieve, not to a particular teaching method, but to the fact that they were born of a liberation struggle. (See, for example, John Bevan's "Each One, Teach One" [1983] in which he compares the successful Nicaraguan campaign to the unsuccessful campaign that was carried out in Honduras at the same time.) The people in Cuba and Nicaragua perceived their campaigns as the means to another end, the creation of a new society in which, as a newly "literate" people, they would have increased economic and political participation. "Now I know how to read and write thanks to our Socialist and democratic Revolution," thousands of Cubans proclaimed in letters to Castro, signifying the triumphant completion of their personal struggle in the literacy campaign (quoted in Kozol, "A New Look" 358–59 and *Children of the Revolution* 140–41). "Revolution and education are the same thing," Castro had long believed (quoted in Samuel Bowles, "Cuban Education and the Revolutionary Ideology" [1971]). For some primary sources that capture the political spirit of Cuba's literacy campaign, see Richard R. Fagen's *Cuba: The Political Content of Adult Education* (1964), a translation of three documents: a poem written to commemorate the death of a *brigadista* shortly after the Bay of Pigs, a teaching manual for literacy workers, and part of an arithmetic workbook also used in the campaign.

While it is certainly important to acknowledge the achievements of these campaigns that are "allied with something else," it should also be noted that they initially aimed for very rudimentary literacy—in the case of Cuba, first- or second-grade competence, then fourth grade, and then the "Battle for the Sixth

Grade" (see Kozol, *Children of the Revolution* 55–56). Their accomplishments will need to be assessed, then, in the context of these low thresholds for literacy. In addition, the fact that the success of these campaigns has been attributed not so much to teaching methods as to political struggles bears consideration in terms of their applicability to basic writing.

The particular political nature of the Cuban and Nicaraguan campaigns is a good reminder that education, including literacy training, whether it takes place in Third World socialist republics or the heartland of America, cannot be neutral. Although the political bias of education may be hidden to those who work within the system that is being promulgated, instruction is never value-free or purely and merely technical. As the writers of the Persepolis manifesto declare, "The act of revealing social reality in order to transform it, or of concealing it in order to preserve it, is political" (Bataille, *A Turning Point for Literacy* [1976] 274). Or, to quote Brian Street, "When students in Tanzania are given text books with such phrases as "Cotton is wealth. Cotton brings money,' . . . they are being subjected to ideological training in the same way as the peasants of Nicaragua, although from a different political perspective" (*Literacy in Theory and Practice* [1984] 204–5). Our point here is not to argue in favor of one form of politics or another, but rather to foreground the danger of assuming that instruction on literacy, or education in general, is apolitical. The danger is that teachers and students may, inadvertently, contribute to reproducing the very conditions that are responsible for generating educational inequalities.

The ideological bias of contemporary American education, and the ways in which schools can be used to perpetuate society's status quo rather than promote social mobility, was exposed in Marxist and radical critiques like Samuel Bowles and Herbert Gintis's *Schooling in Capitalist America* (1976) and Michael W. Apple's scholarship, such as *Ideology and Curriculum* (1979). Such critics have argued that, far from being forces for democratic ends, schools were designed to accomplish just the opposite, the reproduction of class and occupational structures. More recent critics in this tradition have exposed the mechanisms by which such reproduction occurs—ironically by means of students' resistance and mediation. See, for example, Robert B. Everhart's *Reading, Writing and Resistance* (1983); Lois Weis's *Between Two Worlds* (1985); Paul Willis's *Learning to Labour* (1977); and Ira Shor and Paulo Freire's *A Pedagogy for Liberation* (1987). While Shor and Freire see students' resistance to becoming actively involved in their education as the result of the subtle, pervasive domestication of a top-down educational system, Michael Holzman believes that resistance can be born of the recognition that school values cancel out community and family values: "Resistance to the institutions of the dominant society, of which school is merely one, is a form of group identification, a qualification for that material and emotional support from the community that makes life possible, if barely tolerable, at the margin" ("The Social Context of Literacy Education" [1986] 32).

Although as Henry Giroux points out, "within the boundaries of conventional discourse," literacy is often assumed to be removed from power, culture, and politics (see *Theory and Resistance in Education* [1983] 205), there is no doubt that literacy instruction embodies cultural values. Carl F. Kaestle, in his *History of Literacy in America* (1979), points out that in the 1900s, "from McGuffey's readers, to Webster's spellers, to Morses' geographies, children learning to read and write were bombarded with messages that were Protestant, nationalist, nativist, racist, and vigorously procapitalist." And immigrants in the early twentieth century "found the same strings attached to English literacy in America, though thousands accepted it anyway, working their way through reading lessons about the virtues of soap and the rewards of getting to work on time" (17). The question—a question that accounts for Shor and Freire's and Holzman's different interpretation of students' resistance—becomes whether such training is liberatory or constraining, or in the Marxist sense, whether this schooling promotes social mobility or holds it out only as a false promise.

Harvey Graff has argued that in nineteenth-century Canada educators used literacy as a means of social control (*The Literacy Myth* [1979]). The same argument can be made about contemporary educational systems. The literacy instruction we provide in our own time, both in adult literacy campaigns and basic writing classrooms, often perpetuates existing social and economic structures. Stanley Aronowitz, in "Towards Redefining Literacy" (1981), locates the potential for this reproduction in the "back to basics" movement of recent years. This movement, he asserts, emphasizes functional literacy, not critical literacy, and he argues (as we would) that the goals of a "truly public education are not merely functional levels of reading and writing" but critical thought (55). See also Henry Giroux's *Theory and Resistance in Education* (1983), in particular his chapter on "Literacy, Ideology, and the Politics of Schooling," for a critique of the ideologies that he believes characterize current approaches to literacy, and Stanley Aronowitz and Henry Giroux's "The Literacy Crisis" in their *Education Under Siege* (1985).

Of all Third World educators, Paulo Freire is most closely associated with promoting literacy as a means to critical thought, and of all the literature on adult literacy, his work has the most immediate application to the teaching of basic writing. What distinguishes Freire from many other educators involved in adult literacy programs is his strong theoretical understanding of language and learning—or in Ann Berthoff's words, "the urgency of comprehending the significance of illiteracy" (" 'Reading the World . . . Reading the Word' " [1986] 119). Unlike many others, Freire is aware of the complexity of literacy as social practice and the implication of literacy for human growth. He moves us, then, toward the more complex understanding of literacy that is the hallmark of the theorists and researchers treated in the second half of our essay. For Freire, becoming literate means learning to look critically at one's world, learning to read its social context in order to become a subject in creating it, an actor, rather than a passive object or willing recipient whose history is written by others. "It is not enough to know mechanically the meaning of 'Eve saw the vineyard,' " says Freire. "It is necessary to know what position Eve occupies in the social context, who works in the vineyard, and who profits from this work'' (''Literacy and the Possible Dream'' [1976] 71). Although Freire would anoint no particular teaching method, his program of ''conscientization'' has always involved selecting key words and syllables from a people's experience and then providing the occasion for dialectical reflection on those words. (See Ira Shor, ''Learning How to Learn'' [1977] and ''Reinventing Daily Life'' [1977], and also his dialogue about education with Freire, *A Pedagogy for Liberation* [1987].) A teacher's role is to enter into dialogue with students about the themes that are important to them. ''What is at stake here,'' explains Henry Giroux in a brief but insightful discussion of Freire's notion of critical literacy, ''is the goal of giving working-class students and adults the tools they need to reclaim their own lives, histories, and voices'' (*Theory and Resistance in Education* [1983] 227).

The best summary of Freire's approach to literacy can be found in *Pedagogy of the Oppressed* (1970). *Pedagogy in Process* (1983), Freire's correspondence with members of a literacy effort in Africa, gives a better sense, however, of the practical form that his theory can take. See also the references given above on the Cuban and Nicaraguan literacy campaigns, for these efforts drew heavily on Freire's pedagogical theories. A useful volume of commentary on Freire's work is Robert Mackie's *Literacy and Revolution* (1981), which contains a bibliography of books and articles by and about Freire, interviews with him, and philosophical and political readings that provide a context for his work. In the same volume, we recommend Jim Walker's critical appraisal, ''The End of Dialogue,'' which examines some of the political contradictions in Freire's pedagogy. Finally, see Nan Elsasser and Vera P. John-Steiner, who draw on Freire (and Vygotsky) in designing an experimental university composition course, described in their essay, ''An Interactionist Approach to Advancing Literacy'' (1977).

By questioning the accuracy and the reliability of the Great Divide theory (both in its cognitive and in its social, economic, and political manifestations), we do not mean to invalidate the importance of literacy. Rather, to warn against the danger of making unwarranted generalizations about this complex, and, as yet, not fully understood phenomenon, we want to point out the various ways in which the social context affects the acquisition of literacy and interacts with cognitive development. The consequences of this questioning are numerous and important; they vary from the dismantling of the myth that literacy causes cognitive, as well as political, economic, and social advancement (as in Harvey Graff's *The Literacy Myth* [1979]); to a reexamination of the assumption that school is the only or the primary context in which literacy can be achieved (as in Scribner and Cole's *The Psychology of Literacy* [1981]), to the recognition that it might be more appropriate to talk about '' 'configurations of literacy,' a 'plurality of literacies' '' (John F. Szwed, ''The Ethnography of Literacy'' [1981] and Patricia Bizzell, ''Literacy in Culture and Cognition'' [1987]).

For further discussions of the relationship between literacy and schooling see Scribner and Cole, ''Literacy without Schooling'' (1978) and ''Cognitive Consequences of Formal and Informal Education'' (1973), and Jack Goody, Michael Cole, and Sylvia Scribner, ''Writing and Formal Operations'' (1977). See also Shirley Brice Heath's *Ways with Words* (1983), and Fred Erickson's ''School Literacy, Reasoning, and Civility'' (1984), and compare these approaches to David Olson's ''From Utterance to Text'' (1977). Also helpful are Richard Hoggart's *The Uses of Literacy* (1961) and Richard Rodriguez's *Hunger of Memory* (1983), a personal account of a child caught in the clash between the literacy of school and the literacy of home. For discussions of new literacies, ranging from rock music to computer technology, see Robert Pattison, *On Literacy* (1982); Neil Postman, ''The Politics of Reading'' (1970); and Suzanne Scollon and Ron Scollon, ''Run Trilogy'' (1984). We especially recommend, for its sensitive and careful analysis of a Mexican-American child's performance of a narrative and departure from essayist literacy, Adrian T. Bennett's essay, ''Discourses of Power'' (1983), and for its insightful and respectful investigation of street rhymes and the language competence they represent, Perry Gilmore's article, ''Spelling 'Mississippi' '' (1983).

THE *ENABLING* PERSPECTIVE: THE *IMPLICATIONS* OF LITERACY

As the complexity of the phenomenon under investigation is recognized, it becomes apparent that traditional methods of ''reading'' it are no longer adequate. More sophisticated methods of reading literacy produce more sophisticated understandings of it, and more sophisticated understandings expose the need for more sophisticated teaching methods. In this section, we review works that stand out for their acknowledgment of the complexity of literacy as social practice. Although these researchers study literacy in contexts that are quite different from the context of the basic writing classroom, their studies—focusing as they do on literacy as social practice, on the different kinds of literacies that different social practices demand and foster, and on the complex relationship between literacy and schooling—can help basic writing teachers to reexamine and restructure their pedagogical assumptions and practices.

David P. Resnick and Lauren B. Resnick's ''The Nature of Literacy'' (1977) is helpful in putting the issue of literacy and basic writing in perspective. The Resnicks point out that the current definition of literacy is a relatively new one (''If the ability to read aloud a simple and well-known passage were the measure, American would have a few illiterates but hardly a crisis,'' 371), and suggest that ''much of the present difficulty in meeting the literacy standard we are setting for ourselves can be attributed to the relatively rapid extension to large populations of educational criteria that were once applied to only a limited elite'' (371). They conclude that if current literacy standards are to be met, new pedagogical practices must be devised because, given the lower literacy expectations of the past, the ''back to basics'' movement would be counterproductive. (For the inappropriateness of looking at the past in search of solutions for the present, see David K. Cohen, "Loss as a Theme in Social Policy" [1976].)

Among recent studies of literacy, Robert Pattison's well-informed and highly readable *On Literacy* (1982) offers a sobering analysis of the many facile claims about the consequences of literacy. He suggests a helpful distinction between two kinds of literacy: the one, a certain form of higher literacy, which he defines as "mechanical ability with the technologies of language coupled with consciousness of language as a force in human affairs" (vii), and the other, a mechanical literacy (that is close to functional literacy), which he defines as "mechanical skill with the technologies of reading and writing" (174). He argues that the ability to read and write does not necessarily make an individual "literate" because "someone who can read and write may still lack the sensitivity to words that is the essential quality of the literate man in the broadest sense of literate, while someone else who can neither read nor write may demonstrate extraordinary insights into the problems of language" (32). The usefulness of this definition for basic writing teachers is that it invalidates the oral-literate dichotomy, and directs a teacher's attention toward what her students bring with them rather than what they lack, toward their differences not in terms of how they measure up to abstract standards but of how they set up different standards that need to be recognized. More importantly, he inverts the "causal" view of literacy. As Deborah Brandt notes in her excellent review, "Versions of Literacy" (1985): "In Pattison's scheme the flow charts tend to get turned around. Literacy does not empower literacy so much as people empower literacy" (130).

Sylvia Scribner and Michael Cole's anthropological/psychological/social study of the Vai, a West African population of about twelve hundred whose acquisition of literacy is independent of formal schooling, offered them an occasion to test the validity of assumptions made about the psychology of literacy. And it led them to scale down grandiloquent generalizations "about the impact of literacy on history, on philosophy, and on the minds of individual human beings" to the more modest conclusion that "literacy makes some difference to some skills in some contexts" (*The Psychology of Literacy* [1981] 234). When, at the conclusion of their studies, Scribner and Cole tried to bring their "evidence of localized and specific changes into relation with scholars' grand speculations about literacy and thought" (236), they found themselves dissatisfied with the available theories of cognition. Neither the Piagetian view of literacy "as unrelated to basic processes of intellectual development," nor the Bruner and Olson and Greenfield position that sees in literacy " 'an emergent force' that brings into existence entirely new mental structures or processes" (235) proved helpful to describe their results. An intensive investigation and a deepened understanding of the work by Vygotsky and his students that had been unavailable to them when they began their study, and also Goody's more recent work, enabled them to construct the framework of "a practice account of literacy," a framework that guided the way they sought to understand literacy: "Instead of focusing exclusively on the technology of a writing system and its reputed consequences," this framework enabled them to approach literacy "as a set of socially organized practices which make use of a symbol system and a technology for producing and disseminating it" (235).

This way of reading literacy led them to realize that "literacy is not simply knowing how to read and write a particular script but applying this knowledge for specific purposes in specific contexts of use. The nature of these practices, including, of course, their technological aspects, will determine the kinds of skills ('consequences') associated with literacy" (236). In addition to the definition of literacy Scribner and Cole offer, a definition that enables basic writing teachers to examine and to understand their students' particular "practices," the aspect of their work that we think is particularly worth reflecting on and that would benefit teachers and scholars of basic writing to emulate is their testing the accuracy of available definitions as well as the power of available theories to account for the richness of the phenomena they observed. Of their method, historian Harvey Graff has this to say: "An approach that begins with context— of learning, use, need, practice, and relationship—is the best method to which to tie a new research agenda" (*Legacies of Literacy* [1987] 389).

Shirley Brice Heath's *Ways with Words* (1983) documents her attempts to understand the varieties of literacies available to and used by people in three communities in the Carolina Piedmonts—the people in Trackton, in Roadville, and the "Townspeople." As she studies the different ways in which the adults from Trackton and Roadville encourage, validate, and invalidate their children's experimentations with language (their—parents' and children's—"ways with words") according to the communities' understanding of time, place, problem solving, and child rearing, Heath discovers how these literacies, although functional within the communities, do not prepare the children for the specific types of reading and writing tasks that school requires. Like Scribner and Cole, Heath draws on various disciplines (ethnography, anthropology, linguistics, psychology) as tools (in the richest Vygotskyan sense), simultaneously transforming the nature or the configuration of the phenomenon (literacy) and herself (both in terms of her understanding of the phenomenon and of her role as researcher).

"The book is written," says Heath, "for what I call 'learning researchers,' non-academics and academics alike. At the top of the list of such researchers are those teachers at all levels of the curriculum who constantly search out new ways of learning about themselves and their students" (13). To the extent that pedagogy, lest it be reduced to didactics, posits continuous reflection on and critique of the epistemological assumptions at the basis of its theory and practice, basic writing teachers who are concerned about the effectiveness and adequacy of their "ways with words" will find in Heath's book the appropriate challenge and guide. But in also challenging "others," i.e., "parents and community members concerned about their own gaps in knowledge and the need of children today to learn more, faster than ever before" (13), Heath's book makes of literacy a social practice that extends far beyond the classroom and that calls attention to the potential for any discipline to be blind to its own limits. (Heath explains:

"These notes and the descriptions and analyses in the body of the book will raise numerous questions for academic researchers. I hope that these questions will be directed not only to the contents of this book, but *also to their own disciplines' theories and generalizations about how children learn language.*" Emphasis added, (13).)

In *Literacy in Theory and Practice* (1984), Brian V. Street critically reviews the enormous literature on literacy, offers a framework for classifying and understanding it, and then tests his theory against his own anthropological fieldwork in Iran and other recent work on adult literacy in the United States and Britain. He offers two models or ideal types of literacy, the "autonomous" and the "ideological," as a framework for classifying approaches to literacy theory and practice. The autonomous model uncritically associates literacy with economic progress, social mobility, and cognitive development, while the ideological model views literacy as culturally embedded and stresses the importance of socialization in constructing meanings for literacy. As he develops these models, Street challenges a lot of received wisdom about the consequences of literacy. He contends that "what the particular practices and concepts of reading and writing are for a given society depends upon the context; that they are already embedded in an ideology and cannot be isolated or treated as 'neutral' or merely 'technical,' " and "that what practices are taught and how they are imparted depends upon the nature of the social" (1). Street's questioning of assumptions about literacy, his opening up of what is usually taken for granted, is, we think, a valuable model for teachers of basic writing.

Awakening to Literacy, edited by Hillel Goelman, Antoinette Oberg, and Frank Smith (1984), is a collection of fourteen papers delivered by researchers from anthropology, linguistics, psychology, sociology, and education at the 1982 University of Victoria symposium on preschool children and literacy. If it provides rich examples of how researchers from different fields "read" children's "awakening" to literacy, the collection also "awakens" readers to the implication that the increasing understanding of literacy can have for parents, teachers, researchers, theorists, and scholars. (For a more detailed review of this book, see Deborah Brandt's "Versions of Literacy" [1985].)

Much of the current basic writing pedagogy exemplifies how a more sophisticated understanding of basic writing calls into question simplistic and imprisoning definitions of literacy, and how a more sophisticated understanding of literacy contributes to an effective restructuring of the pedagogical scene. A good example of work in this tradition is the scholarship of Mike Rose, which constantly avoids, in fact exposes, the danger of reifying observations and correlations into evaluative categories and causal links. As Andrea Lunsford observes, Rose "tries to release ["remediation" and "literacy"] from reductive definitions and the negative semantic freight they traditionally carry" ("Politics and Practice in Basic Writing" [1987]). In Rose's carefully constructed interdisciplinary approach, sociology, history, and psychology monitor each other's methods and assumptions, and the possible insights they can offer to an understanding of literacy are rigorously tested in terms of a scholarly and humane understanding of basic writers. In "The Language of Exclusion" (1985), Rose denounces "literate" people's lack of reflexivity about their own language use (one of the great "divides" that usually distinguishes basic from "other" writers) and demonstrates how inaccurate definitions of literacy can jeopardize the educational goals of even well-intentioned teachers. In his current work, he is expanding his analysis and critiques of the various causes responsible for a "narrowed model of and curriculum for composing" ("Remedial Writing Courses" [1983]) to an analysis and a somber prediction of the counterproductive effects that the unreflexive adoption of polarization can have for the discipline at large.

As he chronicles his exploration of texts that previous composition pedagogy had deemed unworthy of study—the texts of basic writers—David Bartholomae educates basic writing teachers to look for the "possibilities" rather than the "limits" of their students' literacies. In "Writing on the Margins" (1987), Bartholomae argues that "there is reason to examine the assumptions about the nature of literate skills represented by the decisions we make in placement exams or tracking procedures" (67). He points out that what has guided and still guides our definition of basic writers is the assumption that these students "are defined by what they don't do (rather than what they do), by the absence of whatever is present in literate discourse: cognitive maturity, reason, orderliness, conscious strategies, correctness" (67). Cognitive maturity, reason, conscious strategies— these are some of the features that the Great Divide theory sets up as the *sine qua non* of literacy. Bartholomae's work, like Rose's, demonstrates the subtle and insidious ways in which inaccurate abstract definitions contribute to shaping programs and curricula that perpetuate divisions, and calls attention to the responsibility that teachers, researchers, and theorists have to enact their literacy through an unrelenting reflexivity on the very problems that their own use of language might cause.

Another example of the sensitive and effective pedagogy that an understanding of literacy as social practice can foster is Jay Robinson's "Literacy in the Department of English" (1985). Robinson defines literacy "as an outcome, not a skill, and not (even) a competency" but rather "something that is achieved when competencies are enabled through exercise of the human capacity to make meaning" (485) and suggests that teachers "should invite and help students to develop as ethnographers of thought—as careful and reflective participant observers, critical thinkers of their own thoughts . . . " (492). Clearly teachers who do what Robinson suggests they do must themselves be practitioners of the method they enforce—a method that is obviously borrowed from other disciplines (sociology, anthropology, ethnography) and that requires a reconceptualization and realignment of the traditional teacher-student hierarchical relationship.

Ann E. Berthoff's work enacts a passionate belief in the capacity of human beings to make meanings and to understand themselves as makers of meaning. Like Paulo Freire and I. A. Richards who, with Lev Vygotsky, C. S. Peirce, Kenneth Burke, Maria Montessori, William James, Suzanne K. Langer, and other "dialectical thinkers," have fueled her thinking about the theory and practice of composition and the dialogical nature of understanding, Berthoff upholds a concept of literacy that makes of education "a pedagogy of knowing." For Berthoff, the teacher of basic writers, having recognized that her students, like "all writers, novice and practiced," are "form finders and form creators," must provide "occasions for them to discover *that* they form." She argues that "the challenge in teaching those whose experience of reading and writing has been minimal, or those for whom the habit of reflecting on what they are reading and writing is undeveloped, is to make this power known; to assure that it is accessible and to encourage an understanding of how to control it in the interest of making meaning" ("Recognition, Representation, and Revision" [1987] 545). Like Freire's, Berthoff's pedagogy is one of empowerment. Further examples of pedagogical practices that call into question simplistic conceptions of literacy and invalidate didactic methods can be found in the collections edited by David Bartholomae and Anthony Petrosky, *Facts, Artifacts and Counterfacts* (1986), and by Thomas Newkirk, *Only Connect* (1986). Although he doesn't work specifically with basic writing, William E. Coles, Jr., also sees a connection between literacy and empowerment, between illiteracy and victimization. Coles values writing as a special form of language use that he understands "as the primary means by which all of us run order through chaos, thereby giving ourselves the identities we have" ("Literacy for the Eighties" [1983] 253).

Our review of the vast body of literature on literacy has been guided by our understanding of basic writing—an understanding shaped by what we consider the most fruitful current scholarship on basic writing and our practice as teachers of basic writing. We chose to use our essay to suggest and to enact a method of investigation rather than to cover all the available material. We hope readers will understand the reasons for our choices and will themselves fill in the gaps we have left. Our intention throughout has been to call attention to the connection between reductive views of literacy and reductive, mainly didactic, and ultimately ineffective educational practices, as well as to the role that pedagogy can have in testing, guiding, and raising questions about the usefulness and applicability of current definitions of and research on literacy.

NOTE

We thank Mike Rose and Carolyn Ball for reading an earlier version of this essay and also for inspiring us and others to think seriously about basic writing and literacy theory.

1. We borrow our definitional language from Scribner and Cole's *Psychology of Literacy* (1981). Brian Street also proposes a similar division in *Literacy in Theory and Practice* (1984), which he defines as the "ideological" model and the "autonomous" model.

REFERENCES

Adkins, Arthur W. H. "Orality and Philosophy." *Language and Thought in Early Greek Philosophy.* Ed. Kevin Robb. La Salle, Ill.: The Hegeler Institute, 1983, pp. 207–27.

Anderson, Alonzo B., and Shelley J. Stokes. "Social and Institutional Influences on the Development and Practice of Literacy." *Awakening to Literacy*. Ed. Hillel Goelman, Antoinette Oberg, and Frank Smith. Portsmouth, N.H.: Heinemann Educational Books, 1984, pp. 24–37.

Anderson, C. Arnold. "Literacy and Schooling on the Development Threshold: Some Historical Cases." *Education and Economic Development*. Ed. C. Arnold Anderson and Mary Jean Bowman. Chicago: Aldine Publishing, 1965, pp. 347–62.

Apple, Michael W. *Ideology and Curriculum*. London: Routledge & Kegan Paul, 1979.

Applebee, Arthur N. "Writing and Reasoning." *Rev Ed Res* 54 (1984): 577–96.

Arnove, Robert F., and Jairo Arboleda. "Literacy: Power or Mystification?" *Lit Disc* 4 (1973): 389–414.

Aronowitz, Stanley. "Towards Redefining Literacy." *Soc Pol* 12 (1981): 53–55.

Aronowitz, Stanley, and Henry R. Giroux. *Education Under Siege: The Conservative, Liberal and Radical Debate over Schooling*. South Hadley, Mass.: Bergin & Garvey, 1985.

Bailey, Richard W., and Robin Melanie Fosheim, eds. *Literacy for Life: The Demand for Reading and Writing*. New York: MLA, 1983.

Bataille, Leon, ed. *A Turning Point for Literacy: Adult Education for Development; The Spirit and Declaration of Persepolis*. Oxford, Eng.: Pergamon Press, 1976.

Bartholomae, David J. "Inventing the University." *When a Writer Can't Write: Studies in Writer's Block and Other Composing-Process Problems*. Ed. Mike Rose. New York: Guilford Press, 1985, pp. 134–65.

———. "Released into Language: Errors, Expectations, and the Legacy of Mina Shaughnessy." *The Territory of Language: Linguistics, Stylistics, and the Teaching of Composition*. Ed. Donald A. McQuade. Carbondale: Southern Illinois University Press, 1986, pp. 65–88.

———. "The Study of Error." *CCC* 31 (1980): 253–69.

———. "Writing on the Margins: The Concept of Literacy in Higher Education." *A Sourcebook for Basic Writing Teachers*. Ed. Theresa Enos. New York: Random House, 1987, pp. 66–83.

Bartholomae, David, and Anthony Petrosky, eds. *Facts, Artifacts and Counterfacts: Theory and Method for a Reading and Writing Course*. Upper Montclair, N.J.: Boynton/Cook, 1986.

Bennet, Adrian T. "Discourses of Power, the Dialectics of Understanding, the Power of Literacy." *J Educ* 165 (1983): 53–74.

Berthoff, Ann E. " 'Reading the World . . . Reading the Word': Paulo Freire's Pedagogy of Knowing." *Only Connect: Uniting Reading and Writing*. Ed. Thomas Newkirk. Upper Montclair, N.J.: Boynton/Cook, 1986, pp. 119–30.

———. "Recognition, Representation, and Revision." *A Sourcebook for Basic Writing Teachers*. Ed. Theresa Enos. New York: Random House, 1987, pp. 545–56.

Bevan, John. "Each One, Teach One." *New Inter* (April 1983): 19–20.

Bizzell, Patricia. "The Ethos of Academic Discourse." *CCC* 29 (1978): 351–55.

———. "Literacy in Culture and Cognition." *A Sourcebook for Basic Writing Teachers*. Ed. Theresa Enos. New York: Random House, 1987, pp. 125–37.

Bowles, Samuel. "Cuban Education and the Revolutionary Ideology." *Harvard Educ Rev* 41 (1971): 472–500.

Bowles, Samuel, and Herbert Gintis. *Schooling in Capitalist America*. New York: Basic Books, 1976.

Brandt, Deborah. "Versions of Literacy." *CE* 47 (1985): 128–38.

Cardenal, Fernando, S.J., and Valerie Miller. "Nicaragua 1980: The Battle of the ABCs." *HER* 51 (1981): 1–26.

Clanchy, Michael. *From Memory to Written Record 1066–1307*. London: Edward Arnold, 1979.

Cohen, David K. "Loss as a Theme in Social Policy." *HER* 46 (1976): 553–71.

Cole, Michael, Vera John-Steiner, Sylvia Scribner, and Ellen Souberman, eds. *Mind in Society: The Development of Higher Psychological Processes*. Cambridge, Mass.: Harvard University Press, 1978.

Coles, William E., Jr. "Literacy for the Eighties: An Alternative to Losing." *Literacy for Life: The Demand for Reading and Writing*. Ed. Richard W. Bailey and Robin Melanie Fosheim. New York: MLA, 1983, pp. 248–262.

Cook-Gumperz, Jenny. *The Social Construction of Literacy*. Cambridge: Cambridge University Press, 1986.

Corbett, Edward P. J. "A Literal View of Literacy." *Literacy as a Human Problem*. Ed. James C. Raymond. University: University of Alabama Press, 1982, pp. 137–53.

D'Angelo, Frank. "Literacy and Cognition: A Developmental Perspective." *Literacy for Life: The Demand for Reading and Writing*. Ed. Richard W. Bailey and Robin Melanie Fosheim. New York: MLA, 1983, pp. 97–114.

———. "Luria on Literacy: The Cognitive Consequences of Reading and Writing." *Literacy as a Human Problem*. Ed. James C. Raymond. University: University of Alabama Press, 1982, pp. 154–69.

Delattre, Edwin J. "The Insiders." *Literacy for Life: The Demand for Reading and Writing*. Ed. Richard W. Bailey and Robin Melanie Fosheim. New York: MLA, 1983, pp. 52–62. Reprinted in *A Sourcebook for Basic Writing Teachers*. Ed. Theresa Enos. New York: Random House, 1987, pp. 56–63.

Elsasser, Nan, and Vera P. John-Steiner. "An Interactionist Approach to Advancing Literacy." *HER* 47 (1977): 355–69.

Enos, Theresa, ed. *A Sourcebook for Basic Writing Teachers*. New York: Random House, 1987.

Erickson, Frederick. "School Literacy, Reasoning, and Civility: An Anthropologist's Perspective." *Rev Ed Res* 54 (1984): 525–46.

Everhart, Robert B. *Reading, Writing and Resistance: Adolescence and Labor in a Junior High School*. Boston: Routledge & Kegan Paul, 1983.

Fagen, Richard R. *Cuba: The Political Content of Adult Education*. Stanford, Calif.: The Hoover Institute on War, Revolution, and Peace, Stanford University, 1964.

Farrell, Thomas J. "IQ and Standard English." *CCC* 34 (1983): 470–84.

———. "Literacy, the Basics and All That Jazz." *CE* 38 (1977): 443–59.

Fingeret, Arlene. "Social Network: A New Perspective on Independence and Illiterate Adults." *Adult Ed Q* 33 (1983): 133–46.

Finnegan, Ruth. "Literacy versus Non-literacy: The Great Divide?" *Modes of Thought: Essays on Thinking in Western and Non-Western Societies*. Eds. Robin Horton and Ruth Finnegan. London: Faber and Faber, 1973.

Freire, Paulo. "Literacy and the Possible Dream." *Prospects* 6 (1976): 68–71.

———. *Pedagogy in Process: The Letters to Guinea-Bissau*. Trans. Carman St. John Hunter. New York: Continuum, 1983.

———. *Pedagogy of the Oppressed*. New York: Seabury Press, 1970.

Gilmore, Perry. "Spelling 'Mississippi': Recontextualizing a Literacy-Related Speech Event." *Anthro Ed Q* 14 (1983): 235–55.

Giroux, Henry A. *Theory and Resistance in Education: A Pedagogy for the Opposition.* South Hadley, Mass.: Bergin & Garvey, 1983.

Goelman, Hillel, Antoinette Oberg, and Frank Smith, eds. *Awakening to Literacy.* Portsmouth, N.H.: Heinemann Educational Books, 1984.

Goody, Jack. *The Domestication of the Savage Mind.* Cambridge: Cambridge University Press, 1977.

Goody, Jack, Michael Cole, and Sylvia Scribner. "Writing and Formal Operations: A Case Study among the Vai," *Africa* 47 (1977): 389–404.

Goody, Jack, and Ian Watt. "The Consequences of Literacy." *Literacy in Traditional Societies.* Ed. Jack Goody. Cambridge: Cambridge University Press, 1968, pp. 27–68.

Graff, Harvey J. *Literacy in History: An Interdisciplinary Research Bibliography.* New York: Garland Publishing, 1981.

————. *The Literacy Myth: Literacy and Social Structure in the Nineteenth-Century City.* New York: Academic Press, 1979.

————, ed. *Literacy and Social Development in the West: A Reader.* Cambridge: Cambridge University Press, 1981.

————. *The Legacies of Literacy.* Bloomington and Indianapolis: Indiana University Press, 1987.

Greenberg, Karen L. "Research on Basic Writers: Theoretical and Methodological Issues." *A Sourcebook for Basic Writing Teachers.* Ed. Theresa Enos. New York: Random House, 1987, pp. 187–207.

————. "Response to Thomas J. Farrell, 'IQ and Standard English.' " *CCC* 35 (1984): 455–60.

Harman, David. "Illiteracy: An Overview." *HER* 40 (1970): 226–43.

Hartwell, Patrick. "Response to Thomas J. Farrell. 'IQ and Standard English.' " *CCC* 35 (1984): 461–65.

Havelock, Eric A. *The Greek Concept of Justice: From Its Shadow in Homer to Its Substance in Plato.* Cambridge, Mass.: Harvard University Press, 1978.

————. *Origins of Western Literacy.* Toronto: Ontario Institute for Studies in Education, 1976.

————. *Preface to Plato.* Cambridge, Mass.: Harvard University Press, 1963.

Heath, Shirley Brice. *Ways with Words: Language, Life, and Work in Communities and Classrooms.* Cambridge: Cambridge University Press, 1983.

Himley, Margaret. "Response to Thomas J. Farrell. 'IQ and Standard English.' " *CCC* 35 (1984): 465–68.

Hirsch, E. D., Jr. "Cultural Literacy." *Am Schol* (Spring 1983): 159–72. Reprinted in *A Sourcebook for Basic Writing Teachers.* Ed. Theresa Enos. New York: Random House, 1987, pp. 138–47.

————. "Cultural Literacy Does Not Mean a List of Works." *ADE Bul* 84 (Fall 1986): 1–3.

Hoggart, Richard. *The Uses of Literacy.* Boston: Beacon, 1961.

Holzman, Michael. "Teaching Is Remembering." *CE* 46 (1984): 229–38.

————. "The Social Context of Literacy Education." *CE* 48 (1986): 27–33.

Hull, Glynda A. "Constructing Taxonomies for Error (or Can Stray Dogs Be Mermaids?)." *A Sourcebook for Basic Writing Teachers*. Ed. Theresa Enos. New York: Random House, 1987, pp. 231–44.

Hunter, Carman St. John, and David Harman. *Adult Literacy in the United States: A Report to the Ford Foundation*. New York: McGraw-Hill, 1979.

Kaestle, Carl F. *The History of Literacy in America: An Introduction*. Reston, Va.: White House Conference on Library Information Services, 1979. ERIC ED 176 241.

Kozol, Jonathan. *Children of the Revolution: A Yankee Teacher in the Cuban Schools*. New York: Delacorte Press, 1978.

———. "A New Look at the Literacy Campaign in Cuba." *HER* 48 (1978): 341–77.

———. *Prisoners of Silence: Breaking the Bonds of Adult Illiteracy in the United States*. New York: Continuum, 1980.

Kozulin, Alex, ed. *Thought and Language*. Cambridge, Mass.: MIT Press, 1986.

Lockridge, Kenneth A. *Literacy in Colonial New England: An Enquiry into the Social Context of Literacy in the Early Modern West*. New York: W. W. Norton, 1974.

Lunsford, Andrea A. "Politics and Practices in Basic Writing." *A Sourcebook for Basic Writing Teachers*. Ed. Theresa Enos. New York: Random House, 1987, pp. 246–58.

Luria, A. R. *The Making of Mind: A Personal Account of Soviet Psychology*. Cambridge, Mass.: Harvard University Press, 1979.

Mackie, Robert, ed. *Literacy and Revolution: The Pedagogy of Paulo Freire*. New York: Continuum, 1981.

Miller, Valerie. *Between Struggle and Hope: The Nicaraguan Literacy Crusade*. Boulder, Colo.: Westview Press, 1985.

Newkirk, Thomas. *Only Connect: Uniting Reading and Writing*. Upper Montclair, N.J.: Boynton/Cook, 1986.

Olson, David. "From Utterance to Text: The Bias of Language in Speech and Writing." *HER* 47 (1977): 257–81.

———. "The Languages of Instruction: The Literate Bias of Schooling." *Schooling and the Acquisition of Knowledge*. Ed. R. Spiro. Hillsdale, N.J.: Lawrence Erlbaum Associates, 1978.

Olson, David R., Nancy Torrance, and Angela Hildyard, eds. *Literacy, Language, and Learning: The Nature and Consequences of Reading and Writing*. Cambridge: Cambridge University Press, 1985.

Ong, Walter J., S.J. "Reading, Technology, and Human Consciousness." *Literacy as a Human Problem*. Ed. James C. Raymond. University: University of Alabama Press, 1982, pp. 170–99.

——— "Literacy and Orality in Our Times." *ADE Bul* 58 (1978): 1–7.

———. *Orality and Literacy: The Technologizing of the Word*. London and New York: Methuen, 1982.

Pattison, Robert. *On Literacy: The Politics of the Word from Homer to the Age of Rock*. Oxford: Oxford University Press, 1982.

Postman, Neil. "The Politics of Reading." *HER* 40 (1970): 244–52.

Raymond, James C., ed. *Literacy as a Human Problem*. University: University of Alabama Press, 1982.

Resnick, Daniel P., and Lauren B. Resnick. "The Nature of Literacy: An Historical Exploration." *HER* 47 (1977): 370–85.

Robinson, Jay. "Literacy in the Department of English." *CE* 47 (1985): 482–98.

Rodriguez, Richard. *Hunger of Memory: The Education of Richard Rodriguez*. New York: Bantam Books, 1983.

Rogoff, Barbara, and Jean Lave. *Everyday Cognition: Its Development in Social Context*. Cambridge, Mass.: Harvard University Press, 1984.

Rose, Mike. "The Language of Exclusion: Writing Instruction at the University." *CE* 47 (1985): 341–59.

———. "Remedial Writing Courses: A Critique and a Proposal." *CE* 45 (1983): 109–28. Reprinted in *A Sourcebook for Basic Writing Teachers*. Ed. Theresa Enos. New York: Random House, 1987, pp. 104–24.

Roskelly, Hephzibah. "Redeeming 'Cultural Literacy.' " *Correspondences Four*. Ed. Ann E. Berthoff. Upper Montclair, N.J.: Boynton/Cook, n.d.

Salvatori, Mariolina. " 'Cultural Literacy': A Critical Reading." *Correspondences Four*. Ed. Ann E. Berthoff. Upper Montclair, N.J.: Boynton/Cook, n.d.

Scollon, Ron. "Language, Literacy, and Learning: An Annotated Bibliography." *Literacy, Language, and Learning: The Nature and Consequences of Reading and Writing*. Ed. David R. Olson, Nancy Torrance, and Angela Hildyard. Cambridge: Cambridge University Press, 1985, pp. 412–26.

Scollon, Suzanne B. K., and Ron Scollon. "Run Trilogy: Can Tommy Read?" *Awakening to Literacy*. Ed. Hillel Goelman, Antoinette Oberg, and Frank Smith. Portsmouth, N.H.: Heinemann Educational Books, 1984, pp. 131–40.

Scribner, Sylvia, and Michael Cole. "Cognitive Consequences of Formal and Informal Education." *Science* 182 (1973): 553–59.

———. "Literacy without Schooling: Testing for Intellectual Effects." *HER* 48 (1978): 448.

———. *The Psychology of Literacy*. Cambridge, Mass.: Harvard University Press, 1981.

———. "Unpackaging Literacy." *Variation in Writing: Functional and Linguistic Cultural Differences*. Ed. Marcia Farr Whiteman. Vol. 1 of *Writing: The Nature, Development, and Teaching of Written Communication*. Hillsdale, N.J.: Lawrence Erlbaum, 1981, pp. 71–86.

Shaughnessy, Mina. *Errors and Expectations: A Guide for the Teacher of Basic Writing*. New York: Oxford University Press, 1977.

Shor, Ira. "Learning How to Learn. " *CE* 38 (1977): 640–47.

———. "Reinventing Daily Life: Self-Study and the Theme of Work." *CE* 39 (1977): 502–6.

Shor, Ira, and Paulo Freire. *A Pedagogy for Liberation: Dialogues on Transforming Education*. South Hadley, Mass.: Bergin & Garvey, 1987.

Smith, Frank. "A Metaphor for Literacy: Creating Worlds or Shunting Information?" *Literacy, Language, and Learning: The Nature and Consequences of Reading and Writing*. Ed. David R. Olson, Nancy Torrance, and Angela Hildyard. Cambridge: Cambridge University Press, 1985, pp. 195–213.

Stratton, R. E. "Response to Thomas J. Farrell. 'IQ and Standard English.' " *CCC* 35 (1984): 468–69.

Street, Brain V. *Literacy in Theory and Practice*. Cambridge: Cambridge University Press, 1984.

Szwed, John F. "The Ethnography of Literacy." *Variation in Writing: Functional and Linguistic Cultural Differences*. Ed. Maria Farr Whiteman. Vol. 1 of *Writing: The Nature, Development, and Teaching of Written Communication*. Hillsdale, N.J.: Lawrence Erlbaum Associates, 1981, pp. 13–23.

UNESCO. *The Experimental World Literacy Programme: A Critical Assessment*. Paris: UNESCO Press, 1976.

————. *The Experimental World Literacy Programme Practical Guide to Functional Literacy: A Method of Training for Development*. Paris: UNESCO, 1973.

————. *The World Literacy: Policy, Research and Action*. Ottawa: International Development Research Centre, 1979.

Walker, Jim. "The End of Dialogue." *Literacy and Revolution: The Pedagogy of Paulo Freire*. Ed. Robert Mackie. New York: Continuum, 1981, pp. 120–50.

Warnock, John. "Cultural Literacy: A Worm in the Bud?" *ADE Bul* 82 (Winter 1985): 1–7.

————. "Reply to Hirsch's Comment on 'Cultural Literacy: A Worm in the Bud?' " *ADE Bul* 84 (Fall 1986): 4–5.

Weis, Lois. *Between Two Worlds: Black Students in an Urban Community College*. Boston: Routledge & Kegan Paul, 1985.

Wells, Susan. "Vygotsky Reads *Capital*." *Correspondences Two*. Ed. Ann E. Berthoff. Upper Montclair, N.J.: Boynton/Cook, n.d.

Wertsch, James V. *Vygotsky and the Social Formation of Mind*. Cambridge, Mass.: Harvard University Press, 1985.

Willis, Paul. *Learning to Labour: How Working Class Kids Get Working Class Jobs*. Farnborough, Eng.: Saxon House, 1977.

————. *The World of Literacy: Policy, Research, and Action*. Ottawa: International Development Research Centre, 1979.

Zebroski, James Thomas. "Tropes and Zones." *Correspondences Four*. Ed. Ann E. Berthoff. Upper Montclair, N.J.: Boynton/Cook, n.d.

PART II

Linguistic Perspectives

4

Modern Grammar and Basic Writers

Ronald F. Lunsford

In 1965 Harold B. Allen had high hopes for modern grammar. In an article entitled "From Prairies to Mountains," Allen commented on the potential contributions of linguistics to composition theory: "The Rockies are the heights to which I think the discipline of composition can rise through the uplifting power of new research in rhetoric and the application of new linguistic knowledge" (261). Allen was seconded by other linguists such as Harry Warfel who compared the developments in language study to earlier developments in music ("Structural Linguistics and Composition" [1959]).

Not all linguists, however, were so sure that linguistic studies would prove applicable to the teaching of writing. Such noted linguists as Paul Roberts ("The Relation of Linguistics to the Teaching of English" [1960]) and Robert Lees ("The Promise of Transformational Grammar" [1963]) doubted that it would.

Since these writers expressed their opinions more than twenty years ago, one might think it would be an easy task to decide which viewpoint was correct, or at least more nearly correct. It is not. There is a way in which proponents of either argument can still find evidence to support their claims: linguistics—or the study of modern grammar—can be seen to have contributed very little to the teaching of writing, or it can be seen to be central to that activity, depending upon one's perspective.

I see modern grammar as central. Those who would maintain that grammar is useless to the teacher of writing have been looking at the role of grammar from the wrong perspective. As has so often been the case in matters concerning the teaching of writing, Mina Shaughnessy provides an important corrective in her article "Diving In" (1976). Shaughnessy offers us a fresh viewpoint in this piece by analyzing, not basic writers, but teachers of basic writers. She suggests that as we teachers "develop" to a higher stage of awareness of our students and our task, we will "see that we must grope our ways into the turbulent disciplines of semantics and linguistics for fuller, more accurate data about words and sentences" (238). Shaughnessy is asserting that teachers can benefit from linguistic study regardless of whether they find it useful to teach linguistic concepts to their students.

The research of the last twenty years suggests that grammar is an important tool for the informed teacher of writing regardless of how much of that grammar should (or can) be taught to the student. In the essay to follow, I shall review that research, with sections devoted to traditional grammar, structural and transformational grammar, and discourse theory. In each of these sections, I will cite relevant linguistic bibliographies. Here I would like to mention three important general bibliographies, two treating basic writing and one treating linguistic-composition connections.

The first, Mina Shaughnessy's "Basic Writing" (1976), is important to our concerns in this essay not only because it is the first comprehensive bibliography on basic writing but also because of the prominent role Shaughnessy assigned to language and linguistics. She suggested that the basic writing teacher should be familiar with such classic works in language as those produced by Leonard Bloomfield (*Language* [1933]), Edward Sapir (*Language* [1921]), Benjamin Whorf (*Language, Thought and Reality* [1956]), and Otto Jesperson (*The Philosophy of Grammar* [1965]). She also recommended reading primary works in modern grammar by such writers as James Deese ("The Psychology of Learning and the Study of English" [1971]), John Lyons (*Introduction to Theoretical Linguistics* [1969]), Charles Fries (*The Structure of English* [1952]), Noam Chomsky (*Syntactic Structures* [1957]), Stephen Ullman (*Semantics* [1970]), and Geoffrey Leech (*Semantics* [1974]). (I should note here that Shaughnessy's bibliography is updated by Andrea Lunsford ["Basic Writing Update" (1987)] in the revised and enlarged edition of *Teaching Composition*.)

The most comprehensive bibliography on basic writing instruction to date was compiled by Glynda A. Hull and David J. Bartholomae ("Basic Writing" [1984]). A glance at the checklist at the end of this article will show that many teachers of basic writing have heeded Shaughnessy's advice to learn more about language.

A third general bibliography is W. Ross Winterowd's "Linguistics and Composition" (1976). Winterowd's bibliography is worthy of note because in it he cites very few actual applications of linguistic theory to the teaching of writing, even though this article was published thirty years after the introduction of structural grammar and nearly twenty years after Chomsky introduced transformational grammar. In part, this fact may be attributed to Winterowd's interest, and to his broad definition of linguistics (which becomes even broader in his update, "Literacy, Linguistics, and Rhetoric" [1987]); however, at the time he wrote his original review, there were few linguistic applications to composition— and virtually none to basic writing. Such is not the case today, as my survey will show.

TRADITIONAL GRAMMAR

Though it may seem something of a contradiction in terms to include a section on traditional grammar in a paper devoted to modern grammars, the number of teachers and theoreticians who intuit a connection between grammar and writing warrants its inclusion. Still another reason for including this section is the persistent belief that basic writers must be taught grammar *before* they will be ready to handle the more sophisticated rhetorical matters treated in the college writing classroom.

Much work has been done in the last twenty-five years to determine whether formal grammar instruction improves writing. A logical place to begin, because of the impact it has had on composition theory, is *Research in Written Composition* (1963) by Richard Braddock, Richard Lloyd-Jones, and Lowell Schoer. After surveying the empirical research on the connection between grammar and writing, these researchers concluded that "[t]he teaching of formal grammar has a negligible or, because it usually displaces some instruction and practice in actual composition, even a harmful effect on the improvement of writing" (37–38).

The next significant overview of research conducted on the grammar-composition connection appeared in J. Stephen Sherwin's *Four Problems in Teaching English* (1969). The studies that Sherwin reviewed corroborated the findings of Braddock et al. Three recent studies confirm the findings of these earlier researchers: Anthony R. Petrosky's "Research Roundup" (1977), Dean Memering's "Forward to the Basics" (1978), and Robert J. Connors's "Grammar in American College Composition" (1986).

The evidence is not conclusive for everyone, however. Martha Kolln speaks for formal grammar instruction in her article "Closing the Books on Alchemy" (1981). She challenges the validity of research into the grammar-composition connection on the grounds that research designs have been flawed and that the researchers' definitions of grammar have been questionable. Kolln's challenge can be answered rather easily. Her objections to research design are the standard objections one can raise in regard to any study in the social sciences. None of the studies having to do with grammar-composition connections is flawless, but the mass of evidence represented by the studies does seem to be overwhelming. Her second objection is actually an equivocation. She wishes to show that since many of the experimental treatments in these studies included instruction in putting sentences together, they actually contain "grammar." If we define grammar in this way, then anything having to do with writing will, by definition, involve grammar. This is not what one normally means, however, in speaking of instruction in grammar.

Kolln is not alone in believing that students need some type of instruction in grammar. Though they insist that teachers should use only as much grammar as needed to teach writing and that grammar instruction should be given in the context of instruction in writing, Ian S. Fraser and Lynda M. Hodson ("Twenty-one Kicks at the Grammar Horse'' [1978]) do maintain that beginning writers need some set of working terms for discussing their writing. Robert de Beaugrande would seem to agree. In "Forward to the Basics" (1984), he offers a simplified grammar designed to be basic enough to help student writers.

Patrick Hartwell ("Grammar, Grammars, and the Teaching of Writing" [1985]) is not surprised that Kolln, and others, are not convinced by the empirical evidence against grammar instruction. Hartwell asserts that one's approach to the grammar question is determined by the model of the composing process he or she espouses. According to Hartwell, those who "believe in" grammar operate on a model "that is rigidly skills-centered and rigidly sequential" (108). In "A Teacher's Guide to the *Real* Basics" (1977), W. Ross Winterowd came to the same conclusion nearly ten years earlier concerning what teachers should be doing in writing courses.

Before leaving this topic, I should mention the large body of work that deals with the connection between traditional grammar and dialect, and that involves the complicated issue of whether writing courses should be allowed to become agents for enforcing the standards of those who hold power in our society. For a review of this literature, the reader should consult Jenefer M. Giannasi's "Language Varieties and Composition" (1987).

STRUCTURAL AND TRANSFORMATIONAL GRAMMARS

Structural grammar has not produced many applications to the teaching of writing because of the task it set for itself, namely describing linguistic behavior. The key word here is "behavior." Since structuralists did not concern themselves with the linguistic ability that allowed a native speaker to produce that behavior, they had very little to say to the writing teacher who is concerned not so much with the product as with the process that leads to that product.

The structuralist movement can trace its roots to Leonard Bloomfield's *Language* (1933). The two most important figures in translating Bloomfield's work into the theory that has come to be known as structuralism are Charles Fries (*The Structure of English* [1952]) and Nelson Francis (*The English Language* [1963]).

Though they offer little to recommend structural grammar, I will mention two studies that investigated the effect of structural grammar on students' writing. In the first, "Structural Versus Non-Structural Teaching" (1960), Falk Johnson focused on remedial students and found no evidence that students trained in structural grammar wrote better essays than students trained in traditional grammar. In the second study, "Structural Grammar versus Traditional Grammar in Influencing Writing" (1961), Lena Reddick Suggs did conclude that the structural grammar was superior to traditional grammar, but as J. Stephen Sherwin (1969) points out, her study contained serious design flaws.

My pronouncements about the limited applicability of structural grammar may be a bit overstated if one considers tagmemics as a type of structural grammar.

The basic principles of tagmemics are outlined in Kenneth Pike's *Language in Relation to the Unified Theory of the Structure of Human Behavior* (1967). While tagmemic grammars have been rather fertile ground for rhetoricians in the last twenty-five years, the one consistent complaint against applications based on tagmemics is that they require a good deal of sophistication with language. Thus, tagmemics has not led to applications for basic writers.

For more information on tagmemic applications to the teaching of writing, the reader may consult the following works: Kenneth Pike, "A Linguistic Contribution to Composition" (1964) and "Beyond the Sentence" (1964); Alton Becker, "A Tagmemic Approach to Paragraph Analysis" (1965); Richard Young and Alton Becker, "Toward a Modern Theory of Rhetoric" (1965); Richard Young, Alton Becker, and Kenneth Pike, *Rhetoric: Discovery and Change* (1970); James Kinney, "Tagmemic Rhetoric" (1978); Lee Odell, "Another Look at Tagmemic Theory" (1978); and Charles Kneupper, "Revising the Tagmemic Heuristic" (1980).

In 1957, and seemingly overnight, structural grammar gave way to transformational grammar with the publication of Noam Chomsky's *Syntactic Structures*. Transformational grammar differed from structural grammar in one respect that was crucial for those interested in making applications to the composing process. Structural grammar's rigorously empirical approach forbade its user to adopt any perspective at all about his data. Thus, structural grammar is essentially a performance model, a way of formalizing the patterns of utterances that already happen to exist. In contrast, generative transformational grammar is a competence model, a way of formalizing, not just the patterns of given utterances, but the principles governing our understanding of the potentially utterable.

It follows that transformational generative grammar should be more readily applicable to the teaching of writing. But does it follow that teaching a transformational grammar to students will prove more successful than teaching them a traditional grammar? In his article entitled "The Value of Transformational Grammar" (1967), Mark Lester, one of the chief promulgators of transformational grammar (via his text, *Introductory Transformational Grammar of English* [1971]) observed that "there simply appears to be no correlation between a writer's conscious study of grammar and his ability to write" (227).

Lester's point is a valid one. There probably is very little correlation between conscious study of grammar (traditional or transformational) and one's ability to write, if we think of writing as conceptualizing and forming a coherent essay. However, as we all know, in the real world of our classrooms—if to say such is not to contradict oneself utterly—matters of usage are a part of one's ability to write. If we include usage, then some form of transformational grammar may be profitably taught to students.

One researcher who clearly believes that students can benefit from learning a transformational grammar is Suzette Elgin. In a charmingly written essay, "Don't No Revolutions Hardly *Ever* Come by Here" (1978), she argues that transformational grammar does have a place in the writing classroom. Elgin cites a study she undertook with Shirley Ann Rush (*An Experimental and Evaluative Approach to Teaching Basic Writing Skills* [1977]) as evidence that students who are led to deduce transformational rules and then state them in their own language will apply the rules in their own writing.

While Elgin focuses on helping students write their own transformational grammar, most researchers who make connections between transformational grammar and composition concern themselves with what teachers stand to learn from the new grammar. In his article "Linguistics and Error Analysis" (1986), Donald Freeman suggests that the transformational model's concept of linguistic competence, inherent in the deep structure/surface structure analysis, provides teachers with a new way to categorize student errors. This competence model takes cognizance of the fact that speakers and writers know more than their performance demonstrates; it also recognizes the fact that a writer's performance is tied directly to his or her competence and, thus, cannot be changed without a change in that competence.

Freeman presents a sample student essay and attempts to show how a system of error analysis based on a theory of competence would help the teacher understand student errors. His point is that traditional error analysis will often classify as one problem what are in fact several different problems of competence and, conversely, often fail to capture the fact that one flaw in linguistic competence can lead to several different surface errors.

Freeman is building on a tradition of error analysis as a tool in teaching basic writing that goes back to Shaughnessy (*Errors and Expectations* [1977]). David Bartholomae also builds on this tradition in his article "The Study of Error" (1980), in which he finds that "basic writers do not, in general, write immature sentences. . . . In fact, they often attempt syntax whose surface is more complex than that of more successful freshmen writers" (254). According to Bartholomae, the basic writer is not suffering from arrested linguistic competence: "his problem is a problem of performance, or fluency, not of competence" (263). Ann Gebhard also concludes, in "Writing Quality and Syntax" (1978), that the difference between the work of good writers and poor writers is not their competence to produce certain syntactic structures. Both types of writers appear to be competent to produce various structures, but the good writers vary theirs much more frequently than do the poor writers.

Peter J. Gingiss approaches the question of competence from a different angle in "Competence and Performance in Written English" (1982). Gingiss finds that the competence factor of memory partially accounts for differences between students' oral and written abilities.

David Carkeet develops the role of memory as a competence factor more fully than Gingiss in "Understanding Syntactic Errors in Remedial Writing" (1977). Building on the transformational concepts of deep structure and transforms, he shows that remedial writers reduce clauses by means of deletion transformations without being able to hold in memory all of the elements contained in the unreduced structure. Carkeet is not suggesting that formal grammatical instruction will help such student writers, but that teachers who understand the psychological processes involved will have an advantage in instructing these students.

Kenneth Bruffee also deals with memory in his article "Getting Started" (1986). In speaking of transformational grammar, Bruffee offers his opinion that "Chomsky's lasting contribution may be an implication inherent in his transformational grammar, the implication that language is nonlinear and discontinuous" (103). Bruffee applies Chomsky's proposition to the choices a writer makes in the composing process. A writer's choice, at a specific point in a composition, is affected not only by the syntactic structure and word choices that precede it, but also by those that come after it. Bruffee's insight is that basic writers often begin very badly because they have no sense of structure for the sentence they are composing.

Patricia Laurence explores the competence-performance distinction from still another perspective in her article "Error's Endless Train" (1975). She shows how dialect interference from a native language hinders the performance of students attempting to learn English as a second language. Such seemingly simple performance tasks as perceiving what is written on a page may be hindered by one's competence in another language.

Laurence is writing about students who are actually learning English as a second language (ESL). In an article entitled "Krashen's Second-Language Acquisition Theory and the Teaching of Edited American English" (1986), Elizabeth Tricomi draws a comparison between such ESL students and basic writers whose nonstandard dialect may function like a first language to hinder their performance in Edited American English. She explains some problems these students have by referring to the distinction Stephen Krashen makes, in *Principles and Practice in Second Language Acquisition* (1982), between language "acquisition" and language "learning." Rules that have been learned rather than acquired must be applied mechanically at the revision stage. Tricomi suggests that drills and exercises aim at learning rather than acquisition, and while she does not say that all exercises should be done away with, she encourages context-based instruction that will lead to language acquisition.

The articles I have examined to this point provide theoretical insights that should be of use to teachers of writing. However, for the most part, they do not suggest direct applications of those theories. There is one very direct application of modern grammar that I shall turn to now—sentence combining.

Though it is certainly true, as many writers have pointed out, that sentence-combining exercises existed before the advent of transformational grammar, it should be evident that the transformational concept of embedding gave sentence combining a theoretical foundation upon which to build. By the time Chomsky and his followers moved away from this concept, sentence combining had enough momentum to sustain itself.

Those interested in the history of sentence combining should begin with three bibliographies. The first appears in a book, *Sentence Combining and the Teaching of Writing* (1979), edited by a trio who has been instrumental in sentence-combining research: Donald A. Daiker, Andrew Kerek, and Max Morenberg. The book also contains articles by such sentence-combining notables as John Mellon ("Issues in the Theory and Practice of Sentence Combining"), and Kellogg Hunt ("Anybody Can Teach English"). A second bibliography, of sorts, is Lester Faigley's thorough review of sentence-combining research in "Names in Search of a Concept" (1980). The most recent bibliography is that found in William Strong's *Creative Approaches to Sentence Combining* (1986). In this monograph, Strong deals with the major issues involving sentence combining and reviews the major studies in the field.

If we accept the assertion that sentence-combining exercises work to improve syntactic growth and overall quality of writing at the college level (and the research suggests it does), then we must ask whether it also works for basic writers. In his article "Sentence Combining: Back to Basics and Beyond" (1976), William Strong presents a compelling argument that sentence combining is more "basic" than mechanical and grammatical drills. He maintains that sentence-combining exercises "provide a relatively non-threatening context for teaching some transcribing fundamentals—penmanship, punctuation, capitalization, and accurate spelling—as well as some larger matters of mechanics—agreement, pronoun reference, parallelism, and so on" (60).

Rebecca Argall's experience, as reported in her paper "Sentence Combining" (1982), offers confirmation for Strong's observation. Developmental writers given instruction in sentence combining wrote papers that contained fewer sentence errors of various types than the papers written by developmental students in a control group. However, Kathy D. Jackson's study, "The Effect of Sentence Combining Practice on the Reduction of Syntactic Errors in Basic Writing" (1982), did not support the contention that sentence-combining practice leads to fewer mechanical errors.

As his dissertation title indicates ("An Experimental Study of Sentence-Combining as A Means of Increasing Syntactic Maturity and Writing Quality in the Compositions of College-Age Students Enrolled in Remedial English" [1977]), Clarence Waterfall tested for both syntactic growth and overall writing quality in his study. He found that writing quality was affected positively but that syntactic fluency was not. Kathy Masters and Mitchell Masters obtained similar results in their study "The Effect of Sentence Combining Achievement in Basic Writing" (1980).

Diane S. Menendez's findings were exactly opposite to those of Waterfall and the Masters ("The Effect of Sentence-Combining Practice on Remedial College Students' Syntactic Maturity, Punctuation Skills and Reading Ability" [1978]). Students made significant gains in two measures of syntactic maturity, but writing quality was not significantly improved. B. G. Armbrecht achieved similar results in a dissertation entitled "The Effects of Sentence-Combining Practice on the Syntactic Maturity, Quality of Writing, and Reading Comprehension of a Select Group of College Students in Remedial English in Southeast Georgia" (1981).

Two other studies raised questions about the value of sentence-combining exercises for basic writers. Ira Hayes compared sentence-combining instruction to traditional instruction for eleventh graders ("An Experimental Study of Sentence Combining as A Means of Improving Syntactic Maturity, Writing Quality and Grammatical Fluency in the Compositions of Remedial High School Students" [1984]). The sentence-combining group experienced significant growth in two of six measurements of syntactic growth, but a comparison of writing quality favored neither. Joyce Elaine Powell conducted a similar study involving community college students ("The Effects of Sentence Combining on the Writing of Basic Writers in the Community College" [1984]) and found that while the experimental group made gains in syntactic maturity, the control group's writing was judged as significantly better.

As these studies make clear, sentence combining has not been proven to be as effective for basic writers as it has for non–basic writers. However, Strong's argument that sentence combining is basic seems compelling and would suggest that much more work should be done in exploring the effect of sentence combining on basic writers.

Before leaving sentence combining, we should mention a related method of sentence expansion introduced by Francis Christensen—generative rhetoric. As outlined in two seminal articles by Christensen, "A Generative Rhetoric of the Sentence" (1963) and "A Generative Rhetoric of the Paragraph" (1965), and two monographs written with his wife, Bonniejean Christensen, *Notes Toward a New Rhetoric* (1967) and *A New Rhetoric* (1976), Christensen's sentence-level rhetoric consists of a program designed to teach students how to expand sentences using free modifiers.

Unfortunately, there have been relatively few studies of the efficacy of Christensen's theories—and virtually none applying his theories to basic writing. There is one transformational study, however, that connects basic writing research to Christensen's theories. In "Phenomenal Nominals" (1981), Donald Freeman examines the work of basic writers and finds that it contains a high percentage of noun clauses consisting of a nominal and a bound modifier. He recommends that basic writers be instructed in methods of "unpacking" these nominals and producing what Christensen calls free modifiers. Joseph Williams presents a somewhat different view of these nominals in "Non-Linguistics and the Teaching of Style" (1986). Though he would not argue that bound nominals are necessarily effective in communicating, he does argue that most readers associate abstract nominalizations with sophisticated writing.

DISCOURSE THEORY

In speaking of the limitations of transformational grammar, W. Ross Winterowd observed, in "The Grammar of Coherence" (1970), that "[j]ust at the point where it could best serve rhetoric transformational generative grammar fails: it does not jump the double cross (#) that signifies 'sentence boundary . . . ' " (828). Winterowd is right, of course: transformational grammar is a sentence grammar.

If we abide by a technical definition of grammar—see, for example, Connors (1986) 7–8; Fraser and Hodson (1978) 51; and Halliday and Hasan (1976) 1–2—we are constrained to say that grammar must limit itself to the sentence. However, linguistics is not so constrained. Those linguists working in discourse theory have jumped the double cross symbol and, in doing so, have developed a theory that might be rightly labeled as linguistic rhetoric or rhetorical linguistics.

Discourse theory is dedicated to describing how parts of a text relate to each other and how the text itself relates to the context in which it appears. Taken together, these concerns entail the question of how a text comes to have meaning. Much of the primary material of discourse linguistics is rather technical. Two secondary articles may prove helpful in explaining some of the concepts and orienting the reader to possible applications: Stephen P. Witte's "Topical Structure and Revision" (1983) and Lester Faigley's "The Problem of Topic in Texts" (1986).

As Witte points out, discourse linguistics has its roots in the Prague School of Linguistics, with the work of Vilem Mathesius ("On Linguistic Characterology with Illustrations from Modern English" [1928]), Jan Firbas ("On Defining the Theme in Functional Sentence Analysis" [1966]), and František Daneš ("A Three-Level Approach to Syntax" [1964]). That work gave rise to an important book for composition researchers by M.A.K. Halliday and Ruqaiya Hasan, *Cohesion in English* (1976). Halliday and Hasan set themselves the task of analyzing *cohesion*, "a semantic relation between an element in the text and some other element that is crucial to the interpretation of it" (8).

Their work has been seminal for researchers involved in analyzing student texts, and it is beginning to be mined by those looking for ways of teaching coherence. In an article entitled "Coherence, Cohesion, and Writing Quality" (1981), Stephen Witte and Lester Faigley observe that weak writers use fewer cohesive ties and different kinds of ties than do strong writers. Sandra Stotsky examines cohesive ties in her article "Types of Lexical Cohesion in Expository Writing" (1983) and concludes that weak writers will learn to use intricate connectors only when they are exposed to reading materials with such connections.

In her dissertation ("A Study of the Cohesive Devices in the Good and Poor Compositions of Eleventh Graders" [1980]), R. T. Pritchard studied the writing of eleventh graders to see whether there is a correlation between the number of cohesive ties used and the quality of the writing. When good essays and bad essays were viewed as a whole, she found no such correlation. However, when raters were asked to choose problematic sections within essays, they did choose sections which were relatively low in cohesive ties.

Jerome L. Neuner examines this same phenomenon in his essay entitled "Cohesive Ties and Chains in Good and Poor Freshman Essays" (1987). He reviews several other articles having to do with this topic, among them articles by G. A. McCulley ("Writing Quality, Coherence, and Cohesion" [1985]), M. Crowhurst (*Cohesion in Argumentative Prose* [1981]), Roger Cherry and Charles Cooper ("Cohesive Ties and Discourse Structure" [1980]), and Robert J. Tierney and James H. Mosenthal ("Cohesion and Textual Coherence" [1983]). Neuner concludes that there is no one-to-one relationship between the number of cohesive ties and quality of writing. He then goes on to report on his own study that shows a correlation between the length of cohesive chains—a chain is a series of references within a text—and the overall quality of writing.

Another study dealing with cohesive ties and writing quality was published by Ulla Connor and Janice Lauer ("Understanding Persuasive Essay Writing" [1985]). Connor and Lauer performed extensive analyses of the writing of one hundred students and, among other things, found no correlation between number of ties and quality of writing.

However, it may be too soon to say that the matter is answered once and for all. Irmgard Lintermann-Rygh ("Connector Density" [1985]) did find a correlation between the number of ties and writing quality. He explains his ability to do so by saying that he took into consideration the number of "that" clauses, which provide no opportunity for connections, in his total count. In "Static and Dynamic Cohesion" (1986) Carolyn G. Hartnett also found a positive correlation between the number of ties and quality of writing. In order to do so, she had to refine the categories of Halliday and Hasan, suggesting that ties be divided into two types: static (those that hold the reader's attention on the subject) and dynamic (those that forge relationships between units). She found that basic writers used a significantly larger number of static ties than did non–basic writers.

Richard Haswell sheds some light on why research on cohesion continues to be indeterminate. In "Critique: Length of Text and the Measurement of Cohesion" (1988), Haswell points to one of the problems in analyzing cohesion. Previous research has assumed "a linear relation between length [of an essay] and opportunities for writers to make cohesive ties" (428). But Haswell explains that there is no such one-to-one relation because, "according to Halliday and Hasan's account of cohesion, a previous word may count as precursor to more than one coherer" (429). There are simply not as many opportunities for cohesion in a shorter piece as in a longer one, and, thus, studies that present comparisons based on this incorrect assumption are bound to misrepresent the abilities of basic writers, who generally write shorter pieces. Haswell continues his investigation of cohesion in "Textual Research and Coherence: Findings, Intuition, Application" (1989), where he shows that good writers often use different, and less obvious, kinds of coherence devices than do less competent writers.

In "Cohesion Paradigms in Paragraphs" (1983), Robin Bell Markels suggests a modification of Halliday and Hasan's categories. She argues that the "categories of ties formulated by Halliday and Hasan . . . identify necessary but not sufficient conditions for cohesion" (451). She calls for a redefining of cohesion so that a cohesive passage would have a "dominant" term (452). In doing so, Markels would seem to be confusing two terms that Witte and Faigley (81) distinguish so clearly (cohesion and coherence).

Even though Markels's suggestion is not useful in defining cohesion, her article does introduce an important concept in discourse analysis—theme/rheme. M.A.K. Halliday outlines the concept of theme/rheme, with its attendance concerns of given/new, topic/comment, identified/identifier, in his article "Notes on Transitivity and Theme in English: II" (1967). Though he uses different terminology, Tuen A. van Dijk deals with many of these matters in his *Text and Context* (1977). William J. Vande Kopple gives a very accessible introduction to the concept of topic/comment in his article "Something Old, Something New" (1983). These various terms are a bit confusing, but perhaps it will suffice here to say that they all have to do with the ways in which parts of a text interact with one another to create coherence (as opposed to cohesion). As might be imagined, they offer fertile soil for those wishing to analyze the problems of basic writers.

Betty Bamberg uses van Dijk's terminology to analyze essays written by students for the National Assessment of Educational Progress ("What Makes a Text Coherent?" [1983]). She finds that students performing poorly lack both local coherence (van Dijk's term for cohesion) and global coherence (his term for coherence); however, she suggests that students must be instructed in matters of global coherence before instruction in local coherence will have the proper effect.

Two other studies dealing with matters of coherence, in particular as it relates to discourse topic, are Eleanor Wikborg's "Unspecified Topic in University Student Essays" (1985) and George Goodin and Kyle Perkins's "Discourse Analysis and the Art of Coherence" (1982).

With the studies in this section, we have expanded our concern from the confines of the sentence to the whole of a text. Discourse analysis, however, does not limit itself to the text. As Halliday (*Language as a Social Semiotic* [1978]) and van Dijk (1977) show us, a text has meaning in a context. Deborah Brandt ("Text and Context" [1986]) discusses the ways in which writers and readers rely on social context in writing and interpreting texts. She suggests that "[t]echniques of discourse analysis which relate text to context and parts of texts to each other can aid composition teachers in reading students' papers more fully for the interpretation processes which underlie them" (106). Brandt goes on to show that basic writers may bring contexts to bear on what they read and write that are different from those others bring. She invokes Shaughnessy in suggesting that basic writing teachers become familiar with these differing reading and writing processes so that they can understand what students do know rather than focusing on what they do not know.

Dan Foster and Paul Hoffman explore a similar concept in "The Private Worlds of Basic Writers" (1984). They categorize noun clauses of basic writers and advanced writers as (1) those requiring earlier text information, (2) those fully interpretable on their own, (3) those requiring extratextual, readily accessible information, and (4) those requiring extratextual, not easily accessible information. Their study indicates that basic writers write a significantly larger number of noun phrases composed of information requiring extratextual, not easily accessible information than other writers.

Ann M. Johns deals with a similar phenomenon in "The ESL Student and the Revision Process" (1986). Johns points out that many ESL students have problems with coherence because they come from cultures that do not operate on the same schemata, or knowledge frames, as does the English-speaking culture.

CONCLUSION

At the time Professor Allen predicted that modern linguistic applications were going to prove important to composition research, most linguists and composition theorists were looking for a new grammar that would prove useful to students in ways that traditional grammar had seemed to fail. As we have seen, there are those who would claim that transformational grammar can be taught profitably to students. They would maintain that its descriptive approach to the language is useful in helping students see the logic of grammar and usage in ways that prescriptive, traditional grammar could not. They may be right, but we are still awaiting studies to support their claims.

We already have ample evidence, however, that modern grammar is an important tool for teachers of writing. The competence-performance distinction inherent in transformational grammar provides teachers with much insight into the composing processes of their students, suggesting new ways of analyzing errors and offering remedies.

Discourse analysis, another type of modern linguistics, is also proving a useful tool. The work of Halliday and Hasan has given rise to a plethora of articles analyzing student texts that may well contribute significantly to the evolving definition of basic writing. Though there is no suggestion that discourse analysis be taught to students, it is clear that its principles provide insights valuable to teachers of writing.

If Professor Allen's high hopes have not been fulfilled in the ways in which he might have imagined, it is nevertheless clear that his optimism was warranted.

REFERENCES

Allen, Harold B. "From Prairies to Mountains: Linguistics and Composition." *CE* 26 (1965): 260–66.

Argall, Rebecca S. "Sentence Combining: An Incisive Tool for Proofreading." ERIC, 1982. ED 214 186.

Armbrecht, B. G. "The Effects of Sentence-Combining Practice on the Syntactic Maturity, Quality of Writing, and Reading Comprehension of a Select Group of

College Students in Remedial English in Southeast Georgia." Diss. Georgia State University, 1981.

Bamberg, Betty. "What Makes a Text Coherent?" *CCC* 34 (1983): 417–29.

Batholomae, David. "The Study of Error." *CCC* 31 (1980): 253–69.

Becker, Alton L. "A Tagmemic Approach to Paragraph Analysis." *CCC* 16 (1965): 237–42.

Bloomfield, Leonard. *Language*. New York: Holt, 1933.

Braddock, Richard, Richard Lloyd-Jones, and Lowell Schoer. *Research in Written Composition*. Champaign, Ill.: NCTE, 1963.

Brandt, Deborah. "Text and Context: How Writers Come to Mean." *Functional Approaches to Writing: Research Perspectives*. Ed. Barbara Couture. London: Francis Pinter, 1986, pp. 93–107.

Bruffee, Kenneth. "Getting Started." *Territory of Language: Linguistics, Stylistics, and the Teaching of Composition*. Ed. Donald A. McQuade. Carbondale: Southern Illinois University Press, 1986, pp. 103–13.

Carkeet, David. "Understanding Syntactic Errors in Remedial Writing." *CE* 38 (1977): 682–95.

Cherry, Roger, and Charles Cooper. "Cohesive Ties and Discourse Structure: A Study of Average and Superior Texts at Four Grade Levels." Unpublished manuscript. Dept. of Learning and Instruction, State University of New York at Buffalo, 1980.

Chomsky, Noam. *Syntactic Structures*. The Hague: Mouton, 1957.

Christensen, Francis. "A Generative Rhetoric of the Paragraph." *CCC* 16 (1965): 144–56.

———. "A Generative Rhetoric of the Sentence." *CCC* 14 (1963): 155–61.

Christensen, Francis, and Bonniejean Christensen. *A New Rhetoric*. New York: Harper and Row, 1976.

———. *Notes Toward a New Rhetoric: Nine Essays for Teachers*. New York: Harper and Row, 1967.

Connor, Ulla, and Janice Lauer. "Understanding Persuasive Essay Writing: Linguistic/Rhetorical Approach." *Text* 5 (1985): 309–26.

Connors, Robert J. "Grammar in American College Composition: An Historical Overview." *The Territory of Language: Linguistics, Stylistics, and the Teaching of Composition*. Ed. Donald A. McQuade. Carbondale: Southern Illinois University Press, 1986, pp. 3–22.

Crowhurst, M. *Cohesion in Argumentative Prose*. Los Angeles: American Educational Research Association, 1981.

Daiker, Donald A., Andrew Kerek, and Max Morenberg, eds. *Sentence Combining and the Teaching of Writing*. Oxford, Ohio: L & S Books, 1979.

Daneš, František. "A Three-Level Approach to Syntax." *Travaux Linguistiques de Prague* 1 (1964): 225–40.

de Beaugrande, Robert. "Forward to the Basics: Getting Down to Grammar." *CCC* 35 (1984): 358–67.

Deese, James. "The Psychology of Learning and the Study of English." *The Learning of Language*. Ed. Carroll E. Reed. New York: Appleton-Century-Crofts, 1971, pp. 157–85.

Elgin, Suzette Haden. "Don't No Revolutions Hardly *Ever* Come by Here." *CE* 39 (1978): 784–89.

Elgin, Suzette Haden, and Shirley Ann Rush. *An Experimental and Evaluative Approach to Teaching Basic Writing Skills*. Long Beach: The California State University and Colleges, 1977.

Faigley, Lester. "Names in Search of a Concept: Maturity, Fluency, Complexity, and Growth in Written Syntax." *CCC* 31 (1980): 291–300.

———. "The Problem of Topic in Texts." *The Territory of Language: Linguistics, Stylistics and the Teaching of Composition*. Ed. Donald A. McQuade. Carbondale: Southern Illinois University Press, 1986, pp. 123–41.

Firbas, Jan. "On Defining the Theme in Functional Sentence Analysis." *Travaux Linguistiques de Prague* 1 (1966): 267–80.

Foster, Dan, and Paul Hoffman. "The Private Worlds of Basic Writers." ERIC, 1984. ED 263 584.

Francis, Nelson. *The English Language*. New York: Norton, 1963.

Fraser, Ian S., and Lynda M. Hodson. "Twenty-one Kicks at the Grammar Horse." *EJ* 67.9 (1978): 49–54.

Freeman, Donald C. "Linguistics and Error Analysis: On Agency." *The Territory of Language: Linguistics, Stylistics and the Teaching of Composition*. Ed. Donald A. McQuade. Carbondale: Southern Illinois University Press, 1986, pp. 165–73.

———. "Phenomenal Nominals." *CCC* 32 (1981): 183–88.

Fries, Charles. *The Structure of English*. New York: Harcourt, 1952.

Gebhard, Ann O. "Writing Quality and Syntax: A Transformational Analysis of Three Prose Samples." *RTE* 12 (1978): 211–31.

Giannasi, Jenefer J. "Language Varieties and Composition." *Teaching Composition: Twelve Bibliographical Essays*, rev. and enl. ed. Ed. Gary Tate. Fort Worth: Texas Christian University Press, 1987, pp. 227–64.

Gingiss, Peter J. "Competence and Performance in Written English." *Southwest Journal of Linguistics* 5 (1982): 203–9.

Goodin, George, and Kyle Perkins. "Discourse Analysis and the Art of Coherence." *CE* 44 (1982): 57–63.

Halliday, M.A.K. "Notes on Transitivity and Theme in English: II." *Journal of Linguistics* 3 (1967): 199–244.

———. *Language as a Social Semiotic: The Social Interpretation of Language and Meaning*. Baltimore: University Park Press, 1978.

Halliday, M.A.K., and Ruqaiya Hasan. *Cohesion in English*. London: Longman, 1976.

Hartnett, Carolyn G. "Static and Dynamic Cohesion: Signals of Thinking in Writing." *Functional Approaches to Writing: Research Perspectives*. Ed. Barbara Couture. London: Francis Pinter, 1986, pp. 142–53.

Hartwell, Patrick. "Grammar, Grammars, and the Teaching of Grammar." *CE* 47 (1985): 105–27.

Haswell, Richard H. "Critique: Length of Text and the Measurement of Cohesion." *RTE* 22 (1988): 428–33.

———. "Textual Research and Coherence: Findings, Intuition, Application." *CE* 51 (1989): 305–19.

Hayes, Ira. "An Experimental Study of Sentence Combining as a Means of Improving Syntactic Maturity, Writing Quality and Grammatical Fluency in the Compositions of Remedial High School Students." Diss. Columbia University Teachers College, 1984.

Hull, Glynda A., and David J. Bartholomae. "Basic Writing." *Research in Composition and Rhetoric: A Bibliographic Sourcebook.* Ed. Michael G. Moran and Ronald F. Lunsford. Westport, Conn.: Greenwood Press, 1984, pp. 265–302.

Hunt, Kellogg W. "Anybody Can Teach English." *Sentence Combining and the Teaching of Writing.* Ed. Donald A. Daiker, Andrew Kerek, and Max Morenberg. Oxford, Ohio: L & S Books, 1979, pp. 149–56.

Jackson, Kathy Diane Dunn. "The Effect of Sentence Combining Practice on the Reduction of Syntactic Errors in Basic Writing." Diss. Auburn University, 1982.

Jesperson, Otto. *The Philosophy of Grammar.* New York: Norton, 1965.

Johns, Ann M. "The ESL Student and the Revision Process: Some Insights From Schema Theory." *JBW* 5 (1986): 70–80.

Johnson, Falk S. "Structural Versus Non-Structural Teaching." *CCC* 11 (1960): 214–15.

Kinney, James. "Tagmemic Rhetoric: A Reconsideration." *CCC* 29 (1978): 141–45.

Kneupper, Charles W. "Revising the Tagmemic Heuristic: Theoretical and Pedagogical Considerations." *CCC* 31 (1980): 160–68.

Kolln, Martha. "Closing the Books on Alchemy." *CCC* 32 (1981): 139–51.

Krashen, Stephen. *Principles and Practice in Second Language Acquisition.* Oxford, Eng.: Pergamon Press, 1982.

Laurence, Patricia. "Error's Endless Train: Why Students Don't Perceive Errors." *JBW* 1 (1975): 23–42.

Leech, Geoffrey. *Semantics.* Middlesex, England: Pelican, 1974.

Lees, Robert B. "The Promise of Transformational Grammar." *EJ* 52.5 (1963): 327–30, 345.

Lester, Mark. *Introductory Transformational Grammar of English.* New York: Holt, 1971.

———. "The Value of Transformational Grammar." *CCC* 18 (1967): 227–31.

Lintermann-Rygh, Irmgard. "Connector Density—An Indication of Essay Quality." *Text* 5 (1985): 347–57.

Lunsford, Andrea. "Basic Writing Update." *Teaching Composition: Twelve Bibliographical Essays*, rev. and enl. ed. Ed. Gary Tate. Fort Worth: Texas Christian University Press, 1987, pp. 207–26.

Lyons, John. *Introduction to Theoretical Linguistics.* Cambridge: Oxford University Press, 1969.

McCulley, G. A. "Writing Quality, Coherence, and Cohesion." *RTE* 19 (1985): 269–82.

Markels, Robin Bell. "Cohesion Paradigms in Paragraphs." *CE* 45 (1983): 450–64.

Masters, Kathy, and Mitchell Masters. "The Effect of Sentence Combining Achievement in Basic Writing." *J Inst Psych* 7 (1980): 53–60.

Mathesius, Vilem. "On Linguistic Characterology with Illustrations from Modern English." *A Prague School Reader of Linguistics.* Ed. Josef Vachek. Bloomington: Indiana University Press, 1964, pp. 59–67.

Mellon, John C. "Issues in the Theory and Practice of Sentence Combining: A Twenty-Year Perspective." *Sentence Combining and the Teaching of Writing.* Ed. Donald A. Daiker, Andrew Kerek, and Max Morenberg. Oxford, Ohio: L & S Books, 1979, pp. 1–38.

Memering, Dean. "Forward to the Basics." *CE* 39 (1978): 553–61.

Menendez, Diane Susan. "The Effect of Sentence-Combining Practice on Remedial

College Students' Syntactic Maturity, Punctuation Skills and Reading Ability.''
Diss. Indiana University, 1978.

Neuner, Jerome L. "Cohesive Ties and Chains in Good and Poor Freshman Essays.''
RTE 21 (1987): 92–105.

Odell, Lee. "Another Look at Tagmemic Theory: A Response to James Kinney.'' *CCC*
29 (1978): 146–52.

Petrosky, Anthony R. "Research Roundup: Grammar Instruction—What We Know.''
EJ 66.9 (1977): 86–88.

Pike, Kenneth. "Beyond the Sentence.'' *CCC* 15 (1964): 129–35.

———. *Language in Relation to a Unified Theory of the Structure of Human Behavior*.
2nd ed. Paris: Mouton, 1967.

———. "A Linguistic Contribution to Composition.'' *CCC* 15 (1964): 82–88.

Powell, Joyce Elaine. "The Effects of Sentence Combining on the Writing of Basic
Writers in the Community College.'' Diss. East Texas State University, 1984.

Pritchard, R. T. "A Study of the Cohesive Devices in the Good and Poor Compositions
of Eleventh Graders.'' Diss. University of Missouri, 1980.

Roberts, Paul. "The Relation of Linguistics to the Teaching of English.'' *CE* 22 (1960):
1–9.

Sapir, Edward. *Language*. New York: Harcourt, 1921.

Shaughnessy, Mina. "Basic Writing.'' *Teaching Composition: 10 Bibliographic Essays*.
Ed. Gary Tate. Fort Worth: Texas Christian University Press, 1976, pp. 137–67.

———. "Diving In: An Introduction to Basic Writing.'' *CCC* 27 (1976): 234–39.

———. *Errors and Expectations: A Guide for the Teacher of Basic Writing*. New York:
Oxford University Press, 1977.

Sherwin, J. Stephen. *Four Problems in Teaching English*. Scranton, Penn.: For NCTE
by International Textbook Company, 1969.

Stotsky, Sandra. "Types of Lexical Cohesion in Expository Writing: Implication .for
Developing the Vocabulary of Academic Discourse.'' *CCC* 34 (1983): 430–46.

Strong, William. *Creative Approaches to Sentences Combining*. Urbana, Ill.: ERIC and
NCTE, 1986.

———. "Sentence Combining: Back to Basics and Beyond.'' *EJ* 65.2 (1976): 56, 60–
64.

Suggs, Lena Reddick. "Structural Grammar Versus Traditional Grammar in Influencing
Writing.'' *EJ* 50.3 (1961): 174–78.

Tierney, Robert J., and James H. Mosenthal. "Cohesion and Textual Coherence.'' *RTE*
17 (1983): 215–29.

Tricomi, Elizabeth Taylor. "Krashen's Second-Language Acquisition Theory and the
Teaching of Edited American English.'' *JBW* 5 (1986): 59–69.

Ullman, Stephen. *Semantics: An Introduction to the Science of Meaning*. Oxford, Eng.:
Basil-Blackwell, 1970.

Vande Kopple, William J. "Something Old, Something New: Functional Sentence Perspective.'' *RTE* 17 (1983): 85–99.

van Dijk, Tuen A. *Text and Context: Explorations in the Semantics and Pragmatics of
Discourse*. London and New York: Longman, 1977.

Warfel, Harry R. "Structural Linguistics and Composition.'' *CE* 20 (1959): 205–13.

Waterfall, Clarence Malan. "An Experimental Study of Sentence-Combining as a Means
of Increasing Syntactic Maturity and Writing Quality in the Compositions of

College-Age Students Enrolled in Remedial English.'' Diss. Utah State University, 1977.

Whorf, Benjamin. *Language, Thought and Reality*. Ed. John B. Carroll. New York: Wiley, 1956.

Wikborg, Eleanor. "Unspecified Topic in University Student Essays." *Text* 5 (1985): 359–70.

Williams, Joseph. "Non-Linguistics and the Teaching of Style." *Territory of Language: Linguistics, Stylistics and the Teaching of Composition*. Ed. Donald A. McQuade. Carbondale: Southern Illinois University Press, 1986, pp. 174–91.

Winterowd, W. Ross."The Grammar of Coherence." *CE* 31 (1970): 828–38.

———. "Linguistics and Composition." *Teaching Composition: 10 Bibliographical Essays*. Ed. Gary Tate. Fort Worth: Texas Christian University Press, 1976, pp. 197–222.

———. "Literacy, Linguistics, and Rhetoric." *Teaching Composition: 12 Bibliographical Essays*, rev. and enl. ed. Ed. Gary Tate. Fort Worth: Texas Christian University Press, 1987, pp. 265–90.

———. "A Teacher's Guide to the *Real* Basics." *Lang Arts* 54 (1977): 625–30.

Witte, Stephen P. "Topical Structure and Revision: An Exploratory Study." *CCC* 34 (1983): 313–35.

Witte, Stephen P., and Lester Faigley. "Coherence, Cohesion, and Writing Quality." *CCC* 32 (1981): 189–204.

Young, Richard E., and Alton L. Becker. "Toward a Modern Theory of Rhetoric: A Tagmemic Contribution." *HER* 25 (1965): 450–68.

Young, Richard E., Alton L. Becker, and Kenneth Pike. *Rhetoric: Discovery and Change*. New York: Harcourt, 1970.

5

Dialects and Basic Writers

Michael Montgomery

From the beginning, a disproportion of students identified as basic writers have not been middle-class whites and have spoken varieties of English often differing from those of traditional, mainstream college students and composition teachers. Inevitably their writing has also differed, especially in grammar (i.e., in word forms and sentence structure), but often in spelling and in rhetoric as well. Because these students were assumed to be simply transferring speech habits to their writing, such forms as *five mens*, *she run away*, and *he sick* were labeled as "dialect," and the belief arose that students could be taught to avoid them by improving their speech or by having them memorize rules and paradigms of "standard English."

However, it has turned out that teachers, course designers, linguists, and other experts have found no easy, foolproof way to help students avoid these patterns. Widely diverging views on the definition, significance, and source of this "dialect problem" and on the most effective response to it have made all these issues controversial and difficult to resolve. Beyond interpreting the literature, the job of teachers has been complicated by individual variation in the frequency and type of dialect forms that their students write. However else basic writers might differ from their traditional counterparts in rhetorical skills, educational backgrounds, and levels of experience, their dialect patterns have raised crucial issues for basic writing researchers, teachers, and students, and have generated a considerable literature. This essay will, in reviewing this literature, attempt both to summarize and synthesize; it will be most convenient to use the broad term "dialect forms" for features like those in the first paragraph although, as will be explained, the features have sources beyond just the student's speech.

Beyond the 1950s, teachers unfamiliar with the language patterns of basic writers often found dialect problems more serious, frequent, and persistent than they were prepared for. Yet they believed it was their duty to teach something called "standard English." As public school integration and open admission colleges sent more minority and nontraditional students into classrooms, there appeared an unprecedented series of interpretive articles and research articles, not to mention countless workshops and conference presentations, apprising the composition profession about "dialects," "standard English," and related topics. Descriptive sociolinguistic studies of speech patterns of minority groups, especially of blacks in northern cities, began to appear (most notably William Labov's *Language in the Inner City* [1972] and Walter Wolfram's *A Sociolinguistic Description of Detroit Negro Speech* [1969]). Linguists tried to explain the nature and source of dialect forms, and pedagogical and political controversies arose over how teachers should evaluate them.

Broadly speaking, the term "dialect" refers to any variety of speech distinctive in pronunciation, grammar, or vocabulary and used by a specific geographical, social, or other definable group. Everyone speaks a dialect, many more than one; here, as in the linguistic literature, the term is used descriptively, without pejorative connotations, and does not contrast directly with "standard English." Any dialect has variations but is sufficiently homogeneous and identifiable to be valid for speech. It is less clearly applicable to writing, because far less variation in spelling or grammar occurs or is permitted than in speech, and forms of written English are not usually associated with a group of writers.

The variety of written English drawing most attention, "standard English," is seen in two ways: descriptively (more on this below), for the English of business, government, and society at large; and prescriptively, for the English that schools are supposed to teach. The term itself has been the focus of contention because some believe the concept incorporates social and cultural prejudices or because it refers to an abstract entity spoken by no one and codified nowhere. As a result, alternative labels have arisen for the formal writing English students are expected to use, labels like "Standard Written English," "Edited Written English," "Edited American English," or even "Academic English" (the last term encompassing rhetorical and other conventions expected of writers in American higher education). Though cumbersome, such terms underscore the fact that writing is a conventional system of language that is not merely a transcription of speech, and they imply what research has in fact revealed—that some types of writing problems are exhibited by many types of students, regardless of their speech backgrounds.

Dialect forms of basic writers tend to be features of social dialects (associated with social class, ethnic group, and other such factors), not geographical dialects. Controversy has flared from time to time over how closely dialect forms correlate with ethnic groups and whether they deserve a label such as "Black English." (Raven I. McDavid, Jr., takes the skeptical view in a 1973 essay, "Go Slow in Ethnic Attributions.") Dissension has reached far beyond linguistic terminology to encompass the language attitudes, social aspirations and sensitivities, and ideological views of minority groups having their language formally labeled.

(Geneva Smitherman's " 'God Don't Never Change': Black English from a Black Perspective" [1973] and Juanita Williamson's "Selected Features of Speech: Black and White" [1970] are essays on these issues by black scholars from different generations and perspectives.) Linguists have tried to define such terms as "Southern English," "Chicano English," and "Black English": Paul Brandes and Jeutonne Brewer's *Dialect Clash in America* (1977) contains useful chapters on many ethnic varieties of American English; William Stewart's "Observations (1966) on the Problems of Defining Negro Dialect" (1971) delineates definitional issues for "Black English." But these researchers have found that social, regional, and ethnic dialects are distinguished by the relative combination of features and the degree to which features occur, not by the absolute presence or absence of them. Walter A. Wolfram and Ralph W. Fasold's *The Study of Social Dialects* (1974), and Brandes and Brewer's volume, though both now somewhat dated, remain the most comprehensive discussions and best compendiums of features of social and ethnic dialects; for a review of research on the relation between black and white speech in the Southern United States, see the introduction to Michael Montgomery and Guy Bailey's 1986 book *Language Variety in the South*. Clearly, there is no consensus of what these dialect labels refer to.

One linguistic fact has become clear: social or ethnic dialect might intrude in writing in the form of vocabulary, idiomatic expressions, and spelling, but most often it involves rules for grammatical features—verb forms, syntactic patterns, especially inflectional suffixes (past tense, plural, possessive, etc.), and others. (Shaughnessy's *Errors and Expectations* [1977], based on personal observations, is still the best catalog and discussion of the range of these.) Social dialect is "deeper," based on rules more integral to the unconscious grammatical system than are regional dialect forms. The latter usually involve isolated vocabulary forms (e.g., *fixing to*, *nowheres*) that are more superficial elements of language, more accessible to conscious awareness and manipulation. Clearly, students could more easily be taught to avoid regional dialect forms while social dialect forms are potentially more difficult for students to overcome.

Paradoxically, the main issues surrounding dialects and basic writers involve a very short list of features, fewer than ten of any frequency (Ralph Fasold and Walter Wolfram's "Some Linguistic Features of Negro Dialect" [1970] and James Funkhouser's "A Various Standard" [1973] are two of many sources exemplifying the common ones), and all presenting little or no hindrance to the successful conveyance of meaning.

A list of the more commonly cited "dialect" patterns follows, the first four being far more common than all others:

1. Absence of past tense and past participle *-ed* (*They play five games last night, They have play five games*)
2. Absence of third-person-singular ending *-s* (*She work at the station*);
3. Absence of plural ending *-s* (*five car*)
4. Absence of possessive endings *-'s, -s'* (*my friend car*)

5. Overuse of one of the suffixes above (*I have runned five miles*; this is often termed "hypercorrection")

6. Spelling words with omitted final consonant (*bol* for *bold*)

7. Use of *it* in a sentence to express the existence of something (*It's a book on the table*)

8. Absence of linking verb or helping verb *be* (*My mother working downtown, My mother downtown*)

9. Use of *be* as a main verb (*She be tired*) or as the first auxiliary verb (*They be waiting for me*)

10. Use of what is known as the "double subject" construction (*My mother, she taught me to cook*)

A teacher might reasonably ask, "What's the controversy about? Why do we hear so much about dialects?" The number is so small that the "dialect problem" of basic writers might seem exaggerated and the attention given to it undeserved and misguided.

There are at least three answers. First, stated above, dialect forms in writing, whatever their source, are stigmatized, persistent, and common. Second, since dialect forms are more frequent in the writing of minority students, it is difficult to single them out for correction without singling out minority writers for special instruction, which many teachers and schools have been reluctant to do (and which has been the subject of at least one court case—Charles Joiner's *Martin Luther King Junior Elementary School Children et al. vs. Ann Arbor School District Board: Memorandum Opinion and Order* [1979]). Third, traditional error correction has had little impact on them, in part because many writers cannot rely on their speech and their ears to correct their work. Dialect forms are deceptive—countless English teachers, schooled in traditional grammar with its emphasis on paradigms, cannot see why this same approach doesn't work with basic writers. Dialect problems look misleadingly like misspellings or problems in memorizing past tense verb forms. This situation has produced a variety of pedagogical experiments.

It would appear that a common interest in understanding the linguistic patterns of basic writers would create a natural meeting ground for composition experts and linguists. But the concerns and emphases of the two groups have often differed, and the challenge of understanding each other's perspectives has sometimes frustrated both sides.

Linguists have been busy describing the correlation of dialect features with the social background, geographical location, and especially ethnic identification of speakers (as in the sociolinguistic studies mentioned above). They have often been preoccupied with abstract questions about the nature of the linguistic system in which dialect forms occurred and with historical questions about their origin in older forms of English or in pidgin and creole English. When linguists seek answers to these questions, as fascinating and important as they are, they often do not provide the information teachers could translate into daily classroom practice. Faced with students having immediate, seemingly intractable problems in writing basic grammatical forms of English, teachers naturally want immediate applications.

When linguists do address the desires of writing teachers, their voices often conflict. Different camps of linguists—most prominently linguistic geographers (led by Raven I. McDavid and his followers), sociolinguists (William Labov, Walt Wolfram, and others), and creolists (principally William Stewart and J. L. Dillard)—clash sharply in answering the questions in the previous paragraph. Teachers know neither who to believe nor why they cannot get a direct answer to such an "obviously simple" question as "How can I get my students to use past-tense verb endings?" Consequently, many teachers have never quite been able to see the importance of distinguishing dialect forms from other "errors" in their students' writing.

Having provided this backdrop, we now turn to the three areas of concern touched on above regarding dialects and basic writing: the linguistic issues, including the question of "dialect interference"; the social and political issues, especially with regard to the concept of "standard English"; and the pedagogical issues.

The literature on these topics, especially dialect interference (a term introduced around 1970), is massive, but it deals mostly with primary- and secondary-level students and with reading rather than writing. Most of it falls outside our purview and is excluded. Much of the pedagogical literature on dialect deals with understanding or altering the speech of students and is also excluded. The material on college writers and dialects has been covered in part in other literature reviews: Jenefer Giannasi's "Dialects and Composition" (1976), Bruce Cronnell's "Dialect and Writing" (1983), Sarah Bobson's "Nonstandard Dialects" (1974), and the "Students' Right to Their Own Language" statement from the College Conference on Composition and Communication (1974), although most of these sources date from the early 1970s.

LINGUISTIC ISSUES

Researchers have proposed five different but overlapping sources for dialect problems in writing: (1) speech patterns, the native language system of the writer; (2) developmental factors, having to do with the age and experience of the writer (i.e., dialect forms tend to decrease with age, regardless of the speech patterns of the individual); (3) constraints on cognitive processing that produce written forms that do not correspond to the spoken language; (4) complexity of the written rules of English and the difficulty of mastering exceptions to these rules; and (5) the physical act of writing itself, and the demands placed on the writer by the mechanics of writing.

Careful, systematic research to enable us to identify and categorize the source(s) of dialect in writing has been limited, and much remains to be done.

We would expect this research at the least to compare writing and speech for single groups of students or for pairs of groups in order to compare, for instance, black students and white students; however, traditional error count/error analysis studies of the writing of single groups outnumber comparative studies, and anecdotal observational reports constitute most of the literature on the question of dialect transfer from speech to writing. More often than not, the comparative research has been marked by methodological shortcomings like poorly defined linguistic categories and questionable sampling and elicitation techniques, making it difficult to refine our understanding of spoken language influence on writing. Daniel Morrow in "Dialect Interferences in Writing" (1985) offers a trenchant, well-targeted critique of the assumptions and methodology of much of the dialect interference research mentioned below.

Research has tended to find relative rather than absolute differences between blacks and whites in dialect usage in writing. Marilyn Sternglass, in "Close Similarities in Dialect Features of Black and White College Students in Remedial Composition Classes" (1974), studies twenty-one grammatical features in the essays of 304 remedial students, one-quarter of whom were black; she found that "with the exception of one linguistic feature, invariant *be*, there was no *qualitative* difference in the nonstandard features produced by white and black students, but there was a *quantitative* difference" (271). On the other hand, Barbara Wright, in "Hypercorrections and Dialect Forms in the Composition of Native Born College Students from Georgia" (1985), found eleven nonstandard morphological and syntactic features distinctive of black writers. J. J. Collins, in "Deviations from Standard English in Written Compositions of Disadvantaged College Freshmen and Regular Admissions Students at Glassboro State College" (1971), found that special admission students (nearly all black) displayed much higher degrees of writing problems (including the features on our list) than regular students but very few differences in kind. Such studies suggest no sharp distinctions between groups of writers, but they have the methodological problem of comparing the writing of students whose speech has been assumed, from the students' race, to have certain features.

Other comparisons have used loosely defined, overly broad categories and concepts. Samuel Kirschner and Howard Poteet, in "Non-standard English Usage in the Writing of Black, White, and Hispanic Remedial English Students in an Urban Community College" (1973), found no difference in the mean number of nonstandard sentences or in the rank order of error types in the writing of whites, blacks, and Hispanics, but they compared types of errors like "wrong word" and "punctuation" rather than more careful categories. Myrna Hammons, in "Aspects of Written Language of College Freshmen in Oklahoma, according to Race and Sex" (1973), found differences between white, Indian, and black students in Oklahoma but in areas that tell us little about possible dialect influence—syntactic maturity, use of nominal constructions, and "areas of nonstandard usage" such as "nouns, verbs, adjective-adverbs," and so on.

Two studies have compared speech and writing within one ethnic group. For thirty white students in Memphis, Bondie Armstrong's "A Study of Dialect and Its Interference with Learning to Write" (1983) found no significant relationship between the frequency of "deviations from the standard oral language" and the frequency of "deviations from the standard written language" (with "standard" defined as the prescriptions of the *Harbrace College Handbook*). James L. Funkhouser's "Black English" (1976), a study better conceived to describe the transfer of specific features from speech to writing, studied forty-one black students in St. Louis, finding that "the conventions of writing force the dialect features examined to undergo regular changes, leaving the dialect, however, as an identifiable pattern" and identifying the different linguistic constraints controlling the use of dialect forms in speech and writing.

Other researchers have examined the writing problems of students, more in the interest of categorizing and ranking these problems than in throwing light on the question of dialect and interference. Nancy Terrebonne, in "The Black English Vernacular in the Writing of Young Adults from Dayton, Ohio" (1975), and Della Whittaker, in "A Content Analysis of Black English Markers in Compositions of Community-College Freshmen" (1972), attempted to correlate grammatical problems in writing of black students and other factors such as age, sex, ACT (American College Test) scores, and racial isolation. Only Terrebonne found a significant correlation—with motivation (which she defines as "the desire to assimilate both culturally and economically to the Middle Class"); a more important finding of hers is "an apparent implicational relationship . . . among seven key features" that may enable us to say precisely how far along individual students are in mastering the appropriate forms of written English. Among traditional studies producing taxonomies of "deviations" from the essays of black writers is Olin Briggs's "A Study of Deviations from Standard English in Papers of Negro Freshmen at an Alabama College" (1968).

Although these early studies on "dialect interference" came to no consensus and often lacked the rigor of empirical research, they make clear that researchers were working in a theoretical vacuum. More than the transfer of speech was involved, and a narrow, inaccurate view of the relation between speech and writing was being assumed. Competing sources of dialect forms, the second, third, and fourth sources listed above, were becoming evident and suggested that problems identified as dialect interference occurred for many writers, regardless of their speech, and that, for anyone, learning to write was akin to learning a second language. This observation is also made by Mina Shaughnessy in her well-known *Errors and Expectations* (1977):

Most students, whether they started out speaking Chinese or BEV [Black English Vernacular] or Navajo, seem to end up in freshman English with a common stock of errors that appear most often to arise directly from interference from other languages and dialects, from problems of predictability within the system called formal English, or from the difficulties associated with writing rather than speaking English. (157)

But to find how these sources were related and what theory of language learning or language production could account for all of them, researchers had to turn to specialists in language acquisition, reading, and other fields for a broader, more theoretical perspective.

One sound empirical study informed by language acquisition theory is Marcia Farr Whiteman's research in Maryland, reported in "Dialect Influence in Writing" (1981). Although based on high school students, its rigorous comparison of features and its findings give it a place in this review. Whiteman investigated how speech differed from writing for both blacks and whites and how blacks differed from whites in both speech and writing. She concluded that there was "a general acquisitional strategy causing the omission of some inflectional suffixes in writing (as well as in a number of other communication contexts). That is, whether or not these same inflectional suffixes are omitted in the speech of the unskilled writer, they are frequently omitted in his/her writing. We cannot, however, totally discount the role of dialect influence in writing, since there are significant differences in suffix omission in writing between dialect groups" (164).

An ambitious and influential essay drawing on reading theory, Patrick Hartwell's "Dialect Interference in Writing: A Critical View" (1980), contends that speaking and writing are fundamentally different, unrelated cognitive processes and that the issues of spoken language influence on writing has received too much attention. Instead, Hartwell connects writing problems to reading problems and says that "all apparent dialect interference in writing is reading related. More precisely, apparent dialect interference in writing reveals partial or imperfect mastery of a neural coding system that underlies both reading and writing" (108). Hartwell, in stating that "it is precisely the nature of a written standard to be adialectal," agrees with E. D. Hirsch that it is invalid to compare speech directly with writing. Hirsch, in *The Philosophy of Composition* (1977), draws on sociolinguistic theory and research on national written languages to argue that written English is a "grapholect," which, according to Hirsch, is "a different kind of language system" whose character "lies in its very isolation from class and region" and its stability through time (44). It breaks down the barriers of space and time, barriers between social and regional groups and is above any ideological debate over which variety of language should be accepted: "the normative status of a grapholect is an historical-linguistic fact which no ideology can overcome or evade. Once a grapholect has become established, it is as fruitful to resist its conservative and normative power as to tilt at windmills or battle the sea" (45). Morrow's essay mentioned earlier critiques Hartwell's position in detail. Mary Epes's "Tracing Errors To Their Sources" (1985) tests Hartwell's hypothesis but finds that nonstandard speech patterns correlate much more closely with dialect use in writing than different reading comprehension levels do.

To summarize, there is a partial match between an individual's speech and writing, but obviously more is involved. To account fully for the source(s) of written dialect, four fundamental points that research on dialect interference has established must be taken into account:

1. No one writes the way he or she speaks. Spelling or other aspects of writing are not based on pronunciation. Some written grammatical markers like the apostrophe have no counterpart in pronunciation. Thus, writing is not a transcription of speech but a system of explicit formal signals that everyone must learn (a point made most strongly by Hartwell and Hirsch).

2. Only some of a person's spoken dialect forms—most commonly grammatical forms—occur in that person's writing. Many grammatical forms (e.g., *ain't*, multiple negation) are filtered out—possibly because they are more stigmatized and easier to avoid. The suffixes most often absent are "redundant" signals, since grammatical concepts of past tense, plurality, and so on are normally indicated by word order and other words in the sentence. Whiteman and Funkhouser have found that these occur less in writing than in speech for dialect speakers.

3. Forms not occurring in anyone's speech sometimes occur in writing. Most often, these are tentative forms revealing how writers are grappling with the finer points of formal writing in a transitional stage on their way to mastering written structures and their exceptions. Among these are "hypercorrections," overuses or overapplications of partially learned language rules (*two mens*, *had runned*) that reveal the complexity of the rules of written English, the difficulty of mastering exceptions, and the insecurity of writers; Jerrie Scott's "Mixed Dialects in the Composition Classroom" (1986) illustrates how individual students develop "interdialect" forms typical of neither spoken nor written English. A case of this is anomalous relative clauses with *in which* frequently written by basic writers but not occurring in speech, structures like *I have a math teacher in which I like very much*.

4. Other written forms that seemingly reflect spoken dialects occur in the writing of individuals who do not speak them. This casts the most doubt on the simplistic view that written dialect forms are transferred from speech. Whiteman found that some white writers omitted inflections two to four times more often in writing than in speech, although not as often as blacks, who omitted them frequently in speech also. In short, the same dialect forms occurred for all types of writers, although much less for senior high school students than for their junior high counterparts, indicating that developmental and processing factors are at work here in the mastery of these written forms.

As a result, "dialect interference" has not yet been defined satisfactorily. The notion ignores how the individual learner produces forms that do not represent his/her speech patterns. We can predict very little, if anything, about how a person will write by knowing that person's speech. For this reason, Whiteman and others have advocated adoption of "dialect influence" as a more appropriate term.

At least three articles deal with problems of Hispanic students writing English in the college classroom. Jon Amastae, in "The Writing Needs of Hispanic Students" (1982), says that Hispanic writers have few special language problems and that teachers should make no special allowances for them. Celia Merrill, in

"Contrastive Analysis and Chicano Compositions" (1976), contrasts the written English of ninety-three Chicano freshmen with standard English. Ricardo Garcia, in "A Linguistic Frame of Reference for Critiquing Chicano Compositions" (1975), explains different types of Spanish interference that occur when Mexican-American students write English.

Many other researchers have written about the need to look beyond the narrow bounds of linguistic forms (the preoccupation of dialect interference research) to understand the larger dimensions of the linguistic behavior of basic writers and the ways this behavior may differ from and conflict with the school's. To them, differences not only in language, but in culture, rhetoric, and even thought patterns are related to the dialects of basic writers. Basic writers are viewed not just as facing a conflict in language patterns that require learning and ability to switch linguistic codes, but also as facing a conflict of culture. Thomas Kochman's *Rappin' and Stylin' Out* (1972) is an early anthology of articles examining urban minority cultures.

Grace Cooper, in "Black Stylistic Features in Student Compositions" (1977), says that black students will come in conflict with rhetorical demands of the writing classroom because of stylistic features found in the black cultural tradition: imagery, rhythmic patterns, and "personal involvement" (first-person orientation) that are characteristic of black speech and writing. In a 1981 article ("Black Language and Holistic Cognitive Style"), she adds features of "holistic cognitive style" such as "the lack of distance, practical method of classification, use of transitional features, and strong preference for concrete images" to this list (206).

Michael Linn, in "Black Rhetorical Patterns and the Teaching of Composition" (1975), emphasizes that "one of the dominant features of black culture is a continuing reliance on oral expression" (150), especially in ritualized verbal play and performance, and that teachers may find their students have cultural conflicts when trying to write impersonal, deductive academic prose. Thus, for inner-city black students with a keener sense of group oral communication than middle-class speakers, this knowledge can be exploited by teachers who begin a composition course with group writing projects.

Desley Noonan-Wagner's "Possible Effects of Cultural Differences on the Rhetoric of Black Basic Skills Writers" (1981), like other dialect interference studies, found that black basic writers had dialect problems similar to whites, but to a greater degree. More interestingly, she found that black writers used sixteen rhetorical features significantly more often than personal point of view.

Joseph Keller, in "Sentence Fragments, Black English, and Prosody" (1978), says that the rhythm of black dialect emphasizes "the affective or dramatic content" (159) and because it therefore tends "to stress subordinate clauses and even phrases just as much as independent clauses" (159), it frequently leads black dialect speakers to write sentence fragments. Since the standard dialect "sacrifices the affective in both its spoken and written realizations" (159), dialect speakers have to learn there is a trade-off in using the standard forms.

When turning to the question of evaluating dialect patterns, linguists have often said more about the attitudes of teachers than the practices of students. For many linguists, students' using nonstandard forms is less problematic than teachers' condemning these forms as illogical corruptions and considering some dialects of English (and by extension their speakers) as deprived, judgments that can have very damaging effects on minority students. This case is presented most convincingly and poignantly in William Labov's famous 1969 essay, "The Logic of Nonstandard English." Labov and other linguists have often said that the learning difficulties dialect speakers may have are not as crucial as teachers' perception of these learning difficulties. They have frequently pointed out and vigorously campaigned for the view that each dialect of English has value, validity, and grammar, although this view clearly flies in the face of the training and inclinations of many teachers. They have done this in the hope that teachers, and the public, will develop respect for such varieties as "Black English," since, linguistically, each dialect of a language is legitimate (reflecting the social background and identity of its users), adequate (based on a system of rules), and functional (used for various purposes), not deviant, careless, or incorrect, and in no sense are dialects corruptions of standard English. Dialects differ in their use, in their structure, and in the sociology of their speakers, but they are equally grammatical.

POLITICAL ISSUES

Dialect forms differ fundamentally from other problems of mechanics (like punctuation) and usage (like subject-verb agreement) in that, to a greater degree, they are associated with the social and ethnic characteristics of their writers. The consequent political issues involve two questions: the significance of dialect problems (i.e., the status of the writers' dialects), and the teachers' approach to them. At the center of these issues is "standard English," variously defined. In correcting students' native language patterns and in expecting them to use "standard English," teachers become cultural brokers, interpreting the values and realities of the larger, mainstream society, and diagnosticians, helping student writers understand and bridge the gap between it and their home culture. While teachers have long been called on to play these roles, the reevaluation of the students' own language and culture (the two are inseparable) calls not only for reorienting teachers (courses in linguistics and dialects became part of their training) but also for redefining what is appropriate for teachers to do. For teachers the situation requires a balancing of their tendency to censure stigmatized dialect with an appreciation of ethnic patterns of culture and language. Personal attitudes toward dialect forms have to be separated from effective correction of them, and dialect forms have to be viewed objectively, not as simple corruptions of normal written patterns but as forms with historical legitimacy and functions in the students' speech. In sum, basic writers, often nontraditional students with minority backgrounds, raise new questions about the precise roles, rights, and responsibilities of teachers, students, and institutions in the teaching of literacy skills.

Teaching "standard English" implies that one variety of English is superior to, or at least more useful than, others. What is "standard English": a social code devised by the privileged elements of society to determine which people to admit to membership? a set of conventions arising from the need for efficient communication between the diverse elements of a society? an idealized version of the language characterized by logic and clarity of meaning? These are three of the many ways of viewing the term in addition to the descriptive sense referring to the English of business, government, education, and society at large. Does requiring students to use "standard English" mean the depreciation of their language background in the process? Even if it does, is this not a necessary price to pay, since many students want to learn language patterns different from those in the level of society from which they came? These and related questions have filled the literature, especially in the early 1970s, with views running the gamut, and with professional and personal agendas often coming into play.

The issues came to a head in the early 1970s, resulting in the passage and publication by the College Conference on Composition and Communication of a resolution and supporting a thirty-two-page position paper provocatively titled "Students' Right to Their Own Language" (1974). Continuing debate and repeated attempts to reverse or modify the resolution indicate the importance and sensitivity of the issues. Tackling questions of the status of varieties of English head on, it began: "We affirm the students' right to their own patterns and varieties of language—the dialects of their nurture or whatever dialects in which they find their own identity and style. Language scholars long ago denied that the myth of a standard American dialect has any validity. The claim that one dialect is unacceptable amounts to an attempt of one social group to exert its dominance over another" (ii). The statement saw the teaching of "standard English" as a political act, inseparable from promoting national and middle-class values that differ from those of minority communities.

Several authors quickly raised practical considerations. For instance, Garland Cannon, in "Multidialects" (1973), pointed out four major problems in implementing the resolution, including the lack of teacher training and adequate descriptions of dialects. Lawrence Freeman, in "The Students' Right to Their Own Language" (1975), discussed how far the legal implications of the "right" of students extend.

The same period witnessed strenuous efforts to establish the heritage of minority dialects, efforts focusing almost entirely on Black English because of the ferment of integration and the low status of this variety of English. The title of J. L. Dillard's polemical and highly reviewed volume *Black English* (1972) led the way in making a case for the language of black Americans. A representative shorter essay in this vein is Orlando Taylor's "An Introduction to the Historical Development of Black English and Implications for American Education" (1969).

The chief political issue thus became the relationship between "standard English" and the home dialect of students. Views on the extent to which dialect should be accepted in schoolwork and should (or could) be discussed with students can be grouped in three general positions: (1) the first dialect of students should be replaced by a second, "standard English"; (2) the first dialect of students should be respected but all students should be taught the same second dialect; and (3) the first dialect should be permitted and appreciated in class (based on adherence to linguistic and cultural pluralism, represented by the CCCC position above). These positions and their philosophical bases are discussed at length in Brandes and Brewer and in Wolfram and Fasold's *The Study of Social Dialects in the United States* (1974).

The second position, which came to be known as bidialectalism, begins with the view that the first and third positions are untenable and tries to steer the middle course of accepting all dialects, making no value judgments about their legitimacy and grammaticality, but helping students appreciate the social and functional differences between them. The theoretical basis for bidialectalism is realism, since every individual is already bidialectal or multidialectal, speaking more than one variety of English, each of which is functionally differentiated and evaluated. It recognizes that competence in formal written English is a mandatory skill for anyone wishing to graduate from a university and succeed in the postgraduate world. Mary Bruder and Luddy Hayden's "Teaching Composition" (1973) describes the bidialectal approach, its assumptions, and its class objectives and then discusses methods and techniques for achieving the objectives.

Opponents attacked bidialectalism on pedagogical, methodological, and political grounds. They said bidialectalists tried to have it both ways, that they tried to tell students that their language patterns were legitimate and valuable and had important historical antecedents, but at the same time that the academic and business world required another variety called standard English. Since value judgments about the two were inevitable, this approach tended to confuse both teachers and students and to be viewed as hypocritical (as by James Sledd, as discussed below). Bidialectalism assumes that language varieties can be discussed in an English classroom as dispassionately and clearly as organic compounds in a chemistry classroom, and that students will understand in a nonprejudicial way, but it is extraordinarily difficult to discuss stigmatized, nonstandard language without students' involving their language attitudes. Many found it too cumbersome and confusing to implement in the classroom.

Rodolfo Jacobson, in "The Teaching of English to Speakers of Other Languages and/or Dialects" (1970), believes that bidialectalism, or the teaching of a second dialect, has been largely uninformed by a methodology based on the nature of language. According to him, such a methodology must consider aspects of the learners' psychology (considering their motivation), social awareness (explaining the social utility of the new dialect), culture (understanding the inseparability of students' dialect from their culture and history), as well as language (acknowledging the students' language to be patterned and to have its own grammar).

Politically, bidialectalism was attacked by the middle-class black community because it accepted that black speech had a unique history as a product of black culture, that it developed differently from other American dialects. Many in this community supported the eradicational view that all students should have their first dialect replaced by standard English.

But the most piercing criticism has come from James Sledd, primarily in two articles: "Bidialectalism" (1969), and "Doublespeak" (1972). Sledd attacks bidialectalism because it accepts that some varieties of language are superior to others not on linguistic grounds but on the grounds of who their speakers are or are not, and because it fosters the illusion that if speakers of minority dialects change their speech, they would no longer be discriminated against. He contends that efforts should be undertaken to rid society of its prejudices against minority dialects and to teach literacy skills to minority students. Richard W. Bailey's "Write off Versus Write on" (1973) surveys the issues and agrees with Sledd's criticism of bidialectalism: "the argument for bidialectalism—for the painstaking and systematic teaching of standard English—finally reduces itself to the naked fact of prejudice against some forms of spoken English reflecting social and racial prejudice against the people who utter such forms" (438).

The argument regarding racial prejudice has been challenged by Thomas Farrell in his "A Defense for Requiring Standard English" (1986). In fact, Farrell argues that requiring all students to learn standard English is "the only truly non-racist position" and that "the failure to require students to learn standard English is *in effect* racist." In this essay as well as in other pieces such as "Literacy, the Basics, and All That Jazz" (1977), "IQ and Standard English" (1983), and "Two Comments on James Sledd's 'In Defense of the Students' Right' " (1984), Farrell argues forcefully against bidialectalism, asserting that students learn "propositional thinking by mastering and controlling . . . the grammar of standard English" ("IQ and Standard English" [478]). The exchanges over the years between Sledd and Farrell have made for exciting and informative reading, and it seems inevitable that the issue will continue to generate debate among teachers.

PEDAGOGICAL ISSUES

Options for dealing with dialects in the basic writing classroom derive from views on three issues discussed above: the source and importance of written dialect problems, the status of students' native dialect(s), and the goals of the instructional program. Many writers who have presented general guidelines and principles for working with basic writers have discussed the priority of treating dialect problems and their explicit handling in the classroom. As persistent as dialect in writing often is, developing literacy skills and maintaining student interest and motivation have been emphasized far more than helping students overcome writing dialect. Karen Hornick's brief "Teaching Writing to Linguistically Diverse Students" (1986) is a valuable outline of fourteen factors found to encourage improved writing from students who speak nonstandard English, including positive teacher attitudes, regular writing practice, and writing for personal purposes. Judith Nembhard's "A Perspective on Teaching Black Dialect Speaking Students to Write Standard English" (1983) discusses eight components of an effective writing program for freshman writers who use black dialect. Other essays offering a general perspective for teachers are Barbara Quint Gray and Virginia Slaughter's "Writing" (1980), Darnell Williams's "Teaching Writing Skills to Dialectically Different Students" (1973), and Carol E. Reed's "Teaching Teachers About Teaching Writing to Students of Varied Linguistic Social and Cultural Groups" (1981).

The foregoing items stress the importance of teachers having positive attitudes toward the students' language and culture, of teachers being sensitive to the insecurity of basic writers, of using students' own cultural experiences for writing and discussion topics, and of selecting reading materials students can easily relate to. In the same spirit, Doris Ginn, in "A Threat to the Black Dialect" (1975), argues that many black basic writers learn to write well only if teachers develop positive attitudes, become aware of historical implications of black dialect, and use a combined linguistic-cognitive approach that recognizes the value of black cultural identity and cultural experiences.

Other articles and essays have commented on dialect's place in writing instruction. Mary Epes et al.'s "Investigating Error in the Writing of Nontraditional College Students" (1978) advocates that teachers separate editing (including work with dialect features) from composing and concentrate on composing to increase rhetorical development and fluency in writing and to improve student attitudes toward writing. Allison Wilson, in "Black Dialect and the Freshman Writer" (1985), calls for working with the correction of dialect as an editing activity following inventing and revising. This point is made as well by Alice Horning in *Teaching Writing as a Second Language* (1987) and by Elizabeth Tricomi in "Krashen's Second-Language Acquisition Theory and the Teaching of Edited American English" (1986), two ambitious attempts to apply second-language acquisition theory to basic writing instruction.

In a 1974 essay titled "Black Dialect? or Black Face?," Constance Weaver says that the usual compulsion of teachers to correct mechanics should be replaced by emphasis on students' writing being coherent and interesting. Hartwell (1980) finds no place for attention to dialect problems at all: "dialect interference in writing . . . does not exist, . . . [and] pedagogies for teaching writing skills to native speakers of English that assume much interference are theoretically wrong, pedagogically unsound, and socially unwise" (101).

An important issue is the extent to which teachers can rely on the ear of students for self-correction to correct their writing. Since linguistic research shows that writers sometimes use grammatical forms that are not in their speech, this has theoretical support and has been adopted as the approach by Barbara

Nauer, in "Soundscript" (1976). It also has received empirical support in David Bartholomae's "The Study of Error" (1980), which shows that when students read their papers aloud, they often pronounce word endings that were not present in the writing (261). In fact, he found some writers able to correct unconsciously nearly all errors as they read them. This ability implies that writers often have at least a passive competence in and acquaintance with a dialect other than their own that they can draw on to their advantage.

Methods of dealing with written dialect problems directly by discussing them as such with students have to date used a simple contrast between speech (the first dialect) and writing (the second dialect) and have presumed a simple relation between the two; these methods are based either on contrastive foreign-language teaching methodology or on the traditional paradigm method. The only research comparing the effectiveness of different methods is Carol Richert's "A Comparative Study of the Teaching of Standard English as a Second Dialect to Speakers of Black English in College" (1979). Textbooks and teachers that deal with dialect explicitly face important, challenging issues of labeling and presenting the two dialects, not exaggerating the importance of dialect differences, and handling the value-laden concept of dialect in a consistent, easily comprehensible way without confusing or demeaning the student. They need to distinguish dialect from other writing problems and to distinguish types of dialect problems. Barbara Quint Gray, in "Dialect Interference in Writing" (1975), identifies three types of dialect-related difficulties that teachers need to recognize: invisibly rule-based, visibly rule-based, and non–rule-based, each with its own pedagogical implications.

As early as William Stewart's "Foreign Language Teaching Methods in Quasi-Foreign Language Situations" (1964), the teaching of standard English imported practices from foreign-language teaching—pattern practice, drillwork, contrasting paradigms, etc. By the early 1970s a professional field of specialization, SESD, the teaching of standard English as a second dialect, had developed, and by the early 1980s a newsletter of this name was regularly addressing the issues of the field. While teaching standard English as a second dialect has obvious similarities to teaching English as a second language (each has the goal of teaching new language patterns not native to the student, and students' mastery of the second dialect or language is directly related to their acculturation to the second language or dialect culture), there are clear differences in the motivation of students. Jacobson (1970) says that second-language methods can go only so far, because the vocabulary of dialects of English coincide with Edited Written English, but grammar and pronunciation do not.

Nonetheless, published techniques for teaching dialect speakers to write standard English rely on foreign-language or English-as-a-second-language approaches. One early, good example of this is Carol Reed's "Adapting TESL Approaches to the Teaching of Written Standard English as a Second Dialect to Speakers of American Black English Vernacular" (1973).

Two master's thesis have developed complete courses based on a similar approach. Stephen Jones, in "The Use of Foreign Language Methodology in Teaching Written Edited American English to Speakers of Black English" (1975), designs and advocates the "package method" of drilling grammar and teaching written English. Wendy Reynoso's "Standard English Acquisition" (1984) is a manual to teach standard forms to dialect users using a proofreading approach based on contrastive analysis.

Composition handbooks and workbooks largely ignore dialect forms and have a very limited view of the dialect-based dimensions of other usage problems such as subject-verb agreement. That is, few books treat dialect forms differently from other grammatical problems that students may have, if they treat them at all.

A survey of books giving them some attention reveals the problems of labeling and explaining these forms for composition students. These difficulties are easy to appreciate, given the sensitivity and complexity of the issues surrounding the subject, and given the challenge of presenting grammatical information to students comprehensibly, accurately, and usefully. Several labels and explanations are used, most approaches using a formal contrastive presentation.

Some materials label dialect as "spoken" forms and contrast them with written forms such as Mary Epes et al.'s *The Comp-Lab Exercises* (1980) and Cora Robey et al.'s *Handbook of Basic Writing Skills* (1978). Others give them a social label—"community dialect" or "nonstandard," such as Constance Gefvert et al.'s *Keys to American English* (1975) and Teresa Glazier's *The Least You Should Know about English* (1982). Still others use the stylistic label "informal," and J. L. Dillard et al., in *How to Score with English* (1986), use "nonstandard or less formal." James Heffernan and John Lincoln, in *Writing: A College Handbook* (1986), give them a blanket label—"ethnic and regional dialects." Other texts use a combined approach. The social and stylistic designations, especially the label "standard," formally receive cursory definitions (Gefvert et al.'s nine-page introduction to geographical and regional dialects in this country is an impressive exception to this), though these textbooks clearly assign more worth to the native dialects of students than their counterparts did no more than ten years earlier.

How is the difference between dialect and standard forms explained? For instance, with regard to supplying the past tense -*ed*, Robey et al. say that "sometimes the ending is not clearly heard in speech, but it always appears in writing" (71). Diana Hacker and Betty Renshaw in *A Practical Guide for Writers* (1982: 352–55) give a long, carefully reasoned comparison, citing the nature of speech and presenting the findings of linguists without using linguistic terminology. Explanations often include a statement about the prestige of standard, written forms and the importance of using these forms to achieve the widest possible communication. Finally, the dialect forms are usually contrasted with the standard written forms, either in side-by-side paradigms (as of the *be* verb) or in pairs of sentences. One source that discusses a placement test for discriminating different types of dialect speakers is Daisy Crystal's "Dialect Mixture and Sorting Out the Concept of Freshman English Remediation" (1972).

This review has outlined the principal linguistic, pedagogical, and political issues involving dialects and basic writers and discussed in the literature over the past twenty years. Although these issues continue to be debated, though most often not in print, our understanding of the nature of dialects, the political realities of dealing with them in the classroom, and the pedagogical options has increased markedly. To many questions, however, we still need research and answers; among these questions are the following: (1) Why do some spoken forms *not* get transferred to writing? (2) How competent are dialect speakers in switching between dialects? (3) What accounts for the individual variation with which dialect forms occur? (4) What does the presence of dialect forms in writing tell us about the sequence of development that basic writers are progressing through? (5) How can we maximize students' native language resources to teach them to self-correct without being preoccupied with rules? (6) What is precisely the degree of dialect influence from various sources? Answers will tell us much about the nature of language learning and are crucial to the continuing development of literacy theory.

REFERENCES

Amastae, Jon. "The Writing Needs of Hispanic Students." *The Writing Needs of Linguistically Different Students.* Ed. Bruce Cronnell. Los Alamitos, Calif.: SWRL Educational Research and Development, 1982, pp. 99–127.

Armstrong, Bondie. "A Study of Dialect and Its Interference with Learning to Write." Diss. Memphis State University, 1983.

Bailey, Richard W. "Write off Versus Write on: Dialects and the Teaching of Composition." *Varieties of Present-Day English.* Ed. Richard W. Bailey and Jay L. Robinson. New York: Macmillan, 1973, pp. 384–411.

Bartholomae, David. "The Study of Error." *CCC* 31 (1980): 253–69.

Bobson, Sara, comp. "Nonstandard Dialects: An Annotated Bibliography of ERIC References." *ERIC Document* 905 227 (1974).

Brandes, Paul, and Jeutonne Brewer. *Dialect Clash in America: Issues and Answers.* Metuchen, N.J.: Scarecrow, 1977.

Briggs, Olin D. "A Study of Deviations from Standard English in Papers of Negro Freshmen at an Alabama College." Diss. University of Alabama, 1968.

Bruder, Mary Newton, and Luddy Hayden. "Teaching Composition: A Report on a Bidialectal Approach." *Lang L* 23 (1973): 1–15.

Cannon, Garland. "Multidialects: The Student's Right to His Own Language." *CCC* 24 (1973): 382–85.

College Conference on Composition and Communication. "Students' Right to Their Own Language." [Special Issue] *CCC* 25 (Fall 1974): 1–32.

Collins, J. J. "Deviations from Standard English in Written Compositions of Disadvantaged College Freshmen and Regular Admissions Students at Glassboro State College." Diss. Temple University, 1971.

Cooper, Grace. "Black Language and Holistic Cognitive Style." *W J B l Studies* 5 (1981): 201–7.

———. "Black Stylistic Features in Student Compositions." *ERIC Document* 153 235 (1977).

Cronnell, Bruce. "Dialect and Writing." *J Res Dev Ed* 17 (1983): 58–64.

Crystal, Daisy. "Dialect Mixture and Sorting Out the Concept of Freshman English Remediation." *Flor For L Rep* 10 (1972): 1–2, 43–46.

Dillard, J. L. *Black English: Its History and Usage in the United States.* New York: Random House, 1972.

Dillard, J. L., et al. *How to Score with English.* Dubuque: Kendall/Hunt, 1986.

Epes, Mary. "Tracing Errors to Their Sources: A Study of the Encoding Processes of Adult Basic Writers." *JBW* 4.1 (1985): 4–33.

Epes, Mary, Carolyn Kirkpatrick, and Michael G. Southwell. *The Comp-Lab Exercises.* Englewood Cliffs: Prentice-Hall, 1980.

Epes, Mary, et al. "Investigating Error in the Writing of Nontraditional College Students." *Eric Document* 168 018 (1978).

Farrell, Thomas J. "A Defense for Requiring Standard English." *P/T* 7 (1986): 165–79.

———. "IQ and Standard English." *CCC* 34 (1983): 470–84.

———. "Literacy, the Basics, and All That Jazz." *CE* 38 (1977): 443–59.

———. "Two Comments on James Sledd's 'In Defense of the Students' Right.' " *CE* 46 (1984): 821–22.

Fasold, Ralph W., and Walter A. Wolfram. "Some Linguistic Features of Negro Dialect." *Teaching English in the Inner City.* Ed. Ralph W. Fasold and Roger W. Shuy. Washington: Center for Applied Linguistics, 1970, pp. 41–86.

Freeman, Lawrence D. "The Students' Right to Their Own Language: Its Legal Bases." *CCC* 26 (1975): 25–29.

Funkhouser, James L. "Black English: From Speech to Writing." Diss. St. Louis University, 1976.

———. "A Various Standard." *CE* 34 (1973): 806–10, 819–27.

Garcia, Ricardo L. "A Linguistic Frame of Reference for Critiquing Chicano Compositions." *CE* 37 (1975): 184–88.

Gefvert, Constance, Richard Raspa, and Amy Richards. *Keys to American English.* New York: Harcourt Brace Jovanovich, 1975.

Giannasi, Jenefer M. "Dialects and Composition." *Teaching Composition: 10 Bibliographical Essays.* Ed. Gary Tate. Fort Worth: Texas Christian University Press, 1976, pp. 275–304.

Ginn, Doris O. "A Threat to the Black Dialect: An Approach That Works." *ERIC Document* 106 874 (1975).

Glazier, Teresa Ferster. *The Least You Should Know about English: Basic Writing Skills,* 2nd ed. New York: Holt, Rinehart and Winston, 1982.

Gray, Barbara Quint. "Dialect Interference in Writing: A Tripartite Analysis." *JBW* 1.1 (1975): 14–22.

Gray, Barbara Quint, and Virginia B. Slaughter. "Writing." *Teaching Basic Skills in College.* Ed. Alice Stewart Trillin et al. San Francisco: Jossey-Bass, 1980, pp. 12–91.

Hacker, Diana, and Betty Renshaw. *A Practical Guide for Writers.* Boston: Little, Brown, 1982.

Hammons, Myrna Adcock. "Aspects of Written Language of College Freshmen in Oklahoma, according to Race and Sex: Negro, American Indian, and Caucasian.'' Diss. University of Tulsa, 1973.

Hartwell, Patrick. "Dialect Interference in Writing: A Critical View.'' *RTE* 14 (1980): 101–18.

Heffernan, James A. W., and John E. Lincoln. *Writing: A College Handbook*, 2nd ed. New York: Norton, 1986.

Hirsch, E. D., Jr. *The Philosophy of Composition*. Chicago: University of Chicago Press, 1977.

Hornick, Karen. "Teaching Writing to Linguistically Diverse Students.'' *ERIC Document* 275 792 (1986).

Horning, Alice S. *Teaching Writing as a Second Language*. Carbondale: Southern Illinois University Press, 1987.

Jacobson, Rodolfo. "The Teaching of English to Speakers of Other Languages and/or Dialects: An Oversimplification.'' *TESOL Q* 4 (1970): 241–54.

Joiner, Charles W. *Martin Luther King Junior Elementary School Children et al. vs. Ann Arbor School District Board: Memorandum Opinion and Order*. Detroit, 1979.

Jones, Stephen C. "The Use of Foreign Language Methodology in Teaching Written Edited American English to Speakers of Black English.'' Thesis. East Carolina University, 1975.

Keller, Joseph. "Sentence Fragments, Black English, and Prosody: Conflict in Composition.'' *EE* 9 (1978): 158–64.

Kirschner, Samuel A., and G. Howard Poteet. "Non-standard English Usage in the Writing of Black, White, and Hispanic Remedial English Students in an Urban Community College.'' *RTE* 7 (1973): 351–55.

Kochman, Thomas, ed. *Rappin' and Stylin' Out: Communication in Urban Black America*. Urbana: University of Illinois Press, 1972.

Labov, William. *Language in the Inner City: Studies in the Black English Vernacular*. Philadelphia: University of Pennsylvania Press, 1972.

———. "The Logic of Nonstandard English.'' *Monograph Series on Languages and Linguistics* 22. Ed. James Alatis. Washington, D.C.: Georgetown University Press, 1969, pp. 1–43.

Linn, Michael D. "Black Rhetorical Patterns and the Teaching of Composition.'' *CCC* 26 (1975): 149–53.

McDavid, Raven I., Jr. "Go Slow in Ethnic Attributions: Geographical Mobility and Dialect Prejudices.'' *Varieties of Present-Day English*. Ed. Jay L. Robinson and Richard W. Bailey. New York: Macmillan, 1973, pp. 258–73.

Merrill, Celia. "Contrastive Analysis and Chicano Compositions.'' *ERIC Document* 136 291 (1976).

Montgomery, Michael, and Guy Bailey, eds. *Language Variety in the South: Perspectives in Black and White*. Tuscaloosa: University of Alabama Press, 1986.

Morrow, Daniel Hibbs. "Dialect Interference in Writing: Another Critical View.'' *RTE* 19 (1985): 154–80.

Nauer, Barbara. "Soundscript: A Way to Help Black Students to Write Standard English.'' *CE* 36 (1976): 586–88.

Nembhard, Judith P. "A Perspective on Teaching Black Dialect Speaking Students to Write Standard English.'' *J Negro Ed* 52 (1983): 75–82.

Noonan-Wagner, Desley. "Possible Effects of Cultural Differences on the Rhetoric of Black Basic Skills Writers.'' Thesis. University of Houston, 1981.

Reed, Carol E. "Adapting TESL Approaches to the Teaching of Written Standard English as a Second Dialect to Speakers of American Black English Vernacular." *TESOL Q* 7 (1973): 289–307.

———. "Teaching Teachers about Teaching Writing to Students from Varied Linguistic Social and Cultural Groups." *Variation in Writing: Functional and Linguistic-Cultural Differences.* Ed. Marcia Farr Whiteman. Hillsdale, N.J.: Lawrence Erlbaum, 1981, pp. 153–66.

Reynoso, Wendy Demko. "Standard English Acquisition." *ERIC Document* 246 693 (1984).

Richert, Carol M. "A Comparative Study of the Teaching of Standard English as a Second Dialect to Speakers of Black English in College." Thesis. Florida Atlantic University, 1979.

Robey, Cora L., Alice M. Hedrick, and Ethelyn H. Morgan. *Handbook of Basic Writing Skills.* New York: Harcourt Brace Jovanovich, 1978.

Scott, Jerrie. "Mixed Dialects in the Composition Classroom." *Language Variety in the South: Perspectives in Black and White.* Ed. Michael Montgomery and Guy Bailey. Tuscaloosa: University of Alabama Press, 1986, pp. 333–47.

Shaughnessy, Mina P. *Errors and Expectations: A Guide for the Teacher of Basic Writing.* New York: Oxford University Press, 1977.

Sledd, James H. "Bidialectalism: The Linguistics of White Supremacy." *EJ* 58.9 (1969): 1307–15, 1329.

———. "Doublespeak: Dialectology in the Service of Big Brother." *CE* 33 (1972): 439–56.

Smitherman, Geneva. " 'God Don't Never Change': Black English from a Black Perspective." *CE* 34 (1973): 828–33.

Sternglass, Marilyn S. "Close Similarities in Dialect Features of Black and White College Students in Remedial Composition Classes." *TESOL Q* 8 (1974): 271–83.

Stewart, William A. "Foreign Language Teaching Methods in Quasi-Foreign Language Situations." *Non-standard Speech and the Teaching of English.* Ed. William A. Stewart. Washington, D.C.: Center for Applied Linguistics, 1964, pp. 1–15.

———. "Observations (1966) on the Problems of Defining Negro Dialect." *Flor For L Rep* 9.1 (1971): 47–49, 57.

Taylor, Orlando. "An Introduction to the Historical Development of Black English and Implications for American Education." *ERIC Document* 035 863 (1969).

Terrebonne, Nancy G. "The Black English Vernacular in the Writing of Young Adults from Dayton, Ohio." Diss. Louisiana State University, 1975.

Tricomi, Elizabeth Taylor. "Krashen's Second-Language Acquisition Theory and the Teaching of Edited American English." *JBW* 5.2 (1986): 59–69.

Weaver, Constance. "Black Dialect? or Black Face?" *ERIC Document* 091 713 (1974).

Whiteman, Marcia Farr. "Dialect Influence in Writing." *Variation in Writing: Functional and Linguistic-Cultural Differences.* Ed. Marcia Farr Whiteman. Hillsdale, N.J.: Lawrence Erlbaum, 1981, pp. 153–66.

Whittaker, Della. "A Content Analysis of Black English Markers in Compositions of Community-College Freshmen." Diss. University of Maryland, 1972.

Williams, Darnell. "Teaching Writing Skills to Dialectically Different Students." *J Negro Ed* 43 (1973): 329–31.

Williamson, Juanita. "Selected Features of Speech: Black and White." *CLAJ* 12 (1970): 420–33.

Wilson, Allison. "Black Dialect and the Freshman Writer." *JBW* 4.1 (1985): 44–54.
Wolfram, Walter A. *A Sociolinguistic Description of Detroit Negro Speech*. Washington,
    D.C.: Center for Applied Linguistics, 1969.
Wolfram, Walter A., and Ralph W. Fasold. *The Study of Social Dialects in the United
    States*. Englewood Cliffs: Prentice-Hall, 1974.
Wright, Barbara Helen White. "Hypercorrections and Dialect Forms in the Compositions
    of Native Born College Students from Georgia." Diss. City University of New
    York, 1985.

6

TESL Research and Basic Writing

Sue Render

Most research in ESL (English as a second language) composition is relatively recent and has been influenced by theoretical and empirical research in second-language acquisition and in English composition. This chapter will provide some historical perspective on language acquisition theory and a very brief introduction to current acquisition theory. The rest of the chapter will concentrate on research, and to a lesser extent, on pedagogical articles on ESL composition. This chapter is intended to complement other chapters in this book; it therefore does not include research about native language composition.

Language acquisition research is useful not only to ESL composition teachers but also to teachers of basic writing, for learning to write academic English can be compared to acquiring a second dialect or language. Patricia Silber, in "Teaching Written English as a Second Language" (1979), discusses some of the differences between oral and written language and builds a case for treating written language as a second language. The case is eloquently and strongly presented by Alice Horning in *Teaching Writing as a Second Language* (1987). She cites several scholarly works to support her view that for basic writers, the written code is a second language.

In the following discussion of these issues, a few linguistic terms are unavoidable. L1 represents first or native language and L2 represents second language. The target language (TL) is the language being studied. Other terms are defined as they come up.

CONTRASTIVE ANALYSIS, ERROR ANALYSIS, AND INTERLANGUAGE

Contrastive analysis was a popular theory in the middle of this century. It was based, at least partially, on the belief from behaviorist psychology that language is a set of habits. Contrasting a student's native language with the target language would predict areas of difficulty and provide a basis for writing teaching materials. Errors in the student's target language performance were thought to be caused by "interference" or "negative transfer" from the student's native language habits. Of interest here is the idea that language is a set of habits and that if teaching materials are structured to prevent students from making errors, then students will not form error-causing habits. This is one principle behind the substitution drills and transformation drills used in the audio-lingual method and transferred almost directly to controlled-writing teaching materials.

Contrastive analysis became controversial in the late sixties and early seventies. For the arguments against the predictive or strong version of contrastive analysis, see Ronald Wardhaugh's "The Contrastive Analysis Hypothesis" (1970). A recent discussion, Virginia Gathercole's "Some Myths You May Have Heard about First Language Acquisition" (1988), identifies three common misconceptions about first-language acquisition and cautions against assuming them in theories of second-language acquisition.

An explanatory or weak version of contrastive analysis developed as researchers began to collect and examine language acquirers' errors to determine areas of difficulty. This is now called error analysis. Error analysis revealed that, excluding pronunciation, the majority of errors were not caused by interference from the acquirers' native language. Jack C. Richards, in "A Non-Contrastive Approach to Error Analysis" (1971), discusses errors common to students with different backgrounds, and he suggests possible causes of these errors.

Because negative transfer did not cause the majority of errors, and for other, very complex reasons such as the influence of transformational-generative grammar theory, the habit-formation theory about language acquisition was questioned. Researchers suggested that a second-language acquirer develops a systematic language somewhere between the native language and the target language. In 1972, Larry Selinker called this systematic language, which changes as the acquirer becomes more competent in the target language, *interlanguage*. S. P. Corder discusses this process in "Idiosyncratic Dialects and Error Analysis" (1971), as does William Nemser in "Approximate Systems of Foreign Language Learners" (1971). In "Interlanguage," Selinker discusses *fossilization*, which occurs when the acquirers "internally as it were, know that they know enough of the TL in order to communicate. And they stop learning" (217). For more on these ideas, see the collection of essays, *Interlanguage* (1984), edited by Alan Davies, C. Criper, and A.P.R. Howatt, and see *Error Analysis and Interlanguage* (1981) by S. P. Corder. S. N. Sridhar, in "Contrastive Analysis, Error Analysis and Interlanguage" (1975), shows how these three areas of research are related to and complement each other.

Error analysis is a research tool for exploring these questions. Those interested in conducting an error analysis can consult several sources. For cautions about error analysis, see Jacquelyn Schachter's "An Error in Error Analysis" (1974) and Schachter's and Marianne Celce-Murcia's "Some Reservations Concerning

Error Analysis'' (1977). Lewis Mukattash's ''Problems in Error Analysis'' (1981) provides useful descriptions of procedures and difficulties.

CONTRASTIVE RHETORIC

Closely related to contrastive analysis is the concept of contrastive rhetoric. In ''Cultural Thought Patterns in Inter-Cultural Education'' (1966), Robert Kaplan stated, ''Rhetoric . . . is not universal . . . , but varies from culture to culture and even from time to time within a given culture'' (2). With this important article, Kaplan introduced the idea of contrastive rhetoric to language teachers. To quote from Kaplan's ''Contrastive Rhetorics'' (1983), ''I am concerned with the notion that speakers of different languages use different devices to present information, to establish the relationships among ideas, to show the centrality of one idea as opposed to another, to select the most effective means of presentation'' (140).

The field has become much more complex since Kaplan's 1966 article. Just how complex is suggested by Diane Houghton and Michael Hoey in ''Linguistics and Written Discourse'' (1983). They write that contrastive rhetoric has to do with discourse theory, traditional rhetorical theory, and language universals. It ''presupposes two kinds of interconnected input—work on the development of a universal theory of discourse, and description of the written discourses of individual languages'' (4). Houghton and Hoey discuss these in some detail and provide an extensive bibliography. Their essay is in the *Annual Review of Applied Linguistics 1982* (1983), edited by Robert Kaplan et al. This volume is devoted to contrastive rhetoric and has essays about Hindi, American Indian languages, German, Korean, Chinese, and Japanese. All have good bibliographies.

Bernard A. Mohan and Winnie Au-Yeung Lo voice a dissenting view concerning contrastive rhetoric in ''Academic Writing and Chinese Students'' (1985). They ask, ''Is the discourse organization of academic writing in English culture-specific, or is it universal?'' (516). By citing examples of translated Chinese, they question the statements of Kaplan (among others), who claims that Chinese prose tends to be indirect. They point out that native-speaking students also have trouble with organization and attribute the majority of non-native students' organizational problems to developmental factors or to the emphasis of prior instruction. For a reaction to their article, see Joan Gregg's ''Comments on Bernard A. Mohan and Winnie Au-Yeung Lo's 'Academic Writing and Chinese Students' '' (1986).

Several studies use contrastive analysis and/or contrastive rhetoric to discuss particular languages. The information they offer is important, for negative transfer still accounts for at least a large minority of errors and for nonstandard rhetorical patterns. Teachers who are aware of such differences can use the information appropriately to inform their students. As Betty Rizzo and Santiago Villafane write in ''Spanish Language Influences on Written English'' (1975), ''It may make a great deal of difference to a student to know that he has not been dumb, but that he has simply been using one system of logic where another is called for'' (71).

For Chinese, see "Contrastive Rhetoric" (1985) by Carolyn Matalene. For Japanese, see "Some Contrastive Features of English and Japanese" (1961) by Yuichi Mito. For Arabic see "The Least You Should Know About Arabic" (1983) by Karyn Thompson-Panos and Maria Thomas-Ružić; see also Margaret Sue Scott and G. Richard Tucker's "Error Analysis and English-Language Strategies of Arab Students" (1974).

LANGUAGE ACQUISITION

Pedagogical methods in teaching English as a second language (TESL) are determined by hypotheses about language acquisition that come from case studies and empirical research. For surveys and comments on such research, see Judith Chun's "A Survey of Research in Second Language Acquisition" (1980), Karl Krahnke and Mary Ann Christison's "Recent Language Research and Some Language Teaching Principles" (1983), and Ann Raimes's "Traditional and Revolution in ESL Teaching" (1983).

Stephen Krashen's "Monitor Model for Second-Language Acquisition" (1978) brings together a considerable amount of current empirical research on language acquisition and presents a set of hypotheses that account for the findings of that accumulated research and that may also be applied to the acquisition of formal, written English. First is his hypothesis that there is a distinction between acquired language and learned language: acquired language is subconscious and is acquired from "comprehensible input," whereas learned language is conscious knowledge about language and is learned from rules, paradigms, memorized patterns, etc. Speaking and writing, as opposed to mechanical drills, come from a person's acquired language. Conscious correction of language comes from a person's learned knowledge of language, which is only available as an editing device or a monitor.

Intake that makes acquisition possible, according to Krashen, is *meaningful* language at and just above a person's present level of competence. In "The Input Hypothesis" (1980), Krashen states "a necessary condition to move from stage i to stage $i+1$ is that the acquirer understand input that contains $i+1$, where 'understand' means that the acquirer is focused on the meaning and not the form of the utterance" (170). The concept of $i+1$ depends upon a prior "natural order" hypothesis, which states that "second language acquirers acquire (not learn) grammatical structures in a predictable order" (169). (For a thorough discussion of acquisition order, see *Language Two* [1982] by Heidi Dulay, Marina Burt, and Stephen Krashen.) This order varies somewhat for individuals, and it is not always possible to know exactly where any one individual is. Thus, "roughly tuned" intake, rather than carefully ordered intake, may be more effective because it reviews i and has a greater chance of hitting $i+1$. This is especially applicable to classroom situations. The intake becomes more complex as the students progress. Understandable intake implies the necessity of simplified language, but Jacquelyn Schachter (in "Nutritional Needs of Language Learners" [1983]) disagrees, arguing that simplification is only one means of providing the necessary intake.

Acquired language can be monitored, under certain conditions, by learned knowledge about language or the monitor. The conditions, according to Krashen, are necessary knowledge, time, and focus on form. There is not time to use the monitor when speaking, and "over-users" who try to do so lack fluency, produce false starts, and therefore have difficulty communicating. The "under-user" doesn't use conscious learning, but depends on "feel." The "optimal-user" uses the monitor when appropriate, such as proofreading a paper. Krashen's description of the "over-user" fits those basic writers who concentrate on form or surface error. Donald M. Morrison and Graham Low take issue with Krashen's perception of monitor use and argue for a much more complex and broader view of the monitor's role in "Monitoring and the Second Language Learner" (1983). While Krashen posits a distinct separation between what is learned and what is acquired, not everyone agrees. Earl Stevik, in "The Levertov Machine" (1980), argues that some of what is learned can "seep" into what is acquired.

In addition to distinguishing between learning and acquisition, Krashen also distinguishes between aptitude, which "may be related directly to conscious learning," and attitude, which "refers to the acquirers' orientations toward speakers of the target language as well as personality factors" ("The Monitor Model" 8–9). In *Second Language Acquisition and Second Language Learning* (1981), which brings together much of Krashen's work, he writes that "the acquirer must not only understand the input but must also, in a sense, be 'open' to it." (21). As regards aptitude, an illuminating survey by Joy Reid, in "The Learning Style Preferences of ESL Students" (1987), identifies preferences among four learning styles—kinesthetic, tactile, visual, and auditory—according to nationality. As regards aptitude, the degree of openness depends on attitude, which includes amount and kind of motivation, and the level of anxiety. For a more thorough discussion of motivation, see Earl Stevick's *Memory, Meaning and Method* (1976), and for a sensitive and perceptive discussion on anxiety, see Stevick's *Teaching Languages* (1980). His comments about what the student risks psychologically may be applied to basic writing students as well as language students. See also Karen Foss and Armeda C. Reitzel's "A Relational Model for Managing Second Language Anxiety" (1988) for a model adapted from the discipline of speech communication.

A powerful determiner of attitude, motivation, and anxiety is how a student feels about and adjusts to the culture of the language he or she desires to acquire. Basic writers entering academia are, in a sense, entering a subculture different from their own. In "Improving Student Writing" (1984), Brigid Ballard discusses the cultural adjustment native and non-native students must make when entering academia. John H. Schumann, in "The Acculturation Model for Second-Language Acquisition" (1978), discusses the very complex issue of acculturation, including social factors, affective factors (such as language shock and culture shock), and personality factors. Less detailed but more readable than Schumann's article is "Affective Factors in Second Language Learning" (1981) by H. Douglas Brown.

Lynn M. Goldstein, in "Standard English: The Only Target for Nonnative Speakers of English?" (1987), reports that Hispanic ESL students in a study showed interference not only from their native language but also from the Black English they heard in their neighborhoods. Students' cultures also play an important part in language acquisition, according to James Paul Gee. He asserts, in "Dracula, the Vampire Lestat, and TESOL" (1988), that language acquisition requires not just knowing grammar and words but also becoming "enculturated"—learning the perspectives and the ways of displaying them that a culture allows and values in its speakers. For a complementary viewpoint, see Karen Ann Watson-Gegeo's "Ethnography in ESL: Defining the Essentials" (1988).

Applications of acquisition theory to classroom practice are made by Julia S. Falk in "Language Acquisition and the Teaching and Learning of Writing" (1979), Helmut Esau and Michael Keene in "A TESOL Model for Native-Language Writing Instruction" (1981), W. Ross Winterowd in "From Classroom Practice into Psycholinguistic Theory" (1983), and Elizabeth Taylor Tricomi in "Krashen's Second-Language Acquisition Theory and the Teaching of Edited American English" (1986).

Also, Linda Blair writes about the role of the monitor in "ESL Students and Writing Acquisition Theory" (1983), and Barbara Kroll argues for the application of acquisition theory in "Sorting Out Writing Problems" (1978). Krashen, in *Writing* (1984), comments, "If second language acquisition and the development of writing ability occur in the same way, writing ability is not learned but acquired via extensive reading in which the focus of the reader is on the message, i.e., reading for genuine interest and/or pleasure" (23). He summarizes L1 composition research that supports that idea. While there is no research in L2 composition that has explored causation between increased reading and improved writing, there is research that shows a correlation between L2 reading ability and writing ability. See "The Relationship of Pleasure Reading and Second Language Writing Proficiency" (1986) by Michael Janopoulos, and two doctoral dissertations, "The Reading and Writing Relationship" (1987) by Pratin Pimsarn, and "English as a Second Language (ESL) Development" (1986) by Dagmar Acuna. More research is necessary, but the pedagogical implication is that ESL writing courses should include extensive reading.

ESL COMPOSITION

In the 1960s, the audio-lingual method was predominant, and teaching materials were designed to help students practice correct habits. Writing, especially at the lower levels, was often seen as an activity to reinforce other language skills. Thus, writing was controlled to provide practice of particular language features and to prevent students from making errors. Making errors, it was believed, was practicing incorrect habits. Since students make errors when composing, free composition was seen as an error-reinforcing activity. In 1963, Anita Pincas wrote, "Since free composition relies on inventiveness, on creativeness, it is in direct opposition to the expressed ideals of scientific habit-forming teaching methods which strive to prevent error from occurring" ("Structural Linguistics and Systematic Composition Teaching to Students of English as a Foreign Language" 185).

Writing materials that strove to prevent error from occurring (controlled writing) took several forms. For beginners, assignments might require exact copying of a short passage of prose. Later on, students might be asked to change a piece from past to future tense, make singular subjects plural with the subsequent changes of pronouns and verbs, or change a dialogue from direct to indirect form.

Another type of controlled writing was the composition frame from which, to make sentences, the students selected the appropriate words from little boxes. For example, if students chose a plural subject, they would need to select a plural verb. K. W. Moody gives several examples in "Controlled Composition Frames" (1965). Other techniques, such as having students respond to a series of related questions or having them fill in the blanks in a prose passage, are described by Gerald Dykstra in "Eliciting Language Practice in Writing" (1964).

Not everyone agreed with the concept of controlled writing. Its proponents defended it by listing disadvantages of free composition, one of which was discouragement for the learner because of numerous corrections on returned papers. Christina Bratt Paulston argued for controlled writing in "Teaching Writing in the ESOL Classroom" (1972), which provides an overview of the subject. She dismissed free composition, arguing in favor of controlled writing because it allowed "a careful grading and sequencing of the language patterns" and had the student concentrate on "one thing at a time" (37). Her strongest argument was that students who were in a controlled writing program were more motivated than the students who were in a free composition program. However, Paulston admitted that in a comparison of the two groups, "the findings concerning increased proficiency were inconclusive" (38).

Paulston's inconclusive findings are understandable in the light of current language acquisition hypotheses. The focus on form in controlled writing would promote learning rather than acquisition. However, given the importance of attitude in language acquisition, controlled writing may be worth exploring as a supplementary exercise in the basic writing classroom because it enables students to feel successful. Donna Gorrell writes about its use in "Controlled Composition for Basic Writers" (1981). Another article that describes exercises is Vivian Horn's "Using the 'Ananse Tales Technique' for Composition" (1974).

Some articles discuss using controlled composition to make students aware of transitional and organizational patterns. Nancy Arapoff, in "Controlled Rhetoric Frames" (1968), advocates the use of frames arranged so as to have students

make selections "on the basis of how successfully they contribute to the coherence, variety, precision, unity, and emphasis of the essay" (28). Elaine
Dehghanpisheh, in "Bridging the Gap Between Controlled and Free Composition" (1979), argues for teaching exposition rather than description or narration
and describes "controlled rhetoric" exercises.

Teachers who used controlled writing were concerned with helping their students make the transition from controlled writing to free composition. Nancy
Arapoff, in "Writing" (1967), had her students move from controlled to free
by converting dialogues into various prose forms. In "An Experience Approach
to Teaching Composition" (1976), Thomas Buckingham and William Pech describe a method of moving from controlled to free by providing structured
experiences (photos, slides, field trips) for discussion and writing topics.

As mentioned above, not everyone agreed with the concept of controlled
writing. Edward Erazmus emphasized quantity over correctness in "Second
Language Composition Teaching at the Intermediate Level" (1960). Eugène
Brière, one of the first to do empirical research in ESL composition, described
in "Quantity before Quality in Second Language Composition" (1966) a study
in which ESL university students showed improvement after a one-semester
course of free composition. The study had no control group and too many
variables (as Brière points out), but the improvement was significant. It may
have been due to the reading the students were doing for their other classes, but
it indicated, at the least, that more research was needed before accepting controlled composition as the only method.

The debate between controlled and free composition is summarized by Ann
Raimes in "Composition" (1976). Raimes states that the division between the
two is unnatural and describes a course based on assignments that limit the
rhetorical and syntactic focus of the students' free compositions. (For another,
very different discussion of carefully structured assignments, see "Communicative Writing" [1979] by Sandra McKay.) Barry Taylor also argues for teaching
free composition, even to beginning students. He gives reasons and sample
lessons in "Teaching Composition to Low-Level ESL Students" (1976).

In that same year, 1976, Vivian Zamel's important article "Teaching Composition in the ESL Classroom" discussed the almost complete lack of empirical
research. She claimed similarities between very advanced ESL students and
English composition students, and she therefore suggested that "the results of
experimentation in English composition classes have as much to say to the ESL
teacher as to the English teacher" (67). Zamel pointed in particular to research
about the process approach to writing instruction.

ESL teachers therefore began to study and write about the writing processes
of their own students. Barry Taylor, in "Content and Written Form" (1981),
argues for the process approach and extensive daily reading. Vivian Zamel, in
two different studies, "Writing" (1982) and "The Composing Processes of
Advanced ESL Students" (1983), examines the composing processes of proficient, university-level (sophomore and above) ESL students. Her results are

similar to those of studies done with L1 students, and Zamel argues persuasively for the process approach.

In partial contrast, Ann Raimes, in her 1985 study of "What Unskilled ESL Students Do as They Write," found several differences between her subjects and their L1 counterparts, basic writers. Raimes reminds us that "the process of writing in an L2 is startlingly different from writing in our L1" (232). From her study she concludes that "attention to process is thus necessary but not sufficient" (250).

Some in the profession go further than "not sufficient." Joy Reid and Daniel Horowitz both argue against exclusive use of process. Reid, in "Comments on Vivian Zamel's 'The Composing Process of Advanced ESL Students' " (1984), states that the teaching implications derived from Zamel's study may not be applicable to ESL students in preuniversity intensive language programs. Reid points out in "The Radical Outliner and the Radical Brainstormer" (1984) that some students do better and are more comfortable working from outlines. In "Process, Not Product" (1986), Horowitz acknowledges the merit of process techniques, but gives strong reasons against "embracing an overall approach which, in its attempt to develop . . . students' writing skills, creates a classroom situation that bears little resemblance to the situations in which those skills will eventually be used" (144).

Several people have written about teaching process techniques. Nancy Pfingstag describes modeling the process in "Showing Writing" (1984). Sandra McKay discusses purpose, audience, voice, and invention in "A Focus on Prewriting Strategies" (1982), and invention is the focus of Ruth Spack's "Invention Strategies and the ESL College Composition Student" (1984). Ruth Spack and Catherine Sadow's "Student-Teacher Working Journals in ESL Freshman Composition" (1983) is especially helpful on journal use in the classroom. Finally, teachers interested in process might consider Cynthia Watson's employment of models in "The Use and Abuse of Models in the ESL Writing Class" (1982).

SKILLS

Referring to the questions of what can or should be taught, this section concentrates on works that describe or discuss the teaching of particular aspects of written English. These works include articles on organization, cohesion and coherence, sentence structure and sentence combining, vocabulary, and spelling. This is not to imply that all or any of the above can be completely described, or that what is described and taught can be acquired and used by the student to produce text. One hopes, however, that students can use some of what they learn to monitor their written work and that some of what they learn (such as vocabulary taught in context) will become acquired.

One skill students must have if they are to succeed in college is the ability to organize their writing effectively and appropriately. Students need to recognize not only that organizational patterns, stylistic features, and forms of support common in their own cultures may or may not be appropriate for English prose (see the above section on contrastive rhetoric), but also that organization and style vary from discipline to discipline within academia. (For a discussion of two variations, see H. G. Widdowson's "Literary and Scientific Uses of English" [1974].)

The academic communities have been surveyed and the writing of the technical disciplines studied in order to learn more about the writing students will need to do in the university. Perhaps the most useful of the surveys is Daniel Horowitz's "What Professors Actually Require" (1986), which reports on writing assignments collected from several professors. Technical writing has received considerable attention because of the large proportion of ESL students who go into the sciences. Jane Friederichs and Herbert Pierson discuss question patterns in "What Are Science Students Expected to Write?" (1981), and Susan Hill, Betty Soppelsa, and Gregory West discuss organization in "Teaching ESL Students to Read and Write Experimental-Research Papers" (1982). For a more detailed linguistic study, see "Formal Written Communication and ESL" (1974) by Larry Selinker and Louis Trimble.

Organization of nontechnical prose has traditionally been taught through the use of models, and a good discussion of this technique is in "A Second Look at Teaching Reading and Composition" (1967) by Donna Carr. In "Functional Exercises" (1981), Cristin Carpenter and Judy Hunter also use reading to teach organization, but instead of using models, their individualized exercise packets have students use content from their other courses. In a related essay (1988), Marguerite Ann Snow and Donna M. Brinton examine the adjunct program of the University of California–Los Angeles, in which ESL courses share content bases and assignments with "content courses," and report that the relevance of the content increases reading and writing skills. Ruth Spack, in "Initiating ESL Students into the Academic Discourse Community" (1988), argues against ESL as a technical writing course and for its traditional humanities orientation.

Ann Johns has taught organization not from reading but, using schema theory, from reader expectations. Her "The ESL Student and the Revision Process" (1986) presents an interesting technique that draws from research in reading comprehension. Patricia Carrell, in "Content and Formal Schemata in ESL Reading" (1987), says that students' comprehension is aided more by their cultural familiarity with content than by their readings' clear organizations. Christine Pearson Casanave, in "Comprehension Monitoring in ESL Reading" (1988), suggests that teachers investigate ESL students' "strategy schemata," their methods of notetaking and annotating their reading, to understand linguistic development. Teresa Pica, Richard Young, and Catherine Doughty (1987) have found that comprehension is more dependent upon familiarity with and redundancy of input than upon its grammatical complexity.

Related to organization are the concepts of cohesion and coherence. The two are not the same, and cohesion may need some definition. M.A.K. Halliday and Ruqaiya Hasan, in *Cohesion in English* (1976), write, "Cohesion occurs where the INTERPRETATION of some element in the discourse is dependent on that of another" (4). They demonstrate this in their first example: "Wash and core six cooking apples. Put them into a fireproof dish" (2). Cohesion in that pair of sentences is established by the relationship between "six cooking apples" and the referring item "them." This is only one type of many cohesive ties that are categorized and discussed in detail in *Cohesion in English*. While that book is quite readable, it may give more than most nonlinguists need to know about the subject. For a good summary of the work, see Stephen Witte and Lester Faigley's "Coherence, Cohesion, and Writing Quality" (1981). They discuss Halliday and Hasan's theory of cohesion from the perspectives of research, distinct from coherence, teaching implications, and analysis of student essays. Ulla Connor also discusses using cohesion theory for analysis of student essays. She describes her method in "A Study of Cohesion and Coherence in English as a Second Language Students' Writing" (1984).

Patricia Carrell, in "Cohesion Is Not Coherence" (1982), takes issue with Halliday and Hasan's work. She interprets their work as associating cohesion with coherence and argues that coherence is caused by content, not by cohesive devices. Cohesive devices, she argues, are an "effect of coherence." However, in separate responses of the same title, "Comments on Patricia Carrell's 'Cohesion Is Not Coherence,' " Mohsen Ghadessy (1983) and Dorothy Rankin (1984) disagree with Carrell's interpretation of Halliday and Hasan but agree that cohesion and coherence are not the same.

For studies of cohesion in ESL student writing, see Paula Ellen Lieber's 1980 dissertation, "Cohesion in ESL Students' Expository Writing," and Robin Cameron Scarcella's 1984 dissertation, "Cohesion in the Writing Development of Native and Non-Native English Speakers." For pedagogical essays on cohesive devices, see "Using Connectives in Elementary Composition" (1972) by Vivian Horn, and Robert Weissberg's "Given and New" (1984), in which he discusses the topic and comment structure of sentences from technical prose. For a helpful essay on coherence, see "Coherence and Academic Writing" (1986) by Ann Johns, who sees coherence as both text-based and reader-based.

In addition to organization and coherence, ESL and basic writing teachers must be concerned with matters such as syntax, vocabulary, and spelling. Syntax is often taught through sentence combining. The question, of course, is does sentence combining help ESL students to develop syntactic maturity? Two studies indicate that it does. Ruth Crymes reports positive results with nominalizations in "The Relation of Study about Language to Language Performance" (1971), and Bernard Klassen reports positive results from a comprehensive sentence-combining program in "Sentence-Combining Exercises as an Aid to Expediting Syntactic Fluency in Learning English as a Second Language" (1977).

These results and those from experiments with native speakers have encouraged sentence combining in ESL classrooms. Patrick Kameen discusses a variety of exercises in "A Mechanical, Meaningful, and Communicative Framework for ESL Sentence Combining Exercises" (1978), and David M. Davidson provides a good, overall discussion in "Sentence Combining in an ESL Writing Program" (1977). Vivian Zamel expresses some caution in "Re-evaluating Sentence-Combining Practice" (1980). She argues that since sentence combining depends upon a preexisting linguistic ability that ESL students may not have, the students should first be introduced to the necessary grammatical concepts.

Perhaps more frustrating to ESL students than their struggles with syntax is their lack of English words with which to express themselves. Theorists and methodologists have attempted to address this need by writing about issues such as what is involved in knowing a word, how people learn words, and which words should be taught. The literature (but not empirical research) on the subject is extensive, so the works mentioned here will serve only as an introduction.

Jack Richards, in "The Role of Vocabulary Teaching" (1976), explains the linguistic assumptions about knowing a word. His clear discussion of multiple meanings, semantic value, network of associations, derivations and register restraints (i.e., temporal, geographical, discourse, and social variations) gives one a sense of richness for each word and implies a variety of teaching approaches. In *Teaching English to Speakers of Other Languages* (1978), Betty Wallace Robinett discusses some of the above, refers to word lists based on frequency counts (with a caution about their weaknesses), and gives a useful discussion of words that are often used together (collocation). Josef Rohrer, in "Learning Styles and Teaching Vocabulary" (1980), discusses vocabulary teaching methods for five learning styles that he believes to be "universal thinking behaviors" (281). Finally, Anne Martin suggests criteria for identification and selection of academic vocabulary in "Teaching Academic Vocabulary to Foreign Graduate Students" (1976).

Spelling is another frustration for both students and their teachers. It is a particular problem for some ESL students because their misspellings can interfere with communication. Causes of ESL students' misspellings are discussed by G. W. Abbot in "Intelligibility and Acceptability in Spoken and Written Communication" (1979) and by Muhammad Ibrahim in "Patterns in Spelling Errors" (1978). Sanford Schane discusses the regularity of English orthography in "Linguistics, Spelling, and Pronunciation" (1970), as does D. S. Taylor in "English Spelling" (1981). If spelling is taught in ESL classes, it is usually taught with pronunciation, as part of vocabulary study, or by itself. The emphasis seems to be on the regularity of spelling patterns. See "The Teaching of Spelling" (1976) by Ovaiza Sally, who offers some empirical evidence for the effectiveness of her described program, and "An Integrated Approach to Pronunciation and Spelling in ESL Curricula" (1976) by Clifford Hill and John Rittershofer.

ERROR

While we know that students make errors as part of the process of acquiring the written code, we don't know whether or not teacher responses to errors help students to make fewer errors. However, since students often demand error correction, teachers usually feel obliged to respond to errors at some point in the writing process. The general consensus seems to be that responses to errors should be consistently selective and systematic. This implies the development of an error hierarchy, but that would be different for each class and possibly each student.

Before such a hierarchy can be developed, it is necessary to determine what kinds of errors students make. Articles mentioned in the error analysis and contrastive rhetoric sections will be helpful here, as will J. F. Green's error classification in "Preparing an Advanced Composition Course" (1967) and Victor Wyatt's classification in "An Analysis of Errors in Composition Writing" (1973). Wyatt, though, does not include lexical errors, a necessary category.

Three criteria have been suggested for developing an error hierarchy: those errors that are most frequent, those that cause misunderstanding of communication, and those that stigmatize the learner. The most frequent errors are considered to be the most serious by David Palmer in "Expressing Error Gravity" (1980). Jeannette Ludwig favors the second criterion in "Native-Speaker Judgments of Second-Language Learners' Efforts at Communication" (1982). She reviewed twelve studies (from different languages) of native speaker reactions to error. Roughly generalizing, for the studies varied in form, she found that errors that decreased comprehensibility were the most irritating to native speakers. Marina Burt used native speakers to discover what kinds of grammatical errors decreased comprehensibility. In "Error Analysis in the Adult ESL Classroom" (1975), she found that errors that affected "overall sentence organization" interfered with communication, and she labeled these errors "global." Errors that affected only one part of a sentence did not tend to interfere with communication and were labeled "local." (James Hendrickson used a global versus local error hierarchy in "The Effects of Error Correction Treatments upon Adequate and Accurate Communication in the Written Compositions of Adult Learners of English as a Second Language" [1977]. He found no significant difference in improvement between a group that had only global errors corrected and a group that had all errors corrected. A hierarchy is no guarantee that error correction will be effective. It may, though, reduce work for the teacher and reduce confusion for the student.)

Aziz Khalil also used native-speaker judgment of comprehensibility as a measure of error seriousness in a study reported in "Communicative Error Evaluation" (1985). He found that lexical errors decreased intelligibility more than grammatical errors, but the grammatical errors used in his study tended to be local. A different approach to error seriousness was taken by Roberta Vann, Daisy Meyer, and Frederick Lorenz in "Error Gravity" (1984). They studied faculty reactions to sentence-level errors and found that word order (often a global error), *it*-deletion (when *it* should be the subject), relative clause error, and word choice were the least acceptable to university faculty.

The third criterion is discussed by James Hendrickson in his comprehensive survey "Error Correction in Foreign Language Teaching" (1978), which refers to the literature on errors that "stigmatize the learner from the perspective of native speakers" (391). In this article, he surveys the literature on error correction and provides some historical perspective.

Once teachers decide which errors to respond to, i.e., establish some sort of hierarchy, they must decide on a method of response. Four methods of error marking (errors corrected by the teacher, errors coded by the teacher, errors marked with a highlighter pen, and the number of errors per line written in the margin) were tested by Thomas Robb, Steven Ross, and Ian Shortreed. Reporting in "Salience of Feedback on Error and Its Effect on EFL Writing Quality" (1986), they found that all four groups improved, and that differences in improvement were negligible. In fact, improvement may have been due to writing practice and/or the six other English-language classes the students were taking.

In spite of the uncertainty about effectiveness of error response, there has been a proliferation of methods. A very useful reference work on the subject is *The Gooficon* (1972) by Marina Burt and Carol Kiparsky. They provide classification and explanations of errors and include pedagogical suggestions. Other articles about methods are Maryruth Bracy Farnsworth's "The Cassette Tape Recorder" (1974), Fred Davidson's "Teaching and Testing ESL Composition through Contract Learning" (1984), Michael Witbeck's "Peer Correction Procedures for Intermediate and Advanced ESL Composition Lessons" (1976), and P. R. Sheal and Susan Wood's "Proof-Reading as a Means of Reducing Student Errors" (1981).

Lack of method is the concern of Vivian Zamel after she studied the "comments, reactions and markings" of fifteen teachers on 105 compositions. In "Responding to Student Writing" (1985), her comments are critical, but she makes several constructive suggestions for paper marking.

EVALUATION

Testing in an ESL writing program serves at least four purposes: placement, diagnosis, evaluation of teaching methods, and evaluation of student progress. Whatever the purpose of the test, it must be an accurate, unbiased measure of a student's writing competence or some feature thereof. The central problems concern defining writing competence, ensuring reader reliability, developing valid testing instruments, and determining the correlation of measurements of specific features, such as syntactic maturity, to overall writing competence.

Testing instruments and measures fall roughly into four categories: holistic, analytic, primary trait, and objective. The strengths and weaknesses of these categories are discussed by Kyle Perkins in "On the Use of Composition Scoring Techniques, Objective Measures, and Objective Tests to Evaluate ESL Writing Ability" (1983). Holistic, analytic, and objective scoring will be discussed here.

For holistic scoring, one or more readers assign a simple grade based on an overall impression of the composition. In order for the grades or scores to be reliable, the readers must base their impressions on agreed-upon criteria of competent writing. Also, the writing topic (the testing instrument) must be within the student's conceptual abilities and must be free of cultural bias. Sybil Carlson and Brent Bridgeman discuss defining writing competence in "Testing ESL Student Writers" (1986), a thorough introduction to the topic in general. They also provide a synthesis of the surveys done by ESL researchers to determine what criteria professors use when grading student writing. The most valuable part of their essay, however, is the section on writing assessment parameters in which they discuss several considerations of topic selection and topic pretesting.

Topic selection and reader reliability are also of key importance to analytic scoring. For analytic scoring, the reader assigns an individual score to each of four or five components (organization, content, vocabulary, mechanics, etc.) and totals these to reach an overall score. A good analytic scoring tool is the ESL Composition Profile developed by Holly Jacobs, Stephen Zinkgraf, Deanna Wormuth, V. Faye Hartfiel, and Jane Hughey. They discuss the profile in *Testing ESL Composition* (1981), which is a useful reference for test development, interpretation of test scores, and training readers.

While holistic and analytic scoring are useful for placement and evaluation of student progress, analytic scoring is more useful, though more time-consuming, for diagnosis and evaluation of teaching methods. There is such a wide variety of objective measures that objective scoring might be adapted, with caution, to any evaluation purpose that did not take content into consideration.

Several ESL studies have contributed to an accumulation of data on objective scoring. These studies include "The Construction of a Second Language Acquisition Index of Development" (1977) by Diane Larsen-Freeman and Virginia Strom, "An ESL Index of Development" (1978) by Diane Larsen-Freeman, "Syntactic Skill and ESL Writing Quality" (1979) by Patrick Kameen, "Using Objective Methods of Attained Writing Proficiency to Discriminate among Holistic Evaluations" (1980) by Kyle Perkins, "Composition Correctness Scores" (1981) by Dean Brodkey and Rodney Young, and "Holistic Evaluation of ESL Compositions" (1984) by Taco Justus Homburg. These studies vary widely in format, but most of them found that measures of or related to the number of error-free T-units, the length of error-free T-units, the length of T-units, and the number of errors were useful discriminators between compositions that were also holistically scored. Some measures discriminated between good and poor compositions but not between two levels of good compositions. What surfaces for objective evaluation of ESL writers is the necessity of taking error into account.

Objective scoring can be too time-consuming. The thought of calculating the average length of error-free T-units for each placement composition of seventy incoming students would turn most teachers pale. Brodkey and Young describe a simple error count system that is not time-consuming but acknowledge that it may misplace good writers who make a large number of minor errors. David Davidson, in "Assessing Writing Ability of ESL College Freshmen" (1978), describes a sentence-combining test as a placement or diagnostic tool and argues that a correlation exists between syntactic maturity and quality of ESL writing.

In addition to time, consistency of student writing must be considered. In "Short-Term Changes in EFL Composition Skills" (1979), Bradford Arthur found fluency and errors of individual students varied widely between compositions. Stephen Witte, in "The Reliability of Mean T-Unit Length" (1983), found that the mean T-unit length was not stable for inexperienced writers. Thus, more than one sample of a student's writing may be needed for a valid score. On T-units, see also Stephen Gaies's discussion on applications and limitations in "T-Unit Analysis in Second Language Research" (1980).

CONCLUSION

While teachers have been writing about ESL composition pedagogy for a long time, research in the field is relatively recent. Because existing research studies usually use small groups of students and because most studies are not replicated elsewhere, their conclusions have limited value. More research is needed in all areas of ESL composition, and the careful studies that have been done deserve replication.

REFERENCES

Abbot, G. W. "Intelligibility and Acceptability in Spoken and Written Communication." *Engl Lang Teach J* 33 (1979): 168–75.

Acuna, Dagmar B. "English as a Second Language (ESL) Development: An Investigation into the Relationship of the Students' Reading Comprehension and Writing Ability at the College Level in Puerto Rico." *DAI* 47 (1986): 1201A. New York University.

Arapoff, Nancy. "Controlled Rhetoric Frames." *Engl Lang Teach J* 23 (1968): 27–36.
———. "Writing: A Thinking Process." *TESOL Q* 1 (1967): 33–39.

Arthur, Bradford. "Short-Term Changes in EFL Composition Skills." *On TESOL '79*. Ed. Carlos A. Yorio, Kyle Perkins, and Jacquelyn Schachter. Washington, D.C.: Teachers of English to Speakers of Other Languages, 1979, pp. 330–42.

Ballard, Brigid. "Improving Student Writing: An Integrated Approach to Cultural Adjustment." *Common Ground: Shared Interests in ESP and Communication Studies*. Ed. Ray Williams, John Swales, and John Kirkman. English Language Teaching Documents 177. Oxford, Eng.: Pergamon, 1984, pp. 43–53.

Blair, Linda. "ESL Students and Writing Acquisitions Theory." ERIC, 1983. ED 242 196.

Brière, Eugène. "Quantity before Quality in Second Language Composition." *Lang L* 16 (1966): 141–51.

Brodkey, Dean, and Rodney Young. "Composition Correctness Scores." *TESOL Q* 15 (1981): 159–67.

Brown, H. Douglas. "Affective Factors in Second Language Learning." *The Second Language Classroom: Directions for the 1980's*. Ed. James E. Alatis, Howard

B. Altman, and Penelope M. Alatis. New York: Oxford University Press, 1981, pp. 111–29.

Buckingham, Thomas, and William C. Pech. "An Experience Approach to Teaching Composition." *TESOL Q* 10 (1976): 55–65.

Burt, Marina K. "Error Analysis in the Adult ESL Classroom." *TESOL Q* 9 (1975): 53–63.

Burt, Marina K., and Carol Kiparsky. *The Gooficon: A Repair Manual for English.* Rowley, Mass.: Newbury, 1972.

Carlson, Sybil, and Brent Bridgeman. "Testing ESL Student Writers." *Writing Assessment: Issues and Strategies.* Ed. Karen L. Greenberg, Harvey S. Wiener, and Richard A. Donovan. New York: Longman, 1986, pp. 126–52.

Carpenter, Cristin, and Judy Hunter. "Functional Exercises: Improving Overall Coherence in ESL Writing." *TESOL Q* 15 (1981): 425–34.

Carr, Donna H. "A Second Look at Teaching Reading and Composition." *TESOL Q* 1 (1967): 30–34.

Carrell, Patricia L. "Cohesion Is Not Coherence." *TESOL Q* 16 (1982): 479–88.

———. "Content and Formal Schemata in ESL Reading." *TESOL Q* 21 (1987): 461–81.

Casanave, Christine Pearson. "Comprehension Monitoring in ESL Reading: A Neglected Essential." *TESOL Q* 22 (1988): 285–302.

Chun, Judith. "A Survey of Research in Second Language Acquisition." *Readings on English as a Second Language: For Teachers and Teacher Trainees*, 2nd ed. Ed. Kenneth Croft. Cambridge, Mass.: Winthrop, 1980, pp. 181–98.

Connor, Ulla. "A Study of Cohesion and Coherence in English as a Second Language Students' Writing." *Papers in Linguistics: International Journal of Human Communications* 17 (1984): 301–16.

Corder, S. P. *Error Analysis and Interlanguage.* Oxford: Oxford University Press, 1981.

———. "Idiosyncratic Dialects and Error Analysis." *IRAL* 9 (1971): 147–59.

Crymes, Ruth. "The Relationship of Study about Language to Language Performance: With Special Reference to Nominalization." *TESOL Q* 5 (1971): 217–30.

Davidson, David M. "Assessing Writing Ability of ESL College Freshmen." *Teaching English as a Second Language and Bilingual Education: Themes, Practices, Viewpoints.* Ed. Richard L. Light and Alice H. Osman. Washington, D.C.: Teachers of English to Speakers of Other Languages, 1978, pp. 86–101.

———. "Sentence Combining in an ESL Writing Program." *JBW* 1 (1977): 49–62.

Davidson, Fred. "Teaching and Testing ESL Composition through Contract Learning." ERIC, 1984. ED 245 560.

Davies, Alan, C. Criper, and A.P.R. Howatt, eds. *Interlanguage.* Edinburgh: Edinburgh University Press, 1984.

Dehghanpisheh, Elaine. "Bridging the Gap Between Controlled and Free Composition: Controlled Rhetoric at the Upper-Intermediate Level." *TESOL Q* 13 (1979): 509–19.

Dulay, Heidi, Marina Burt, and Stephen Krashen. *Language Two.* New York: Oxford University Press, 1982.

Dykstra, Gerald. "Eliciting Language Practice in Writing." *Engl Lang Teach J* 19 (1964): 23–26.

Erazmus, Edward T. "Second Language Composition Teaching at the Intermediate Level." *Lang L* 10 (1960): 25–31.

Esau, Helmut, and Michael L. Keene. "A TESOL Model for Native-Language Writing Instruction: In Search of a Model for the Teaching of Writing." *CE* 43 (1981): 694–710.

Falk, Julia S. "Language Acquisition and the Teaching and Learning of Writing." *CE* 41 (1979): 436–47.

Farnsworth, Maryruth Bracy. "The Cassette Tape Recorder: A Bonus or a Bother in ESL Composition Correction." *TESOL Q* 8 (1974): 285–91.

Foss, Karen A., and Armeda C. Reitzel. "A Relational Model for Managing Second Language Anxiety." *TESOL Q* 22 (1988): 437–54.

Friederichs, Jane, and Herbert D. Pierson. "What Are Science Students Expected to Write?" *Engl Lang Teach J* 35 (1981): 407–10.

Gaies, Stephen J. "T-Units Analysis in Second Language Research: Applications, Problems, and Limitations." *TESOL Q* 14 (1980): 53–60.

Gathercole, Virginia. "Some Myths You May Have Heard about First Language Acquisition." *TESOL Q* 22 (1988): 407–35.

Gee, James Paul. "Dracula, the Vampire Lestat, and TESOL." *TESOL Q* 22 (1988): 201–25.

Ghadessy, Mohsen. "Comments on Patricia Carrell's 'Cohesion Is Not Coherence.' " *TESOL Q* 17 (1983): 685–87.

Goldstein, Lynn M. "Standard English: The Only Target for Nonnative Speakers of English?" *TESOL Q* 21 (1987): 417–36.

Gorrell, Donna. "Controlled Composition for Basic Writers." *CCC* 32 (1981): 308–16.

Green, J. F. "Preparing an Advanced Composition Course." *Engl Lang Teach J* 21 (1967): 141–50.

Gregg, Joan. "Comments on Bernard A. Mohan and Winnie Au-Yeung Lo's 'Academic Writing and Chinese Students: Transfer and Developmental Factors.' " *TESOL Q* 20 (1986): 354–57.

Halliday, M.A.K., and Ruqaiya Hasan. *Cohesion in English*. London: Longman, 1976.

Hendrickson, James Michael. "The Effects of Error Correction Treatments upon Adequate and Accurate Communication in the Written Compositions of Adult Learners of English as a Second Language." *DAI* 37 (1977): 7002A. Ohio State University.

———. "Error Correction in Foreign Language Teaching: Recent Theory, Research and Practice." *Mod Lang J* 62 (1978): 387–98.

Hill, Clifford A., and John S. Rittershofer. "An Integrated Approach to Pronunciation and Spelling in ESL Curricula." *On TESOL '76*. Ed. John F. Fanselow and Ruth H. Crymes. Washington, D.C.: Teachers of English to Speakers of Other Languages, 1976, pp. 117–28.

Hill, Susan S., Betty F. Soppelsa, and Gregory K. West. "Teaching ESL Students to Read and Write Experimental-Research Papers." *TESOL Q* 16 (1982): 333–47.

Homburg, Taco Justus. "Holistic Evaluation of ESL Compositions: Can It Be Validated Objectively?" *TESOL Q* 18 (1984): 87–107.

Horn, Vivian. "Using Connectives in Elementary Composition." *Engl Lang Teach J* 26 (1972): 154–59.

———. "Using the 'Ananse Tales Technique' for Composition." *TESOL Q* 8 (1974): 37–42.

Horning, Alice S. *Teaching Writing as a Second Language*. Carbondale: Southern Illinois University Press, 1987.

Horowitz, Daniel M. "Process, Not Product: Less Than Meets the Eye." *TESOL Q* 20 (1986): 141–44.

———. "What Professors Actually Require: Academic Tasks for the ESL Classroom." *TESOL Q* 20 (1986): 445–62.

Houghton, Diane, and Michael Hoey. "Linguistics and Written Discourse: Contrastive Rhetorics." *Annual Review of Applied Linguistics 1982*. Ed. Robert B. Kaplan et al. Rowley: Newbury, 1983, pp. 2–22.

Ibrahim, Muhammad H. "Patterns in Spelling Errors." *Engl Lang Teach J* 32 (1978): 207–12.

Jacobs, Holly L., et al. *Testing ESL Composition: A Practical Approach*. Rowley, Mass.: Newbury, 1981.

Janopoulos, Michael. "The Relationship of Pleasure Reading and Second Language Writing Proficiency." *TESOL Q* 20 (1986): 763–68.

Johns, Ann M. "Coherence and Academic Writing: Some Definitions and Suggestions for Teaching." *TESOL Q* 20 (1986): 247–65.

———. "The ESL Student and the Revision Process: Some Insights from Schema Theory." *JBW* 5 (1986): 70–80.

Kameen, Patrick T. "A Mechanical, Meaningful, and Communicative Framework for ESL Sentence Combining Exercises." *TESOL Q* 12 (1978): 395–401.

———. "Syntactic Skill and ESL Writing Quality." *On TESOL '79*. Ed. Carlos A. Yorio, Kyle Perkins, and Jacquelyn Schachter. Washington, D.C.: Teachers of English to Speakers of Other Languages, 1979, pp. 343–50.

Kaplan, Robert B. "Contrastive Rhetorics: Some Implications for the Writing Process." *Learning to Write: First Language/Second Language*. Ed. Aviva Freedman, Ian Pringle, and Janice Yalden. New York: Longman, 1983, pp. 139–61.

———. "Cultural Thought Patterns in Inter-Cultural Education." *Lang L* 16 (1966): 1–20.

Kaplan, Robert B., et al., eds. *Annual Review of Applied Linguistics: 1982*. Rowley, Mass.: Newbury, 1983.

Khalil, Aziz. "Communicative Error Evaluation: Native Speakers' Evaluation and Interpretation of Errors of Arab EFL Learners." *TESOL Q* 19 (1985): 335–51.

Klassen, Bernard. "Sentence-Combining Exercises as an Aid to Expediting Syntactic Fluency in Learning English as a Second Language." *DAI* 37 (1977): 6258A. University of Minnesota.

Krahnke, Karl J., and Mary Ann Christison. "Recent Language Research and Some Language Teaching Principles." *TESOL Q* 17 (1983): 625–49.

Krashen, Stephen. "The Input Hypothesis." *Current Issues in Bilingual Education*. Ed. James E. Alatis. Georgetown University Roundtable on Languages and Linguistics, 1980. Washington, D.C.: Georgetown University Press, 1980, pp. 168–80.

———. "The Monitor Model for Second-Language Acquisition." *Second Language Acquisition and Foreign Language Teaching*. Ed. Rosario C. Gingras. Washington, D.C.: Center for Applied Linguistics, 1978, pp. 1–26.

———. *Second Language Acquisition and Second Language Learning*. Oxford, Eng.: Pergamon, 1981.

———. *Writing: Research, Theory, and Applications*. Language Teaching Methodology Series. Oxford, Eng.: Pergamon, 1984.

Kroll, Barbara. "Sorting Out Writing Problems." *On TESOL '78*. Ed. Charles H. Blatchford and Jacquelyn Schachter. Washington, D.C.: Teachers of English to Speakers of Other Languages, 1978, pp. 176–82.

Larsen-Freeman, Diane. "An ESL Index of Development." *TESOL Q* 12 (1978): 439–48.

Larsen-Freeman, Diane, and Virginia Strom. "The Construction of a Second Language Acquisition Index of Development." *Lang L* 27 (1977): 123–34.

Lieber, Paula Ellen. "Cohesion in ESL Students' Expository Writing: A Descriptive Study." *DAI* 41 (1980): 657A. New York University.

Ludwig, Jeannette. "Native-Speaker Judgments of Second-Language Learners' Efforts at Communication: A Review." *Mod Lang J* 66 (1982): 274–83.

McKay, Sandra. "Communicative Writing." *TESOL Q* 13 (1979): 73–80.

———. "A Focus on Prewriting Strategies." *On TESOL '81*. Ed. Mary Hines and William Rutherford. Washington, D.C.: Teachers of English to Speakers of Other Languages, 1982, pp. 89–95.

Martin, Anne V. "Teaching Academic Vocabulary to Foreign Graduate Students." *TESOL Q* 10 (1976): 91–97.

Matalene, Carolyn. "Contrastive Rhetoric: An American Writing Teacher in China." *CE* 47 (1985): 789–808.

Mito, Yuichi. "Some Contrastive Features of English and Japanese." *Lang L* 11 (1961): 71–76.

Mohan, Bernard A., and Winnie Au-Yeung Lo. "Academic Writing and Chinese Students: Transfer and Developmental Factors." *TESOL Q* 19 (1985): 515–34.

Moody, K. W. "Controlled Composition Frames." *Engl Lang Teach J* 19 (1965): 146–55.

Morrison, Donald M., and Graham Low. "Monitoring and the Second Language Learner." *Language and Communication*. Ed. Jack C. Richards and Richard W. Schmidt. London: Longman, 1983, pp. 228–49.

Makuttash, Lewis. "Problems in Error Analysis." *Papers and Studies in Contrastive Linguistics*. Ed. Jacek Fisiak. The Polish-English Contrastive Project 13. Poznań: Adam Michiewicz University; Washington, D.C.: Center for Applied Linguistics, 1981, pp. 261–74.

Nemser, William. "Approximate Systems of Foreign Language Learners." *IRAL* 9 (1971): 115–23.

Palmer, David. "Expressing Error Gravity." *Engl Lang Teach J* 34 (1980): 93–96.

Paulston, Christina Bratt. "Teaching Writing in the ESOL Classroom: Techniques of Controlled Composition." *TESOL Q* 6 (1972): 33–59.

Perkins, Kyle. "On the Use of Composition Scoring Techniques, Objective Measures, and Objective Tests to Evaluate ESL Writing Ability." *TESOL Q* 17 (1983): 651–71.

———. "Using Objective Methods of Attained Writing Proficiency to Discriminate among Holistic Evaluations." *TESOL Q* 14 (1980): 61–69.

Pfingstag, Nancy. "Showing Writing: Modeling the Process." *TESOL Newsletter Supplement No. 1: Writing and Composition* 18 (1984): 1–3.

Pica, Teresa, Richard Young, and Catherine Doughty. "The Impact of Interaction on Comprehension." *TESOL Q* 21 (1987): 737–58.

Pimsarn, Pratin. "The Reading and Writing Relationship: A Correlational Study of English as a Second Language Learners at the Collegiate Level." *DAI* 47 (1987): 2974A. North Texas State University.

Pincas, Anita. "Structural Linguistics and Systematic Composition Teaching to Students of English as a Foreign Language." *Lang L* 12 (1962): 185–94.

Raimes, Ann. "Composition: Controlled by the Teacher, Free for the Student." *On TESOL '76*. Ed. John F. Fanselow and Ruth H. Crymes. Washington, D.C.: Teachers of English to Speakers of Other Languages, 1976, pp. 183–94.

———. "Tradition and Revolution in ESL Teaching." *TESOL Q* 17 (1983): 535–52.

———. "What Unskilled ESL Students Do as They Write: A Classroom Study of Composing." *TESOL Q* 19 (1985): 229–58.

Rankin, Dorothy S. "Comments on Patricia Carrell's 'Cohesion Is Not Coherence.' " *TESOL Q* 18 (1984): 158–61.

Reid, Joy. "Comments on Vivian Zamel's 'The Composing Process of Advanced ESL Students: Six Case Studies.' " *TESOL Q* 18 (1984): 149–53.

———. "The Learning Style Preferences of ESL Students." *TESOL Q* 21 (1987): 87–111.

———. "The Radical Outliner and the Radical Brainstormer: A Perspective on the Composing Process." *TESOL Q* 18 (1984): 529–33.

Richards, Jack C. "A Non-Contrastive Approach to Error Analysis." *Engl Lang Teach J* 25 (1971): 204–19.

———. "The Role of Vocabulary Teaching." *TESOL Q* 10 (1976): 77–89.

Rizzo, Betty, and Santiago Villafane. "Spanish Language Influences on Written English." *JBW* 1 (1975): 62–71.

Robb, Thomas, Steven Ross, and Ian Shortreed. "Salience of Feedback on Error and Its Effect on EFL Writing Quality." *TESOL Q* 20 (1986): 83–95.

Robinett, Betty Wallace. *Teaching English to Speakers of Other Languages: Substance and Technique*. Minneapolis: University of Minnesota Press; New York: McGraw-Hill, 1978.

Rohrer, Josef. "Learning Styles and Teaching Vocabulary." *Current Issues in Bilingual Education*. Ed. James E. Alatis. Georgetown University Roundtable on Languages and Linguistics, 1980. Washington, D.C.: Georgetown University Press, 1980, pp. 280–88.

Sally, Ovaiza. "The Teaching of Spelling." *Engl Lang Teach J* 30(1976): 219–24.

Scarcella, Robin Cameron. "Cohesion in the Writing Development of Native and Non-Native English Speakers." *DAI* 45 (1984): 1386A. University of Southern California.

Schachter, Jacquelyn. "An Error in Error Analysis." *Lang L* 24 (1974): 205–14.

———. "Nutritional Needs of Language Learners." *On TESOL '82: Pacific Perspectives on Language Learning and Teaching*. Ed. Mark A. Clarke and Jean Handscombe. Washington, D.C.: Teachers of English to Speakers of Other Languages, 1983, pp. 175–89.

Schachter, Jacquelyn, and Marianne Celce-Murcia. "Some Reservations Concerning Error Analysis." *TESOL Q* 11 (1977): 441–51.

Schane, Sanford. "Linguistics, Spelling, and Pronunciation." *TESOL Q* 4 (1970): 137–41.

Schumann, John H. "The Acculturation Model for Second-Language Acquisition." *Second Language Acquisition and Foreign Language Teaching*. Ed. Rosario C. Gingras. Washington, D.C.: Center for Applied Linguistics, 1978, pp. 27–50.

Scott, Margaret Sue, and G. Richard Tucker. "Error Analysis and English-Language Strategies of Arab Students." *Lang L* 24 (1974): 69–97.

Selinker, Larry. "Interlanguage." *IRAL* 10 (1972): 209–31.

Selinker, Larry, and Louis Trimble. "Formal Written Communication and ESL." *JTWC* 4 (1974): 81–91.

Sheal, P. R., and Susan Wood. "Proof-Reading as a Means of Reducing Student Errors." *Engl Lang Teach J* 35 (1981): 405–7.

Silber, Patricia. "Teaching Written English as a Second Language." *CCC* 30 (1979): 296–300.

Snow, Marguerite Ann, and Donna M. Brinton. "Content-Based Language Instruction: Investigating the Effectiveness of the Adjunct Model." *TESOL Q* 22 (1989): 553–74.

Spack, Ruth. "Initiating ESL Students into the Academic Discourse Community: How Far Should We Go?" *TESOL Q* 22 (1988): 29–51.

———. "Invention Strategies and the ESL College Composition Student." *TESOL Q* 18 (1984): 649–70.

Spack, Ruth, and Catherine Sadow. "Student-Teacher Working Journals in ESL Freshman Composition." *TESOL Q* 17 (1983): 575–93.

Sridhar, S. N. "Contrastive Analysis, Error Analysis and Interlanguage: Three Phases of One Goal." *Stud Lang L* 1 (1975): 60–94. Rpt. in *Readings on English as a Second Language: For Teachers and Teacher Trainees*, 2nd ed. Ed. Kenneth Croft. Cambridge, Mass.: Winthrop, 1980, pp. 91–119.

Stevick, Earl W. "The Levertov Machine." *Research in Second Language Acquisition*. Ed. Robin C. Scarcella and Stephen D. Krashen. Rowley, Mass.: Newbury, 1980, pp. 28–35.

———. *Memory, Meaning and Method: Some Psychological Perspectives on Language Learning*. Rowley, Mass.: Newbury, 1976.

———. *Teaching Languages: A Way and Ways*. Rowley, Mass.: Newbury, 1980.

Taylor, Barry P. "Content and Written Form: A Two-Way Street." *TESOL Q* 15 (1981): 5–13.

———. "Teaching Composition to Low-Level ESL Students." *TESOL Q* 10 (1976): 309–20.

Taylor, D. S. "English Spelling: A Help Rather Than a Hindrance." *Engl Lang Teach J* 35 (1981): 316–21.

Thompson-Panos, Karyn, and Maria Thomas-Ružić. "The Least You Should Know About Arabic: Implications for the ESL Writing Instructor." *TESOL Q* 17 (1983): 609–23.

Tricomi, Elizabeth Taylor. "Krashen's Second-Language Acquisition Theory and the Teaching of Edited American English." *JBW* 5 (1986): 59–69.

Vann, Roberta J., Daisy E. Meyer and Frederick O. Lorenz. "Error Gravity: A Study of Faculty Opinion of ESL Errors." *TESOL Q* 18 (1984): 427–40.

Wardhaugh, Ronald. "The Contrastive Analysis Hypothesis." *TESOL Q* 4 (1970): 123–30.

Watson, Cynthia B. "The Use and Abuse of Models in the ESL Writing Class." *TESOL Q* 16 (1982): 5–14.

Watson-Gegeo, Karen Ann. "Ethnography in ESL: Defining the Essentials." *TESOL Q* 22 (1988): 575–92.

Weissberg, Robert C. "Given and New: Paragraph Development Models from Scientific English." *TESOL Q* 18 (1984): 485–500.

Widdowson, H. G. "Literacy and Scientific Uses of English." *Engl Lang Teach J* 28 (1974): 282–92.

Winterowd, W. Ross. "From Classroom Practice into Psycholinguistic Theory." *Learning to Write: First Language/Second Language*. Ed. Aviva Freedman, Ian Pringle, and Janice Yalden. New York: Longman, 1983, pp. 237–46.

Witbeck, Michael C. "Peer Correction Procedures for Intermediate and Advanced ESL Composition Lessons." *TESOL Q* 10 (1976): 321–26.

Witte, Stephen P. "The Reliability of Mean T-Unit Length: Some Questions for Research in Written Composition." *Learning to Write: First Language/Second Language*. Ed. Aviva Freedman, Ian Pringle, and Janice Yalden. New York: Longman, 1983, pp. 171–77.

Witte, Stephen P., and Lester Faigley. "Coherence, Cohesion and Writing Quality." *CCC* 32 (1981): 189–204.

Wyatt, Victor. "An Analysis of Errors in Composition Writing." *Engl Lang Teach J* 27 (1973): 177–86.

Zamel, Vivian. "The Composing Processes of Advanced ESL Students: Six Case Studies." *TESOL Q* 17 (1983): 165–87.

———. "Re-evaluating Sentence-Combining Practice." *TESOL Q* 14 (1980): 81–90.

———. "Responding to Student Writing." *TESOL Q* 19 (1985): 79–101.

———. "Teaching Composition in the ESL Classroom: What We Can Learn from Research in the Teaching of English." *TESOL Q* 10 (1976): 67–76.

———. "Writing: The Process of Discovering Meaning." *TESOL Q* 16 (1982): 195–209.

PART III

Pedagogical Perspectives

7

Basic Writing Courses and Programs

Michael D. Hood

The proliferation of basic writing courses and the growth of basic writing programs are a response to the decline in the level of preparedness of entering college freshmen. "For, even in the most prestigious colleges and universities," as Barbara Quint Gray and Virginia B. Slaughter (1981) note, "more students than ever before read and write at a level that was formerly regarded as inadequate for college" ("Writing" 14). In fact, according to Betty Bamberg (1978), nearly half of the freshmen at Berkeley and Los Angeles, the two largest campuses of the University of California, which admits only the top 12.5 percent of California high school students, are required to take Subject A, a remedial composition course ("Composition Instruction Does Make a Difference" 47). And in a recent national survey of 1,269 colleges and universities (1983), Marie J. Lederman, Susan R. Ryzewic, and Michael Ribaudo report that more than nine out of ten institutions now offer basic writing courses (*Assessment and Improvement of the Academic Skills of Entering Freshmen*).

Several factors explain the decline in student writing ability. First, students traditionally bound for college are not as well prepared as they once were. Martha Maxwell (1979), for example, accounts for the absolute drop in Scholastic Aptitude Test and College Entrance Examination Board scores because of the declining rigor of high school education, resulting from automatic promotion, grade inflation, and an erosion in the reading level for high school textbooks and in enrollment in high school English courses (*Improving Student Learning Skills*). "Willy-nilly," to quote the blunt language of *Newsweek* (1975), "the U.S. education system is spawning a generation of semi-literates" ("Why Johnny Can't Write" 58).

Second, the policy of open admissions at most two-year and many four-year colleges has made college accessible to students who, in the past, would never have considered higher education. Mina Shaughnessy (1977), characterizing open admissions students at City University of New York in the mid-seventies, states that they are "students whose difficulties with the written language seemed of a different order from those of the other groups, as if they had come, you might say, from a different country, or at least through different schools" (*Errors and Expectations* 2).

And third, because of declining enrollments, colleges not only are admitting students to whom they would have denied admission in the past, but in order to improve the retention rate of such students, they are requiring increasing numbers of freshmen to take courses in basic writing, reading, and mathematics. This trend in remediation will in all probability continue well into the next century, for, as Harold L. Hodgkinson (1986) points out, the number of students graduating from American high schools will decline each year until the year 2000, and the freshman class of 2000 "will prove very difficult to educate because of the larger proportions who are poor, who do not speak English, and who have physical handicaps" ("Reform?" 274).

Just as courses and programs in basic writing have grown in an attempt to meet the needs of both traditional and nontraditional students, so has interest in their design, implementation, and effectiveness. One approach to examining the growing body of scholarship dealing with basic writing courses and programs is to discuss it in terms of what Susan S. Obler (1983) refers to as the five major patterns of effective programs (for underprepared students), which include "thorough assessment, systematic instruction, careful staffing, consistent evaluation, and centralized program coordination" ("Programs for the Underprepared Student" 22).

In the context of basic writing programs, "thorough assessment" involves evaluating students for placement, diagnosis, and proficiency. While there is general agreement about the importance of assessment, experts disagree about the relative merits of objective tests and writing samples as the basis for placement in writing courses. "Systematic instruction" includes both teaching methodology and course design. The disagreement over course design is the result of differing views about two issues: language acquisition and the purpose for basic writing courses. That is, do students improve more readily when writing is taught hierarchically as a sequence of discrete skills, or when it is taught holistically as an organic process? And are basic writing courses intended primarily to meet the demand for certification or to promote liberal learning? "Careful staffing" refers to both the instructional faculty and support services such as writing laboratories and peer tutoring. "Consistent evaluation" involves not only the methods for evaluating both courses and programs, but also the issue of whether or not courses and programs in basic writing are effective. And "centralized program coordination" pertains to administration. Two frequently debated issues relating to administration of basic writing courses and programs concern the place of basic writing courses in the college curriculum and whether or not such courses ought to carry college credit. This essay, then, will review scholarship relevant to assessment, course design, evaluation, and administration of basic writing courses and programs.

ASSESSMENT

Assessment in basic writing programs generally involves evaluating students for three different purposes: for placement, done before the course begins to determine who should enroll; for diagnosis, done at the beginning of the course to discover each student's particular instructional needs; and, for proficiency, usually done near or at the end of the course to determine whether or not a student has fulfilled the minimal requirements for writing competency. Before reviewing each of these purposes, however, I call the reader's attention to Rosentene B. Purnell's "A Survey of the Testing of Writing Proficiency in College" (1982), which summarizes the testing trends in each of these areas of evaluation. Purnell reports that placement and diagnostic testing are widely accepted and on the rise, that most campuses set the freshman year as the point of competency assessment, that the majority of schools use a writing sample in their testing program, and that most of those using a writing sample use holistic scoring methods.

Other surveys of assessment procedures can be found in three dissertations that review basic writing programs; they are Gretchen N. Vik's "Developmental Composition in College" (1976), Allison Wilson's "A Survey of College-Level Remedial Writing Programs" (1980), and Etta M. Stewart's "Remedial Freshman English Composition Course and Program Offerings in Selected Four-Year Colleges and Universities" (1982). Also see William Lutz's annotated bibliography of writing assessment in *Writing Assessment* (1986), edited by Karen L. Greenberg, Harvey S. Wiener, and Richard A. Donovan.

Placement, according to D. A. Frisbie (1982), is the "process of making the best possible match between a student's current achievement status and the prerequisites of various alternate course sequences" ("Methods of Evaluating Course Placement Systems" 133). Making the "best possible match" is important for both student and school, for the student because it improves learning and reduces frustration and for the school because it uses resources more efficiently and has the potential to improve retention of marginal students. Measuring a student's "current achievement status" in writing for placement in a basic writing program is done in one of two ways: either by the use of indirect measures (objective tests), or by a combination of indirect measures and direct measures (a writing sample).

Indirect measures or objective tests used for placement in basic writing courses fall into two categories—those tests administered by the institution that are either institution-designed or published tests, and standardized tests such as the Scholastic Aptitude Test (SAT) or the College Entrance Examination Board (CEEB) taken by students prior to enrolling in college. Writing about an institution-designed test in "A Successful Placement Test for Basic Writing" (1980), Nancy

W. Johnson explains how to construct a valid and reliable multiple-choice examination that "will provide the same, or nearly the same, information about a student's knowledge of grammar and rhetoric that a writing sample will" (97–98). Since the test has been used for placement of basic writers at Northern Virginia Community College, Johnson notes that classes are more homogeneous, that the course-completion rate is higher, that there has been a sizable reduction in the number of students who add and drop, and that there is a significant correlation between the test score and course grade. In regard to published tests administered by the institution, Barbara Quint Gray and Virginia B. Slaughter ("Writing" [1980]) provide an excellent review of those tests used by various City University of New York (CUNY) campuses, in addition to indicating the cutoff scores for each test and their placement equivalencies in the CUNY programs (21–22). Essays are read only for those students "whose objective scores cluster at the dividing point between two different levels" (22). Standardized tests are used exclusively for determining placement in the expository writing programs, for example, at both New York University (NYU) and the University of California (UC) at Berkeley. Paula Johnson in "Writing Face to Face" (1979) points out that all freshmen at NYU are placed according to their SAT verbal score into one of three levels of expository writing: Honors (650 and above), Regular (500–649), and Developmental (500 and below). And Sabina Thorne Johnson in "Remedial English" (1972) reports that any student admitted to UC Berkeley with a CEEB-ECT score below 550 is required to enroll in Subject A, remedial English, during the first quarter.

While indirect measures of writing ability may seem more practical when large numbers of students must be considered for placement in writing courses, they are, it is generally agreed, a less valid measure of writing performance than a writing sample. In contrast to a multiple-choice test, a writing sample "involves students in the entire complex activity of generating and sustaining writing" (Gray and Slaughter 23). Because holistic evaluation permits large numbers of writing samples to be scored quickly and reliably, more and more schools are turning to a writing sample in addition to objective measures for placement of students in writing courses. (For an overview of methods of holistic grading, see Charles R. Cooper, "Holistic Evaluation of Writing" [1977], and for a discussion of the comparative merits of these methods see Lee Odell and Charles R. Cooper, "Procedures for Evaluating Writing" [1980].)

For example, the writing program at CUNY, as described by Gray and Slaughter, has adopted (in conjunction with the objective tests mentioned above) general impression marking that requires readers to rank essays on a six-point scale according to a carefully specified criteria (given in full on 25–26). David Bartholomae ("Teaching Basic Writing" [1979]) explains that students at the University of Pittsburgh are placed in basic writing as a result of their scores on the Nelson-Denney Reading Test and on an essay holistically scored. The "range-finders" or criteria for evaluating the essay include type and frequency of error, coherence, and ability to draw general conclusions (106–7). In designing the basic writing program at Ohio State University, Andrea A. Lunsford and Sara Garnes ("Anatomy of a Basic Writing Program" [1979]) required students to write an essay that was marked for coherence, basic sentence combining, sentence sense, usage and agreement, and spelling. Students weak in coherence were placed in the two-course sequence (100.01 and 100.02); those who were not, enrolled in 100.02. Lunsford and Garnes turned to a holistically scored writing sample because the ACT (American College Test) English Test at the lower scores (below 15) did not correlate with the student writing ability. (Also see Edward M. White and Leon L. Thomas, "Racial Minorities and Writing Skills Assessment" [1981], who demonstrate that the Test of Standard Written English [TSWE] does not correlate with minority writing ability.) And at J. Sargeant Reynolds Community College, the writing placement test, according to Arthur L. Dixon ("Basic Writing at J. Sargeant Reynolds Community College" [1980]), consists of having students correct errors in ten sentences and write a ten-sentence paragraph that is holistically scored. "The paragraph," Dixon points out, "is a better indication of skills and can either confirm or reverse the preliminary judgment made on the basis of [ten] sentences" (36).

Research confirms that the practice of using *both* indirect and direct measures of writing ability is the best method for placing students in writing courses. Robert G. Noreen ("Placement Procedure for Freshman Composition" [1977]), after comparing qualities evident in a well-written essay with possible means of testing those qualities, concluded that "the best measure of composition ability appears to be a combination of a writing sample, reliably evaluated, and an objective test which would focus on the *critical skills* necessary to produce an effective essay" (142). And Donna Gorrell ("Toward Determining a Minimal Competency Entrance Examination for Freshman Composition" [1983]) discovered that the best predictors of success in English 101 (at Illinois State University), as determined by a holistic rating of the final essay for English 101, were a holistic rated placement essay and the ACT English score.

Diagnosis, the second aspect of assessment, is undertaken after students have been placed in basic writing courses. Its purpose is to determine the specific needs of individuals so that a program of instruction can be tailored to meet those needs. Rexford Brown presents an overview of diagnostic testing in "Choosing or Creating an Appropriate Writing Test" (1980), in which he (1) points out that neither standardized multiple-choice tests nor holistically scored essays are adequate for diagnostic purposes and (2) reviews the Educational Testing Service's Composition Evaluation Scales (CES) and the National Assessment's "primary trait" scoring as diagnostic measures of writing. At CUNY, for example, instructors use the Hunter College Writing Profile and Score Key, which pinpoints problem areas in a student's writing. The Profile is particularly helpful because it evaluates subskills that correlate with the criteria on CUNY's holistic assessment scale (Gray and Slaughter 26–29). At Surry Community College, as reported by Milton G. Spann and Virginia Foxx ("Basic Writing Programs of the Western North Carolina Consortium" [1980]), students in basic writing begin with a test to determine their areas of strength and weakness. Students with diagnosed weaknesses are required to complete self-contained, instructional modules that treat the specific skills needing improvement. In the basic writing program at American River College, Helen Mills ("Language and Composition" [1976]) explains that students, after a writing and a sentence pretest, begin either with sentence, paragraph, or essay writing. Muriel Harris in "Individualized Diagnosis" (1978), however, points out that diagnosis should go beyond identifying a student's initial writing deficiencies to include ongoing diagnosis during instruction and diagnosis of student attitudes toward writing. Harris's interest in both the cognitive and affective domains has merit, for, as Obler points out, "the strategies that appear to achieve the greatest success combine basic skills testing with assessment of attitudes toward learning, sometimes including self-concept" (23).

Measuring writing proficiency, the third aspect of assessment, is done in several ways. Course grades have been a traditional method; in fact, Allison Wilson, in "A Survey of College-Level Remedial Writing Programs" (1980), reports that nearly half of the respondents used standard letter grades to evaluate writing performance. The difficulty with course grades, however, is that they are rarely based on clearly articulated standards that inform program-wide evaluation. English faculty acting independently not only have different standards about what constitutes minimal competency, but also, as Joseph Williams makes clear in "Reevaluating Evaluating" (1978), they may call for one style of writing while being unaware that they prefer another.

Another method for measuring writing proficiency is through testing. "Measuring Writing Ability by Using Proficiency Tests," the third chapter of *Teaching and Assessing Writing* (1985) by Edward M. White, presents an excellent overview of various proficiency testing models along with the benefits and drawbacks of each. And Karen L. Greenberg, in "Competency Testing" (1982), provides writing teachers with essential information relevant to this type of testing, taking up such matters as test validity and reliability, establishing a minimum score, and providing help for those who fail. In those programs that test for minimal writing competency, the point at which a student takes the writing proficiency test will vary from program to program. It may be during the freshman year or sometime later in the student's career. (See, for example, Sarah Warshauer Freedman and William S. Robinson's description of a junior-level proficiency test in "Testing Proficiency in Writing at San Francisco State University" [1982].) However, students in many basic writing courses, before taking the next course in the writing sequence, must pass a writing proficiency test. For example, at LaGuardia Community College, all students in English 100 (Fundamentals of Effective Writing) must pass an exit examination to be eligible for English 101. The criteria for the examination, the procedures for its administration and grading, and the process for appeal are outlined by Roberta S. Matthews in "The Evolution of One College's Attempt to Evaluate Student Writing" (1978). Other essays that describe exit examinations for basic writing courses include "With

No Apology'' (1978) by Rosemary Hake and "Testing Basic Writers' Proficiency" (1983) by Kathleen E. Kiefer. Also see "Teaching Basic Writing" (1979), in which David Bartholomae reviews the criteria of the exit examination for basic writing courses at the University of Pittsburgh.

A third method for assessing writing proficiency is by the writing portfolio. Rather than taking an examination, students submit a sampling of their best work done over the course of a semester to be evaluated anonymously by instructors in the writing program. Two essays outlining the procedures for and benefits of the portfolio system as a means of establishing minimum standards for writing are "The Portfolio System" (1978) by James E. Ford and Gregory Larkin and "Portfolios as a Substitute for Proficiency Examinations" (1986) by Peter Elbow and Pat Belanoff.

COURSE DESIGN

There are two orientations around which it is possible to group courses in basic writing. The first orientation is analytic. From this perspective, it is assumed that writing can best be taught when it is divided into discrete skills. Courses reflecting this orientation are generally form centered, emphasize correctness, and are organized so that students move from less to more complex skills as the course progresses. The second orientation is synthetic and holistic. From this perspective, it is assumed that writing can best be taught by engaging students in questions of substance. Courses reflecting this orientation are idea centered and organized so that students learn the conventions of academic discourse, in part by composing a response to their reading of serious texts. From the perspective of the first orientation, English is perceived as a socializing discipline to help students meet the demands of certification; from the perspective of the second orientation, English is perceived as an individuating discipline that promotes liberal learning and liberation. Essays that discuss these two contradictory impulses of basic writing courses include "What Happens When Basic Writers Come to College?" (1986) by Patricia Bizzell; "Reconsidering the Links Between Teaching and Assessing Writing" (chapter 1) in *Teaching and Assessing Writing* (1985) by Edward M. White; "Assignments for Basic Writers" (1986, 92–94) by Andrea A. Lunsford; "An Introduction to Basic Writing" (1980) by Lawrence N. Kasden; "Deciphering the Academic Hieroglyph" (1978) by Louise Yelin; and "An Exhortation for Teachers of English in Open-Admissions Programs" (1974) by Joan Baum.

Analytically designed courses tend to follow one of four patterns. The first pattern organizes instruction by sentence, paragraph, and essay writing. The basic writing program at Northern Illinois University, for example, has, at its center, a course organized by this pattern. According to Vernon E. Lattin ("A Program for Basic Writing" [1978]), "students must demonstrate writing proficiency in three areas: the sentence, the paragraph, and the essay. An examination for each area is given at five-week intervals *en masse* to all students" (314).

Arthur L. Dixon ("Basic Writing" [1980]) explains that students placed in the basic writing course at J. Sargeant Reynolds Community College study basic grammar, standard grammar and usage, sentence combining, and finally paragraph writing. And as Helen Mills ("Language and Composition" [1976]) points out in describing the basic writing program at American River College, students master writing step by step through sequential instruction in sentence, paragraph, and essay writing.

As a variation on the above, some courses focus only on one of these units of discourse. For example, Jacqueline Griffin ("Remedial Composition at an Open-Door College" [1969]) reports that the basic writing courses at Essex County College deal exclusively with sentence combining. Janice N. Hays ("Teaching the Grammar of Discourse" [1980]) also describes a sentence-level basic writing course; students learn the strategies for manipulating basic sentence patterns that are analogous to the strategies for manipulating larger units of discourse such as the paragraph and essay. The two courses in the basic writing program at Ohio State, designed by Andrea Lunsford and Sara Garnes ("Anatomy of a Basic Writing Program" [1979]), focus on paragraph-level skills. Also see the third chapter of Lunsford's dissertation, "An Historical, Descriptive, and Evaluative Study of Remedial English in American Colleges and Universities" (1977). And in "The COMP-LAB Project" (1979), Mary Epes, Carolyn Kirkpatrick, and Michael G. Southwell point out that since the burden of explaining grammatical concepts is the responsibility of the writing laboratory at York College, CUNY, instructors in the classroom are able to devote time to teaching composition, namely free writing and theme writing in which students isolate, support, and develop main ideas. Also see *An Evaluation of the COMP-LAB Project* (1980) by Epes and colleagues.

A second pattern of analytically designed courses organizes instruction by the rhetorical modes, which are usually ordered hierarchically so that students progress from the concrete to the abstract. Harvey S. Wiener ("Basic Writing" [1980]), for example, first instructs students at the City University of New York, LaGuardia, in the construction of sensory detail, which is followed by having them write paragraphs of description, narration, and illustration. For a more complete outline of this course, see Appendix A ("Suggested Day Plans" 249–56) of Wiener's *The Writing Room* (1981). In the rhetoric program at Boston University's College of Basic Studies, according to Harry Crosby ("The Rhetoric Program" [1980]), students, after being taught the conventions of the five-paragraph theme, write papers informed by the rhetorical modes, including narration, description, definition, process analysis, classification, and comparison-contrast; argumentation is taught second semester. Essays are marked according to a "Theme Analysis Blank" that rates each essay according to purpose, structure, substance, style, conventions, and mechanics. In "Teaching the Thinking Process" (1976), Ann Petrie similarly combines a strict form of the essay with five essay patterns that she terms personal, proposal, critical, contrast-comparison, and evaluation. And Jeanne Desy ("Reasoned Writing for Basic Students" [1976]) has students write paragraphs or papers using "modes of informal reasoning" in the following order of difficulty: causal analysis, induction, deduction, analogy, and decision making. Also see Richard A. Shine's dissertation, "The Remediation Conundrum" (1979), which presents a curriculum for basic writers based on "a sequence of carefully phrased assignments that builds cumulatively in complexity on the cognitive, stylistic, linguistic, and rhetorical levels" (1439A).

Thomas J. Farrell ("Developing Literacy" [1978]; "Literacy, the Basics, and All That Jazz" [1977]; and "Open Admissions, Orality, and Literacy" [1974]), whose ideas are based on the work of Walter J. Ong, offers an interesting variation on the rhetorical-modes approach to course design. Because Farrell believes that individuals "recapitulate the history of the race with respect to the development of the communications arts, moving from narrative to rhetoric to logic" ("Developing Literacy" 50), he focuses on the use of detail in fictional or autobiographical narratives and on such rhetorical concerns as organization, stating a purpose, narrowing the topic, and writing appropriately for a particular audience. Editing, in Farrell's view, should be taught only after students achieve fluency. The course described by Marie Ponsot ("Total Immersion" [1976]) is based on a similar theoretical perspective. Students first read literature in the oral tradition and write fables, parables, and riddles, moving from narrative to thesis (moral). In the second half of the course, students reverse the order by stating the thesis first and then supporting it by a narrative. For a detailed outline of such a course, see Chapter 15 of *Beat Not the Poor Desk* (1982) by Marie Ponsot and Rosemary Deen.

A third pattern of analytically designed courses organizes instruction around a hierarchy of cognitive skills. That is, students are directly involved in the development of cognitive skills as a part of writing (and reading) instruction. For example, Anna Berg and Gerald Coleman, in "A Cognitive Approach to Teaching the Developmental Student" (1985), describe the "Cognitive Project" at Passaic County Community College in which students receive training in twelve cognitive processes that underlie basic reading and writing skills. And Karl K. Taylor ("*Doors* English" [1979]) requires students in basic writing at Illinois Central College to perform concrete cognitive exercises to ensure that they understand the concept behind each of the rhetorical modes. For a more detailed treatment of this approach, see Taylor's dissertation, "If Not Grammar, What?" (1978).

A fourth pattern of analytically designed courses could be characterized as comprehensive. That is, such a pattern deals with word- and sentence-level concerns (spelling, vocabulary, syntax, punctuation, and grammar); patterns of organization (rhetorical modes); the paragraph, essay, and research paper; and the writing process (prewriting, composing, and editing). Mina Shaughnessy, in the final chapter of *Errors and Expectations* (1977), outlines the three-course sequence in such a program (284–90). for detailed descriptions of the courses that Shaughnessy's outline suggests, see Gray and Slaughter (27–44), and Virginia B. Slaughter and Harvey S. Wiener, "Basic Skills Programs at the City University of New York" (1981).

The holistic orientation is the second orientation around which it is possible to group courses in basic writing. Holistically designed courses, although their surface features may differ, are based on four assumptions: first, that language is acquired unconsciously rather than consciously learned; second, that reading ("comprehensible input") is integral to writing improvement; third, that writing needs to be tied to a writer's sense of meaning, purpose, and social context (i.e., meaning takes precedence over form); and fourth, that errors in writing can be seen as evidence of competence and a sign of progress. Two excellent discussions of this perspective are available in Karen L. Greenberg's "Research on Basic Writers" (1987) and Stephen D. Krashen's *Writing* (1984).

Holistically designed courses tend to fall into one of two categories: those that emphasize reading so that students will acquire the language and conventions of academic discourse, and those that emphasize interaction with the social context so that students will become conscious of oppressive social structures. David Bartholomae in "Teaching Basic Writing" (1979) describes two holistically designed courses at the University of Pittsburgh that emphasize reading in order to make the language and methods of the academy available to basic writing students. Basic Writing, a one-semester course, deals with a single issue (such as identity and change); requires students to read several primary texts relating to this issue; and encourages students, through numerous writing assignments, to become conscious of the writing experience, to analyze writing as a problem-solving procedure, to see writing as a way of knowing, and to discover a method for analyzing their own writing for error. Basic Writing and Reading, a two-semester course, attempts to teach students, in addition to the above, how to compose readings for primary texts. In "Facts, Artifacts, and Counterfacts" (1987), Bartholomae and Anthony R. Petrosky present a more extensive theoretical account of the connection between reading and writing underlying the Basic Writing and Reading course. In addition, two articles that describe courses for adult basic writers and readers based on the model developed by Bartholomae are "Building Thought on Paper" (1983) by Elaine O. Lees and "Conflict and Power" (1987) by Nicholas Coles and Susan V. Wall.

Other essays in the literature of basic writing emphasize the importance of reading in course design. Marilyn S. Samuels, for example, in "Norman Holland's 'New Paradigm' " (1978), describes a basic writing course taught at City College, CUNY and at Case Western Reserve University in which students were involved in "a combined program of writer/reader consciousness-raising, frequent writing, and frequent reader feedback" (55). Such a course, as Samuels points out, is based on the assumption that acts of reading, like those of writing, are acts of making meaning through which the self is accommodated to the other. In "Reading, Listening, Writing" (1985), David Rankin outlines a course that requires students, while using a tape recorder, to engage in reading and listening while working through the composing process. Rankin's method is based on the assumptions that language acquisition is largely unconscious and that "an effective learning process is situational, integrative, and holistic, in the sense that absorption and reproduction of the principles of the model [anything to be imitated] depend upon an understanding of it as a gestalt" (51). Also relevant is Alice S. Horning's essay, "The Connection of Writing to Reading" (1978).

Elaine P. Maimon, in an essay ("Cinderella to Hercules" [1980]) in which she attempts to demythologize writing across the curriculum and to explain the value of such programs to basic writers, argues that getting back to basics means "a renewed commitment to teaching students to write, to read, and to think about content" (4). Two basic writing programs that engage students in reading and thinking about content are those at New York University and at the University of California at Berkeley. The program at NYU, described by Paula Johnson ("Writing Face to Face" [1979]), groups second-semester basic writing students with other freshmen writers according to their areas of interest, and requires them to do reading and writing in either the humanities, social sciences, or natural sciences. The program at Berkeley, described by Sabina T. Johnson ("Remedial English" [1972]), is centered around a content course that engages students in reading and writing about language as a subject.

A second type of holistically designed basic writing course emphasizes interaction with the social context. An interesting example of this type of course is described by Kyle Fiore and Nan Elsasser in " 'Strangers No More' " (1982). The course, based on Lev Vygotsky's theory of language acquisition and Paulo Freire's pedagogy of liberation, involved a class of all women at the College of the Bahamas in reading and writing about feminist concerns. Fiore and Elsasser discovered that "through the investigation of a generative theme, students can advance their reading and writing skills, recognize links between their own lives and the larger society, and develop ways of using their newfound writing skills to intervene in their own environment" (127). A helpful supplementary essay is "An Interactionist Approach" (1977) by Nan Elsasser and Vera P. John-Steiner. Other works that deal with this perspective as it pertains to basic writing course design include Virginia A. Perdue's dissertation, "Writing As an Act of Power" (1984), which examines Paulo Freire's pedagogy as an alternative to either product or process approaches to basic writing; Susan V. Wall's ERIC document, "A Sequence of Assignments for Basic Writing" (1980), which describes a course designed to help students understand that writers create meaning through choices informed by their intention; Louise Yelin's essay, "Deciphering the Academic Hieroglyph" (1978), which examines the connection between Marxist literary theory and basic writing course design; and Adrienne Rich's essay, "Teaching Language in Open Admissions" (1973), which presents the view that the teacher of language is someone "who is trying to aid others to free themselves through the written word, and above all through learning to write it for themselves" (268).

To conclude this section dealing with course design, I would call the reader's attention to two essays. The first is "Remedial Writing Courses" (1983) by

Mike Rose, in which he offers a five-point critique of basic writing courses. He argues that they may limit writing growth in five ways: by being self-contained, by requiring students to write on simple topics to aid in the correction and elimination of error, by encouraging error vigilance and presenting reductionist models in composing, by separating writing from reading and thinking, and by narrowing exploratory discourse and misunderstanding discourse structures. (Also see Rose's "The Language of Exclusion" [1985] and Jeffrey Youdelman's "Limited Students" [1978].) The second essay is "Literacy Education and the Basic Writer" (1986) by Christopher Gould and John Heyda. Based on a survey of 221 colleges and universities offering courses in basic writing, Gould and Heyda conclude that their survey "portrays the basic writing course, as it is taught on a good many campuses, as a theoretically impoverished enterprise, sustained by a narrowly instrumental vision of literacy—one that has been challenged successfully at more advanced levels of English study" (17). Rose's critique, by and large, is aimed at the weaknesses and limitations of analytically designed courses even though, as the Gould-Heyda survey indicates, these analytically designed courses still prevail on most college campuses. I would assert, however, based on the above review of holistically designed courses, that such courses are a step in the right direction because they suggest an appropriate response to each of Rose's objections.

COURSE AND PROGRAM EVALUATION

Evaluation of basic writing courses and programs is especially important because such courses and programs are often seen as peripheral to the purpose of a college or university and, thus, need to demonstrate their effectiveness. In addition to justifying the allocation of resources, evaluation is essential to the reconsideration and adjustment of course and program goals that inform decisions regarding assessment and course design, and that ultimately determine the quality of writing instruction.

Evaluation of writing instruction and program effectiveness has been informed by two very different and competing paradigms. The dominant paradigm is quantitative: it imitates the scientific method and is primarily concerned with objectively measuring short- and long-term gains in student performance. The alternative paradigm is qualitative: it imitates the techniques of ethnography, placing emphasis on interviewing, attitude surveys, and observation of student and teacher performance. The most commonly used quantitative method for measuring gains in writing performance is based on the pretest-posttest model. Geoffrey Akst and Miriam Hecht in "Program Evaluation" (1981) present a helpful introduction to this approach by describing eight different pretest-posttest designs of varying degrees of complexity. Paul B. Diederich's *Measuring Growth in English* (1974) and Charles Cooper's "Measuring Growth in Writing" (1975) outline reliable methods for evaluating writing and explain how the results from these methods can be placed in the context of the pretest-posttest model to be used for growth measurement and program evaluation. And Stephen P. Witte and Lester Faigley, in Chapter 2 of *Evaluating College Writing Programs* (1983), suggest the complexities and difficulties involved in pretest-posttest program evaluations by reviewing four major university studies.

Studies done in basic writing using the pretest-posttest model are mostly limited to short-term measures of course effectiveness and of the relative merits of two instructional methods. Examples of such studies include "Teaching English Composition to Developmental Students at the College Level" (1984) by Ruby M. Lewis, "An Analysis of the Effects of Two Methods of Teaching Remedial Composition" (1981) by Betty J. Overton, "Interpreting Growth in Writing" (1980) by Susan P. McDonald, "A Comparative Study of Two Approaches to Teaching Freshman Remedial Composition" (1975) by Michael A. Miller, and "A Comparative Study of a Laboratory Approach Versus a Conventional Approach to Teaching Developmental Freshman Composition" (1973) by William V. Rakauskas.

However, Edward M. White, in the tenth chapter of *Teaching and Assessing Writing* (1985), is critical of the pretest-posttest model for evaluating writing courses and programs. In addition to "gain scores," White suggests that other desirable student outcomes—such as improved grades, a lower dropout rate, and a willingness to take other English courses—be used for course and program evaluation. For a more detailed examination of similar criteria for program evaluation, see the sixth chapter of *Improving Student Learning Skills* (1979) by Martha Maxwell. Studies that evaluate courses in basic writing according to some of the criteria enumerated by White and Maxwell include "Measurable Improvement in the Writing of Remedial College Students" (1978) by Andrea Lunsford, "Evaluating Teaching Methods in Composition" (1975) by Doris G. Sutton, "The Effects of Two Methods of Compensatory Freshman English" (1974) by Doris G. Sutton and Daniel S. Arnold, and "Assessing the Effectiveness of Remedial College Courses" (1972) by Amiel T. Sharon.

Witte and Faigley in the second chapter of *Evaluating College Writing Programs* (1983) are also critical of the pretest-posttest model for evaluating writing programs. As an alternative to this model, they describe (in Chapter 3) a qualitative approach for evaluating college writing programs that accounts for the cultural and social context of the program, its institutional context, its structure and administration, its curriculum, and its pedagogy.

The CCCC Committee on Teaching and Its Evaluation in Composition ("Evaluating Instruction in Writing" [1982]) criticizes pretest-posttest models of evaluation as well, pointing out that they "appear of limited value when we seek to determine the overall effectiveness of writing programs, courses, and teachers" (215). The committee describes and offers examples of six qualitative instruments, based on an analogy with steps in the writing process, to be used for course and program evaluation. Unfortunately, little has been reported about the use of qualitative measures in the evaluation of basic writing courses and programs. Elizabeth Metzger's essay, "A Scheme for Measuring Growth in College Writing" (1978), however, is an exception. Metzger outlines the scheme for evaluating the writing program at State University of New York at Buffalo, which involves both qualitative measures (student evaluation of courses, reports by each teacher on the progress of one student, the coordinator's evaluation of teachers, and examination of the students' writing anxiety) and one quantitative measure (measurement of growth in writing samples). She describes in detail the measurement of writing and of writer anxiety.

Another type of qualitative evaluation is based on the impressions and experience of a single observer rather than on a carefully designed instrument. Several essays falling into this category address the issue of whether or not composition instruction for basic students in the larger context of remedial education is worthwhile. See, for example, Geoffrey Wagner's "On Remediation" (1976) and Barbara Quint Gray's response, "On Remediation at the City University of New York" (1978); "How to Kill a College" (1978) by Theodore L. Gross; "The Miserable Truth" (1980) by Mina Shaughnessy; "The Long Walk to Room 114" (1986) by R. C. Reynolds; and "Survival of the Fittest" (1988) by Hephzibah Roskelly.

ADMINISTRATION OF COURSES AND PROGRAMS

In regard to administration of basic writing programs, two issues are most frequently discussed and debated: first, whether or not basic writing courses should be taught in a separate skills program or come under the auspices of the English department, and second, whether or not college credit should be given for courses in basic writing.

Education specialists, by and large, have argued for a separate academic division for basic skills that effectively integrates instruction, counseling, and other support services into one program. Those who support this view include John E. Roueche and R. Wade Kirk (*Catching Up* [1974]), K. Patricia Cross (*Accent on Learning* [1976]), John E. Roueche and Jerry J. Snow (*Overcoming Learning Problems* [1977]), Milton G. Spann ("Building a Developmental Education Program" [1977]), Mary Kathryn Grant and Daniel R. Hoeber (*Basic Skills Programs* [1978]), and Janice Rank ("One That Works!" [1979]). Opponents of the integrated skills model argue, however, that students need to be part of the traditional academic community from the beginning. For the description of a successfully developed basic writing program achieved largely under the direction of the English department, see Gray and Slaughter ("Writing" 87–89), and for an account of the difficulties that can develop between a separate basic skills program and the English department over writing instruction, see Elissa S. Guralnick's "The New Segregation" (1978), George H. Jensen in "Bureaucracy and Basic Writing Programs" (1988), using the Jan Kemp incident at the University of Georgia as an example, examines "the kinds of political issues that arise in basic writing programs that are administratively separate from a traditional academic department of college'' (31).

Excellent discussions of the issues involved in the debate over awarding credit for basic writing courses are found in the chapter on administration in Gretchen N. Vik's dissertation, "Developmental Composition in College" (1976), and in the second chapter of Martha Maxwell's *Improving Student Learning Skills* (1979). Also see Margaret S. Butler's "A Study of Credit Remedial English Courses in the Two-Year Colleges" (1980), which not only discusses the issue of awarding credit, but also addresses other administrative concerns from financing remedial programs to identification of remedial English in the school catalog.

CONCLUSION

"Holisticism," according to Edward M. White ("Holisticism" [1984]), "argues against reductionism and denies that the whole is only the sum of its parts" (400), it "says that the human spirit and its most significant form of expression (writing) must be seen and understood not in parts, but as a whole, face to face as it were, almost sacramentally" (409). If there is a trend in recent scholarship dealing with courses and programs in basic writing, it is toward what White refers to as holisticism. Holisticism, in its various manifestations, has had and is having a profound impact on all phases of writing instruction: it has revolutionized placement and proficiency examinations for writing courses; it has radically influenced course design so that instruction in some programs is no longer based exclusively on analytic and hierarchical models; and it is beginning to change methods for course and program evaluation by insisting that qualitative measures have their place alongside quantitative ones. Considerably more work needs to be done, however, in program evaluation not only in terms of designing better instruments for assessing the short- and long-term efforts of writing instruction, but also in terms of developing and testing models for program evaluation that may have wide application and eventually wide acceptance.

REFERENCES

Akst, Geoffrey, and Miriam Hecht. "Program Evaluation." *Teaching Basic Skills in College*. Ed. Alice Stewart Trillin and associates. San Francisco: Jossey-Bass, 1981, pp. 261–96.

Bamberg, Betty. "Composition Instruction Does Make a Difference: A Comparison of the High School Preparation of College Freshmen in Regular and Remedial English Classes." *RTE* 12 (1978): 47–59.

Bartholomae, David. "Teaching Basic Writing: An Alternative to Basic Skills." *JBW* 2.2 (1979): 85–109.

Bartholomae, David, and Anthony R. Petrosky. *Facts, Artifacts and Counterfacts: Theory and Method for a Reading and Writing Course*. Upper Montclair, N.J.: Boynton/Cook, 1986. Rpt. as "Facts, Artifacts, and Counterfacts: A Basic Reading and

Writing Course for the College Curriculum." *A Sourcebook for Basic Writing Teachers*. Ed. Theresa Enos. New York: Random House, 1987, pp. 275–306.

Baum, Joan. "An Exhortation for Teachers of English in Open-Admissions Programs." *CCC* 25 (1974): 292–97.

Berg, Anna, and Gerald Coleman. "A Cognitive Approach to Teaching the Developmental Student." *JBW* 4.2 (1985): 4–23.

Bizzell, Patricia. "What Happens When Basic Writers Come to College?" *CCC* 37 (1986): 294–301.

Brown, Rexford. "Choosing or Creating an Appropriate Writing Test." *Basic Writing: Essays for Teachers, Researchers, and Administrators*. Ed. Lawrence N. Kasden and Daniel R. Hoeber. Urbana, Ill.: NCTE, 1980, pp. 105–16.

Butler, Margaret S. "A Study of Credit Remedial Courses in the Two-Year Colleges in the United States." *DAI* 41 (1980): 1043A. Indiana University of Pennsylvania.

CCCC Committee on Teaching and Its Evaluation in Composition. "Evaluating Instruction in Writing: Approaches and Instruments." *CCC* 33 (1982): 213–29.

Coles, Nicholas, and Susan V. Wall. "Conflict and Power in the Reader-Responses of Adult Basic Writers." *CE* 49 (1987): 298–314.

Cooper, Charles R. "Holistic Evaluation of Writing." *Evaluating Writing: Describing, Measuring, Judging*. Ed. Charles R. Cooper and Lee Odell. Urbana, Ill.: NCTE, 1977, pp. 3–31.

———. "Measuring Growth in Writing." *EJ* 64.3 (1975): 111–20.

Cooper, Charles R., and Lee Odell, eds. *Evaluating Writing: Describing, Measuring, Judging*. Urbana, Ill.: NCTE, 1977.

Crosby, Harry. "The Rhetoric Program at Boston University's College of Basic Studies." *Basic Writing: Essays for Teachers, Researchers, and Administrators*. Ed. Lawrence N. Kasden and Daniel R. Hoeber. Urbana, Ill.: NCTE, 1980, pp. 74–87.

Cross, K. Patricia. *Accent on Learning: Improving Instruction and Reshaping the Curriculum*. San Francisco: Jossey-Bass, 1976.

Desy, Jeanne. "Reasoned Writing for Basic Students: A Course Design." *JBW* 1.2 (1976): 4–19.

Diederich, Paul B. *Measuring Growth in English*. Urbana, Ill.: NCTE, 1974.

Dixon, Arthur L. "Basic Writing at J. Sargeant Reynolds Community College." *Basic Writing: Essays for Teachers, Researchers, and Administrators*. Ed. Lawrence N. Kasden and Daniel R. Hoeber. Urbana, Ill.: NCTE, 1980, pp. 35–44.

Donovan, Timothy R., and Ben W. McClelland, eds. *Eight Approaches to Teaching Composition*. Urbana, Ill.: NCTE, 1980.

Elbow, Peter, and Pat Belanoff. "Portfolios as a Substitute for Proficiency Examinations." *CCC* 37 (1986): 336–39.

Elsasser, Nan, and Vera P. John-Steiner. "An Interactionist Approach to Advancing Literacy." *HER* 47 (1977): 355–69.

Enos, Theresa, ed. *A Sourcebook for Basic Writing Teachers*. New York: Random House, 1987.

Epes, Mary, Carolyn Kirkpatrick, and Michael G. Southwell. "The COMP-LAB Project: An Experimental Basic Writing Course." *JBW* 2.2 (1979): 19–37.

———, and others. *An Evaluation of the COMP-LAB Project: Final Report*. ERIC, 1980. ED 194 909.

Farrell, Thomas J. "Developing Literacy: Walter J. Ong and Basic Writing." *JBW* 2.1 (1978): 30–51.

————. "Literacy, the Basics, and All That Jazz." *CE* 38 (1977): 443–59.

————. "Open Admissions, Orality, and Literacy." *J Youth Ado* 3 (1974): 247–60.

Fiore, Kyle, and Nan Elsasser. " 'Strangers No More': A Liberatory Literacy Curriculum." *CE* 44 (1982): 115–28.

Ford, James E., and Gregory Larkin. "The Portfolio System: An End to Backsliding Writing Standards." *CE* 39 (1978): 950–55.

Freedman, Aviva, and Ian Pringle, eds. *Reinventing the Rhetorical Tradition.* Conway, Ark.: L & S Books, 1980.

Freedman, Sarah Warshauer, and William S. Robinson. "Testing Proficiency in Writing at San Francisco State University." *CCC* 33 (1982): 393–98.

Frisbie, D. A. "Methods of Evaluating Course Placement Systems." *Educ Eval Pol Anal* 4 (1982): 133–40.

Gorrell, Donna. "Toward Determining a Minimal Competency Entrance Examination for Freshman Composition." *RTE* 17 (1983): 263–74.

Gould, Christopher, and John Heyda. "Literacy Education and the Basic Writer: A Survey of College Composition Courses." *JBW* 5.2 (1986): 8–27.

Grant, Mary Kathryn, and Daniel R. Hoeber. *Basic Skills Programs: Are They Working?* Washington, D.C.: American Association for Higher Education, 1978.

Gray, Barbara Quint. "On Remediation at the City University of New York." *CE* 39 (1978): 631–34.

Gray, Barbara Quint, and Virginia B. Slaughter. "Writing." *Teaching Basic Skills in College.* Ed. Alice Stewart Trillin and associates. San Francisco: Jossey-Bass, 1980, pp. 12–90.

Greenberg, Karen L. "Competency Testing: What Role Should Teachers of Composition Play?" *CCC* 33 (1982): 366–76.

————. "Research on Basic Writers: Theoretical and Methodological Issues." *A Sourcebook for Basic Writing Teachers.* Ed. Theresa Enos. New York: Random House, 1987, pp. 187–207.

Greenberg, Karen L., Harvey S. Wiener, and Richard A. Donovan, eds. *Writing Assessment: Issues and Strategies.* New York: Longman, 1986.

Griffin, Jacqueline. "Remedial Composition at an Open-Door College." *CCC* 20 (1969): 360–63.

Gross, Theodore L. "How to Kill a College: The Private Papers of a Campus Dean." *Sat Rev* 4, February 1978: 12–20.

Guralnick, Elissa S. "The New Segregation: A Recent History of EOP at the University of Colorado, Boulder." *CE* 39 (1978): 964–74.

Hake, Rosemary. "With No Apology: Teaching to the Test." *JBW* 1.4 (1978): 39–62.

Harris, Muriel. "Individualized Diagnosis: Searching for Causes, Not Symptoms of Writing Deficiencies." *CE* 40 (1978): 318–23.

Hays, Janice N. "Teaching the Grammar of Discourse." *Reinventing the Rhetorical Tradition.* Ed. Aviva Freedman and Ian Pringle. Conway, Ark.: L & S Books, 1980, pp. 145–55.

————, et al. *The Writer's Mind: Writing as a Mode of Thinking.* Urbana, Ill.: NCTE, 1983.

Hodgkinson, Harold L. "Reform? Higher Education? Don't Be Absurd!" *Kappan* 68 (1986): 271–74.

Horning, Alice S. "The Connection of Writing to Reading: A Gloss on the Gospel of Mina Shaughnessy." *CE* 40 (1978): 264–68.

Jensen, George. "Bureaucracy and Basic Writing Programs; or, Fallout from the Jan Kemp Trial." *JBW* 7.1 (1988): 30–37.

Johnson, Nancy W. "A Successful Placement Test for Basic Writing." *Basic Writing: Essays for Teachers, Researchers, and Administrators*. Ed. Lawrence N. Kasden and Daniel R. Hoeber. Urbana, Ill.: NCTE, 1980, pp. 91–104.

Johnson, Paula. "Writing Face to Face." *JBW* 2.2 (1979): 7–18.

Johnson, Sabina Thorne. "Remedial English: The Anglocentric Albatross?" *CE* 33 (1972): 670–85.

Kasden, Lawrence N. "An Introduction to Basic Writing." *Basic Writing: Essays for Teachers, Researchers, and Administrators*. Ed. Lawrence N. Kasden and Daniel R. Hoeber. Urbana, Ill.: NCTE, 1980, pp. 1–9.

Kasden, Lawrence N., and Daniel R. Hoeber, eds. *Basic Writing: Essays for Teachers, Researchers, and Administrators*. Urbana, Ill.: NCTE, 1980.

Kiefer, Kathleen E. "Testing Basic Writers' Proficiency: An Effective Model." ERIC, 1983. ED 235 496.

Krashen, Stephen D. *Writing: Research, Theory, and Applications*. Language Teaching Methodology Series. Oxford, Eng.: Pergamon Institute of English, 1984.

Lattin, Vernon E. "A Program for Basic Writing." *CE* 40 (1978): 312–17.

Lederman, Marie Jean, Susan Remmer Ryzewic, and Michael Ribaudo. *Assessment and Improvement of the Academic Skills of Entering Freshmen: A National Survey*. New York: City University of New York Instructional Resource Center, 1983.

Lees, Elaine O. "Building Thought on Paper with Adult Basic Writers." *The Writer's Mind: Writing as a Mode of Thinking*. Ed. Janice N. Hays et al. Urbana, Ill.: NCTE, 1983, pp. 145–51.

Lewis, Ruby M. "Teaching English Composition to Developmental Students at the College Level: A Free Writing/Language Study Approach Versus a Structured Writing/Language Study Approach." *DAI* 45 (1984): 2788A. Kansas State University.

Lunsford, Andrea. "Assignments for Basic Writers: Unresolved Issues and Needed Research." *JBW* 5.1 (1986): 87–99.

———. "An Historical, Descriptive, and Evaluative Study of Remedial English in American Colleges and Universities." *DAI* 38 (1977): 2743A. Ohio State University.

———. "Measurable Improvement in the Writing of Remedial College Students." ERIC, 1978. ED 155 725.

Lunsford, Andrea, and Sara Garnes. "Anatomy of a Basic Writing Program." *JBW* 2.2 (1979): 38–51.

Lutz, William. "Bibliography." *Writing Assessment: Issues and Strategies*. Ed. Karen L. Greenberg, Harvey S. Wiener, and Richard A. Donovan. New York: Longman, 1986, pp. 183–91.

McDonald, Susan Peck. "Interpreting Growth in Writing." *CCC* 31 (1980): 301–10.

Maimon, Elaine P. "Cinderella to Hercules: Demythologizing Writing Across the Curriculum." *JBW* 2.4 (1980): 3–11.

Matthews, Roberta S. "The Evolution of One College's Attempt to Evaluate Student Writing." *JBW* 1.4 (1978): 63–70.

Maxwell, Martha. *Improving Student Learning Skills: A Comprehensive Guide to Successful Practices and Programs for Increasing the Performance of Underprepared Students*. San Francisco: Jossey-Bass, 1979.

Metzger, Elizabeth. "A Scheme for Measuring Growth in College Writing." *JBW* 1.4 (1978): 71–81.

Miller, Michael A. "A Comparative Study of Two Approaches to Teaching Freshman Remedial Composition in a Comprehensive Community College." *DAI* 35 (1975): 7083A. University of Kansas.

Mills, Helen. "Language and Composition: Three Mastery Learning Courses in One Classroom." *JBW* 1.2 (1976): 44–59.

Noreen, Robert G. "Placement Procedures for Freshman Composition: A Survey." *CCC* 28 (1977): 141–44.

Obler, Susan S. "Programs for the Underprepared Student: Areas of Concern." *A New Look at Successful Programs*. Ed. John E. Roueche. San Francisco: Jossey-Bass, 1983, pp. 21–30.

Odell, Lee, and Charles R. Cooper. "Procedures for Evaluating Writing: Assumptions and Needed Research." *CE* 42 (1980): 35–43.

Overton, Betty J. "An Analysis of the Effects of Two Methods of Teaching Remedial Composition." *DAI* 42 (1981): 118A. George Peabody College for Teachers of Vanderbilt University.

Perdue, Virginia A. "Writing As an Act of Power: Basic Writing Pedagogy As Social Practice." *DAI* 45 (1984): 441A. University of Michigan.

Petrie, Ann. "Teaching the Thinking Process in Essay Writing." *JBW* 1.2 (1976): 60–67.

Ponsot, Marie. "Total Immersion." *JBW* 1.2 (1976): 31–43.

Ponsot, Marie, and Rosemary Deen. *Beat Not the Poor Desk; Writing: What to Teach, How to Teach It, and Why*. Upper Montclair, N.J.: Boynton/Cook, 1982.

Purnell, Rosentene B. "A Survey of the Testing of Writing Proficiency in College: A Progress Report." *CCC* 33 (1982): 407–10.

Rakauskas, William V. "A Comparative Study of a Laboratory Approach Versus a Conventional Approach to Teaching Developmental Freshman Composition at The University of Scranton." *DAI* 34 (1973): 1657A. Temple University.

Rank, Janice. *One That Works! An Integrated Program of Basic Skills*. ERIC, 1979. ED 173 762.

Rankin, David. "Reading, Listening, Writing: An Integrated Approach to Teaching Exposition." *JBW* 4.2 (1985): 48–57.

Reynolds, R. C. "The Long Walk to Room 114: The Realities of Teaching Remedial English in College." *Chron Higher Ed* 15 October 1986: 104.

Rich, Adrienne. "Teaching Language in Open Admissions: A Look at the Context." *Harvard Engl Stud* 4 (1971): 257–73.

Rose, Mike. "The Language of Exclusion: Writing Instruction at the University." *CE* 47 (1985): 341–59.

———. "Remedial Writing Courses: A Critique and a Proposal." *CE* 45 (1983): 109–28.

Roskelly, Hephzibah. "Survival of the Fittest: Ten Years in a Basic Writing Program." *JBW* 7.1 (1988): 13–29.

Roueche, John E., Ed. *A New Look at Successful Programs*. San Francisco: Jossey-Bass, 1983.

———. *New Directions for Higher Education: Increasing Basic Skills by Developmental Studies*. San Francisco: Jossey-Bass, 1977.

Roueche, John E., and R. Wade Kirk. *Catching Up: Remedial Education*. San Francisco: Jossey-Bass, 1974.

Roueche, John E., and Jerry J. Snow. *Overcoming Learning Problems: A Guide to Developmental Education in College*. San Francisco: Jossey-Bass, 1977.

Samuels, Marilyn S. "Norman Holland's 'New Paradigm' and the Teaching of Writing." *JBW* 2.1 (1978): 52–61.

Sharon, Amiel T. "Assessing the Effectiveness of Remedial College Courses." *J Exp Educ* 41 (1972): 60–62.

Shaughnessy, Mina P. *Errors and Expectations: A Guide for the Teacher of Basic Writing*. New York: Oxford University Press, 1977.

———. "The Miserable Truth." *JBW* 3.1 (1980): 109–14.

Shine, Richard A. "The Remediation Conundrum: A Workshop/Tutorial Experiment in Developmental Writing." *DAI* 40 (1979): 1439A. University of Massachusetts.

Slaughter, Virginia B., and Harvey S. Wiener. *Basic Skills Programs at the City University of New York: Writing*. ERIC, 1981. ED 207 073.

Spann, Milton G. "Building a Developmental Education Program." *New Directions for Higher Education: Increasing Basic Skills by Developmental Studies*. Ed. John E. Roueche. San Francisco: Jossey-Bass, 1977, pp. 23–39.

Spann, Milton G., and Virginia Foxx. "Basic Writing Programs of the Western North Carolina Consortium." *Basic Writing: Essays for Teachers, Researchers, and Administrators*. Ed. Lawrence N. Kasden and Daniel R. Hoeber. Urbana, Ill.: NCTE, 1980.

Stewart, Etta M. "Remedial Freshman English Composition Course and Program Offerings in Selected Four-Year Colleges and Universities Accredited by the Southern Association of Colleges and Schools." *DAI* 43 (1982): 1855A. McNeese State University.

Sutton, Doris G. "Evaluating Teaching Methods in Composition." ERIC, 1975. ED 120 730.

Sutton, Doris G., and Daniel S. Arnold. "The Effects of Two Methods of Compensatory Freshman English." *RTE* 8 (1974): 241–49.

Taylor, Karl K. "*Doors* English—The Cognitive Basis of Rhetorical Models." *JBW* 2.2 (1979): 52–66.

———. "If Not Grammar, What?—Taking Remedial Writing Instruction Seriously." *DAI* 39 (1978): 168A. University of Illinois, Urbana.

Trillin, Alice Stewart, and associates, eds. *Teaching Basic Skills in College*. San Francisco: Jossey-Bass, 1981.

Vik, Gretchen N. "Developmental Composition in College." *DAI* 36 (1976): 8037A. University of Florida.

Wagner, Geoffrey. "On Remediation." *CE* 38 (1976): 153–58.

Wall, Susan V. "A Sequence of Assignments for Basic Writing: Problems 'Beyond the Sentence.' " ERIC, 1980. ED 186 937.

White, Edward M. "Holisticism." *CCC* 35 (1984): 400–409.

———. *Teaching and Assessing Writing: Recent Advances in Understanding, Evaluating, and Improving Student Performance*. San Francisco: Jossey-Bass, 1985.

White, Edward M., and Leon L. Thomas. "Racial Minorities and Writing Skills Assessment in the California State University and Colleges." *CE* 43 (1981): 276–83.

"Why Johnny Can't Write." *Newsweek* 8 December 1975: 58–63.

Wiener, Harvey S. "Basic Writing: First Days' Thoughts on Process and Detail." *Eight Approaches to Teaching Composition*. Ed. Timothy R. Donovan and Ben W. McClelland. Urbana, Ill.: NCTE, 1980, pp. 87–99.

———. *The Writing Room: A Resource Book for Teachers of English*. New York: Oxford University Press, 1981.

Williams, Joseph. "Re-evaluating Evaluating." *JBW* 1.4 (1978): 7–17.

Wilson, Allison. "A Survey of College-Level Remedial Writing Programs at Selected State-Supported Institutions Currently Admitting the Underprepared." *DAI* 40 (1980): 4881A. Columbia University Teachers College.

Witte, Stephen P., and Lester Faigley. *Evaluating College Writing Programs*. Carbondale, Ill.: Southern Illinois University Press, 1983.

Yelin, Louise. "Deciphering the Academic Hieroglyph: Marxist Literary Theory and the Practice of Basic Writing." *JBW* 2.1 (1978): 13–29.

Youdelman, Jeffrey. "Limiting Students: Remedial Writing and the Death of Open Admissions." *CE* 39 (1978): 562–72.

8

Computers and Writing Instruction

Stephen A. Bernhardt and Patricia G. Wojahn

Few topics in the past ten years have seized the attention of composition researchers and teachers as computers have. Though mainframe technology offered possibilities for electronic text processing for some years, these large systems had always been oriented not toward words but numbers. The advent of the personal computer, a machine perfectly adapted to writing, signaled the start of a new era in composition teaching, one marked by a new emphasis on medium.

Continuing interest in computers and composition is evidenced in the emergence of several journals and newsletters: *Collegiate Microcomputer*, *Computers and Composition*, *Computer-Assisted Composition Journal*, *Creative Word Processing in the Classroom*, and *Research in Word Processing Newsletter* (addresses in list of references). The Assembly on Computers in English (ACE), a special interest group of the National Council of Teachers of English (NCTE), has its own well-attended meetings and sponsored panels at the NCTE convention, as well as a widely subscribed *ACE Newsletter*. Conferences devoted to computers and composition are held with increasing frequency, with publication of the proceedings a regular occurrence (Lillian Bridwell and Donald Ross, Special Issue of *Computers and Composition* [1985]; Lisa Gerrard, *Writing at Century's End: Essays on Computer-Assisted Composition* [1987]). Extensive bibliographies on computers and composition include Margaret L. Lansing, *Computers and Composition* (1984a); Paula Reed Nancarrow, Donald Ross, and Lillian Bridwell, *Word Processors and the Writing Process* (1984); Hugh Burns, "Computers and Composition" (1987); Jeanne Luchte, "Computer Programs in the Writing Center: A Bibliographical Essay" (1987); and Helen J. Schwartz and Lillian S. Bridwell, "A Selected Bibliography on Computers and Composition" (1984; updated, 1987).

While the use of computers in teaching writing has its start in computer-assisted instruction (CAI), especially grammar practice, growth in computer use has largely been away from drill and practice toward uses as either heuristic devices or simply tools for writing. Marc S. Tucker in "Computers in the Schools" (1985) describes the growing recognition that the machine is most appropriately used as a tool—as a word processor, a graphics processor, a spreadsheet, or a database.

This shift—from drill and practice or programming toward applications—is documented in Henry J. Becker's survey of research: *How Schools Use Micro-computers* (1985) and "Reports from the 1985 National Survey" (1986). Between 1983 and 1985, for instance, the use of computers for word processing in public schools increased from about 7 percent of total time to 15 percent, with the trend filtering down from universities to high schools to elementary schools. It is not unusual on university campuses today to find that the major use of personal computers is word processing, with estimates running as high as 90 percent of time on some campuses (Judith Axler Turner, "Drive to Require Students to Buy Computers Slows" [1987]).

In this chapter, we will review the uses of computers in teaching composition, paying particular attention to their applications in basic writing classes. We will of necessity be concerned generally with research on composition at the university level, and not solely with basic writing, since much of what has been written can be applied equally well to both general and basic writing classes. When a study of students or classes below the university level had particular relevance to basic writing, we will include it in the review. For reasons of space, we will not cover several applications of computers: as electronic gradebooks, as test generators, or as aids to generating stock comments on student papers.

The review itself is organized around what we see as the movement in the field from the machine as tutor to machine as tool. We will first consider CAI, where software is expected to do the teaching; then consider various heuristic applications, where the machine is intended to help students through the composing process; and then consider word processing applications and studies of the effects of computers on individual writers, where the software simply serves as a tool for the writer. Finally, we will examine studies of whole classes using computers and consider the implications of computers for the future of composition teaching.

COMPUTER AS TUTOR

The default setting for many who consider applications of computers to basic writers has been CAI, specifically grammar programs. PLATO (developed at the University of Illinois) and TICCIT (developed at Brigham Young University) represent such applications, each system having numerous programs offering grammar exercises and writing instruction among a broad array of programs. For discussions of these mainframe applications, see Donald Alderman, Lola Appel, and Richard Murray, "PLATO and TICCIT" (1978); Gayle Byerly,

"CAI in College English" (1978); W. B. Macgregor, *PLATO and the English Curriculum* (1982); and Elray Pedersen, "TICCIT Will Gladly Learn and Gladly Teach Composition Skills" (1985).

Textbook companies are currently bringing CAI to market, primarily as inducements to buy certain handbooks or rhetorics. Little, Brown has its *Diagnostic Program*; CBS College Publishing offers *The Holt Writing Tutor*; Scott, Foresman offers *StudyWare: Workbook of Current English*; Simon and Schuster offers software to accompany Troyka's *Handbook for Writers*; and Harcourt Brace offers *Caret Patch*. These commercial programs share an emphasis on correction of common errors. Other CAI programs have a specific focus: with basic writers in mind, Terri Paul and Don Payne discuss a CAI spelling program that compiles profile data and assists with the development of individualized lessons ("Computer-Assisted Instruction: Teaching and Learning from the Basic Writer" [1983]); Louis Marchesano describes MACH, a paragraph development program for basic writers ("Process CAI: A Bridge between Theory and Practice in Writing Instruction" [1986]).

The machine is quite efficient at presenting grammatical instruction: it is tireless and patient, good at keeping tabs on right and wrong answers, and good at randomly selecting items from a large database so sessions are in some sense individualized. The newer programs offer flexibility and control, so the student does not get locked into long sequences of instruction. While some programs tend to be more testing than instruction, as Michael G. Southwell has pointed out in "Microcomputers and Writing Instruction" (1987), it is possible to provide explanations and examples at various depths within the program, so that students who do not understand an item can access instructional text. Anne Auten encourages English teachers to consider CAI in her "ERIC/RCS Report" (1984), and William Oates provides evidence in "An Evaluation of Computer-Assisted Instruction for English Grammar Review" (1981) that CAI can produce gains in scores on grammar tests, though he does not establish a connection between grammar tests and writing.

Others are much more suspicious of the value of CAI for writing instruction. In "Computer Promises, Computer Realities" (1984), Lee Otto warns that most language arts programs have a poor research base and are conceived, tested, and marketed under a process of systematic reductionism. B. Cronnell (*Computer-Based Practice in Editing* [1982]) and Craig Etchison ("Who's Making the Decisions?" [1985]) both worry about the reduction of language study to sentence skills, arguing for keeping language whole. Such arguments bring us up against fundamental assumptions about how people learn language and improve writing skills, evoking a long tradition of arguments about the connection of grammar instruction and writing ability.

It is likely that CAI software in English will continue to be seen as an adjunct to instruction and not a replacement for traditional instruction. Often, the software will be developed within specific institutions with specific goals in mind, such as that developed at the University of Minnesota–Duluth to be integrated with their freshman composition course (Thomas Bacig, Donald Larmouth, and Kenneth Risdon, "A Comprehensive Computer-Aided Program in Writing" [1985]). The best software will involve whole, purposeful texts in an attempt to model how writers edit text and will provide scaffolding that moves students from tutorial and practice with sample language toward practice with their own language, so that transfer is not a simple hope but a condition of instruction. Progress has been made in the development of such software at the University of Pittsburgh; see Robert Glaser, Alan Lesgold, and David Bartholomae, *Using Cognitive Research and Computer Technology to Improve Writing Skill in Low-Performing College Students* (1985); Glynda Hull, "The Use of Microcomputers in Basic Writing" (1985); and Glynda Hull and William Smith, "Error Correction and Computing" (1985).

THE COMPUTER AS WRITING AID

Reflecting the general shift in the field toward process instruction, many computer-based writing aids provide strategies for inventing, drafting, revising, and editing. Common programs are of two sorts: (1) prompt programs that help students create, develop, and structure ideas, and (2) text-analysis programs that help students analyze and edit texts. Some software integrates word processing as well as prewriting, revising, and editing programs to provide a complete writing environment. With process software, the computer can ask students questions, make comments, and offer suggestions. Never really interacting in the sense of knowing and responding to content, the computer merely waits for responses or searches for certain words or phrases to which it has stock responses. For general discussions of computerized writing aids in composition classrooms, see Lillian Bridwell and Donald Ross, "Integrating Computers into a Writing Curriculum" (1984); Fred Kemp, "The User-Friendly Fallacy" (1987) and "Getting Smart with Computers: Computer-Aided Heuristics for Student Writers" (1987); Stephen Marcus, "Real-Time Gadgets with Feedback" (1984); Robert Shostak, "Computer-Assisted Composition Instruction: The State of the Art" (1982); and Mark Waldo, "Computers and Composition: A Marriage Made in Heaven?" (1985).

Most writing aids are designed to encourage students to develop their composing processes and to internalize the thinking patterns encouraged by computerized aids. In "Do Writers Talk to Themselves? (1985), Colette Daiute explains how interaction with the computer can increase writers' objectivity and heighten awareness of their composing processes. James Strickland suggests in "Prewriting and Computing" (1985) that good writing aids *model* good writing teachers—they "direct creativity, suggest strategies, play audience, and dislodge writer's block" (69).

As invention tools, computerized writing aids can help students formulate and investigate topics through an open-ended inquiry approach, with questions and comments that encourage students to consider what they know and do not know about a topic. Students type in responses, and a printed record of the computer-student dialogue can then guide students as they draft. Of course, since the computer cannot comprehend the semantic content of responses, the quality of the prewriting session is largely determined by the student.

Prewriting programs such as PREWRITE (Mimi Schwartz, "Computer Writing Made Easier" [1985]) and QUEST (James Strickland, "Prewriting and Computing" [1985]) use general heuristic questions. FREE is based on Peter Elbow's "freewriting and synthesis cycles" (Strickland [1985]); another program uses "visual synectics" to help students think metaphorically about their topics (Dawn Rodrigues and Raymond Rodrigues, "Computer-Based Creative Problem Solving" [1984]). The best programs, and PREWRITE is an example, allow teachers to edit the prompt question files for specific assignments. For an overview of invention programs, see Ellen McDaniel, "Bibliography of Text-Analysis and Writing-Instruction Software" (1987), and Raymond Rodrigues and Dawn Rodrigues, "Computer-Based Invention: Its Place and Potential" (1984).

To help students through the drafting stage, revision prompt programs offer questions and suggestions to assist students in developing and arranging ideas. Programs such as ORGANIZE encourage students to establish an approach, analyze an audience, and arrange ideas according to such patterns of development as cause and effect, comparison and contrast, description, and definition (Helen Schwartz, "Teaching Writing with Computer Aids" [1984]). Colette Daiute's *Catch* prompts students to focus on the "organizational, semantic, and logical aspects of their texts" ("Physical and Cognitive Factors in Revising" [1986] 147).

Still other programs focus on the editing stage. For example, *Writer's Workbench* identifies a long list of prose features, including nominalizations, sexist terms, *to be* verbs, and abstract, passive, inflated, overused, or vague words. It prints the first and last sentence of each paragraph and provides a quantitative analysis of work, sentence, and paragraph length (Lawrence T. Frase et al., "Theory and Practice in Computer-Aided Composition" [1985]; Kathleen Kiefer and Charles R. Smith, "Improving Students' Revising and Editing: The Writer's Workbench System" [1984]). Less powerful microcomputer text analyzers such as GRAMMATIK, HOMER, and *MacProof* do essentially the same things, counting and tagging what the computer can recognize. In "Matching Software and Curriculum" (1986), Joyce Kinkead describes a number of text-analysis programs, stressing the need to match software and composition program goals. Such programs have proliferated in educational and business markets within the last three years.

The most recent developments in computer-assisted writing software have been integrated packages that aid students throughout the entire writing process. *Writer's Helper: Stage II* features prewriting programs as well as prompts to help students outline and arrange supporting sentences into rough essay form. An important design feature of *Writer's Helper* is that the results of prewriting can be ported to common word processors so students can continue drafting and revising into finished texts. Drafts can then be checked with the text-analysis programs (William Wresch, "Questions, Answers, and Automated Writing" [1984]). Deborah Holdstein's HOLTCOMP also helps students prewrite, draft, and rewrite various types of assignments, in part by making prewriting responses viable as students compose (Ellen McDaniel, "A Comparative Study of the First-Generation Software" [1986]).

Still another integrated system, *HBJ Writer* (formerly WANDAH) consists of a word processor, several prewriting aids, and revising/editing aids for style, organization, and mechanics. One freewriting prompt causes the screen to blink when students pause for more than a few seconds, a feature some will find useful and others unnerving. Another prewriting aid makes use of "invisible" writing on a blank screen so students cannot edit until they have written at least 100 words. In addition, a "commenting facility" allows students to react to each other's work. (Morton P. Friedman, "WANDAH—A Computerized Writer's Aid" [1985]; Ruth Von Blum and Michael E. Cohen, "WANDAH: Writing Aid *and* Author's Helper" [1984]). A limiting design feature in *HBJ Writer* is that the student is locked into the integrated word processor, which is supposed to be simple but is in reality a rather clumsy editor that produces files that only *HBJ Writer* can read or write. Students will find that their editing and formatting demands quickly outgrow the program, and they will be forced to find another word processor (David Partenheimer, "One View of *WANDAH: HBJ Writer*" [1987]).

Research on the effects of computerized writing aids suggests they have some value. Interactive programs may be particularly helpful for beginning writers who experience difficulty in creating and evaluating texts (Carl Bereiter and Marlene Scardamalia, "From Conversation to Composition: The Role of Instruction in a Developmental Process" [1982]). In an early study of prewriting heuristics, college students who used the programs generated more and better ideas than a control group (Hugh L. Burns and George H. Culp, "Stimulating Invention in English Composition through Computer-Assisted Instruction" [1980]). Moreover, students reported that the programs helped them consider topics from different angles and that some of their best ideas came after the prewriting sessions (Hugh Burns, "Computer-Assisted Prewriting Activities" [1982]). In a Georgia State University study, three groups of college freshmen were compared, one working with a computer-based prewriting program, another with a human tutor, and the third using classroom instruction alone. The computer group outperformed the others on all posttest measures except fluency (Philip D. Gilles, "The Utilization of Computer Technology as a Means of Teaching and Evaluating Prewriting Processes" [1983]). In another comparative study, junior high students using a revision prompt program made significantly more revisions of all types than did students using a word processor alone (Colette Daiute, "Physical and Cognitive Factors in Revising" [1986]). Pretests and posttests of college students using *Writer's Workbench* suggest it can improve skill in editing for clarity and directness (Kathleen Kiefer and Charles R. Smith, "Textual Analysis with Computers: Tests of Bell Laboratories' Computer Software" [1983]). Students in the *Writer's Workbench* study also reacted favorably to the computers: approximately 80% would welcome using the computer for another course. Holistic scores of essays, however, suggest that students in experimental groups did not write better than students in control groups.

Not everyone is convinced that interactive programs really do help students write better. In "Some Ideas about Idea Processors" (1987), David N. Dobrin articulates in intelligent ways the distinction between the easy manipulation of symbols on a screen and the difficult cognitive task of reformulating ideas; he is critical of so-called idea processors that make it possible for a student to shift hierarchies in an outline without considering the resulting major redefinitions of coherence in the discourse. Earl Woodruff found that an interactive questioner seemed to interfere with the composing process of thirty-six eighth graders. In addition, some students began relying on the computer to prompt them to continue writing ("Computers and the Composing Process: An Examination of Computer-Writer Interaction" [1982]). Edward Vockell warns that many prewriting programs cause students to waste potential learning time because the programs are not compatible with the students' word processors ("The Computer and Academic Learning Time" [1987]). Lawrence Frase et al. (1985) found that students demonstrated great variability in how they used the programs and in how much revision the programs triggered, suggesting that the programs prove more valuable for some students than others. Christine Hult's comparative study of two matched sections of freshman English, one using word processors and text-analysis programs to write, the other using pen and paper, indicated that computer use did not necessarily improve students' ability to edit: with the exception of spelling, the two groups were similar in the number and kinds of errors ("The Effects of Word Processing on the Correctness of Student Writing" [1985]). As Lillian Bridwell and Ann Duin report, "Some of the best programs and studies . . . have failed to show that using computer-assisted instruction achieves miraculous results" ("Looking In Depth at Writers: Computers as Writing Medium and Research Tool" [1985] 116).

Critics of text-analysis programs state that the programs direct students' attention to minor errors, away from more important writing concerns. In "Pitfalls in Electronic Writing Land" (1984), Lawrence Oliver complains that the computer's advice, concentrated as it is on "surface features," isolates discourse "from its intended meaning, purpose, and audience" (95). He suggests that *Writer's Workbench*, for example, promotes a single style of writing and that students, unlike the technical writers for whom it was designed, are not able to determine the appropriateness of the computer's analysis and advice. In "Style Analyzers Once More" (1986), David Dobrin warns that those who can accurately analyze the analysis are those who do not need the program. He believes the programs can be distracting and even dangerous for the uninformed. Donald Ross discusses in "Realities of Computer Analysis of Compositions" (1985) the limits of text-analysis programs and suggests how they might be made more useful than current offerings.

At the largest level, critics of artificial intelligence research such as Hubert L. Dreyfus (*What Computers Can't Do: A Critique of Artificial Intelligence* [1979]), Hubert L. Dreyfus and Stuart E. Dreyfus (*Mind over Machine: The Power of Human Intuition and Expertise in the Era of the Computer* [1986]), and Joseph Weizenbaum (*Computers and Human Reason* [1976]) show us just how far researchers are from creating programs that really understand natural language. Teachers who use text-analysis software quickly discover that the programs are extremely limited in the problems they recognize and the help they offer. It *is* possible with these programs to get a general reading on nominal versus verbal styles through examining the rates of passives, *to be* verbs, prepositional phrases, and nominalizations. But it takes a teacher who understands the syntactic correlates of verbal styles and who can communicate this understanding in useful and intelligent ways to students who are often poorly versed in the terms or methods of stylistic grammar. In the hands of uninformed students or poorly prepared teachers, the use of text-analysis software often leads to useless or even harmful decontextualized generalizations about avoiding forms of *to be* or using active verbs.

Most researchers underscore the need for heuristic software that reflects what we know about writing (Bruce T. Pedersen, Cynthia L. Selfe, and Billie J. Wahlstrom, ''Computer-Assisted Instruction and the Writing Process: Questions for Research and Evaluation'' [1984]). Such software will encourage students to internalize strategies for writing; at the same time it will treat writing as a complex, idiosyncratic process, with instruction tailored to various composing strategies.

THE COMPUTER AS WORD PROCESSOR

While some researchers question the value of CAI and heuristic software for teaching writing, there is widespread agreement that the computer with word processing software makes a very good writing tool, especially for encouraging revision. Colette Daiute describes how the computer frees writers from physical and psychological constraints that inhibit revision processes (''The Computer as Stylus and Audience'' [1983]; *Writing and Computers* [1985]). Many researchers have noted that the machine allows writers to revise without recopying or retyping whole texts. Elizabeth Sommers and James L. Collins conclude in *What Research Tells Us about Composing and Computers* (1984) that word processing brings about five important changes: (1) students develop into more fluid writers, (2) revision is more intensive, more varied, and sustained over longer periods of time, (3) illegible handwriting is no longer a problem, (4) students are more willing to revise, and (5) students develop a deeper understanding of the writing process. Given the research of the past several years, however, we should be skeptical of these findings (with the obvious exception of that related to handwriting). While both students and teachers *say* that word processing encourages substantial revision, consistent effects of word processing on revision strategies have proven difficult to establish, through either case or experimental studies.

We have a great wealth of anecdotal and self-report data from teachers and students suggesting that students appreciate the revision capabilities of word processing. In "Computers and Basic Writers" (1985), Dawn Rodrigues reports that her students learned to revise more readily by concentrating first on content and structure before moving on to style and mechanical editing. Linda Hunter, too, found that her basic writing students quickly became comfortable with the computer and found it an encouragement to revision ("Basic Writers and the Computer" [1983]). Marian Arkin and Brian Gallagher report impressive gains for their basic writers in grade point averages, noting their students gained a sense of accomplishment and an appreciation for their revising processes ("Word Processing and the Basic Writer" [1984]). Lynn Veach Sadler and Wendy Tibbetts Greene, in "Computer-Assisted Composition at Bennett College" (1985), noted that students thought they revised more freely because of word processing. Sadler and Greene also claim that their students wrote longer essays, that the opportunities for revising resulted in better writing through successive drafts, and that the students came to see themselves more as writers.

Several researchers have reported on teaching writing with computers to learning disabled students. A large project at the General College of the University of Minnesota issued a generally favorable report (Trudy Dunham, *Learning Disabled College Writers Project* [1987]). Glen Kleiman and Mary Humphrey reported their learning disabled, fourteen- to sixteen-year-old students wrote more, edited more, and wrote better using word processing, noting a progression of attention during revision from spelling, to words and sentences, and finally to ideas and organization ("Word Processing in the Classroom" [1982]). Laurie Fais and Richard Wanderman found more improvement on active-expressive tasks than on passive-receptive tasks such as error correction (*A Computer-Aided Writing Program for Learning Disabled Adolescents* [1987]). Lillian Bridwell-Bowles ("Writing with Computers: Implications from Research for the Language Impaired" [1987]) and Charles A. MacArthur ("The Impact of Computers on the Writing Process" [1988]) review the literature on learning disabled students and conclude with favorable recommendations. Positive evaluations have been reported for economically disadvantaged college students in Wayne Moore's "Word Processing in First-Year Comp" (1985), for developmental learners in Tom Mac Lennan's "Beyond Drill and Skill" (1986), and for dyslexic students in Valerie Arms's "A Dyslexic Can Compose on a Computer" (1984).

Apparently, students across the range of composition classes feel very positive about word processing. R. J. Kurth reported that his ninth graders wrote more substantial, longer essays and had better attitudes (*Word Processing and Composition Revision Strategies* [1987]). Lillian Bridwell, Geoffrey Sirc, and Robert Brooke, in "Revising and Computing" (1985), report that their upper division students liked word processing and felt it improved their writing. Paula R.

Feldman, working with business students, found that the computer helped turn her students' composing processes into a "qualitatively better, more rewarding experience," noting that her students seemed more willing to experiment with language and phrasing (*Using Microcomputers for College Writing* [1984] 4). In "Word-Processing in Freshman Composition" (1986), Paul Cohen reports very positive reactions, with students finding composing and editing to be easier with the computer than with pen and paper. The ease of revision is nicely captured by James V. Catano in his characterization of electronic text as *fluid* in "Computer-Based Writing: Navigating the Fluid Text" (1985). There is no doubt that students feel the word processor makes their texts more fluid, more subject to revision.

In addition to facilitating text revisions, Colette Daiute hypothesizes that "the interactiveness of the text editor stimulates writers to take a reader's point of view and thus evaluate their writing and find their own mistakes" ("The Computer as Stylus and Audience" [1983] 134). Other researchers echo this point, arguing that (1) seeing text on screen can help students evaluate it and see the need for refinement (Marian Arkin and Brian Gallagher "Word Processing and the Basic Writer" [1984]; Paula R. Feldman, *Using Microcomputers for College Writing* [1984]; Gail G. Womble, "Revising and Computing" [1985]) or that (2) seeing a text that is neat, though not free of errors, convinces students they can control their writing (James Nash and Lawrence Schwartz, "Making Computers Work in the Writing Class" [1985]). Other researchers, however, argue that the screen is difficult to work with and that writers are not able to see problems as easily (Christina Haas and John R. Hayes, "What Did I Just Say?" [1986]; Jeanette Harris, "Student Writers and Word Processing" [1985]; Margaret L. Lansing, *Student Writers and Word Processors* [1984]).

In spite of the consistently positive self-report data from students and teachers on the benefits to drafting and revising that word processing provides, the data from case studies is at best equivocal. In an early study of four inexperienced college writers, "The Word Processor and Revision Strategies" (1983), Richard M. Collier found that the computer tended to increase the number and complexity of revisions, with a slight increase in length; the revisions, however, did not appear to affect ratings of quality. Several other researchers suggest that word processors encourage attention to sentence-level editing, rather than to the higher-level reorganization of ideas. Studying six college writers, Jeanette Harris (1985) found they made *fewer* revisions with word processing than when revising by hand; she found no evidence that the machine encouraged students to experiment to take risks at macrostructural levels. She noted that her less experienced writers, those who did not typically revise, seemed even less inclined to do so on the computer. That her students all wrote drafts on paper before using the machine may have influenced their behavior. Bridwell, Sirc and Brooke, in case studies of five upper-level university writers (1985), found a "tremendous increase" in the number of surface-level changes (at least in part due to typographical errors because of lack of experience with sensitive keyboards). Their students also showed an increased concern with how texts looked—format—but not necessarily with what texts said. A couple of their subjects used the word processor to revise *less* than they normally would, since they didn't like writing and the computer allowed them to finish faster.

Randall G. Nichols gathered similar data on five college basic writers, who tended to compose in more frequent sessions of shorter duration, producing more words in less time than when composing by hand (''Word Processing and Basic Writers'' [1986]). Nichols saw no evidence that the computer led these basic writers to revise more, to take the reader's point of view, to write more, or to write better. Though the writers tended to suffer frequent interruptions because of problems operating the machine, they still finished more quickly than when composing by hand. Linda Hunter, too, found that her basic writers tended not to use the high-level editing capabilities of the computer (''Basic Writers and the Computer'' [1983]).

A few studies of small groups of students report improvements in student writing as an effect of word processing. Wendy C. Beserra's six college-level basic writers wrote better essays on the computer than by hand, devoting more time to the four essay tasks (''Effects of Word Processing upon the Writing Processes of Basic Writers'' [1986]). B. King, J. Birnbaum, and J. Wageman report their ten college basic writers wrote better with word processing (''Word Processing and the College Basic Writer'' [1984]); George Moberg, in an informal study, found a higher passing rate on his school's writing assessment for remedial writers who used word processing (''Remedial Writing on Computers'' [1987]). But E. J. Posey's thirteen first-year basic writers, who wrote posttests by hand, did not attain higher quality ratings than a control group (''The Writer's Tool: A Study of Microcomputer Word Processing to Improve the Writing of Basic Writers'' [1986]).

What is clear from these case studies is that there is no clear pattern of a single effect of the machine on student writing processes. Bridwell, Sirc, and Brooke argue that ''the way the machine is used is not a function of the computer by itself, the writer by herself, or the task by itself—all three interrelate'' (1985: 192). The case studies reported by Cynthia L. Selfe in ''The Electronic Pen'' (1985) demonstrate this differential adaptation of composing styles to the technology, with some students choosing to compose on screen and others not, and with important differences among the strategies of those who do. Andrea Herrmann also found differential use of the machine, characterizing some high school writers as remaining marginally proficient with the machine; others as becoming technically proficient though with little effect on their composing habits; and still others as productive learners, who were both technically proficient with the machine and who used it in productive ways to enhance their writing (''An Ethnographic Study of a High School Writing Class Using Computers'' [1987]). Margaret L. Lansing notes important differences in two writers, one of whom she characterized as a planner, the other a reviser. She argues that the word processor may be much more useful to a writer who emphasizes multiple drafts and revision as an overall strategy (*Student Writers and Word Processors* [1984]). M. Bryson found that word processing benefited high-ability students more than low-ability students (*Augmented Word Processing: The Influence of Task Characteristics and Mode of Presentation on Writers' Cognition* [1986]). We may conclude with some certainty that the technology in and of itself will not miraculously change well-established writing/revising behaviors in student writers. Instead of a simple correlation between the two variables—use of the machine and increased revision—the relation appears to be multivariate, involving individual composing styles, the nature of the writing task and situational constraints, and the influence of teaching approaches, all of which interact with the influence of the machine.

We are only beginning to see controlled studies that compare full classes of students using computers with traditionally taught classes. Milton Teichman and Marilyn Poris (*Word Processing in the Classroom: Its Effects on Freshman Writers* [1985]) found that among freshman, computers decreased writing anxiety in three of four trials, though not significantly, and increased scores on the Test of Standard Written English. Most importantly, in three of four trials, the use of computers enhanced the quality of student writing. Repeated measures analysis tended to show that growth in computer essay writing tended to occur in curvilinear spurts, rather than in simple linear progression.

In "A Comparative Study of the Quality and Syntax of Compositions by First Year College Students Using Handwriting and Word Processing" (1985), Craig Etchison compared four sections of composition using word processing with four traditional sections. Two pretest and two posttest essays were written by each student, with time allowed for revisions. Though the word-processing students began the term with scores well below the control group, by the end of the term they scored above the control group, with gains on mean holistic scores more than five time those of the control students. T-unit analysis showed the main identifiable difference to be added length.

The present authors with Penny Edwards reported on a comparative study at Southern Illinois University–Carbondale. Twelve sections of computer-assisted freshman composition were matched by teacher with twelve control sections. The study measured both in-class and take-home revision skills, allowing students to do their posttest writing on the computer. Results favored the computer students, who improved an in-class writing sample upon revision (especially high-level discourse features) to a significantly greater extent than did the regular students. The teacher and the teacher's interaction with the instructional method (using computers or not) were found to be stronger influences over student revision than the computer alone, though the computer still accounted for significant gains. Those experimental students who chose to compose on word processors for the posttest had much higher revision scores than those students who chose to write by hand (Stephen A. Bernhardt, Penny Edwards, and Patti Wojahn, "Teaching College Composition with Computers: A Program Evaluation Study" [1989]).

Several recent studies have carefully investigated the influence of computers and found improved writing quality as compared with traditional methods. Carole McAllister and Richard Louth found significantly improved paragraph writing among 102 basic college writers ("The Effect of Word Processing on the Quality of Basic Writers' Revisions" [1988]). Barbara Anne Pivarnik found improvement among seventy-six low achieving eleventh grade students in her dissertation research ("The Effect of Training in Word Processing on the Writing Quality of Eleventh Grade Students" [1985]). Virginia Juettner also found improved writing in her dissertation study of high school students ("The Word Processing Environment and Its Impact on the Writing of a Group of High School Students" [1987]). V. J. Cirello's dissertation study of tenth grade remedial students who used computers showed they wrote more, wrote longer sentences, and wrote better on two of three writing tasks ("The Effect of Word Processing on the Writing Abilities of Tenth Grade Remedial Writing Students" [1986]). Diane D. Hammar's dissertation reported that using microcomputers to help eleventh graders who had failed the New York State Regents exam was effective in improving their writing, though not as effective as the best traditional methods taught by experienced teachers ("The Effectiveness of Computer-Assisted Writing Instruction for Juniors Who Have Failed the Regents Competency Test in Writing" [1986]).

Gilbert Storms compared five sections of students who chose computer sections of introductory composition with five traditional sections at Miami University of Ohio. The interdisciplinary research team took a broad approach to evaluation, relying on classroom and lab logs, observation, questionnaires, interviews, case studies, and writing samples. They found that teachers did not have to spend large amounts of time showing students how to use computers (IBM PCs with PC-Write), that the computers did not create a barrier between students or between teachers and students, that the teachers believed they could teach more effectively with computers than without, and that teachers in experimental sections assigned more in-class writing. While students in computer sections spent more time planning and drafting, they believed revising was easier on the computer and spent less time at it than control students. The researchers found no qualitative improvement in the essays of the computer students (*Report on the Department of English Computer Classroom and Laboratory 1985–86* [1986]).

Gail Hawisher in "The Effects of Word Processing on the Revision Strategies of College Freshmen" (1987) reports on twenty word-processing college students who wrote four essays on the computer and four by hand. She found the machine did not increase revision, that there was no relation between revisions and quality ratings, and that there were no differences between essays composed on machine and those composed by hand.

Paul Cohen reports that a large group of students using word processing made 34% more revisions on an end-of-term essay than did control students, even though they wrote with pen and paper. Although the use of the computer did not result in higher grades, Cohen does believe the revising behaviors encouraged by the computer transfer to other writing situations ("Word-Processing in Freshman Composition" [1986]). Delores Shriner, too, reports more risk taking and more revisions among her first-year writers at the University of Michigan, but no differences from her control group in overall writing quality ("Risk Taking, Revising, and Word Processing" [1988]). Catherine A. Coulter reports findings of no difference for her sixty-two college freshmen at the University of Oklahoma on writing quality, or type and frequency of revisions ("Writing with Word Processors: Effects on Cognitive Development, Revision, and Writing Quality" [1986]). John A. Cross and Bob J. Curey studied three freshman composition classes at Indiana University of Pennsylvania with half the students in each class using word processors. Measures of attitude, performance, process strategies, and grades were inconsistent across the groups. They conclude that the effects of word processing vary with the writer and with general factors related to the teacher and class (*The Effects of Word Processing on Writing* [1984]).

What is repeatedly suggested by both the case studies and the experimental studies of larger groups is that students enjoy using word processing in their composition courses; they also believe it enhances their writing and revision. Writing teachers, too, remain enthusiastic about using the computer and believe it can help students become better writers, though they are often cautious about claiming to see immediate improvements in student writing. We should continue to see the data on positive attitudes as an important argument for teaching with computers, but we need to document through longitudinal studies the persistence of such attitudes and their effects on writing performance.

Examining both case studies and experimental studies of whole classes, the most we can conclude is that the data are inconsistent on word processing leading to increased revision, higher level revision, or improved writing. Part of the inconsistency is a result of research designs that are either not well conceived or not comparable with other studies, making it difficult to generalize (Gail Hawisher, "Studies in Word Processing" [1986]). Recent research is improving in this respect; we are seeing careful dissertations and better designed studies. These do tend to support word processing, especially for basic writers.

But we must conclude that in spite of the machine's potential for significantly enhancing revision, it remains very difficult to change the persistent habits of student composing, habits that equate revision with surface tinkering and error correction. For many students, writing is not a pleasurable activity, and the increased ease of revision with the machine may lead students to spend less overall time with their writing, rather than leading them to exploit those features of word processing that make it useful for experimenting with ideas in a fluid medium.

We might still place some hope in the hypothesis of D. N. Perkins that word processing represents an area of "low road" transfer, so that continual use of word processors year after year might result in "a gradual broadening of students' range and power" ("The Fingertip Effect" [1985] 14). Such skill development would be in contrast to "high road" transfer, where what is learned transfers in an immediate and purposeful way, via mindful abstraction and application of learned principles to new contexts. Such a position would lead us to refuse to place too much emphasis on attempts to document improved student writing in one semester. A broader approach to evaluating the effectiveness of computers would take into account attitudes of students and teachers, persistence and transfer of learning, influence on behavior in other courses, and the relationship of word processing to larger goals of writing instruction and university education.

THE COMPUTER LAB AS A TEACHING ENVIRONMENT

While it is important to document the changes word processing brings about in student attitudes, behaviors, and skills, it is critical to consider research that concentrates on the changes the technology brings about in the classroom environment: to the patterns of interaction, the roles of teachers and students, and the nature of assignments and completion strategies. When we think about the effects of computers on writing, we need to think about both how they change the writing processes and products of our students *and* how they change the nature of instruction. These two areas of concern are linked—the potential of the technology for enhancing the writing of our students is at least partially dependent on how we adapt our roles and instructional strategies to take advantage of the machine environment. When we learn how the machine can change instruction and begin to match our teaching strategies with the technology, we may begin to see more consistent research findings on the value of the computer in teaching writing. When teaching strategies and the technology are mismatched, we encourage the difficulties described by Charles Suhor and Valerie Jester in their "ERIC/RCS Report: Computer Caveats" (1984). We need to recognize the importance of teacher influence in successful integration of computers: the enthusiasm of individual teachers and the strategies they employ to teach writing with computers influence student attitudes, work habits, revision strategies, and ultimately the successful use of the machine.

One of the most important shifts in classroom roles that the computer brings about is the decentering of the teacher and the consequent individualization of instruction (Elizabeth A. Sommers, "Integrating Composing and Computing" [1985]). Instead of front-and-center teaching to a full group, the teacher in a lab environment moves about, works with students individually as they write, and generally coordinates and facilitates individual learning (Ronald A. Sudol, "Applied Word Processing" [1985]). John C. Thoms's "Observations on a New Remedial Language Arts Course" (1987) is particularly apt here: he found his own role as teacher redefined as he moved about, helping students in various ways while they pursued different kinds of learning through individualized activities. Dawn Rodrigues, too, states as her most important finding that the lab encouraged her basic writers to move from dependence on her help to independence ("Computers and Basic Writers" [1985]). Judith M. Newman in "Online" (1984) describes the teacher's role in a lab environment as encouraging students to find ways of answering their own questions. Students in a lab often rely on other students, who may be less intimidated by the technology than the teacher is and better suited to solving technical difficulties. We see in this situation a radical role reversal, with students assuming expert roles and teachers assuming the role of learner or co–problem solver.

One result of the individualized learning in the lab is an increased reliance on collaborative learning. In "An Emerging Rhetoric of Collaboration" (1986), Cynthia Selfe and Billie J. Wahlstrom describe the new patterns of etiquette in their computer lab. Other researchers also stress the emergence of a collaborative community in the workshop model that informs their teaching with computers (Valerie Arms, "Engineers Becoming Writers" [1987]; Pamela B. Farrell, "Writer, Peer Tutor, and the Computer: A Unique Relationship" [1987]; Dawn Rodrigues [1985]; and Ronald A. Sudol [1985]).

Many researchers argue that teachers should intentionally structure their class-room activities to encourage students to experiment with new revising strategies through word processing. In "Accordion Writing" (1984), Jamieson McKenzie recommends expanding essays from the inside out, followed by compression as editing takes place. Sudol stresses the possibilities for "additive revision" as students revise by juxtaposing new versions with original versions, comparing for effects before deleting ("Applied Word Processing" [1985]). James Nash and Lawrence Schwartz use staged assignments that incorporate new source material into existing essays ("Making Computers Work" [1985]). Colette Daiute (*Writing and Computers* [1985]), Christine Hult and Jeanette Harris (*A Writer's Introduction to Word Processing* [1987]), Helen J. Schwartz (*Interactive Writing* [1985]), and Ronald A. Sudol (*Textfiles* [1987]) all describe activities that can help teachers develop strategies for exploiting the potential of the computer in a writing classroom. Perhaps the best discussion of how computers can change the nature of assignments is presented by Brian Gallagher in *Microcomputers and Word Processing Programs* (1985). He suggests making assignments that stretch out over a term, with students using the computer for storing various drafts that are recombined in a series of texts, some of which exist only electronically, some of which get printed and reprinted in various forms.

Four articles are particularly good at helping teachers figure out how to be productive in a machine environment. Christine Hult offers advice for avoiding problems with poor writers ("The Computer and the Inexperienced Writer" [1988]). Paul LeBlanc uses a case study approach to recommend strategies for adapting instruction to individual composing styles ("How to Get the Words Just Right: A Reappraisal of Word Processing and Revision" [1988]). Marcia Curtis offers a good critical review of some of the negative research on revising with computers, suggesting that revision not be isolated from teaching strategies in such studies ("Windows on Composing: Teaching Revision on Word Processors" [1988]). And Andrea Herrmann usefully discusses training programs for teachers new to computers ("Teaching Teachers to Use Computers as Writing Tools" [1988]). *Critical Perspectives on Computers and Composition Instruction* (1989), edited by Gail Hawisher and Cynthia Selfe, similarly focuses on how teachers can achieve an appropriate fit between the available technology and the existing knowledge base concerning composition teaching.

A few teachers have begun to experiment with applications other than word processing. Elaine O. Lees, in "Proofreading with the Ears" (1985), discusses how her basic reading and writing students benefited from proofreading with a Kurzweil Reading Machine, which read aloud their printed texts. Her students spent more time and corrected more errors with the voice machine than when proofing on their own. We should expect to see other applications to writing of voice machine technology, with the potential to encourage the development of direct dictation skills (see Jeanne W. Halpern and Sarah Liggett, *Computers and Composing* [1984] and Michael Spooner, "ERIC/RCS Report: Dictating to the Machine: Voice Activated Computer Technology" [1988]).

Communications also promises to figure importantly in writing classrooms. Helen Schwartz recognized quite early the potential of an electronic bulletin board for organizing prewriting exercises, peer collaboration, and peer revision in an introductory literature class ("SEEN" [1984]). In "An Interdisciplinary Program Linking Computers and Writing Instruction" (1985), Muriel Harris and Madelon Cheek describe a service the Purdue University Writing Lab has provided to electrical engineering students who submit drafts of their reports via electronic mail. Don Payne describes a similar setup in "Computer-Extended Audiences for Student Writers" (1987), with high school students sending their texts to university students in a teaching methods course. Taking communications technology a step further, Edward M. Jennings describes in "Paperless Writing" (1987) how he kept all student work in electronic files so it would be constantly available for teacher and student commentary. His experiments with on-line teaching bring into question many traditional assumptions about how writing is taught, what a conference is, who has authority, and what constitutes a classroom.

We should expect to see within a few years startling advances in the development of writers' environments. In "A Framework for a Cognitive Theory of Writing" (1980), Allan Collins and Dedre Gentner describe one such "idea" environment, wherein a writer would have access to expert advice and guidance from the machine throughout the writing process. James A. Levin, Marcia J. Boruta, and Mary T. Vasconcellos describe another such environment in "Microcomputer-Based Environments for Writing" (1983). ACCESS (A Computer Composition Educational Software System), currently being developed by Donald Ross and Sheldon Fossum at the University of Minnesota, represents another project to provide software to support a computerized writing classroom. Minicomputer-based systems under development at Carnegie Mellon present an environment through multiple screens on a large monitor to give students access to assignments, the course syllabus, readings, note and citation files that can be built from the readings, writing aids, and a class bulletin board, in addition to full word processing functions. And whole new environments have been created in the past year with the advent of hypermedia software, such as Project Jefferson at the University of Southern California. Such environments raise many questions: How much tolerance for reading electronic text do students have? How is reading on screen different from reading in books? What are the advantages of searching for information physically in libraries, books, and magazines versus searching through electronic databases? Will we find that some students adapt well to learning within the screen environment while others feel handicapped?

COMPUTERS AND COMPOSITION: A POSTSCRIPT

We are not facing questions about whether the computer should be used in schools for writing or for teaching composition. The computer is with us on campus, in programs for basic writers as well as advanced. Each semester, more of our students arrive already familiar with the advantages of word processing. Each course we teach with word processing generates a group of students who continue to expect machine resources throughout their academic careers. On every campus, increasing funds are being spent to enhance computer resources, especially microcomputers, which are proving increasingly popular with students and faculty across the disciplines.

So the questions we face are not so much *whether* we should use computers, but how. How can computers be used to help students understand and enhance their own writing strategies? How can teachers structure assignments to encourage students to take advantage of the machine's efficiency for revising prose? How should lab time be structured to take advantage of collaborative possibilities and the redefined roles of teachers and students? How can the computer help us create writing environments that help students build texts through increasingly complex interactions of writer, text, machine, and multiple sources of information? Research has only begun to suggest answers to such questions, for basic writers and for student writers in general.

REFERENCES

ACE Newsletter. Ed. Tom Decker. Westview Centennial Secondary School, North York, Ontario, Canada M3N 1W7.

Alderman, Donald L., Lola R. Appel, and Richard T. Murray. "PLATO and TICCIT: An Evaluation of CAI in the Community College." *Educ Tech* (April 1978): 40–44.

Arkin, Marian, and Brian Gallagher. "Word Processing and the Basic Writer." *Conn Eng J* 15 (Spring 1984): 60–66.

Arms, Valerie. "A Dyslexic Can Compose on a Computer." *Educ Tech (January 1984): 39–41.*

———. *"Engineers Becoming Writers: Computers and Creativity in Technical Writing Classes." Writing at Century's End: Essays on Computer-Assisted Composition.* Ed. Lisa Gerrard. New York: Random House, 1987, pp. 64–78.

Auten, Anne. "ERIC/RCS Report: Computers in English: How and Why." *EJ* (January 1984): 54–56.

Bacig, Thomas, Donald Larmouth, and Kenneth Risdon. "A Comprehensive Computer-Aided Program in Writing." *Selected Papers from the Conference on Computers in Writing: New Directions in Teaching and Research.* Spec. issue of *Computers and Composition.* Ed. Lillian Bridwell and Donald Ross. Houghton: Michigan Technological University, 1985; pp. 1–22.

Becker, Henry J. *How Schools Use Microcomputers: Summary of the First National Survey*. Baltimore: Johns Hopkins University; Center for Social Organization of Schools, March 1985.

———. "Reports from the 1985 National Survey." *Instructional Uses of School Computers* (June 1986): 1–11.

Bereiter, Carl, and Marlene Scardamalia. "From Conversation to Composition: The Role of Instruction in a Development Process." *Advances in Instructional Psychology*, vol. 2. Ed. Robert Glaser. Hillsdale, N.J.: Lawrence Erlbaum Associates, 1982, pp. 1–64.

Bernhardt, Stephen A., Penny Edwards, and Patricia Wojahn. "Teaching College Composition with Computers: A Program Evaluation Study." *Written Communication* 6 (1989): 108–33.

Beserra, Wendy C. "Effects of Word Processing upon the Writing Process of Basic Writers." Diss. New Mexico State University, 1986.

Bridwell, Lillian, and Ann Duin. "Looking In Depth at Writers: Computers as Writing Medium and Research Tool." *Writing On-Line: Using Computers in the Teaching of Writing*. Ed. James L. Collins and Elizabeth A. Sommers. Upper Montclair, N.J.: Boynton/Cook, 1985, pp. 115–21.

Bridwell, Lillian, Geoffrey Sirc, and Robert Brooke. "Revising and Computing: Case Studies of Student Writers." *The Acquisition of Written Language: Response and Revision*. Ed. Sarah W. Freedman. Norwood, N.J.: Ablex Publishing Corporation, 1985, pp. 172–94.

Bridwell, Lillian, and Donald Ross. "Integrating Computers into a Writing Curriculum; or Buying, Begging, and Building." *The Computer in Composition Instruction*. Ed. William Wresch. Urbana, Ill.: NCTE, 1984, pp. 107–19.

———, eds. *Selected Papers from the Conference on Computers in Writing: New Directions in Teaching and Research*. Spec. issue of *Computers and Composition*. Houghton: Michigan Technological University, 1985.

Bridwell-Bowles, Lillian. "Writing with Computers: Implications from Research for the Language Impaired." *Topics in Language Disorders* 7 (1987): 78–85.

Bryson, M. "Augmented Word Processing: The Influence of Task Characteristics and Mode of Presentation on Writers' Cognition." ERIC, 1986. ED 276 016.

Burns, Hugh. "Computer-Assisted Prewriting Activities." *Computers in Composition Instruction*. Ed. Joseph Lawlor. Los Alamitos, Calif.: SWRL Educational Research and Development, 1982, pp. 19–29.

———. "Computers and Composition." *Teaching Composition: Twelve Bibliographic Essays*, rev. and enl. ed. Ed. Gary Tate. Fort Worth: Texas Christian University Press, 1987, pp. 378–400.

Burns, Hugh L., and George H. Culp. "Stimulating Invention in English Composition through Computer-Assisted Instruction." *Educ Tech* (August 1980): 5–10.

Byerly, Gayle A. "CAI in College English." *Comp Hum* 12 (1978): 281–85.

Catano, James V. "Computer-Based Writing: Navigating the Fluid Text." *CCC* 36 (1985): 309–16.

Cirello, V. J. "The Effect of Word Processing on the Writing Abilities of Tenth Grade Remedial Writing Students." Diss. New York University, 1986.

Cohen, Paul. "Word-Processing in Freshman Composition: A New Study." NCTE 76th Annual Convention. San Antonio, 22 November 1986.

Collegiate Microcomputer. Rose-Hulman Institute of Technology, Terre Haute, IN 47803.

Collier, Richard M. "The Word Processor and Revision Strategies." *CCC* 34 (1983): 149–55.

Collins, Allan, and Dedre Gentner. "A Framework for a Cognitive Theory of Writing." *Cognitive Process of Writing*. Ed. Lee W. Gregg and Erwin R. Steinberg. Hillsdale, N.J.: Lawrence Erlbaum Associates, 1980, pp. 51–72.

Computer-Assisted Composition Journal (CACJ). Ed. Lynn Veach Sadler and Wendy Tibbetts Greene. Methodist College, 5400 Ramsey Street, Fayetteville, NC 28301–1499.

Computers and Composition. Ed. Cynthia Selfe and Gail Hawisher. Humanities Department, Michigan Technological University, Houghton, MI 49331.

Coulter, Catherine A. "Writing with Word Processors: Effects on Cognitive Development, Revision, and Writing Quality." Diss. University of Oklahoma, 1986.

Creative Word Processing in the Classroom (CWP): A Teacher's Guide and Newsletter. P.O. Box 590727, San Francisco, CA 94159.

Cronnell, B. *Computer-Based Practice in Editing*. ERIC, 1982 ED 220 869.

Cross, John A., and Bob J. Curey. "The Effects of Word Processing on Writing." ERIC, 1984. ED 247 921.

Curtis, Marcia. "Windows on Composing: Teaching Revision on Word Processors." *CCC* 39 (1988): 337–44.

Daiute, Colette. "The Computer as Stylus and Audience." *CCC* 34 (1983): 134–45.

———. "Do Writers Talk to Themselves?" *The Acquisition of Written Language: Response and Revision*. Ed. Sarah W. Freedman. Norwood, N.J.: Ablex Publishing Corporation, 1985, pp. 133–59.

———. "Physical and Cognitive Factors in Revising: Insights from Studies with Computers." *RTE* 20 (1986): 141–59.

———. *Writing and Computers*. Menlo Park, Calif.: Addison-Wesley, 1985.

Dobrin, David N. "Some Ideas about Idea Processors." *Writing at Century's End: Essays on Computer-Assisted Composition*. Ed. Lisa Gerrard. New York: Random House, 1987, pp. 95–107.

———. "Style Analyzers Once More." *Comp Comp* 3.3 (1986): 22–31.

Dreyfus, Hubert L. *What Computers Can't Do: A Critique of Artificial Intelligence*, 2nd ed. New York: Harper and Row, 1979.

Dreyfus, Hubert L., and Stuart E. Dreyfus. *Mind over Machine: The Power of Human Intuition and Expertise in the Era of the Computer*. New York: Free Press, 1986.

Dunham, Trudy. *Learning Disabled College Writers Project, Evaluation Report, 1985–86* (General College, University of Minnesota, Minneapolis). ERIC, 1987. ED 286 188.

Etchison, Craig. "A Comparative Study of the Quality and Syntax of Compositions by First Year College Students Using Handwriting and Word Processing." Diss. Indiana University of Pennsylvania, 1985.

———. "Who's Making the Decisions—People or Machines?" *Comp Comp* 2.4 (1985): 17–26.

Fais, Laurie, and Richard Wanderman. *A Computer-Aided Writing Program for Learning Disabled Adolescents*. ERIC, 1987. Ed 293 273.

Farrell, Pamela B. "Writer, Peer Tutor, and the Computer: A Unique Relationship." *WCJ* 8 (1987): 29–33.

Feldman, Paula R. *Using Microcomputers for College Writing—What Students Say*. ERIC, 1984. Ed 244 298.

Frase, Lawrence T., Kathleen E. Kiefer, Charles R. Smith, and Mary L. Fox. "Theory and Practice in Computer-Aided Composition." *The Acquisition of Written Language: Response and Revision*. Ed. Sarah W. Freedman. Norwood, N.J.: Ablex Publishing Corporation, 1985, pp. 195–210.

Freedman, Sarah Warshauer, ed. *The Acquisition of Written Language: Response and Revision*. Norwood, N.J.: Ablex Publishing Corporation, 1985.

Friedman, Morton P. 'WANDAH—A Computerized Writer's Aid." *Selected Papers from the Conference on Computers in Writing: New Directions in Teaching and Research*. Spec. issue of *Computers and Composition*. Ed. Lillian Bridwell and Donald Ross. Houghton: Michigan Technical University, 1985, pp. 113–24.

Gallagher, Brian. *Microcomputers and Word Processing Programs: Research Report Monograph Number 9*. City University of New York, 1985. (Available from Instructional Resource Center, Office of Academic Affairs, CUNY, 535 E. 80th Street, New York, NY 10021.)

Gerrard, Lisa, ed. *Writing at Century's End: Essays on Computer-Assisted Composition*. New York: Random House, 1987.

Gilles, Philip D. "The Utilization of Computer Technology as a Means of Teaching and Evaluating Prewriting Processes." Diss. Georgia State University, 1983.

Glaser, Robert, Alan Lesgold, and David Bartholomae. *Using Cognitive Research and Computer Technology to Improve Writing Skill in Low-Performing College Students* (Grant 830–0355). An Interim Project Report to the Ford Foundation. Prepared by Glynda Hull, Research Associate. University of Pittsburgh, Learning Research and Development Center, December 1985.

Haas, Christina, and John R. Hayes. "What Did I Just Say? Reading Problems in Writing with the Machine." *RTE* 20 (1986): 22–35.

Halpern, Jeanne W., and Sarah Liggett. *Computers and Composing: How the New Technologies Are Changing Writing*. Carbondale and Edwardsville: Southern Illinois University Press, 1984.

Hammar, Diane D. "The Effectiveness of Computer-Assisted Writing Instruction for Juniors Who Have Failed the Regents Competency Test in Writing." Diss. University of Rochester, 1986.

Harris, Jeanette. "Student Writers and Word Processing: A Preliminary Evaluation." *CCC* 36 (1985): 323–30.

Harris, Muriel, and Madelon Cheek. "An Interdisciplinary Program Linking Computers and Writing Instruction." *Coll Micro* 3 (1985): 213–23.

Hawisher, Gail. "The Effects of Word Processing on the Revision Strategies of College Freshmen." *RTE* 21 (1987): 145–59.

———. "Studies in Word Processing." *Comp Comp* 4.1 (1986): 6–31.

Hawisher, Gail, and Cynthia Selfe, eds. *Critical Perspectives on Computers and Composition Instruction*. Wolfeboro, N.H. Teachers College Press, 1989.

Herrmann, Andrea. "An Ethnographic Study of a High School Writing Class Using Computers: Marginally, Technically Proficient, and Productive Learners." *Writing at Century's End: Essays on Computer-Assisted Composition*. Ed. Lisa Gerrard. New York: Random House, 1987, pp. 79–91.

———. "Teaching Teachers to Use Computers as Writing Tools." *Eng Ed* 20 (1988): 215–29.

Hull, Glynda. "The Use of Microcomputers in Basic Writing." *Selected Papers from the Conference on Computers in Writing: New Directions in Teaching and Re-*

search. Spec. issue of *Computers and Composition*. Ed. Lillian Bridwell and Donald Ross. Houghton: Michigan Technological University, 1985, pp. 185–93.

Hull, Glynda A., and William L. Smith. "Error Correction and Computing." *Writing On-Line: Using Computers in the Teaching of Writing*. Ed. James L. Collins and Elizabeth A. Sommers. Upper Montclair, N.J.: Boynton/Cook, 1985, pp. 89–101.

Hult, Christine. "The Effects of Word Processing on the Correctness of Student Writing." *Research in Word Processing Newsletter* (November 1985): 1–4.

———. "The Computer and the Inexperienced Writer." *Comp Comp* 5 (1988): 29–37.

Hult, Christine, and Jeanette Harris. *A Writer's Introduction to Word Processing*. Belmont, Calif.: Wadsworth, 1987.

Hunter, Linda. "Basic Writers and the Computer." *Focus* 9.3 (1983): 22–27.

Jennings, Edward M. "Paperless Writing: Boundary Conditions and Their Implications." *Writing at Century's End: Essays on Computer-Assisted Composition*. Ed. Lisa Gerrard. New York: Random House, 1987, pp. 11–20.

Juettner, Virginia, "The Word Processing Environment and Its Impact on the Writing of a Group of High School Students." Diss. University of Arizona, 1987.

Kemp, Fred. "Getting Smart with Computers: Computer-Aided Heuristics for Student Writers." *WCJ* 8 (1987): 3–10.

———. "The User-Friendly Fallacy." *CCC* 38 (1987): 32–39.

Kiefer, Kathleen, and Charles R. Smith. "Improving Students' Revising and Editing: The Writer's Workbench System." *The Computer in Composition Instruction*. Ed. William Wresch. Urbana, Ill.: NCTE, 1984, pp. 65–82.

———. "Textual Analysis with Computers: Tests of Bell Laboratories' Computer Software." *RTE* 17 (1983): 201–14.

King, B., J. Birnbaum, and J. Wageman. "Word Processing and the College Basic Writer." *The Written Word and the Word Processor*. Ed. T. Martinez. Philadelphia: Delaware Valley Writing Council, 1984.

Kinkead, Joyce. "Matching Software and Curriculum: A Description of Four Text-Analysis Programs." *Comp Comp* 3.3 (1986): 33–55.

Kleiman, Glen, and Mary Humphrey. "Word Processing in the Classroom." *Compute!* (March 1982): 96–99.

Kurth, R. J. *Word Processing and Composition Revision Strategies*. ERIC, 1987. ED 283 195.

Lansing, Margaret L. *Computers and Composition: A Bibliography of Research and Practice*. ERIC, 1984. ED 249 499.

———. *Student Writers and Word Processors: A Case Study*. ERIC, 1984. ED 249 491.

Lawlor, Joseph. *Computers in Composition Instruction*. Los Alamitos, Calif.: SWRL Educational Research and Development, 1982.

LeBlanc, Paul. "How to Get the Words Just Right: A Reappraisal of Word Processing and Revision." *Comp Comp* 5 (1988): 29–43.

Lees, Elaine O. "Proofreading with the Ears: A Case Study of Text-to-Voice Performance of a Student's Writing." *Coll Micro* 3 (1985): 339–44.

Levin, James A., Marcia J. Boruta, and Mary T. Vasconcellos. "Microcomputer-Based Environments for Writing: A Writer's Assistant." *Classroom Computers and Cognitive Science*. Ed. Alex Wilkinson. New York: Academic Press, 1983.

Luchte, Jeanne. "Computer Programs in the Writing Center: A Bibliographical Essay." *WCJ* 8 (1987): 11–19.

McAllister, Carole, and Richard Louth. "The Effect of Word Processing on the Quality of Basic Writers' Revisions." *RTE* 22 (1988): 417–27.

MacArthur, Charles A. "The Impact of Computers on the Writing Process." *Exceptional Children* 54 (1988): 536–42.

McDaniel, Ellen. "Bibliography of Text-Analysis and Writing-Instruction Software." *Journal of Advanced Composition* 7 (1987): 139–70.

———. "A Comparative Study of the First-Generation Software." *Comp Comp* 3.3 (1986): 7–21.

Macgregor, W. B. *PLATO and the English Curriculum.* ERIC, 1982. ED 227 484.

McKenzie, Jamieson. "Accordion Writing—Expository Composition and the Word Processor." *EJ* (September 1984): 56–58.

MacLennan, Tom. "Beyond Drill and Skill: Computers and Developmental Learners." NCTE 76th Annual Convention. San Antonio, 22 November 1986.

Marchesano, Louis. "Process CAI: A Bridge between Theory and Practice in Writing Instruction." *Coll Micro* 4 (1986): 83–87.

Marcus, Stephen. "Real-Time Gadgets with Feedback: Special Effects in Computer-Assisted Writing." *The Computer in Composition Instruction.* Ed. William Wresch. Urbana, Ill.: NCTE, 1984, pp. 120–30.

Moberg, George. "Remedial Writing on Computers: Evaluation by Students and Faculty of a Pilot Study Project, Fall 1985." *Comp Comp* 4 (1987): 35–51.

Moore, Wayne. "Word Processing in First-Year Comp." *Comp Comp* 3.1 (1985): 55–60.

Nancarrow, Paula Reed, Donald Ross, and Lillian Bridwell. *Word Processors and the Writing Process.* Westport, Conn.: Greenwood Press, 1984.

Nash, James, and Lawrence Schwartz. "Making Computers Work in the Writing Class." *Educ Tech* (May 1985): 19–21.

Newman, Judith M. "Online: Some Reflections on Learning and Computers." *Lang Arts* 61 (1984): 414–17.

Nichols, Randall G. "Word Processing and Basic Writers." *JBW* 5.2 (1986): 81–97.

Oates, William. "An Evaluation of Computer-Assisted Instruction for English Grammar Review." *Stud Lang L* 3 (1981): 193–200.

Oliver, Lawrence. "Pitfalls in Electronic Writing Land." *Eng Ed* 16 (1984): 94–100.

Otto, Lee. "Computer Promises, Computer Realities." *Class Comp L* (March 1984): 60+.

Partenheimer, David. "One View of *WANDAH: HBJ Writer.*" *WCJ* 8 (1987): 55–58.

Paul, Terri, and Don Payne. "Computer-Assisted Instruction: Teaching and Learning from the Basic Writer." *WI* 2 (1983): 193–99.

Payne, Don. "Computer-Extended Audiences for Student Writers: Some Theoretical and Practical Implications." *Writing at Century's End: Essays on Computer-Assisted Composition.* Ed. Lisa Gerrard. New York: Random House, 1987, pp. 21–26.

Pedersen, Bruce T., Cynthia L. Selfe, and Billie J. Wahlstrom. "Computer-Assisted Instruction and the Writing Process: Questions for Research and Evaluation." *CCC* 35 (1984): 98–101.

Pedersen, Elray L. 'TICCIT Will Gladly Learn and Gladly Teach Composition Skills." *Selected Papers from the Conference on Computers in Writing: New Directions in Teaching and Research.* Spec. issue of *Computers and Composition.* Ed. Lillian

Bridwell and Donald Ross. Houghton: Michigan Technological University, 1985, pp. 233–41.

Perkins, D. N. "The Fingertip Effect: How Information-Processing Technology Shapes Thinking." *Info Tech Ed* (August–September 1985): 11–17.

Pivarnik, Barbara Anne. "The Effect of Training in Word Processing on the Writing Quality of Eleventh Grade Students." Diss. University of Connecticut, 1985.

Posey, E. J. "The Writer's Tool: A Study of Microcomputer Word Processing to Improve the Writing of Basic Writers." Diss. New Mexico State University, 1986.

Research in Word Processing Newsletter. Ed. Bradford A. Morgan and James M. Schwartz. South Dakota School of Mines and Technology, 501 E. St. Joseph, Rapid City, SD 57701–3995.

Rodrigues, Dawn. "Computers and Basic Writers." *CCC* 36 (1985): 336–39.

Rodrigues, Dawn, and Raymond Rodrigues. "Computer-Based Creative Problem Solving." *The Computer in Composition Instruction*. Ed. William Wresch. Urbana, Ill.: NCTE, 1984, pp. 34–46.

Rodrigues, Raymond J., and Dawn Wilson Rodrigues. "Computer-Based Invention: Its Place and Potential." *CCC* 35 (1984): 78–86.

Ross, Donald. "Realities of Computer Analysis of Compositions." *Writing On-Line: Using Computers in the Teaching of Writing*. Ed. James L. Collins and Elizabeth A. Sommers. Upper Montclair, N.J.: Boynton/Cook, 1985, pp. 105–13.

Sadler, Lynn Veach, and Wendy Tibbetts Greene. "Computer-Assisted Composition at Bennett College." *Selected Papers from the Conference on Computers in Writing: New Directions in Teaching and Research*. Spec. issue of *Computers and Composition*. Ed. Lillian Bridwell and Donald Ross. Houghton: Michigan Technological University, 1985, pp. 243–56.

Schwartz, Helen J. *Interactive Writing*. New York: Holt, Rinehart and Winston, 1985.

———. "SEEN: A Tutorial and User Network for Hypothesis Testing." *The Computer in Composition Instruction*. Ed. William Wresch. Urbana, Ill.: NCTE, 1984, pp. 47–62.

———. "Teaching Writing with Computer Aids." *CE* 46 (1984): 239–47.

Schwartz, Helen J., and Lillian S. Bridwell. "A Selected Bibliography on Computers and Composition." *CCC* 35 (1984): 71–77; updated, *CCC* 38 (1987): 453–57.

Schwartz, Mimi. "Computer Writing Made Easier." *Comp Comp* 2.2 (1985): 7–8.

Selfe, Cynthia L. "The Electronic Pen: Computers and the Composing Process." *Writing On-Line: Using Computers in the Teaching of Writing*. Ed. James L. Collins and Elizabeth A. Sommers. Upper Montclair, N.J.: Boynton/Cook, 1985, pp. 55–66.

Selfe, Cynthia, and Billie J. Wahlstrom. "An Emerging Rhetoric of Collaboration: Computers, Collaboration and the Composing Process." *Coll Micro* 4 (1986): 289–95.

Shostak, Robert. "Computer-Assisted Composition Instruction: The State of the Art." *Computers in Composition Instruction*. Ed. Joseph Lawlor. Los Alamitos, Calif.: SWRL Educational Research and Development, 1982, pp. 5–18.

Shriner, Delores. "Risk Taking, Revising, and Word Processing." *Comp Comp* 5 (1988): 43–53.

Sommers, Elizabeth A. "Integrating Composing and Computing." *Writing On-Line: Using Computers in the Teaching of Writing*. Ed. James L. Collins and Elizabeth A. Sommers. Upper Montclair, N.J.: Boynton/Cook, 1985, pp. 3–10.

Sommers, Elizabeth A., and James L. Collins. *What Research Tells Us about Composing and Computers*. ERIC, 1984. ED 249 497.

Southwell, Michael G. "Microcomputers and Writing Instruction." *A Sourcebook for Basic Writing Teachers*. Ed. Theresa Enos. New York: Random House, 1987, pp. 584–93.

Spooner, Michael. "ERIC/RCS Report: Dictating to the Machine: Voice Activated Computer Technology." *Eng Ed* 20 (1988): 109–15.

Storms, Gilbert. *Report on the Department of English Computer Classroom and Laboratory 1985–86*. Miami University of Ohio. August 11, 1986. Unpublished report to Stephen Day, Dean, College of Arts and Science.

Strickland, James. "Prewriting and Computing." *Writing On-Line: Using Computers in the Teaching of Writing*. Ed. James L. Collins and Elizabeth A. Sommers. Upper Montclair, N.J.: Boynton/Cook, 1985, pp. 67–74.

Sudol, Ronald A. "Applied Word Processing: Notes on Authority, Responsibility and Revision in a Workshop Model." *CCC* 36 (1985): 331–35.

———. *Textfiles: A Rhetoric for Word Processing*. San Diego: Harcourt Brace Jovanovich, 1987.

Suhor, Charles, and Valerie Jester. "ERIC/RCS Report: Computer Caveats." *Eng Ed* 16 (1984): 181–85.

Teichman, Milton, and Marilyn Poris. *Word Processing in the Classroom: Its Effects on Freshman Writers*. ERIC, 1985. ED 276 062.

Thoms, John C. "Observations on a Remedial Language Arts Course." *Writing at Century's End: Essays on Computer-Assisted Composition*. Ed. Lisa Gerrard. New York: Random House, 1987, pp. 55–63.

Tucker, Marc S. "Computers in the Schools: Has the Revolution Passed or Is It Yet to Come?" Speech presented to the Association of American Publishers at their Annual Meeting, Ryetown, New York, January 1985. (Paper available from Carnegie Forum on Education and the Economy, Suite 301, 1001 Connecticut Ave., NW, Washington, D.C. 20036.)

Turner, Judith Axler. "Drive to Require Students to Buy Computers Slows." *Chron Higher Ed* 4 (February 1987): 1 + .

Vockell, Edward L. "The Computer and Academic Learning Time." *Clearing House* 61 (1987): 72–75.

Von Blum, Ruth, and Michael E. Cohen. "WANDAH: Writing Aid AND Author's Helper." *The Computer in Composition Instruction*. Ed. William Wresch. Urbana, Ill: NCTE, 1984, pp. 154–73.

Waldo, Mark. "Computers and Composition: A Marriage Made in Heaven?" *Coll Micro* 3 (1985): 351–56.

Weizenbaum, Joseph. *Computers and Human Reason*. San Francisco: W. H. Freeman, 1976.

Womble, Gail G. "Revising and Computing." *Writing On-Line: Using Computers in the Teaching of Writing*. Ed. James L. Collins and Elizabeth A. Sommers. Upper Montclair, N.J.: Boynton/Cook, 1985, pp. 75–82.

Woodruff, Earl. "Computers and the Composing Process: An Examination of Computer-Writer Interaction." *Computers in Composition Instruction*. Ed. Joseph Lawlor. Los Alamitos, Calif.: SWRL Educational Research and Development, 1982, pp. 31–45.

Wresch, William, ed. *The Computer in Composition Instruction: A Writer's Tool*. Urbana,
    Ill.: NCTE, 1984.
————. "Questions, Answers, and Automated Writing." *The Computer in Composition
    Instruction*. Ed. William Wresch. Urbana, Ill.: NCTE, 1984, pp. 143–53.

9

Writing Laboratories and Basic Writing

Donna Beth Nelson

> ...I am trying to help you create a place where you will talk and write—
> not to fulfill a requirement—but because you have *something to say*, where
> you will learn to talk and write better—not to get a grade—but because you
> have *somebody to hear* and respond to what you say.
>
> *From Dialogue to Discourse*, 1972, p. 8

In this simple statement to her students, Lou Kelly—the first person to provide a process for working with basic writers in writing laboratories, and according to an editor's note in the *Writing Center Journal*, "perhaps the steadiest, most ardent proponent of one-on-one teaching of writing anywhere" (1.1:19)—describes the core of the pedagogical philosophy upon which her lab at the University of Iowa operates. Kelly's lab, which dates back to the 1930s, was founded upon the belief that individualized writing instruction meant sitting down individually with students, face to face, to talk about their writing; it meant that students would gain confidence and competence through collaboration—and by actually writing. This philosophy of instruction still persists at Iowa, and has been adopted by numerous labs all over the country, most of which have been established since the early 1970s.

The one-on-one approach used by writing labs has proved successful not only for basic writers, but for average and even gifted writers as well. This success, according to the literature surveyed for this chapter, can be attributed to a writing lab pedagogy based upon sound principles of conferencing and upon current composition theory—which works for writers of varying abilities. In "The Idea of a Writing Center" (1984), Stephen M. North states that the object of a writing lab is to make sure that writers—and not necessarily their texts—change as a result of tutoring. Since writing is viewed as a process, the teaching takes place as much as possible during writing—during the activity being learned.

When a writing lab is conceived as a place where all students can be helped in this manner, rather than as a " 'bonehead place' where idiots, failures, and illiterates go and, presumably, sit in Comma Corners or Noun Nooks" (to borrow a phrase from Muriel Harris's "Growing Pains" [1982] 8), all students will benefit—and basic writers won't be as likely to slink through the writing lab doorway, feeling embarrassed or as though they are being punished for some misdeed.

As is by now apparent, this chapter's focus is the process-oriented lab, where students come by referral or of their own volition to sit with a tutor who helps them to improve their writing process. In "Writing Labs Are More Than Redemption Centers" (1986), Elray Pedersen complains that too often writing labs have not been conceived so broadly, but rather as mere "fix-it repair shops, post-mortem editing and proofreading parlors, whose work it is to free rough drafts of fragments, rid tentative texts of run-ons, clear completed compositions of comma faults, and deliver unedited discourse from misspellings" (3). The majority of the literature concurs that such labs are too limited in purpose, as they emphasize errors rather than the extensive and complex process of writing. Articles that explain why the Iowa writing lab and other labs across the country have come to believe that they should be full-service centers are Lou Kelly's "One on One, Iowa City Style" (1980) and Muriel Harris's "Growing Pains" (1982).

While the process-oriented lab is generally held in highest repute, it is not regarded as the only useful or successful kind of lab. Proponents of autotutorial labs, for example, claim that self-teaching materials provide an excellent way for students to learn about the basic rules of punctuation—when to add -*s* to a verb, and so on—despite the fact that the materials are unable to teach students about the composing process or about organizing their writing. Two articles by Mary Epes, Carolyn Kirkpatrick, and Michael G. Southwell—"The Autotutorial Writing Lab" (1982) and "The COMP-LAB Project" (1979)—provide careful explanations of autotutorial labs.

The fact that labs have been designed with various purposes in mind and that there is some confusion about just what should take place in them is evidenced by the long list of titles such places have been given. In "New Directions for Writing Labs" (1984), Thomas Nash offers an abbreviated list of titles coined by laboratory personnel: the Writing Center, the Writing Laboratory, the Learning Resource Center, the Writing Room, the Developmental Writing Program, the Basic Writers' Laboratory, the Study Skills Center, the Academic Support Center, the Learning Center, the Composition Corner, the Writing Place, the Writing Haven, the Reading and Writing Laboratory, and Reading and Study Skills Lab (RASSL), and the Composition Closet. Throughout this chapter I use the term "writing laboratory," not with the intended connotation of a medical lab where people go because they are ill—but with the same connotation that Nash has for "lab." The term is apt, says Nash, because the process-oriented lab shares some characteristics with the chemistry lab or the biology lab, where the process of investigation complements the formal instruction of the classroom. In the writing lab, students "test" various approaches to composition, often discovering methods by trial and error. The lab serves as an experimentation station where students can try out new procedures under the helpful eyes of their tutors.

It is not my purpose, however, to imply that such interaction, such experimentation, such discovery can take place only within the confines of a writing lab—or that writing lab instruction is superior to, or entirely different from, the type of work that often goes on in a classroom setting. In "Writing Laboratory 'Image' Or How Not to Write to Your Dean" (1982), Irvin Hashimoto says,

It is fairly easy to point out how writing laboratories are better than classes operated in the spirit of prison camps—classes in which teachers lecture and make a few brief comments (in red) on students' papers and students go off to suck on bread soaked in water. On the other hand, many of the best things that go on in writing classes are not necessarily different or do not necessarily have to be different from the best that goes on in writing laboratories. (2)

Hashimoto's point is well taken by many classroom instructors who are making the shift from traditional lecture-discussion formats to conference-centered writing instruction, spending long hours discussing papers one-on-one with their students, and going over students' ideas and early drafts long before the students turn in a final draft. Although the dynamics of a writing lab and a conference-centered classroom are not exactly the same (that is, a classroom teacher will eventually serve as the evaluator of a student's paper whereas a tutor will not), a number of techniques are easily applicable to both situations. Therefore, many of the materials referred to in this chapter should prove useful to instructors of conference-centered classrooms as well as to writing lab tutors.

There is one way in which a conference-centered classroom has a decided advantage over a laboratory setting: in a writing lab a student collaborates with a tutor, but in a classroom a student is able to share experiences and collaborate in a spirit of camaraderie and support with a room full of peers—a community of writers and readers who can greatly enhance a sense of audience awareness. On the other hand, we know that students respond differently to various approaches. We know that many students—especially weak writers—will thrive when their classroom activity is supplemented by a writing tutor who will provide immediate feedback and constant support. And we know that a one-to-one approach is unquestionably the most effective way to help many troubled writers overcome fear about writing, gather information and discover an appropriate structure for it, untangle problematic syntax, and eliminate a multitude of errors.

To date, no books have been written nor bibliographies compiled that specifically address the tutoring of basic writers. This is undoubtedly because, as has already been pointed out, sound writing lab pedagogy applies to teaching all writers, not just basic writers. A number of articles in journals and newsletters and chapters in books do address the topic, however. Taken together, these materials provide a good overview of the possibilities for tutoring basic writers.

We must remember that there is no single formula. How can there be when we've yet to arrive at a definitive description of who, exactly, constitutes our basic writers? Writing lab tutors must become familiar with the research on basic writers in general and then, through a process of trial and error, discover effective methods for helping each student tap into his or her own resources. When this occurs, basic writers can indeed develop into confident, competent, independent writers.

CONFERENCE METHODOLOGY

Although tutoring is an educational practice that is centuries old, a substantial body of literature on the subject has been developing only in recent years, a result of the numerous labs being established all over the nation. The literature clearly shows that good conferences do not happen by chance; they happen as a result of adherence to sound methodology, which often recommends a Rogerian approach of questioning and listening—an approach that works not only for tutoring basic writers, but all writers.

Two excellent books, both with comprehensive bibliographies, thoroughly address questions about conducting tutorials. The first, Muriel Harris's *Teaching One-to-One* (1986), addresses the needs of both classroom instructors and lab personnel. The second, Emily Meyer and Louise Z. Smith's *The Practical Tutor* (1987), provides detailed discussions of ways to deal with particular kinds of students and their problems. This book is notable for its ability to integrate contemporary theory and research into its practical discussions of technique. It also includes many transcripts of sample tutorials, often paring successful with unsuccessful techniques.

I also recommend Joyce S. Steward and Mary K. Croft's *The Writing Laboratory* (1982) for its useful section on conference methodology, and Marian Arkin and Barbara Shollar's *The Tutor Book* (1982) for its careful examination of the process of tutoring, although the book is not devoted exclusively to the tutoring of writing. Thomas J. Reigstad and Donald A. McAndrew's *Training Tutors for Writing Conferences* (1984) provides still another useful analysis of the conference method.

Particularly interesting are studies asserting that the structure of writing conferences should be similar to the structure of interviews as defined by social workers and psychologists. In "The Student-Teacher Conference" (1977), Rosemarie Arbur analyzes the seven stages in the process of an interview or a writing conference, explaining how the entire process may actually extend through several sessions. David Taylor, in "A Counseling Approach to Writing Conferences" (1988), recommends training writing tutors to follow the conference framework used by counselors in order to ease the tutors into the intimacy and openness required for a successful collaborative effort.

In "The Student-Centered Conference and the Writing Process" (1975), Charles R. Duke also compares conferencing to psychological interviews. He recommends using a nondirective approach in favor of a directive approach, since most people are capable of helping themselves if they are freed from emotional obstacles such as intimidation and fear of failure. The term "nondirective" does not mean that the conference will be unplanned but that it will avoid traditional overdirection, provide reassurance, and encourage students to accept responsibility for the writing process. In "Non-Directive Tutoring Strategies" (1988), Kay Satre and Valerie Traub maintain that such conferences provide students with problem-solving strategies that are, in some sense, already in their own possession and that the students become able to employ these strategies on their own in later writing.

Donald Murray is unquestionably one of the strongest advocates of the non-directive conference. In "The Listening Eye" (1979), he explains the questioning approach he uses to lead students through invention/prewriting and revision conferences; his ultimate goal is to teach students to react to their own work in such a way that they write increasingly effective drafts. John Roderick's "Problems in Tutoring" (1982) also stresses the importance of a questioning approach used by tutors who are good listeners. This approach is especially necessary for tutoring basic writers, Roderick points out, for they all too often have low esteem—not just about their writing, but about themselves as well. The approach is successful, he says, as the right questions will draw students out; and the basis of all good writing starts with the writer's belief that he or she has something to say. The article contains several transcripts of conferences that illustrate the effectiveness of the questioning technique. Suzanne E. Jacobs and Adela B. Karliner's "Helping Writers to Think" (1977) also contains transcripts of conferences and claims that the right kind of questioning can result in significant change in the cognitive level of revision a student is able to do.

In "The Nature of Writing Laboratory Instruction for the Developing Student" (1982), Rudolph Almasy further elaborates on the questioning process; the goal, he says, is to lead the student to do the questioning, finally becoming independent of a tutor or teacher. Virginia A. Chappel stresses this goal in "Hands Off" (1982). She recommends a questioning procedure and explains that the conference must be broken into three tasks: focusing, making a diagnosis, and teaching the lesson itself. Anita Brostoff in "The Writing Conference" (1982) explains that while there can be no absolute routine in the questioning procedure, the tutor should move from straightforward, factual questions, to questions about the student's writing ability and experience, to a determination of the problem at hand, to questions about the student's handling of the writing process.

In an earlier article, "An Approach to Conferencing" (1980), Brostoff recommends that the questioning in the first conference be guided by a "preliminary questionnaire" that the student fills out when he or she makes the first appointment. The questionnaire is designed to elicit specific information about the student's quantity and quality of writing experience, attitude toward writing, feelings about his or her ability as a writer, and habits in handling the writing process. In "Writing Center Diagnosis" (1982), Stephen North recommends the use of a similar form, which he calls the "composing profile." Rather than the student filling out the form, however, the tutor and student complete the form together, with the student narrating and the tutor writing. The use of such forms helps establish a foundation that is especially useful when working with basic writers, who often have negative or apprehensive attitudes about writing.

For an article that specifically treats the conferencing of basic writers, see Lou Kelly's "Writing as Learning for Basic Writing Teachers and Their Students" (1984). Kelly, too, advocates a questioning strategy for teaching prewriting, revision, and copyreading. In initial writing lab conferences, however, the basic writer at the University of Iowa uses Kelly's text, *From Dialogue to Discourse* (1972), which she calls a "talking book," a carefully crafted series of "invitations to write." The student answers questions on paper—and the tutor listens. The tutor's responses must assure the student that the tutor is an interested, perceptive reader who wants to hear more. Another article that addresses the nature of conferences for basic writers is Patrick Hartwell's "A Writing Laboratory Model" (1980). Hartwell discusses conferences that focus on various stages in the student's writing, recommends materials that work well for tutoring basic writers, and stresses the importance of having the student talk through his or her perceptions about writing and reading with the tutor. *Peer Tutoring in Basic Writing* (1981), by Jackie Goldsby, is a journal kept by the author while she served as a peer tutor for basic writers. The journal provides a poignant record of her conferences and is especially useful to other beginning peer tutors.

Although the literature overviewed in this section was written primarily for use by writing lab tutors, much of it is easily applicable to classroom instructors who use conference-centered instruction. For detailed descriptions of ways to employ a conference-centered approach in the classroom, see "The Writing Conference" by Thomas Carnicelli (1980), *One-to-One* by Charles W. Dawe and Edward A. Dornan (1984), "One-to-One" by Roger Garrison (1974), *A Writer Teaches Writing* by Donald M. Murray (1985), and "The One-to-One Method of Teaching Composition" by Jo An McGuire Simmons (1984). All of these espouse a conference approach for classroom instruction and describe techniques that are easily adapted to writing lab settings.

CHANGING THE PROCESS

Since the goal of writing laboratories is ultimately to change students' processes of writing, tutors should become familiar with literature that explains the processes, strategies, and stages of development that basic writers share. In saying this I am not suggesting that these characteristics are exactly alike for each basic writer—or even that a great deal is known about these characteristics; nonetheless, common tendencies can be recognized.

A main problem of basic writers is their inability to generate ideas for a paper. But sitting next to that authentic and helpful audience—the tutor—who continuously probes and patiently listens, basic writers learn to handle invention and prewriting. The "Conference Methodology" section of this chapter contains numerous materials on questioning strategies, a number of which aid in invention. I also recommend two additional articles that will help a tutor teach students to generate ideas. In "Hamlet, Polonius, and the Writing Center" (1980), Thomas Nash asserts that writing lab tutors should know how to teach traditional methods of invention, from brainstorming to field theory, and he includes a helpful heuristic that allows the tutor to interact directly with the student during prewriting. Gary A. Olson and John Alton (1982) recommend that writing labs use formal heuristics in their article "Heuristics" and include helpful samples.

Another major problem plaguing basic writers is their lack of effective strategies for drafting and revising. For an understanding of how basic writers handle these processes, tutors should become familiar with Sondra Perl's "The Composing Processes of Unskilled College Writers" (1979) and Sharon Pianko's "A Description of the Composing Processes of College Freshman Writers" (1979). These studies indicate that basic writers tend not to write recursively, as do experienced writers—and that they tend not to reread what they have written as they continue writing. Linda Flower's "Writer-Based Prose" (1979) is also a must-read for tutors of basic writing, since the article explains the failure of basic writers to adapt to the rhetorical problem at hand, instead often allowing their papers to remain as interior monologues that reflect their thought processes.

For ways to help the basic writer become more reader-oriented, I recommend Linda Flower's "Revising Writer-Based Prose" (1981). Here Flower shows how to break up the writing problem, thereby reducing cognitive overload; she concludes that the role of a listener is important in effecting this change. Patrick Hartwell's "The Writing Center and the Paradoxes of Written-Down Speech" (1984) also recommends techniques for helping writing lab students make their prose more reader-based. Hartwell advocates having students read aloud and using a tape recorder. In "Listening and Writing" (1981), Irene Lurkis Clark explains how basic writers can learn to acquire psychological distance from their own discourse by working with a tutor and by reading aloud; her article includes worksheets to aid basic writers as they revise. David Hoddeson in "The Reviser's Voices" (1981) recommends having students read aloud to aid in revision and explains the importance of using dictation as an exercise that will ready students for revision.

We are well aware that basic writers tend to depend upon everyday, spoken language to represent meaning in their written language. Several articles that address this concern conclude that it is too much to expect an abrupt change from spoken to written language as a result of instruction. In "Intimacy and Audience" (1980), Thom Hawkins claims that tutors can supply a "missing link''; they break down the distance between students and classroom teachers—a distance students perceive as being between two language systems. For this reason, Hawkins claims, peer tutors often provide the best social dimension for helping inexperienced and insecure writers revise. James L. Collins, in "Training Teachers of Basic Writing in the Writing Laboratory" (1982), also refers to tutors as "missing links" who help basic writers make the transition to the written code. Collins recommends that tutors respond to basic writing as "dumb readers," since the tendency of basic writers is to write for familiar audiences who have shared experiences with them. Another writer, Walker Gibson, uses the term "dumb reader" in "The Writing Teacher as a Dumb Reader" (1979). He says that to help students see a difference between the spoken and the written code, tutors should respond to the signals on the page, rather than to the students' intentions. In "Exploiting the Writing-Speaking Relationship in the Writing Center" (1987), Virginia Hudson Young recommends similar strategies for tutors and explains the benefits of instructional and noninstructional talk.

Although writer-based prose is not related to cognitive development, other characteristics suggest that basic writers may be arrested in what Jean Piaget and Lev Vygotsky call the egocentric stage of cognitive development, that they tend to be dualistic thinkers, and that they conceptualize and generalize with great difficulty. I recommend three articles by Andrea Lunsford as starting points for the tutor who lacks information about the relationship between basic writing and cognition: "What We Know—and Don't Know—About Remedial Writing" (1978), "Cognitive Development and the Basic Writer" (1979), and "The Content of Basic Writers' Essays" (1980). Lunsford not only gives insight into the issues of cognition, but also offers teaching strategies to bridge the cognitive gap. In "Promoting Cognitive Development in the Writing Center" (1984), Karen Spear discusses specific, sequenced assignments that should be used by writing labs in order to promote cognitive development in basic writers. M. E. Lamb, in "Just Getting the Words Down on Paper" (1982), recommends an activity that will help basic writers avoid cognitive overload. The activity breaks down the students' tasks into smaller units and allows tutors to discuss students' decisions with them. In "Critical Thinking and the Writing Center" (1988), Tracey Baker asserts that critical thinking should not be taught as a separate skill and discusses a variety of methodologies for promoting cognitive development in a writing lab setting.

In general, what we know about getting basic writers to change their strategies for drafting and revising is that it can be done; under the guidance of a writing lab tutor, many basic writers experience success in making macrostructure changes. According to Byron Stay in "When Re-Writing Succeeds" (1983), a tutor helps many basic writers make the same kind of holistic changes researchers previously had associated only with experienced writers. Stay attributes the success to the collaboration that takes place throughout the writing process. Writing lab literature concurs that basic writers, like other writers, need to view writing as a discovery process rather than as a system of rules. For explanations of why formulas inhibit basic writers' thinking and writing development, I recommend Teri Haas's "The Unskilled Writer and the Formula Essay" (1983), and Mike Rose's "Rigid Rules, Inflexible Plans, and the Stifling of Language" (1980).

ANALYZING AND ELIMINATING ERROR

Basic writers tend to be preoccupied with error. They have good reason: in general, they have had a history of convoluted syntax, errors in usage, errors in punctuation, errors in spelling—and low grades on papers. For such students, relegating editing to the final step in the writing process reduces fear of error in the initial stages of composing and allows development of effective strategies for the higher level skills. And for many students, the most effective and most efficient way to deal with this final and troublesome phase of writing is working one-on-one with a tutor, who serves not as an editor but as a guide who leads them to their own discoveries.

As a foundation for dealing with the errors made by basic writers, tutors should become familiar with Mina Shaughnessy's *Errors and Expectations* (1977). This is the most important work we presently have on basic writing, not only because it offers numerous teaching strategies, but because it provides an understanding about the writing that basic writers produce. The book catalogs problems with handwriting, punctuation, syntax, and spelling—and is as much a requisite for those who work individually with basic writers as it is for classroom instructors.

Anyone engaged in tutoring writing for any length of time also should have an understanding of error analysis, a method originally developed for instructing second-language students that has proved equally useful for instructing basic writers. The philosophy of this method is to treat errors not as mistakes to be corrected but as evidence to help discover why the student made the errors and how the student can be moved closer to the "target form" of the language. For good explanations of error analysis, I recommended David Bartholomae's "The Study of Error" (1980), and Barry Kroll and John Schafer's "Error Analysis and the Teaching of Composition" (1978). Muriel Harris's "Mending the Fragmented Free Modifier" (1981) is another careful explanation, which deals specifically with analysis and treatment of sentence fragments.

I highly recommend another article by Muriel Harris, "Individualized Diagnosis" (1982), for an overview of how to use error analysis in a writing lab setting. Harris points out that while searching for causes of errors is not a science, it can be accomplished fairly effectively in a writing lab where the tutor can observe students as they write and can easily ask the reasons for certain choices or constructions. In "All of the Answers or Some of the Questions?" (1982), Lee Ann Leeson explains her method of having writing lab students help in their own error analysis; she claims that helping students discover that their rule diverges from standard English usage takes longer than simply pointing out the errors, but the students will more readily remember the correct forms. "Using

Error-Analysis in the Writing Lab for Correctness and Effectiveness'' (1984) by Helen Rothschild Ewald provides samples of student writing and a partial transcript of a conference to illustrate how to use error analysis in a lab. Ewald also illustrates how error analysis can be used to gain insight into assumptions underlying rhetorical misjudgments as well as into usage or mechanical errors. Doug Hunt's ''Diagnosis for the Writing Lab'' (1982) discusses both formal and informal methods of diagnosing errors in a writing lab. He claims that diagnosis should not stop with the student's paper; the tutor might need to consider the student's attitude toward writing, for example.

It is generally agreed that basic writers will better learn to correct errors that are addressed when they occur within a real context, that is, when the knowledge is gained inductively rather than through drills designed to teach deductively. Richard C. Veit makes the case well in ''Basic Writer'' (1981), an article that focuses upon the importance of tutoring for basic writers. In ''A Blueprint for Writing Lab Exercises'' (1984), Thomas Friedmann agrees that traditional exercises—multiple-choice questions, fill-ins, error-based paragraphs—are incapable of habituating ''correctness'' in basic writers. He concludes by offering a sequence of exercises that can be used successfully in writing labs; the exercises are non–error based and frequently require students to rewrite passages from one form into another.

In addition to a process of drafting, error analysis, and short composing exercises, many writing labs are teaching sentence combining as a way of helping basic writers (and regular-track students) to enhance syntactic maturity. This activity serves as an adjunct to regular composition work and is unlike traditional drills in that it stresses language production over linguistic description and accomplishments over errors. Although numerous sentence-combining texts are on the market, writing lab literature makes several specific recommendations. In ''A Sentence-Combining Laboratory'' (1981), William Stull recommends *The Writer's Options* by Donald Daiker, Andrew Kerek, and Max Morenberg (3rd ed., 1986), because every chapter includes rhetorical as well as syntactic strategies. In a review in the *Writing Lab Newsletter* (1979), Susan Glassman explains her preference for Lee Jacobus's *The Sentence Book* (1980): the text provides students many opportunities to generate their own sentences, which she finds preferable to simply working with the sentences in the book. In ''Sentence-Combining and the Reading of Sentences'' (1980), Marilyn Sternglass explains methods of directing sentence combining (e.g., Frank O'Hare's *Sentencecraft* [1975]) and of nondirected sentence combining (e.g., William Strong's *Sentence Combining* [1973]). She asserts that sentence-combining activities are particularly appropriate for basic writers, and hypothesizes that sentence combining may lead to improved reading comprehension for basic writers. While Sternglass does not specifically address an audience of writing lab personnel, I recommend her article for its information on basic writers. In *The Practical Tutor*, Meyer and Smith recommend sentence combining, but they also offer useful descriptions of other techniques that can be used by tutors to help students improve their syntax.

As is the case with other types of errors, the literature also generally recommends an inductive approach for diagnosing and treating spelling. For a careful discussion of issues regarding the teaching of spelling and for explanations of how to use sensory techniques, mnemonic devices, phonics, word groups—and a few rules—I recommend Ann Dobie's "Orthographical Theory and Practice, or How to Teach Spelling" (1986). In "College Spelling Texts" (1984), Irvin Hashimoto and Roger Clark review a number of spelling texts, finally making the assertion that students should become actively engaged in diagnosing their own spelling problems. Chopeta Lyons, in "Spelling Inventory" (1985), agrees that the more students are involved in the analysis of their own misspelling patterns, the stronger their commitment to correction becomes. Such analysis can be best handled in individual conferences, she claims, that use a data sheet for inventory of personal errors. In "The Teaching of Spelling" (1981), Janice Kleen recommends a much different approach—the tactile kinesthetic method—the intent of which is to help students program words into their automatic spelling systems.

Of course, all the work with diagnosing and treating error cannot be entirely effective until students acquire techniques for proofreading. As these techniques tend to rely upon oral methods, a writing lab is ideally suited to teaching this final step in writing papers. Shelly Samuels's "Emphasizing Oral Proofreading in the Writing Lab" (1984) contains a helpful explanation of why oral proofreading is preferable to silent proofreading. Samuels describes three categories of errors that students can make as they proofread and the ways the tutor should respond to each. In "Helping Students to Proofread" (1986), Mary M. Dossin outlines a sensible eight-step process for teaching writing lab students to proofread orally. Elaine Ware, in "Visual Perception Through 'Window Proofreading' " (1985), offers a supplemental technique to oral proofreading; her writing lab students slowly move a small cardboard "window" across their papers, thereby isolating each word or punctuation mark from the rest of the sentence. The tutors encourage the students to lift up the window periodically to look at a word or punctuation mark within the context of an entire sentence.

PSYCHOLOGICAL CONSIDERATIONS

Because of a history of negative experiences with writing, basic writers sometimes develop psychological characteristics that inhibit their writing process. Although the literature concurs that one-on-one environments generally reduce apprehension, hostility, and apathy, it also acknowledges that tutors may still find themselves dealing with such problems. If psychological problems related to writing are excessive, they must be alleviated before writing problems can be tackled with any degree of success.

For information about writing apprehension, a problem not limited to basic writers, I recommend *When a Writer Can't Write*, edited by Mike Rose (1985). This collection addresses the complex causes of apprehension that lead to blocking and suggests a variety of treatments. An informative article that specifically focuses on anxiety experienced by basic writers is Thomas Reigstad's "Perspectives on Anxiety and the Basic Writer" (1985). Reigstad offers an overview of research on writing anxiety and makes suggestions to help tutors deal with the problem. Other articles that will help tutors handle students' psychological problems are Kevin Davis's "Improving Students' Writing Attitudes" (1988); William O. Shakespeare's "Establishing an Effective Learning Environment" (1986); Mary K. Croft's " 'I Would Prefer Not To' " (1984); and Loretta Cobb's "Practical Techniques for Training Tutors to Overcome Defensive Blocks" (1982).

CONCLUSION

Because the vast majority of writing labs have been established since the early 1970s, writing labs scholarship only recently has come of age. The literature is exciting and reassuring; it corroborates that writing labs across the country are places where countless basic writers—and others—have learned to think of writing, in the words of Lou Kelly, "not as a drudging academic requirement, but a fulfilling dynamic process of sharing their experiences with others"; where they have learned to see their own writing "not as a product to be criticized and graded, but as a means of exploring and understanding their perceptions of the world"; where they have learned to hear their writing "as the voice of the unique human being each of them is and is becoming" ("One on One" 19).

REFERENCES

Almasy, Rudolph. "The Nature of Writing Laboratory Instruction for the Developing Student." *Tutoring Writing: A Sourcebook for Writing Labs*. Ed. Muriel Harris. Glenview, Ill.: Scott, Foresman, 1982, pp. 13–20.

Arbur, Rosemarie. "The Student-Teacher Conference." *CCC* 28 (1977): 338–42.

Arkin, Marian, and Barbara Shollar. *The Tutor Book*. New York: Longman, 1982.

Baker, Tracey. "Critical Thinking and the Writing Center: Possibilities." *WCJ* 8.2 (1988): 37–41.

Bartholomae, David. "The Study of Error." *CCC* 31 (1980): 253–69.

Brostoff, Anita. "An Approach to Conferencing." *WLN* 4.7 (1980): 7–8.

———. "The Writing Conference: Foundations." *Tutoring Writing: A Sourcebook for Writing Labs*. Ed. Muriel Harris. Glenview, Ill.: Scott, Foresman, 1982, pp. 21–26.

Carnicelli, Thomas A. "The Writing Conference: A One-To-One Conversation." *Eight Approaches to Teaching Composition*. Ed. Timothy Donovan and Ben McClelland. Urbana, Ill.: NCTE, 1980, pp. 101–31.

Chappel, Virginia A. "Hands Off: Fostering Self-Reliance in the Writing Lab." *WLN* 6.6 (1982): 4–6.

Clark, Irene Lurkis. "Listening and Writing." *JBW* 3.3 (1981): 81–90.

Cobb, Loretta. "Practical Techniques for Training Tutors to Overcome Defensive Blocks." *WCJ* 3.1 (1982): 32–37.

Collins, James L. "Training Teachers of Basic Writing in the Writing Laboratory." *CCC* 33 (1982): 426–33.

Croft, Mary K. "I Would Prefer Not To: A Consideration of the Reluctant Student." *Writing Centers: Theory and Administration*. Ed. Gary Olson. Urbana, Ill.: NCTE, 1984, pp. 170–81.

Daiker, Donald A., Andrew Kerek, and Max Morenberg. *The Writer's Options: College Sentence Combining*. 3rd ed. New York: Harper and Row, 1986.

Davis, Kevin. "Improving Students' Writing Attitudes: The Effect of the Writing Center." *WLN* 12.10 (1988): 3–6.

Dawe, Charles W., and Edward A. Dornan. Instructor's Manual for *One-to-One: Resources for Conference-Centered Writing*, 2nd ed. Boston: Little, Brown, 1984.

Dobie, Ann B. "Orthographical Theory and Practice, or How To Teach Spelling." *JBW* 5.2 (1986): 41–48.

Dossin, Mary M. "Helping Students to Proofread." *WLN* 11.2 (1986): 3–4.

Duke, Charles R. "The Student-Centered Conference and the Writing Process." *EJ* 64 (1975): 44–47.

Epes, Mary, Carolyn Kirkpatrick, and Michael G. Southwell. "The Autotutorial Writing Lab: Discovering Its Latent Power." *Tutoring Writing: A Sourcebook for Writing Labs*. Ed. Muriel Harris. Glenview, Ill.: Scott, Foresman, 1982, pp. 132–46.

———. "The COMP-LAB Project: An Experimental Basic Writing Course." *JBW* 2.2 (1979): 19–37.

Ewald, Helen Rothschild. "Using Error-Analysis in the Writing Lab for Correctness and Effectiveness." *WLN* 8.5 (1984): 6–8.

Flower, Linda S. "Revising Writer-Based Prose." *JBW* 3.3 (1981): 62–74.

———. "Writer-Based Prose: A Cognitive Basis for Problems in Writing." *CE* 41 (1979): 19–37.

Friedmann, Thomas, "A Blueprint for Writing Lab Exercises." *WLN* 8.5 (1984): 1–4.

Garrison, Roger. "One-to-One: Tutorial Instruction in Freshman Composition." *New Directions for Community Colleges* 2 (1974): 55–84.

Gibson, Walker. "The Writing Teacher as a Dumb Reader." *CCC* 30 (1979): 192–95.

Glassman, Susan. "Book Review." *WLN* 4.2 (1979): 4.

Goldsby, Jackie. *Peer Tutoring in Basic Writing: A Tutor's Journal*. Classroom Research Study no. 4, ed. Gerald Camp. Berkeley: The Regents of the University of California, 1981.

Haas, Teri. "The Unskilled Writer and the Formula Essay: Composing by the Rules." *WCJ* 3.2 (1983): 11–21.

Harris, Muriel. "Growing Pains: The Coming of Age of Writing Centers." *WCJ* 2.1 (1982): 1–8.

———. "Individualized Diagnosis: Searching for Causes, Not Symptoms of Writing Deficiencies." *Tutoring Writing: A Sourcebook for Writing Labs*. Ed. Muriel Harris. Glenview, Ill.: Scott, Foresman, 1982, pp. 53–65.

———. "Mending the Fragmented Free Modifier." *CCC* 28 (1981): 175–82.

———. *Teaching One-to-One: The Writing Conference*. Urbana, Ill.: NCTE, 1986.

Hartwell, Patrick. "The Writing Center and the Paradoxes of Written-Down Speech." *Writing Centers: Theory and Administration*. Ed. Gary A. Olson. Urbana, Ill.: NCTE, 1984, pp. 48–61.

———. "A Writing Laboratory Model." *Basic Writing: Essays for Teachers, Research-*

ers, and Administrators. Ed. Lawrence N. Kasden and Daniel Hoeber. Urbana, Ill.: NCTE, 1980, pp. 63–73.

Hashimoto, Irvin. "Writing Laboratory 'Image' or How Not to Write to Your Dean." *WCJ* 3.1 (1982): 1–10.

Hashimoto, Irvin, and Roger Clark. "College Spelling Texts: The State of the Art." *WCJ* 5.1 (1984): 1–13.

Hawkins, Thom. "Intimacy and Audience: The Relationship Between Revision and the Social Dimension of Peer Tutoring." *CE* 42 (1980): 64–68.

Hoddeson, David. "The Reviser's Voices." *JBW* 3.3 (1981): 81–91.

Hunt, Doug. "Diagnosis for the Writing Lab." *Tutoring Writing: A Sourcebook for Writing Labs.* Ed. Muriel Harris. Glenview, Ill.: Scott, Foresman, 1982, pp. 66–73.

Jacobs, Suzanne, E., and Adela B. Karliner. "Helping Writers to Think: The Effect of Speech Roles in Individual Conferences on the Quality of Thought in Student Writing." *CE* 38 (1977): 489–505.

Jacobus, Lee A. *The Sentence Book.* New York: Harcourt Brace Jovanovich, 1980.

Kelly, Lou. *From Dialogue to Discourse.* Glenview, Ill.: Scott, Foresman, 1972.

——. "One on One, Iowa City Style: Fifty Years of Individualized Instruction in Writing." *WCJ* 1.1 (1980): 4–19.

——. "Writing as Learning for Basic Writing Teachers and Their Students." *JBW* 3.4 (1984): 38–54.

Kleen, Janice. "The Teaching of Spelling: A Success Story." *WLN* 6.4 (1981): 1–2.

Kroll, Barry, and John Schafer. "Error Analysis and the Teaching of Composition." *CCC* 29 (1978): 242–48.

Lamb, M. E. "Just Getting the Words Down on Paper: Results from the Five-Minute Writing Practice" *WCJ* 2.2 (1982): 1–6.

Leeson, Lee Ann. "All of the Answers or Some of the Questions? Teacher As Learner in the Writing Center." *WCJ* 2.2 (1982): 18–23.

Lunsford, Andrea. "Cognitive Development and the Basic Writer." *CE* 41 (1979): 38–46.

——. "The Content of Basic Writers' Essays." *CCC* 31 (1980): 278–90.

——. "What We Know—and Don't Know—About Remedial Writing." *CCC* 29 (1978): 47–52.

Lyons, Chopeta. "Spelling Inventory." *JBW* 4.2 (1985): 80–83.

Meyer, Emily, and Louise Z. Smith. *The Practical Tutor.* New York: Oxford University Press, 1987.

Murray, Donald M. "The Listening Eye: Reflections on the Writing Conference." *CE* 41 (1979): 13–18.

——. *A Writer Teaches Writing,* 2nd ed. Boston: Houghton Mifflin, 1985.

Nash, Thomas. "Hamlet, Polonius, and the Writing Center." *WCJ* 1.1 (1980): 34–40.

——. "New Directions for Writing Labs." *WLN* 9.1 (1984): 2–7.

North, Stephen M. "The Idea of a Writing Center." *CE* 46 (1984): 433–46.

——. "Writing Center Diagnosis: The Composing Profile." *Tutoring Writing: A Sourcebook for Writing Labs.* Ed. Muriel Harris. Glenview, Ill.: Scott, Foresman, 1982, pp. 42–53.

O'Hare, Frank. *Sentencecraft.* Lexington, Mass.: Ginn & Company, 1975.

Olson, Gary A., and John Alton. "Heuristics: Out of the Pulpit and into the Writing Center." *WCJ* 2.1 (1982): 48–56.

Pedersen, Elray. "Writing Labs Are More Than Remediation Centers." *WLN* 10.7 (1986): 3–5.

Perl, Sondra. "The Composing Process of Unskilled College Writers." *RTE* 13 (1979): 317–36.

Pianko, Sharon. "A Description of the Composing Processes of College Freshman Writers." *RTE* 13 (1979): 5–22.

Reigstad, Thomas J. "Perspectives on Anxiety and the Basic Writer: Research, Evaluation, Instruction." *JBW* 4.1 (1985): 68–77.

Reigstad, Thomas J., and Donald A. McAndrew. *Training Tutors for Writing Conferences.* Urbana, Ill.: ERIC Clearinghouse on Reading and Communication Skills and the NCTE, 1984.

Roderick, John. "Problems in Tutoring." *Tutoring Writing: A Sourcebook for Writing Labs.* Ed Muriel Harris. Glenview, Ill.: Scott, Foresman, 1982, pp. 32–39.

Rose, Mike. "Rigid Rules, Inflexible Plans, and the Stifling of Language." *CCC* 31 (1980): 389–401.

———, ed. *When a Writer Can't Write.* New York: Guilford, 1985.

Samuels, Shelly. "Emphasizing Oral Proofreading in the Writing Lab: A Multi-Function Technique for both Tutors and Students." *WLN* 9.2 (1984): 1–4.

Satre, Kay, and Valerie Traub. "Non-Directive Tutoring Strategies." *WLN* 12.8 (1988): 5–6.

Shakespeare, William O. "Establishing an Effective Learning Environment." *WLN* 10.9 (1986): 10–13.

Shaughnessy, Mina. *Errors and Expectations: A Guide for the Teacher of Basic Writing.* New York: Oxford University Press, 1977.

Simmons, Jo An McGuire. "The One-to-One Method of Teaching Composition." *CCC* 35 (1984): 222–29.

Spear, Karen I. "Promoting Cognitive Development in the Writing Center." *Writing Centers: Theory and Administration.* Ed. Gary A. Olson. Urbana, Ill.: NCTE, 1984, pp. 62–76.

Stay, Byron. "When Re-Writing Succeeds: An Analysis of Student Revisions." *WCJ* 4.1 (1983): 15–28.

Sternglass, Marilyn. "Sentence-Combining and the Reading of Sentences." *CCC* 31 (1980): 325–28.

Steward, Joyce S., and Mary K. Croft. *The Writing Laboratory: Organization, Management, and Methods.* Glenview, Ill.: Scott, Foresman, 1982.

Strong, William. *Sentence Combining.* New York: Random House, 1973.

Stull, William L. "A Sentence-Combining Laboratory for Basic Writing Students." *WLN* 5.5 (1981): 1–3.

Taylor, David. "A Counseling Approach to Writing Conferences." *WLN* 12.5 (1988): 10–11.

Veit, Richard C. "Basic Writer: Lab or Tutor?" *New Directions for College Learning Assistance*, vol. 2. Ed. Thom Hawkins and Phyllis Brooks. San Francisco: Jossey-Bass, 1981, pp. 9–14.

Ware, Elaine. "Visual Perception Through 'Window Proofreading.' " *WLN* 9.9 (1985): 8–9.

Young, Virginia Hudson. "Exploiting the Writing-Speaking Relationship in the Writing Center." *WLN* 11.2 (1987): 1–5.

10

Preparing Teachers of Basic Writing

Richard A. Filloy

In the dozen years since Mina Shaughnessy made basic writing a familiar phrase in composition circles, a great deal of attention has been paid to how teachers can best help basic writers improve. Shaughnessy's bibliographic essay "Basic Writing" (1976) and her influential book *Errors and Expectations* (1977) focused attention on the need to understand better the problems facing "severely unprepared" writing students. Subsequent research has both advanced that understanding and led to much useful information on teaching. The wealth of writing and research on how to teach basic writers has not, however, resulted in a similar amount of publication on how to prepare the teacher of basic writers.[1] Several causes probably account for the relative scarcity of publication on training basic writing teachers. First among these is that, following Shaughnessy's description of the teaching of basic writing as "the frontier of a profession," most attention has been focused on describing the territory. It has no doubt seemed premature or presumptuous to some researchers to offer to guide others in territory still so vaguely understood. A second cause is that teacher training programs are often designed and put into place without a public report. If every college or university that offers some training for teachers of basic writing had produced only one document describing that training, the literature would be much richer than it is currently. A third cause is described by Sandra Schor: "The truth is that you learned to teach writing by yourself, and probably there is little one can do to help" ("Preparing Volunteers from Disciplines of Currently Diminished Student Interest to Teach Basic Writing" [1983] 46). Despite Schor's rejection of this approach, it remains true that many teachers must prepare themselves to teach basic writing, finding help where they can. Prospective teachers, directors of composition, deans, and others who need models for preparation of basic writing teachers will thus not find as extensive a literature to guide them as the research in the rest of the field might indicate. Nonetheless, enough has been written to offer useful guidance and to indicate the categories into which subsequent writing is likely to fall.

Preparation for all writing teachers may be roughly divided into two categories. First, there is professional education and training in composition, not primarily aimed at the needs or practice of a particular program. This kind of training most frequently takes place in departments of English or rhetoric as part of a degree program. Descriptions and rationales of such programs constitute one important part of the literature on preparing teachers of basic writing. Such training may also take place in postdegree programs like the Extended Teacher Institutes described by Charles Moran in "Teaching Teachers of Writing" (1982). Such institutes do not generally lead to formal qualifications but, like degree programs, aim to prepare and improve teachers of writing wherever they may teach. Moran describes the minimal setting for such general teacher-improvement programs as the "one-shot, two-hour workshop" in his essay "A Model for Teacher Training Programs in the Field of Writing" (1981). A second kind of training for writing teachers is the preservice or in-service training provided by specific writing programs to instructors who teach in that program. Descriptions of this sort of training provide a second important part of the literature on preparing basic writing teachers. The two kinds of training overlap to the extent that degree programs in composition and rhetoric often use the writing programs of their own institutions as training grounds for prospective teachers and require them to complete preservice or in-service training.

Besides these two broad categories, training for teachers of basic writing can be categorized by the setting in which writing will be taught and the population from which the teachers are drawn. Basic writing is most typically taught in two settings: (1) to individuals by a tutor in a writing laboratory or clinic and (2) to groups by a classroom teacher in a formal course. These two settings involve overlapping groups of teachers. Tutors in writing labs are undergraduates, graduate students, and regular faculty, with the first two groups predominating. Classroom teachers in formal courses are graduate students, part-time faculty, and regular faculty, sometimes including teachers from disciplines other than English. This diversity among teachers calls for equal diversity in their preparation. Training for undergraduate peer tutors in a writing lab is very different from training for faculty members from biology or nursing who will teach a course. In describing the literature on the preparation of basic writing teachers, I will begin with some goals articulated by many writers and applicable to all kinds of training. I will then offer a summary of literature dealing with professional training of writing teachers both in programs leading to degrees and in postdegree programs. A description of writing on preservice and in-service training for classroom teachers will follow. The final sections will describe the preparation of tutors in writing laboratories.

GENERAL GOALS

There have been several attempts to describe the necessary qualities and knowledge a teacher of basic writing must have. William Lutz's article "On Training Teachers of Remedial English" (1973) names seven minimum qualifications needed for competence as a teacher of "disadvantaged" students. They are knowledge of systems of grammar, of dialectology, of rhetoric, of writing, of reading, of writing laboratories, and of working individually with students. Harvey S. Wiener's article "Questions on Basic Skills for the Writing Teacher" (1977) asks ten questions, each of which names a skill basic to the undertaking of teaching writing. These skills are research on writing, evaluation of student writing, identification of objectives, proscription of purse-string pedagogy, instruction in grammar as a tool for growth in writing, development of effective textbooks, development of new teaching strategies, spreading out the teaching of writing across the curriculum, training others to teach writing, and seeing instruction in basic writing as a task worth doing. Joseph Comprone in his article "Graduate Programs for Teachers of Basic Writing" (1981) offers a "general theory for training basic writing teachers." It includes six things that basic writing teachers must be able to do (teach developmentally, diagnose individual writing problems, construct curricula, conduct empirical studies of writings, create supplementary programs, and teach other teachers of writing) and six subject areas with which they should be familiar (the composing process, rhetorical theory and practice, linguistics, cognitive psychology, reading theory and practice, literary theory and practice, and basic learning patterns in disciplines other than English). More recently, Sara Garnes has summarized the necessities for a teacher of basic writing as the "three C's: commitment, curiosity, and confidence" ("Preparing the Ideal Teacher of Basic Writing" [1984] 4). Garnes asserts that commitment depends on having teachers who teach basic writing voluntarily and on an understanding of the development of basic writers. Curiosity, she speculates, may be closely related to an interest in how languages develop (diachronic language study) and in how populations of language users differ (sociolinguistics). Confidence is partly the teacher's belief in herself as a writer and partly the belief in the student's potential for improvement.

Each of these characterizations of the necessary skills of basic writing teachers contains what is probably the most commonly mentioned single piece of advice: basic writing teachers must be writers. In an article subsequent to his "Questions on Basic Skills," Wiener makes this qualification central: "I now believe that the first and most important qualification for teachers of basic writing is that they be practicing writers who apply whatever formal training or finely tuned instincts they have . . . " ("Preparing the Teacher of Writing" [1981] 5). Another exponent of the centrality of the writing teacher's own writing is Charles Moran (1981, 1982), who writes that we "should train writing teachers to be *writers* and to be *editors*" (1982, 420). The importance of the teachers' writing is also emphasized by Sandra Schor in "Preparing Teachers from Disciplines" (1983) in her decision to require regular faculty members from other departments being retained as basic writing teachers to attend and complete the writing assignments in her basic writing class. The assumptions behind demanding that writing teachers write are simple: it is as writers they can best relate to their students' problems and as writers they can fulfill what John L. Ruszkiewicz terms the Great Commandment: teach writing ("The Great Commandment" [1986]).

Emphasis on teachers as writers does not mean, however, that these writers see traditional literary education as inappropriate or unnecessary for teachers of basic writing. Wiener asserts that "the habit of mind nurtured by advanced degree programs, the kinds of insights about writing that such programs in literature cultivate, are what basic writing teachers must bring into the classroom and to a page of a beginner's efforts" (1981, 9). Comprone supports this view with his comment, "the English profession must clearly perceive those ways literary study can be a useful part of a basic writing teacher's broader, more functional knowledge" (1981, 13). John Brereton, in "The Doctorate in Composition at Wayne State University" (1981), explains that the program requires coursework half in composition and half in literature partly because "it seemed sensible to stress the closely interrelated processes of reading literature and writing prose in order to give students a full picture of how language is employed" (17–18). Donald McQuade and Marie Ponsot, in "Creating Communities of Writers" (1981), express a similar view when they write, "Great literature is the generative matrix of writing and reading at whatever level they are learned, and provides the teacher's deductive framework for teaching both writing and the study of literature" (83).

If there is general agreement about the need for teachers of basic writing to be good writers and analytical readers of literature, there is less agreement about how to approach what is often perceived to be at the heart of the basic writer's difficulties: error. It was, of course, Shaughnessy's view in *Errors and Expectations* (1977) that a reconceptualization of error was at the heart of a new approach to teaching basic writing. Some writers, however, have found her position too rigid, aiming as it does primarily at producing students who can write edited American English. In "Toward Defining 'Basic' Once Again" (1985), Charles Timothy Summerlin offers a summary of the dispute over "the importance of competence in standard American English" and strongly supports the view that such competence must be the goal of basic writing instruction, despite the political and moral objections of some theorists. As the lists of goals above make clear, knowledge of linguistics has often been described as an important part of the teacher's preparation to help students achieve that competency. Some writers have been skeptical of the necessity of linguistic training. Moran (1982) says that, of course, "writing teachers should know everything," but when choices must be made he places linguistics after training in "actual writing and editing" (420). A stronger expression of doubt comes from P. A. Ramsey in "Teaching the Teachers to Teach Black-Dialect Writers" (1979), where he considers emphasis on black dialect by writing teachers an excuse for failure and racism. He writes, "The unintending culprits are the linguists who have recently given us a plethora of literature on black dialect. . . . If teachers feel they cannot teach until they have read Sledd, Labov, Dillard, Stewart, Shuy, Feigenbaum, Smitherman to name a few—few of whom agree—then they will never teach these students" (199). Ramsey does not reject standard American English as the goal; but his experience teaching prospective teachers leads him to believe that knowledge of linguistics and dialectology is a relatively unimportant part of a teacher's training. Nevertheless, most writers consider training in linguistics and in grammar a valuable part of a teacher's equipment in diagnosing and responding to error.

PROFESSIONAL TRAINING

Professional training is used here to describe work undertaken not for the purpose of preparing to teach in a particular writing program but as a part of a teacher's general training in the profession. This work is often part of a degree program, but with teachers of basic writing it is also very likely to be postdegree training to enable them to meet needs that have surfaced since their original training.

Although a number of universities are now offering advanced degrees with emphasis on rhetoric and/or composition, relatively few programs have offered descriptions of themselves as they are especially appropriate to the training of teachers of basic writing. Two exceptions are John Brereton's description of the doctorate in composition at Wayne State University (1981) and Joseph Comprone's of the doctoral program at the University of Louisville (1981).

Brereton describes the origins of the program and the choice among models for such training. Rejecting a program similar to those found in schools of education or a program closely tied to training in the social sciences, Wayne State elected to establish a program with coursework in literature and in subjects directly related to composition. These latter are described in some detail. They include classical rhetorical theory, teaching expository writing, survey of research in writing, introduction to syntax, psycholinguistics, and sociolinguistics. Besides this course work, the program emphasizes practical teaching experience. Although the coursework is obviously designed to prepare students for teaching basic writers, the practical experience is even more heavily slanted that way. Students serve as tutors or adjunct instructors at the campus writing workshop that serves students who need extra help with composition. They also teach the writing workshop's remedial course for students who fail Wayne State's junior proficiency examination. Later in their program students are likely to teach the regular university composition courses, but their first experience is likely to be with basic writers. Wayne State's program is not explicitly designed to train teachers of basic writing; but it clearly contains preparation for teaching basic writers and assumes that its graduates will be capable of doing so.

Comprone's description of the University of Louisville's program ties its establishment to the renewed interest in the teaching of basic writing. While the program is not designed exclusively to train basic writing teachers, he makes it clear that the demand for teachers of basic writing, at Louisville and elsewhere, has influenced the program and that the "basic writing teachers have helped shape the courses they take as graduate students in the English Department's Ph.D. in rhetoric and composition" (24). Students in the Louisville program take courses in three areas: rhetoric and pedagogy, linguistics and reading, and literature. Students also have the opportunity for practical experience. They teach basic writers as tutors in a writing clinic or as classroom teachers in the university's developmental writing course. They may also teach regular and advanced composition courses. They also have the opportunity for administrative internships in the writing clinic and as assistant directors of composition. Comprone concludes that the Louisville program is especially well suited for students "who wish to enter the profession at a time when the ability to teach basic writing is important at almost every level of the secondary and college curriculum" (40).

Another sort of professional training is the institute, course, or workshop attended by writing teachers who wish to improve their skills or to learn new skills appropriate to new kinds of students. One example of this sort of training is detailed by McQuade and Ponsot in their report on the Queens English Project (1981). This program aims not to prepare teachers of basic writing at the college level, but to use college faculty to help train local secondary school teachers to teach basic writing. The rationale is that such training could lower the number of students who enter Queens and other City University of New York (CUNY) campuses needing basic writing instruction. Thus the project aims at breaking down unnecessary boundaries between college and secondary school instruction and at identifying approaches that can work in various settings. The emphasis in the training of teachers is on the teachers' own writing. It is used not only to improve their skills as writers, but to lead them inductively to discover the coherent set of skills that they must recognize and help their students master. Participants read their writing aloud to each other and receive commentary from their audiences. The syllabus for the project "differed from a syllabus used in basic writing classes only in the level of work produced" (85). The Queens project also trains undergraduate tutors to help the high school teacher-participants in their basic writing classes. The experience of the Queens project formed the basis of the training Sandra Schor (1983) offered to faculty members from other disciplines. A favorable report on the results of the project by one of the high school teachers who participated is offered by Charles Roemer in "The Queens English Project" (1982).

Moran (1982) reports on a similar kind of training for high school teachers at the Institutes for the Teaching of Writing, offered through the National Endowment for the Humanities by the University of Massachusetts at Amherst. These institutes stressed the writing of the participants and published two volumes of their work. The institute also emphasized the teacher as editor and involved working with a small group of students. This institute was not exclusively focused on teaching basic writing; but being an effective high school writing teacher virtually requires the ability to work with basic writers. Moran (1981) has also reported on similar but less extensive training provided to teachers in shorter time periods.

In reporting on shorter training programs, Moran provides a description of what is probably the most common sort of professional training most writing teachers receive: the single course on teaching writing. Large numbers of teachers of writing in both high schools and colleges have a single course, either graduate or undergraduate, as their only professional training. Moran describes a graduate course that features experience as a tutor in an undergraduate writing course with students ranging from "severe remedial cases to glib, hyper-verbal writers who need to learn to edit" (73). The course also offers readings on topics important to teachers of writing. The course, like most such courses, is not devoted primarily to teaching basic writing, but the tutorials and the readings ensure that it is a part of what is covered. A similar sort of course on the undergraduate level is described by Richard C. Gebhardt in "Training Basic Writing Teachers at a Liberal Arts College" (1981) and "Balancing Theory with Practice in the Training of Writing Teachers" (1977). The course he describes does not involve tutoring other students, concentrating instead on the students' own writing and on an introduction to the subjects important to writing teachers. This course, like many such courses, serves all kinds of prospective writing teachers—elementary, secondary, and collegiate. It also does not focus on basic writing, but it "does address the needs of Findlay's basic writers" (54). As basic writing has become better recognized, it is probable that many such courses have attempted to build in some treatment of the subject. An indication of the incorporation of the concerns of basic writing teachers into more general courses is also given by Charles W. Bridges in "The Basics and the New Teacher in the College Composition Class" (1986) as he describes the training course offered at New Mexico State University. In that course, error and its diagnosis is one of the topics and *Errors and Expectations* is the text used. A similar recognition comes from Nancy R. Comley in "The Teaching Seminar" (1986), where she writes that Shaughnessy's book ought to be required reading for everyone teaching composition. Since they form such a large part of the professional training of writing teachers, it would be valuable to have more reports on the courses for prospective writing teachers from around the country with attention given to how and to what extent they include preparation to teach basic writing.

It is much rarer to find courses devoted exclusively to preparing teachers of basic writing. One report of such a course is Constance J. Gefvert's "Training Teachers of Basic Writing" (1980), which describes a graduate course offered at Virginia Polytechnic Institute. Gefvert gives a detailed description of a fifteen-week course that includes a tutoring internship in the campus writing center. The course relies heavily on *Errors and Expectations* but uses many other readings as well. It includes considerable work on dialect interference, English as a second language, syntax, error analysis, and sentence combining. A much less theoretical course aimed exclusively at preparing basic writing teachers is described by James L. Collins in "Training Teachers of Basic Writing in the Writing Laboratory" (1982). Collins's course used basic writers in an undergraduate writing laboratory as the tutees of secondary English teachers and university teaching assistants. The members of the class worked with the basic writers, and Collins in turn worked with the class members. This approach produced teachers with a very immediate sense of the needs of basic writers, experience in responding to those needs, and guidance and criticism of their responses. It relies, however, on students who are already experienced teachers in some respects.

A similar kind of practicum training is described by Lou Kelly in "Writing as Learning for Basic Writing Teachers and Their Students" (1984). Graduate students at the University of Iowa enroll in this course to learn about the teaching of basic writing through observation of and then personal experience in the university's writing laboratory. Observation and practice are supplemented by a seminar in which discussion of goals, assumptions, and theories takes place. Students from several different programs related to teaching writing enroll in the course.

PRESERVICE AND IN-SERVICE TRAINING FOR CLASSROOM TEACHERS

Because professional training of the sort described above is still relatively new and rare and because the need for teachers of basic writing has grown, many institutions need to offer training to graduate students or faculty members to prepare them for such teaching. In "Anatomy of a Basic Writing Program" (1979), Andrea A. Lunsford and Sara Garnes sketch briefly the preparation of teachers at the beginning of the basic writing program at Ohio State University: a training course studying strategies of basic writers, cognitive development, and realistic expectations. This section describes reports on the preparation offered as a basis for teaching in other basic writing programs.

Richard P. VanDeWeghe describes the process of training teaching assistants (TAs) at the University of Colorado at Denver in "Linking Pedagogy to Purpose for Teaching Assistants in Basic Writing" (1986). This program is of interest partly because all TAs begin by teaching basic writing so that their training for this course often occurs at the beginning of their teaching careers and carries over into their teaching of more advanced courses. The training course features a presemester orientation that introduces TAs to basic writing, its goals, and its population. The bulk of the training, however, is provided in a series of staff workshops with topics such as writing apprehension, assignment making, and peer editing groups.

Irvin Y. Hashimoto's article "Sensitizing Beginning Teachers of Writing" (1984) describes the training for teaching assistants at Idaho State University.

This program emphasizes removing unproductive preconceptions about teaching writing, especially regarding basic writers. The training focuses on reconceptualizing error analysis along lines suggested by Shaughnessy. The program is a gradual one, based on the assumption that it will take these new teachers considerable time to unlearn their prejudices.

Lil Brannon and Gordon Pradl describe training for graduate students teaching expository writing at New York University (NYU) in ''The Socialization of Writing Teachers'' (1984). This training course is not exclusively for teachers of basic writing since the writing course these graduate students teach is required of all NYU undergraduates. Brannon and Pradl's course emphasizes writing teachers as writers using their own writing processes as a guide to helping others. The course is not highly theoretical but aims at offering guidance in assignment making, classroom practice, and commenting on essays.

Many new teachers of basic writing are not graduate students but faculty members enlisted in the effort to improve the writing skills of unprepared students. A number of essays describe programs for preparing these teachers. Sandra Schor (1983) describes how she had colleagues from other departments attend her basic writing class as a preparation for their own teaching. This experience was supplemented by keeping a log and commentary on the class, a weekly seminar on composition theory, and additional meetings after the new faculty began teaching basic writing.

Gebhardt (1981) describes the preparation to teach basic writing in a small English department devoted to teaching writing. Because the department shared a strong consensus about the importance of teaching basic writing, the preparation consisted mostly of meeting to discuss readings on the subject and joint planning of writing curricula. He also describes the seminar offered to Findlay faculty outside the English department to encourage them to include writing instruction in other classes. The seminar was called ''Writing as a Way to Learn'' and focused on two problems common in classes in other disciplines: not thinking about writing and lacking the confidence to teach it. The seminar introduced faculty members to theoretical considerations involving writing and offered practical suggestions. It was attended by about half the college faculty. A second seminar stressed practical techniques of teaching writing.

In ''Recruiting, Training, and Supporting Volunteer Basic Writing Instructors'' (1984), Christopher C. Burnham describes the preparation of faculty members from other disciplines who volunteer to teach basic writing on a rotating basis at Stockton State College in New Jersey. This program uses rotating faculty for 40% of its basic writing instruction. The training program involves three parts: readings on writing and writing pedagogy; a one-day workshop in the spring designed to help new teachers plan their courses over the summer; and a one-day workshop in the fall that involved analyzing the teachers' own writing, critiquing syllabi, discussing support services, offering practical teaching techniques, and evaluating successes and failures in the classroom.

Some teachers of basic writing are neither graduate students nor regular faculty but part-time faculty. This group of teachers are often given the least attention and the least training. Betsy E. Brown and John T. Harwood describe the program at Pennsylvania State University to train part-time faculty in writing in "Training and Evaluating Traditional and Non-Traditional Instructors of Composition" (1984). The program is similar to the one described by Burnham for regular faculty members in using a set of readings for the summer and a two-day orientation program at the beginning of fall term. These are supplemented by a three-term course on teaching writing, which the part-time faculty audit, and by ongoing consultation with the teaching coordinator or one of five experienced assistants. No distinctions between training provided to teachers of developmental writing and teachers of the regular freshman sequence are described. Another account of preparation for part-time faculty comes from Kay Harley, who describes a workshop at Saginaw Valley State College in Michigan in "Training Part-Time Faculty" (1983). She arranged for a four-day workshop in which part-time faculty, none of whom had had any previous training in teaching writing, discussed current research on composition, writing assignments, error analysis, essay evaluation, course design and textbooks. Participants in the workshop were paid $100 for attendance as a recognition of the value of their time. Despite these accounts, however, the training, or lack of it, received by part-time teachers of basic writing remains largely unreported.

TRAINING OF TUTORS

Much of basic writing teaching occurs in tutorial settings in writing laboratories, clinics, and centers. Many of the tutors are already highly trained professionals with advanced degrees; some are graduate students preparing for careers in teaching; and some are undergraduates, commonly called peer tutors. The training of the first two groups is usually part of more extensive training in teaching writing, but peer tutors are more frequently trained only for their specific role. This section considers descriptions of the training offered to such tutors.

In "Training Writing Center Tutors" (1981), Marian Arkin considers the matter of training tutors both theoretically and practically. On the theoretical level, she defines several issues that determine the kind of training a tutor should receive: relationships between tutors and teachers, relationships between the tutor and the academy, the approach to tutoring, the tutor's responsibilities, and the evaluation of tutors. In training tutors, she identifies formal and informal approaches. Formal methods include peer-tutor courses, preservice training, in-service training meetings, training handbooks, training tapes, and proficiency workshops. Informal methods are senior tutors, committees, material acquisition and preparation, tutor logs, and case studies. Most specific programs discussed below use some combination of these.

In "Training Tutors to Talk about Writing" (1982), Stephen M. North describes a course to train tutors for the writing center at State University of New York (SUNY) at Albany. He defines tutoring in writing as "intervention in the composing process'' and the essential skill as ''knowing how to talk about writing'' (434, 439). To further these goals, he has tutors play the roles of tutor and tutee, watch videotapes of tutorials, and observe live tutorials. He also offers them a list of composing ''locations'' at which tutorials are likely to take place: inventing, writing, revising, editing, evaluating, and experiencing the writing process generally. Students also read their own writing aloud and receive comments from their peers. His description of the SUNY Albany program ends by calling for research into what makes an effective tutor.

Kenneth A. Bruffee in ''Staffing and Operating Peer-Tutoring Writing Centers'' (1980) describes the process by which peer tutors at Brooklyn College are recruited and trained. Recruitment is usually by letter, based on recommendations from freshman composition teachers. Students who decide to become tutors enroll in a training course, the first part of which involves ''writing, reviewing grammar, and learning techniques of analysis and evaluation'' (147). The second part of the course involves peer criticism of the writing done by prospective tutors. These peer criticisms aim at teaching the tutors to distinguish and perform three types of readings: ''objective, rhetorically descriptive analysis; evaluative or judgmental response; and reaction to the issues and point of view developed in a paper'' (148). Bruffee's final point is that the experience of tutoring not only helps the basic writer progress as a writer but helps the tutor as well.

Gebhardt (1981) describes two ways that peer tutors are trained at Findlay College. One is through enrolling in the teaching of the writing course described above. The other is through training in the writing center where they observe more experienced tutors and offer general feedback on drafts while they develop their skills as tutors. These tutors are also expected to do some reading on theory and practice of composition instruction and to discuss this in staff meetings.

''Training and Using Peer Tutors'' (1978) by Paula Beck, Thom Hawkins, and Marcia Silver describes peer tutor programs at Nassau Community College in Garden City, New York; the University of California at Berkeley; and Brooklyn College.

Despite such training programs at some institutions, many tutors are largely self-taught; and even those who are trained must learn a good deal for themselves. Some tutors have written of their experiences as tutors and of how and what they learned. In ''An Argument for Peer Tutoring as Teacher Training'' (1981), James E. Anderson, Ellen M. Bommarito, and Laura Seijas briefly describe how their experiences as peer tutors in the writing laboratory at the University of Michigan–Flint led them to career goals as writing teachers. In ''A Peer Tutor Assesses Her Teaching Ability'' (1981), Patricia Roberts describes how her uncertainty about tutoring produced her approach to helping students. A fuller description is offered by Jackie Goldsby in *Peer Tutoring in Basic Writing* (1981). She recounts some of her experiences and uses them to provide insight into the skills needed for tutoring. She also includes copies of the information sheets distributed to students and tutors at the writing center at the University of California at Berkeley. A detailed and intimate study of the relationship between a tutor and a tutee can be found in *Benjamin* (1972) by Thom Hawkins, which describes the author's successful attempt to teach basic reading and writing skills to a nearly illiterate young man.

CONCLUSION

A glance at the references to this essay will make it clear that the City University of New York has produced a very large part of the literature on training teachers of the basic writing. The experience of open admissions and the establishment of a community of teachers and scholars dedicated to teaching basic writing doubtless account for the fact. As more colleges and universities establish programs to teach basic writing, we must hope that more reports of how those programs prepare teachers will be produced. We must similarly hope that institutions offering professional training in teaching writing, whether at the level of the single course or the advanced degree, will describe how the need for teachers of basic writing and the increasing need for all teachers of writing to be able to teach basic writing have led to changes in the preparation offered to prospective writing teachers. Similarly, much more could profitably be written about the specific preparation basic writing programs around the country offer new and continuing teachers. Beyond increasing the descriptive literature lies another sort of research, not yet undertaken with regard to preparing teachers of basic writing. That is the attempt to assess the effectiveness of the preparation they have received. Many kinds of work might be done in this regard: longitudinal studies of the careers of basic writing teachers with various kinds of training, interviews with working teachers to discover their assessment of the preparation they received, statistical studies of the progress of students of teachers trained in different ways. As the field of basic writing grows and reaches maturity, it will doubtless turn its attention to addressing more systematically the question of what sorts of preparation produce the most effective and satisfied teachers of the subject.

NOTE

1. A computer search of the ERIC database conducted as part of the research for this essay discovered only 35 documents dealing with preparation of teachers of basic writing. The search included such related terms as developmental and remedial writing as well as a variety of terms related to teacher training. The search included more than 39,000 documents dealing with teacher training and more than 26,000 dealing with writing.

REFERENCES

Anderson, James E., Ellen M. Bommarito, and Laura Seijas. "An Argument for Peer Tutoring as Teacher Training." *Improving Writing Skills*. Ed. Thom Hawkins and Phyllis Brooks. New Directions for College Learning Assistance 3. San Francisco: Jossey-Bass, 1981, pp. 35–38.

Arkin, Marian. "Training Writing-Center Tutors: Issues and Approaches." *Improving Writing Skills*. Ed. Thom Hawkins and Phyllis Brooks. New Directions for College Learning Assistance 3. San Francisco: Jossey-Bass, 1981, pp. 25–34.

Beck, Paula, Thom Hawkins, and Marcia Silver. "Training and Using Peer Tutors." *CE* 40 (1978): 432–48.

Brannon, Lil, and Gordon Pradl. "The Socialization of Writing Teachers." *JBW* 3.4 (1984): 28–37.

Brereton, John. "The Doctorate in Composition at Wayne State University." *JBW* 3.2 (1981): 14–22.

Bridges, Charles W., ed. *Training the New Teacher of College Composition*. Urbana, Ill.: NCTE, 1986.

——. "The Basics and the New Teacher in the College Composition Class." *Training the New Teacher of College Composition*. Ed. Charles W. Bridges. Urbana, Ill.: NCTE, 1986, pp. 13–26.

Brown, Betsy E., and John T. Harwood. "Training and Evaluating Traditional and Non-Traditional Instructors of Composition." *JBW* 3.4 (1984): 63–73.

Bruffee, Kenneth A. "Staffing and Operating Peer-Tutoring Writing Centers." *Basic Writing: Essays for Teachers, Researchers, and Administrators*. Ed. Lawrence N. Kasden and Daniel R. Hoeber. Urbana, Ill.: NCTE, 1980, pp. 141–49.

Burnham, Christopher C. "Recruiting, Training, and Supporting Volunteer Basic Writing Instructors: A Working Program." *JBW* 3.4 (1984): 14–27.

Collins, James L. "Training Teachers of Basic Writing in the Writing Laboratory." *CCC* 33 (1982): 426–33.

Comley, Nancy R. "The Teaching Seminar: Writing Isn't Just Rhetoric." *Training the New Teacher of College Composition*. Ed. Charles W. Bridges. Urbana, Ill.: NCTE, 1986, pp. 47–57.

Comprone, Joseph. "Graduate Programs for Teachers of Basic Writing: The University of Louisville's Ph.D. in Rhetoric and Composition." *JBW* 3.2 (1981): 23–45.

Garnes, Sara. "Preparing the Ideal Teacher of Basic Writing." *JBW* 3.4 (1984): 4–13.

Gebhardt, Richard C. "Balancing Theory with Practice in the Training of Writing Teachers." *CCC* 28 (1977): 134–40.

——. "Training Basic Writing Teachers at a Liberal Arts College." *JBW* 3.2 (1981): 46–63.

Gefvert, Constance J. "Training Teachers of Basic Writing." *Basic Writing: Essays for Teachers, Researchers, and Administrators*. Ed. Lawrence N. Kasden and Daniel R. Hoeber. Urbana, Ill.: NCTE, 1980, pp. 119–40.

Goldsby, Jackie. *Peer Tutoring in Basic Writing: A Tutor's Journal*. Classroom Research Study 4. Berkeley: Bay Area Writing Project, 1981.

Harley, Kay. "Training Part-Time Faculty." *WI* 3.1 (1983): 26–30.

Hashimoto, Irvin Y. "Sensitizing Beginning Teachers of Writing." *JBW* 3.4 (1984): 55–62.

Hawkins, Thom. *Benjamin: Reading and Beyond*. Columbus, Ohio: Merrill, 1972.

Hawkins, Thom, and Phyllis Brooks, eds. *Improving Writing Skills*. New Directions for College Learning Assistance 3. San Francisco: Jossey-Bass, 1981.

Kasden, Lawrence N., and Daniel R. Hoeber, eds. *Basic Writing: Essays for Teachers, Researchers, and Administrators*. Urbana, Ill.: NCTE, 1980.

Kelly, Lou. "Writing as Learning for Basic Writing Teachers and Their Students." *JBW* 3.4 (1984): 38–54.

Lunsford, Andrea A., and Sara Garnes. "Anatomy of a Basic Writing Program." *JBW* 2.2 (1979): 38–51.

Lutz, William. "On Training Teachers of Remedial English." *FEN* 2.2 (1973): 12–13.

McQuade, Donald, and Marie Ponsot. "Creating Communities of Writers: The Experience of the Queens English Project." *JBW* 3.2 (1981): 79–89.

Moran, Charles. "A Model for Teacher Training Programs in the Field of Writing." *JBW* 3.2 (1981): 64–77.

———. "Teaching Teachers of Writing: Steps toward a Curriculum." *CCC* 33 (1982): 420–25.

North, Stephen M. "Training Tutors to Talk about Writing." *CCC* 33 (1982): 434–41.

Ramsey, P. A. "Teaching the Teachers to Teach Black-Dialect Writers." *CE* 41 (1979): 197–201.

Roberts, Patricia. "A Peer Tutor Assesses Her Teaching Ability." *Improving Writing Skills*. Ed. Thom Hawkins and Phyllis Brooks. New Directions for College Learning Assistance 3. San Francisco: Jossey-Bass, 1981, pp. 39–40.

Roemer, Charles. "The Queens English Project: Camaraderie, Not Competition." *Writing Problems after a Decade of Open Admissions*. Proceedings of the Annual CUNY Association of Writing Supervisors Conference. 3 April 1981. New York: CUNY, 1982, pp. 18–21.

Ruszkiewicz, John J. "The Great Commandment." *Training the New Teacher of College Composition*. Ed. Charles W. Bridges. Urbana, Ill.: NCTE, 1986, pp. 78–83.

Schor, Sandra. "Preparing Volunteers from Disciplines of Currently Diminished Student Interest to Teach Basic Writing." *ADE Bul* 76 (1983): 46–48.

Shaughnessy, Mina P. "Basic Writing." *Teaching Composition: 10 Bibliographical Essays*. Ed. Gary Tate. Fort Worth, Texas: Christian University Press, 1976, pp. 137–67.

———. *Errors and Expectations: A Guide for the Teacher of Basic Writing*. New York: Oxford University Press, 1977.

Summerlin, Charles Timothy. "Toward Defining 'Basic' Once Again." *ADE Bul* 81 (1985): 32–35.

VanDeWeghe, Richard P. "Linking Pedagogy to Purpose for Teaching Assistants in Basic Writing." *Training the New Teacher of College Composition*. Ed. Charles W. Bridges. Urbana, Ill.: NCTE, 1986, pp. 37–46.

Wiener, Harvey S. "Preparing the Teacher of Writing." *JBW* 3.2 (1981): 5–13.

———. "Questions on Basic Skills for the Writing Teacher." *CCC* 28 (1977): 321–24.

Appendix

Selective Bibliography of Basic Writing Textbooks

Mary Sue Ply

The diversity of approaches to the teaching of basic writing is revealed in the variety of basic writing texts. They range across a spectrum of five general categories: all grammar, grammar with some composition, half grammar and half composition, composition with some grammar, and all composition. But these labels do not reflect the different philosophies of authors within a given category. Some texts cling to the notion that basic students' writing consists merely of errors to be corrected, and some approaches to composition are equally prescriptive, with minimal practice in invention. At times, these books ask students to devise a topic sentence or thesis statement somewhat like Athena springing fully grown and armored from the head of Zeus. At the opposite extreme are texts devoting full attention to invention and the individual's ever-evolving writing process. Here idea dictates structure. But here there may also be no treatment of grammar.

Most texts try to balance the students' need to compose clear, cogent prose with their need to produce prose free of distracting errors. For most texts, the balance is uneasy, for composing and editing are at cross-purposes—one liberating, the other restricting; one intellectual, the other mechanical; one stimulating, the other boring and lifeless.

Nevertheless, dedicated teacher-scholars continue to write texts in an effort to meet students' needs. The following appendix surveys these basic writing texts. Some texts that seemed more suitable for 101-level courses were eliminated. Faced with ninety-nine books and limited space, I must restrict the annotations to books copyrighted after 1986, books that presumably reflect current trends in the teaching of basic writing. Not discussed are significant works such as *Composition Five* (Sieben and Anthony), *Steps in Composition* (Troyka and Nudelman), *Basic Writing* (Lorch), and *Stepping Stones* (Eisenberg and Wiener). However, the older texts are listed in a separate bibliography, divided into the same categories as the newer books.

TEXTS THAT FOCUS ONLY ON GRAMMAR

The most successful of the early basic writing texts were devoted entirely to grammar and mechanics. These texts prescribed rules and reinforced them in exercises where students underlined, circled, or labeled elements of grammar. Later texts added a greater variety of exercises, including sentence writing, paragraph editing, and transforming. Some texts moved beyond rules of mere correctness to methods to improve style, with exercises in sentence combining, passage transforming, and copying. A few authors approached grammar inductively, allowing the students to derive the rules for themselves.

Unless specified otherwise, the texts in this section follow a prescriptive approach to grammar with copious and varied exercises. Some offer writing assignments at the end of each chapter, but to practice a particular grammar element, not to compose. Thus, grammar and mechanics are presented as the raison d'être of writing, not an adjunct—even though some critics argue that the teaching of grammar divorced from the students' own writing is fruitless.

Essential College English (Selby, 1987) stresses identifying sentence parts and errors and then editing for correctness. This focus prevents a variety of exercises; moreover, the content of the exercises is not very stimulating.

Mary Epes and Carolyn Kirkpatrick have developed *Editing Your Writing* (1988) for "students . . . working at somewhat more advanced level" than typical of their earlier *COMP-LAB Exercises*. Twelve self-paced and -graded modules, with Error Analysis Charts, focus on errors of spelling, plurals, and writing conventions—surface errors that the authors believe students "can control" more easily than sentence-level errors. Varied exercises reinforce prespective grammar rules.

In contrast, *The Sentence Book* (Jacobus and Miller, 1989) begins with nine chapters on the parts of the sentence, followed by five chapters on connecting words, phrases, and clauses. "Sentence Problems" (e.g., fragments, agreement) precedes units on punctuation and style. The text contains a helpful unit on peer editing but no writing assignments for the students to edit. Copious and varied exercises offer the students practice.

Easy Writer II (Campbell and Meier, 1987) focuses on the sentence—closed sentence combining, punctuation of combined sentences, revision, and open combining—followed by ninety pages of "revising at the word level" and editing for errors. Overly dependent on grammar terminology and labeling exercises, the book emphasizes editing practice, but tear-out pages discourage copying exercises. However, the numerous exercises are lively and informative.

GRAMMAR TEXTS WITH SOME COMPOSITION

Realizing the need to include writing instruction in sentence-level books, many authors have added such material, usually less than one-fourth of the text. Unless noted otherwise, these texts treat grammar and composition as *separate* functions and present grammar completely and clearly in a prescriptive manner with copious exercises varying in degree of complexity.

Students using *Foundation* (Neuberger, 1989) will label every part of simple sentences and draw arrows from modifiers to the words they modify. Other exercises call for sentence combining or for editing or transforming unrelated sentences. The text moves from sentence-level problems to word-level errors to mechanics. Unit 7, "Writing Paragraphs and Essays" (forty-three pages), avoids standard terminology but still offers a traditional approach. Although briefly discussing various invention methods, the text focuses on "the summary page method." Material on eliminating deadwood and passive voice separates the discussion of thesis statements from the practice of writing them.

Some users of *Grassroots* (Fawcett and Sandberg, 1987) have complained about its simplistic grammar exercises. The twenty-six page unit on writing, limited to the paragraph, offers a formulaic approach to the composing process. The text offers only brainstorming for developing topic sentences that students have already derived. The only connection between writing and grammar is the fairly simple writing assignments focusing on the particular grammar rules covered in each grammar unit.

The twenty-page section of writing assignments in John Langan's *Sentence Skills* (1987) gives little explanation of the writing process. With its diagnostic test, achievement test, and progress chart, the text helps students discover their problem areas and do exercises at their own rate, but most require no writing. The text also includes work on sentence combining.

In its forty-seven-page unit "Writing Paragraphs and Essays," *English Fundamentals* (Emery et al., 1985–1987) presents the writing process as a sequence of nine terse steps, with no significant invention strategies and only brief explanations of how to select a subject, derive a thesis, and organize a paper. While the authors follow the nine steps for two sample essays, there are no exercises for the students to practice these techniques. The chapter on paragraphing provides only the usual information about topic sentences, the modes, unity, and coherence, although the chapters on essay tests and study skills are more useful. The grammar portion relies on tear-out identification and revising exercises.

The writing assignments closing each chapter of *Writing Clear Sentences* (Donald et al., 1987) focus on audience and purpose and tie in (although not overtly) with the grammar material. Distinctive drawings and numerous exercises fill grammar chapters moving from the parts of speech and punctuation of simple sentences to coordination and subordination, to mechanics and spelling. The text's concluding twenty-nine pages cover standard material on paragraphing but do not discuss invention.

Glazier opens *The Least You Should Know about English* (1987) with forty-eight pages on spelling and apostrophes and then moves to errors in sentence structure and mechanics. Prescriptive rules are reinforced by numerous "circle" and "correct" exercises containing related sentences numbered individually. Answer keys are included. Proofreading exercises often specify the number and types of errors—assistance the students won't receive in their own writing. In each chapter confusing directions send students to an unspecified writing assignment in the final section, "Eight Steps to Better Writing." These forty-three pages discuss the essay, with material on freewriting but no attention to audience.

The authors of *Just Writing* (Laubheim et al., 1988) advocate a traditional approach to paragraph structure and development, with little attention to audience or purpose. The book presents seven paragraph "types" before moving to "Basic Elements of an Essay." The text does note that more than one "paragraph type" can appear in longer pieces, and it gives some practice in deriving topic sentences and thesis statements, but writing assignments are neither fully explained nor challenging. The grammar chapters, completely divorced from the writing instruction but complete with pretests and posttests, rely excessively on identifying and sentence-writing exercises.

Skills in Sequence (Friedman, 1988) labels chapters as either "Recommended" or "Assign as Needed," thus making the text "paper specific." It is self-paced, with diagnostic tests and answer keys for the interesting exercises. While the editing exercises often specify the number of errors, the author does use a semi-inductive approach to word-level problems, fragments, run-ons, and mechanics. The seventeen-page unit on writing offers an unusual but formulaic approach: "proposition/defense" pieces with two paragraphs of reasons or examples and a thesis with "an argumentative edge."

In *Review and Revise* (1989) Marlene Martin illustrates her own seven-day writing processes (including days for freewriting, researching, brainstorming, drafting, and studying for other classes). This chatty text begins with a chapter on ways to generate ideas: freewriting, focused freewriting, clustering, brainstorming, keeping a Reading and Reaction Journal, and researching (with information on the card catalog and *Readers' Guide*). Chapter 3 explains documentation of sources. The 106 pages on writing are followed by a standard prescriptive handbook organized alphabetically by error (e.g., "ab," "abst," "adj"); it contains very few but also very interesting exercises.

The Complete Sentence Workout Book (Fitzpatrick and Ruscica, 1988) has an unusual structure, beginning with a brief overview of the parts of speech and sentence patterns and a *full* treatment of verb tenses. The authors include some passage-transforming exercises and a preponderance of fairly interesting editing exercises (with a key) but no specific writing assignments. Instead, students must "proofread a rough draft . . . of your own" for the problem treated in the chapter. "The Composing Process" (eighteen pages) offers the journalist's questions, freewriting, and brainstorming for invention; the standard elements of an essay; and twenty challenging writing assignments with specific purposes and audiences.

The title of *A Creative Copybook* (Rockas, 1981) is apt, for it focuses on creative writing. A livelier text than those by Gorrell and by Gonzalez et al., this copybook asks students to copy, transform, imitate, practice (fill in words or even sentences in passages), and then create (with stimulating professional passages serving as springboards for student thinking and writing). However, much of the writing will be personal rather than transactional, nor is there any advice on invention or attention to audience or purpose. Composition is presented inductively in five chapters on the parts of the essay.

The poor layout of the explanatory sections of *Writing for Meaning* (Shea, 1988) makes it seem a forbidding text. However, it depends on a multitude of writing assignments. Chapter 1 discusses listing, writing topic sentences, and then asking and answering questions as methods of development; it offers ten rough-draft exercises leading the students through the writing process. A lengthy Chapter 2 inductively leads students through the parts of the essay, with exercises on writing paragraphs in the context of an essay, writing supporting points for a partial outline, writing follow-up details for partial paragraphs, and revising to add missing details. The 132 pages on writing are followed by two lengthy chapters on sentence logic and mechanics, which rely on minimal grammar apparatus and numerous fill-in and writing exercises.

Writing with Confidence (Meyers, 1988) is notable for its vivid, lengthy editing exercises. It provides a detailed, complete presentation of grammar rules, including a good section on idioms with prepositions, and a variety of exercises. The brief introduction to writing focuses on planning (with brainstorming and freewriting for invention), drafting, and revising/evaluating. Chapter 16 treats paragraphs fairly traditionally. Discussion of a relevant mode (paragraphs and then essays) comes at the end of most of the grammar chapters. Students edit for grammar, thus matching the grammar and writing. These assignments, however, ignore audience analysis.

The title of *Writing, Grammar, and Usage* (O'Hearn, 1989) reflects the sequence of the book. The first section on writing (ninety pages) begins with a surface look at "Writers and the Writing Process"; it mentions invention techniques but offers no practice in any but outlining. Primarily this section reproduces student drafts at varying stages but with end comments rather than detailed marginal notes. The writing assignments in this text are especially good, with attention to specific and varying audiences (e.g., readers of university or city newspapers) and purposes. Since many are case study assignments, students practice both transactional and personal writing. The text includes twenty pages of interesting "Readings for Writing." Excessive grammar jargon mars the prescriptive sections on sentence structure and word forms, which are notable for the lengthy treatment of verbs, the numerous but somewhat dull copying exercises, and the absence of writing assignments.

For Richard Swartz, in *Starting Points* (1987), the first "starting point" is "Begin with Writing," which is amplified by Part 3, "The Paragraph and the Essay." These sixty-seven pages offer practice in listing and in deriving and narrowing the focus; writing assignments lead the students through the varying stages of the writing process for a given topic. The section on paragraphs treats the modes and provides exercises in outlining paragraphs and in analyzing paragraphs for structural problems and then revising them. The text briefly describes the essay as an expanded paragraph, modeled as five paragraphs. Units on "Sentence Skills," "Usage," and "Mechanics" rely primarily on paragraph-editing exercises; writing assignments ask students to apply "everything you have learned about. . . ."

Connections (Adams, 1987), by devoting 120 pages to the concerns of writing, more completely treats the recursive nature of writing. It is the only text in this section to discuss *finding* a topic; the others assume a preexisting topic. The author handles audience, purpose, and revision well, with one six-paragraph essay taken through four versions. Ignoring the modes, the other chapters on paragraphs, details, thesis, unity, and the organization and development of longer pieces (including arguments) contain a variety of exercises allowing students to practice these skills in sample papers and in their own writing. The writing topics are often fresh and challenging. This text does not assume that students possess complex analytical skills; rather, it teaches and develops those skills. The writing chapters alternate with the grammar chapters, but other than "look for errors in . . . ," there is no logical connection of the grammar to the writing process. The book presents grammar inductively, with a wide variety of exercises.

EQUAL TREATMENT OF COMPOSITION AND GRAMMAR

Responding to teachers' demands, the texts in this category offer more instruction in composition. Most have opted for a bifurcated approach, with a clear delineation between the composition and grammar sections. Others integrate in each chapter problems of composition, grammar, mechanics, and perhaps even reading, spelling, and vocabulary. This blend is "organic" when the grammar and syntax sections logically relate to the writing sections. Teachers who select such a book must adopt its overall structure and theoretical concept. Unless noted otherwise, the texts also are complete and prescriptive in their treatment of grammar, with many and varied exercises.

Bifurcated Texts

Better Paragraphs Plus (Ostrom and Cook, 1988) depends on lengthy analyses of paragraphs written by professionals plus a few exercises applying the standard strictures about paragraph organization, development, unity, and coherence. The text devotes little attention to invention, audience, or purpose. Writing assignments, although occasionally trite, often ask students to write persuasively. The sequence of chapters is unusual: two on paragraph structure, then one each on coordination and subordination, paragraph coherence, sentence coherence (faulty modifiers and parallelism), and complex methods of paragraph development. With few exercises, "Concise Guide for Punctuation" merely exemplifies rules. The text does not treat fragments, run-ons, comma splices, verb tenses, or subject-verb agreement. The final chapter, "Planning and Writing a Short Paper," compares paragraph and essay structure and then illustrates the stages of a researched essay. Basically, the text says "This is how it's done" and omits exercises for practicing the stages.

The eight chapters of *A Plan for Writing* (Brereton, 1987) move logically from consideration of six steps in the writing process to paragraphs and five-paragraph essays to sentence style and finally to grammar, word endings, mechanics, and spelling. Students receive much practice in improving topic sentences and thesis statements, but aside from brief discussions of various kinds of invention techniques, they receive little instruction in deriving these generalizations. Although discussed in Chapter 1, the relationship among writer, reader, and subject/text is dropped, even from the persuasion writing assignments in Chapter 3, "The College Essay." This highly traditional and formulaic chapter contains student and professional samples. Chapter 4 offers fourteen exercises in open sentence combining as well as exercises in wordiness and diction. In 107 pages the text covers most of the major grammar and mechanics problems, but with relatively few supporting exercises, especially paragraph editing.

The controlling metaphor in Units 1–2 of *The Writing Clinic* (Loewe, 1988) is that the students' writing is sick and must be diagnosed and then cured in the English class. In Chapter 1 students react to cartoons, poems, essays, and pictures so that "the director of the Clinic (your instructor) [can] prescribe suitable 'treatment' for what ails the 'patients' (your compositions)." Chapter 2 exhorts students to listen, follow directions, pay attention to details, and read. "The Four-Phase Writing Formula" involves assessing the assignment, selecting and limiting the subject, developing the outline, and writing the paper (including revising). Chapter 4 traces a paragraph through these stages; then it presents a standard explanation of the modes. Chapter 5 does much the same for "Writing Essays," but it offers no writing assignments. Units 3 and 4 rely on prescriptive rules about building and polishing sentences and on numerous exercises (some editing but no copying); answers to many exercises conclude the chapters. In Unit 5, students can "Check out of the Clinic" by demonstrating "how much the 'treatment' has improved [their] writing" as they read and emulate professional models. Other than the section on verb tenses, the grammar chapters contain no writing assignments.

Unlike most of the texts in this section, *The Writer's Workplace* (Scarry and Scarry, 1987) begins with two units on grammar: dictionary use and sentence structure. The prescriptive approach uses varied exercises generally containing dull, unrelated sentences, with little paragraph editing. Paragraphing chapters develop the standard concepts through exercises dependent on listing details. Separate chapters on description, narration, process, and comparison and contrast, and a single chapter on definition, classification, and cause-effect ignore audience and purpose. Writing assignments lead students through the stages of devising a topic sentence and then listing and organizing details, but no other invention strategies appear. Chapters on essay modes are better in guiding the students through the writing process, including brainstorming. The text also has a chapter on the essay exam and appendicies on grammar and spelling.

Although *Evergreen* (1988) includes separate chapters on invention techniques and the stages of writing paragraphs and essays (in separate units), Fawcett and Sandberg do not further integrate these concepts into the rest of the book. Instead, the majority of the writing assignments for the two chapters on the modes merely list "Suggested Topics," with no attention to invention, audience, or purpose beyond simply practicing writing. Indeed, except for a brief reference in the section on persuasive paragraphs, the text ignores audience analysis. Coverage of the standard elements of paragraphs and essays is thorough, well illustrated with professional models and exercises. The chapter on the essay exam seems most helpful. Unit 5, "Reviewing the Basics," follows the same approach as the authors' *Grassroots*: prescriptive rules for all major grammar errors, varied exercises, no writing assignments.

The major difference between John Langan's *College Writing Skills with Readings* (1989) and *English Skills* (1989) is that the former focuses on the essay while the latter makes the same basic points about the paragraph before moving to a separate brief section on the essay. Students follow four basic steps that begin with writing, not discovering, a thesis or topic sentence. Material on purpose, audience, and prewriting (brainstorming, freewriting, outlining, listing) is in Part 2, "Other Important Factors in Writing." The book models the five-paragraph essay and treats the modes as separate patterns of development to be emulated. Langan's writing assignments are seldom trite, and he always provides numerous and varied exercises. The grammar apparatus is occasionally written at a simpler, more detailed level in *English Skills*, which also uses inductive "introductory projects" before presenting the rules. Besides the addition of readings organized thematically, *College Writing Skills with Readings* omits the unit on special writing assignments and condenses both the explanatory apparatus and grammar exercises.

The main strengths of *Composing with Confidence* (Meyers, 1989) have been borrowed from *Writing with Confidence*: clear, coherent discussion of grammar with interesting exercises. In Chapter 1 the author treats "Subject, Audience, and Purpose"; "Your Writing Voice"; "The Writing Process"; and "Your Personal Writing Process." Invention techniques are brainstorming, clustering, and freewriting. The unit then moves into a standard approach to the paragraph. The book treats modes in relationship to the paragraph and discusses "compositions" in chapters on exposition, persuasion (with attention to audience), and the essay exam. The practice exercises, with facts for students to use in their compositions, are beneficial, but the occasionally trite paragraph assignments, with little emphasis on purpose or audience, often preclude transactional writing. In the essay assignments, the author avoids this problem.

Because Carolyn H. Fitzpatrick and Marybeth B. Ruscica devote considerable attention to audience and purpose in *The Complete Paragraph Workout Book* (1989), their writing assignments often seem fresh; also, students can practice both personal and transactional writing. After two wordy chapters on the writing process (with prewriting discussed after a full-scale essay revision) and reading skills, the chapters rely on interesting exercises to convey the standard elements of paragraph and essay structure and of revision. The authors discuss one or two modes at the end of each paragraphing chapter, each illustrated by vivid professional examples sometimes used as springboards to composition. The separate chapter on essays includes material on evaluating essays, with suggestions that students critique one another's essays but with no formal procedure for doing so. The essay assignments, often case studies with specific and varied audiences, purposes, and modes, are especially good. The "Grammar Review" (with answers) in Part 2 begins with a brief analysis of parts of speech before three detailed chapters on verb tenses. Then it shifts to a logical sequence of sentence types, major sentence errors, agreement, and punctuation; each chapter is replete with varied exercises, but no writing assignments.

The first chapter of *The Resourceful Writer* (Barnwell, 1987) creates a classroom community through letters to the class and interviews. Next is a chapter on paragraphs and short essays *before* a good chapter describing and practicing five ways of gathering ideas. "Six Steps to Writing Well" treats the composing process, although with little attention to recursiveness. Students practice this process once for each of the modes. The text also has sections on reading and summarizing, using the library, arguing (no emphasis on audience but a hint that many modes can appear in one essay), and writing a research paper.

A Guide to the Whole Writing Process (Blum et al., 1988) is unique in its ability to lead students through keeping a "writer's notebook" (excellent, thorough discussion) to exploring topics (with special emphasis on clustering and questioning) to focusing on a thesis and organizing ideas, to shaping the piece. The book makes the leap from invention to thesis and development that so many texts fail to complete. The text notes that the several "ordering strategies" for ideas can be mixed. Chapters 5–7 ("Shaping and Arranging Ideas," "Strengthening Your Support," and "Inquiring Further") contain many useful analyzing and planning exercises (often for group work) but no assignments for students to write or revise their own paragraphs. The material on "decentering" (consulting other sources—friends and public information) is very good. The chapter on "Revising the Whole Paper" sets up an excellent procedure for peer review and resulting plans for revision; it also suggests that the students have been writing essays, presumably assigned by the teacher. Two lengthy chapters, with answer keys, present typical information and exercises on sentence structure, dictation, grammar, mechanics, and spelling.

An excellent introduction to *Passages* (Nordquist, 1987) aims at "Shaping a Positive Attitude toward Writing." Nine paragraph and four essay chapters, each related to a mode, lead students through four stages of writing: invention, development, rough draft, and revision, with sample invention material reappearing as final drafts. Exercises call for developing and revising other writers' compositions. The author slides imperceptibly into the essay by asking the students to write and then join two contrast paragraphs on the same subject. The text presents the standard elements of structure and coherence inductively. In the interesting "Additional Assignments," audience analysis is not significantly addressed. Part 2, "A Guide to Writing Sentences," provides a complete treatment of syntax, grammar, and spelling, with many sentence-combining and paragraph-editing exercises. The preface notes that the Instructor's Manual integrates the two halves of the book. The text concludes with appendices on diagnostic tests, essay examinations, business writing, and the research paper.

Integrated Texts

In *Creating Compositions* (Wiener, 1987), each chapter in "Part 1: Paragraphs" and "Part 2: The Longer Theme" has these major subdivisions: vocabulary, building composition skills (including sentence development), solving problems in writing (grammar and mechanics), writing a particular kind of paragraph/essay (with writing assignment, student samples, reader response, and revising checklist), professional samples, and a set of more complex assignments. The paragraphing unit treats description, narration, illustration, comparison/contrast, and "using expert testimony"—an excellent analysis of how to read and use statistics, graphs, and expert opinion. The essay unit returns to description and then moves to chapters on process, argument, and the research essay. The author views the four-paragraph essay as analogous to a paragraph with thesis statement, two subtopics and development, and concluding statement. Part 3, "A Mini-book of Nineteen Special Skills," includes material on the card catalog, *Readers' Guide*, quotations, and footnotes that seems to belong in the chapter on research. The ten "prewriting" techniques treated at various points in the text assume a preselected or assigned topic; still, the book offers considerable practice in using the techniques. Audience, with the exception of the peer review sessions, receives no emphasis until "Chapter 7: Process," and none in the chapter on argument. The text's prescriptive approach does not provide an organic blend of grammar and composition skills.

In *Keeping in Touch* (Day et al., 1987) each of the vividly titled chapters (e.g., "Chunky Guacamole: Analytical Writing") opens with pictures or a brief, lively essay serving as a springboard for the student's "Key Essay." Questions for peer review of the Key Essay ensure audience awareness. Each chapter then moves to three series of exercises: "Writing Fluently" (sentence combining and essay development), "Writing Accurately" (grammar or punctuation often presented inductively through copying exercises), and "Writing Logically and Coherently" (more writing topics). This text eschews the usual points about paragraph and essay structure; rather, the students analyze the professional readings and write in response to clear, fresh assignments.

Like *Steps in Composition* (Troyka and Nudelman, 1986), each chapter in Madelyn Timmel Mihm's *Sentence by Sentence* (1989) blends an interesting reading passage, vocabulary, comprehension exercises, and writing assignments; moreover, the copious and varied Language Exercises often allude to the passage. The thematically organized chapters introduce such subjects for thought and writing as handling job interviews, parenting, smoking, enduring stress, and teenagers' working. Avoiding the standard jargon about paragraphs, the text carefully guides the thinking, planning, and developing stages of the early writing assignments, but later chapters offer less assistance, requiring the students to think for themselves. In some chapters the Language Exercises complement the composition, but they begin with capital letters and end marks, subjects and verbs, troublesome pairs of words, and apostrophes before considering major sentence problems like fragments and run-ons (Chapters 7–9) and verb tenses (Chapters 10–12).

Although the blend of grammar and composition is not organic, *Write and Write Again* (Paznik-Bondarin and Baxter, 1987) follows a stages approach to writing. Organized by logically sequenced modes, the chapters all contain a fully analyzed reading selection with a writing assignment using new vocabulary; "Writing and Rewriting" uses the reading passage and related student writing as springboards for a first draft (various invention techniques) and then, after consideration of "What Makes Writing Good?," for a second draft; then follows "Proofreading for Conventions, Grammar, and Punctuation"; and finally comes "Additional Writing Assignments." The "Writing Good" sections consider the standard points of development and structure; however, Chapter 2 offers detailed explanation of the dictionary. This section approaches audience through a discussion of appropriate diction level. Although the text refers occasionally to audience, it seems unable to integrate in-depth audience analysis into the writing assignments. After many varied and interesting exercises, proofreading sections simply instruct the students to edit their second drafts for the particular errors and then recopy. Unusual to this text are the numerous exercises in which students write and then label their own paragraphs for grammar. Also, it makes no attempt to differentiate between paragraphs and essays; instead, students merely respond to the writing assignments at a length suited to the point to be communicated.

The remaining texts in this section do not emphasize reading instruction.

Thomas E. Tyner divides the six "levels" of *College Writing Basics* (1987) as follows: "The Paragraph" (with "The Composition" in Levels 4–6), "The Sentence," and "The Word." The text's subtitle, *A Progressive Approach*, is inappropriate, for the segments on writing paragraphs and essays are traditional in approach and content. Missing is any attention to audience or purpose, and a coherent stages approach, including invention, receives emphasis only in the often uninspired writing assignments in the "Writing Review" section ending each level. *Each* level has prescriptive discussions of sentence combining; correct sentences (fragments and run-ons); verbs; and pronouns, adjectives, and adverbs.

The "lessons" in Part 1 of *The Developing Writer* (McKoski and Hahn, 1988) blend sentence combining and embedding with some work on the paragraph. The integration is awkward, for the lessons usually bounce between sentence combining and freewriting and drafting, with advice to combine sentences in the paragraphs coming at the *end* of a chapter. The six-page Lesson 7, "Writing beyond the Paragraph," analyzes the essay as analogous to the paragraph with three subtopics; however, the thesis is connected to the first body paragraph and there are no introduction and conclusion paragraphs. Part 2 divides twenty-one professional and student essays into four thematic groups; paragraphs describing the students' "identification" with some part of an essay generally do not lead to complex transactional writing. Part 3, a prescriptive section on grammar and mechanics, assigns writing for practice in the grammar rules.

Writing Clear Paragraphs (Donald et al., 1987) slights the essay: an eight-page Chapter 10 describes the essay as an expanded paragraph and also discusses the essay examination. Each chapter has these divisions: organization, sentences, and words. Chapter 1 gives the standard overview of the paragraph and a formula of topic sentence, body, and summary conclusion. Chapters 2–9 focus on the modes. The organization sections are further subdivided: purpose, topic sentence (with no invention strategies), body, conclusion, "Some Do's . . . and Don'ts," and questions for discussion. Each chapter's "Suggested Activities and Assignments" are familiar. The "Writing across the Curriculum" assignments are the best feature of the book: often case studies with specific purposes and audiences, they blend modes and other disciplines (e.g., narration/criminal justice, illustration/psychology). Only here is audience a major concern in this text. Although an organic blend of grammar and composition is often possible (e.g., parallel structure with classification), the authors seldom overtly connect those sections. The text offers many writing and sentence-combining exercises, but few requiring paragraph editing.

The title of *Writer, Audience, Subject* (Ply and Winchell, 1989) reflects its focus on bridging gaps between these elements of the communication triangle. Eight writing chapters guide the students' work on drafts through five stages: getting started, selecting, shaping, revising for clarity and coherence, and editing for correctness. The chapters on the modes ("patterns of thought") treat both paragraphs and essays, with student and professional samples. The students practice twelve invention techniques, each matching a particular kind of writing (e.g., clustering, drawing a spectrum, and drawing a classification ladder for classification). The blend of grammar, sentence combining, and composition is organic (e.g., relative clauses and appositives with "Writing about a Person"). An editing handbook offers more practice primarily in editing and passage transforming exercises. Writing assignments emphasizing purpose and audience allow personal and transactional writing. The text treats "Blending the Patterns," "Doing Field Research," and "Taking Essay Examinations."

COMPOSITION TEXTS WITH SOME GRAMMAR

These texts focus primarily on composition but discuss what is truly "the least you should know" about grammar and mechanics. Some critics might argue that these texts will not be useful for students whose knowledge of English is based on oral sources. Other critics might respond that grammar instruction will not solve the problem, but that adding more reading to the basic writing course might help. Unless stated otherwise, these texts split the discussion of paragraphs and essays and treat the standard paragraphing elements of topic sentence, unity, coherence, order, and development, usually by the modes.

A rigid formula—topic sentence, three supporting points, and reworded topic sentence—dominates the paragraphing portion of *The Practical Writer with Readings* (Bailey and Powell, 1989). Similar formulas describe the "One-Paragraph Essay" (with subtopics), the five-paragraph essay (with occasional references to variations from this model), and even the research paper. This traditional text contains typical information about structure, unity, coherence, and modes, but nothing about audience or invention. The text devotes eighty-six pages to the stages of the research paper. Two sections treat punctuation and sentence problems; however, the few exercises offer unrelated sentences to correct. The text ends with student essays and an appendix on paper format.

Strategies and Structures (Spangler and Werner, 1989) offers a formula for writing mechanical topic sentences and an eleven-sentence formula to organize paragraphs (although page 101 notes that variations are possible). Still, the text leads students through the stages of writing the paragraph (with a topic carried through all the stages over four chapters). Part 3 discusses the modes in paragraphs. Students write only *one* full essay, developed in six stages in six chapters. While omitting audience analysis, Jotting Pages and Worksheets force students to develop each paper's inventing and organizing stages. Further, Evaluation Sheets and explicit instructions force instructors to accept the text's approach to teaching and grading. Part 5 applies writing to keeping a journal, writing a book report, doing a summary, taking an essay exam, and taking a writing skills test. The grammar section presents rules, various exercises, and chapter tests.

The composition section of *The Basic Writer's Rhetoric* (Herman, 1988) is divided according to modes, with each chapter having the following topics: freewriting, analyzing student freewriting, the goal of . . . writing (reading passage), the basic method of . . . writing, and "working papers," which guide the students through parts of the writing process. The often-fresh writing assignments, do, however, ignore audience, as does the entire book. The thirty-eight page grammar section treats the major errors but with few and brief exercises.

Steps to Writing Well (Wyrick, 1987) opens with a good chapter on invention and prewriting, with attention to audience analysis, but the attention is not well maintained in writing assignments or discussions of modes. The text focuses on the essay but still makes the standard points about paragraphing; unusual assignments often ask students to write *bad* (e.g., wordy) paragraphs and then to exchange and correct the papers. In the modes section, exposition and argumentation appear before description and narration. These chapters offer typical advice, fresh writing topics, and at least one student and one professional model. A thirty-four-page chapter on the research paper is helpful. "A Concise Handbook" is just that: forty-one pages of terse rules and brief exercises.

Each unit of *Re: Writing* (Kurilich and Whitaker, 1988) has a concluding section, "If

You Are Using a Word Processor." Other notable features are each writing unit's "Pre-writing Model" for choosing a subject and gathering information, and the resulting "Rough Draft Model" carried through four stages. Unit 1, "Getting Started," explains how to clarify the writing process and the writing assignment. The text does not maintain this first section's stress on audience. The second unit presents the standard points about single-paragraph compositions, and the third models three patterns of the essay: three-paragraph, four-paragraph, and five-paragraph. Unit 3 contains prewriting models for "Five Special Situations" (e.g., observation, pro-con) but no drafts or final copies. "Revising" involves improving development, organization, coherence, and sentences (with diction and combining exercises). The final grammar unit treats the major grammar rules, with many paragraph-editing exercises.

Unlike many texts, *Process and Structure in Composition* (Clouse, 1987) gives much specific, detailed attention to invention, audience, and purpose in writing; it also gives much advice on improving writing, all of it based on sound theory. However, the pages are so packed with ideas and suggestions that they might overwhelm basic writers who are also basic readers. The text is well organized, with separate sections on the paragraph (description, narration, and illustration chapters) and the essay. Two chapters focus on the writer's concerns and on the reader's (revising for clarity). Unit 4, "Writing for a Purpose," presents essay modes: to share, to inform (four patterns in two chapters), and to persuade. Various questionnaires allow students to assess their opportunities to write, their attitudes toward writing, and their opportunities for persuasive writing. The revising and editing unit covers diction, sentence structure and variety, grammar, and mechanics, with many good editing exercises. Appendices on classroom writing (exams and summaries) and business writing conclude the text.

As the title suggests, *Thinking/Writing* (Cavender and Weiss, 1987) emphasizes *thinking* as the basis of *writing*. In a friendly tone, Chapter 1 offers a variety of prewriting and narrowing techniques and discusses writer's voice and audience. Chapter 2 discusses developing generalizations with specifics, while Chapter 3 gives excellent practice in inductive reasoning. Chapter 4 focuses on categorizing. With minimal explanation, these chapters use well-conceived exercises to give students practice in these thinking skills. The book treats the usual elements of paragraph development, with emphasis on mapping for invention and on "Organization: Keeping the Reader on Track." Chapter 7 looks at two kinds of expository essay: personal and objective. More could be done to show how the various paragraph types are integrated into essays, and the chapter on persuasion is not adequately developed. The book concludes with a thirty-two-page grammar appendix and additional professional readings with writing assignments.

Fifteen Steps to Better Writing (Berbrich, 1988) involves making writing more vivid first at the word level (e.g., noun, verbs, prepositions) and then at the sentence level (e.g., combining, verbals, parallel structure). Described in the first two units, these steps include many exercises, the most beneficial being a series of first draft, vocabulary study, and revision using the new words. An unusual Unit 3 provides paragraphs and then detailed instructions for revising specific words and sentences. Unit 4 is an innovative, intriguing approach to teaching composition inductively. It is divided into seven "port-folios" of related passages (e.g., housing, inventions, television), each followed by six case study writing assignments (e.g., taking and interpreting a poll, writing an advertising program) based on information from the portfolio. The assignments often call for trans-actional writing to a variety of audiences. In fact, explicit audience analysis becomes "figuring the angles." In the last unit students work through four assignments requiring increasing independence in the choice of subject, details, and organization. The lively, chatty style, jokes, and puns should appeal to younger students, but the text might not appeal to teachers who want specific instruction in grammar rules and mechanics.

After two good chapters on keeping a journal and generating ideas, *Prentice-Hall Guide to Basic Writing* (Roy and Roy, 1989) defines the paragraph and then presents four chapters on paragraph modes, a chapter defining the expository essay (classification), and three chapters on essay modes. Each chapter leads students through stages of invention (often clustering), derivation of a focus/thesis, analysis of audience and purpose, development, organization, and revision. Student models also follow these stages; however, after detailed instructions for revising a model, the book doesn't include the final version or even ask the students to write it. A lengthy Part 2 discusses the major grammar and mechanics errors (with many editing exercises) before moving to vocabulary, style (including sentence combining), and "tone and image" (concrete and figurative language).

Special features of *Effective Writing* (Greenberg, 1988) are the many group and paired activities (analyzing, writing, reviewing), the suggestions for journal entries ending each chapter, the numerous writing activities and sample papers in various stages, the challenging writing topics, and the well-crafted writing assignments that often pick up earlier writing activities and lead the students through all stages of writing. Audience, purpose, and intention receive adequate attention. This lively text opens with good chapters, "Exploring Your Thoughts and Feelings about Writing" and "Getting Started," emphasizing discovery drafts. The author covers the standard elements of paragraphs and essays in a nontraditional manner. The chapters on sentence style and structure, grammar, and mechanics have good exercises (especially editing student paragraphs) and conclude with readings and related writing assignments. Students can apply their writing skills to double-entry notebooks, summaries, evaluations, essay exams, and researched essays (the treatment of which is a bit brief).

COMPOSITION TEXTS WITH NO GRAMMAR

In recent years this category has contained fewer new texts, presumably because market pressures require at least some grammar, just as there are fewer strictly grammar texts because teachers expect some material on composition.

Paragraph Practice (Sullivan, 1989) includes the standard information about paragraphs and short compositions, which are discussed separately. Chapter 1 discusses clustering with several models for students to emulate. But this and other invention techniques do not appear on subsequent writing assignments. The text gives good practice in writing topic sentences and thesis statements but no information on how to invent them. The modes and persuasion are introduced inductively as the students do paragraph-writing assignments. The text models five-paragraph "short compositions," but most samples eschew that formula. While sometimes interesting, the essay-writing assignments are not sequenced according to writers' cognitive development.

The author's friendly voice pervades *Step by Step* (De Villez, 1984, 1989), giving it a warm, human tone. Chapter 1 contains a helpful discussion of prewriting, many invention strategies, and a lengthy list of brainstorming topics. Chapter 2 takes a paragraph from invention through final copy and then concludes with a checklist for revision. The approach to paragraphing is standard (with modes), but there are no practice exercises. Discovering a thesis and outlining are briefly discussed in Chapter 4, and introductory, concluding, and transitional paragraphs in Chapter 5. The remaining chapters cover the modes at the essay level, persuasion, and the research paper (which is especially well done); the numerous student and professional models often appear without discussion. Invention strategies and audience receive little attention in the modes chapters.

Besides omitting grammar, *The Complete Writer's Workout Book* (Fitzpatrick and Ruscica, 1988) differs from *The Complete Paragraph Workout Book* only in that the former creates a Part 2 on the essay and shifts the writing assignments ending the latter's chapter on the essay to five new chapters on narration, description, exposition (the modes), persuasion, and argumentation. These chapters offer vivid professional models for analysis and imitation. The text distinguishes persuasion as emotional and argumentation as logical.

"CONCLUSION IN WHICH NOTHING IS CONCLUDED"

The line from Samuel Johnson is apt, for no one person can conclude what is best for all students. Each teacher must assess where students are as writers, where they need to be, and what texts, if any, will help to get them there.

REFERENCES

Adams, Peter Dow. *Connections: A Guide to the Basics of Writing*. Boston: Little, Brown, 1987.

Bailey, Edward P., Jr., and Philip A. Powell. *The Practical Writer with Readings*, 2nd ed. New York: Holt, 1989.

Barnwell, William H. *The Resourceful Writer: A Basic Writing Course*. Boston: Houghton Mifflin, 1987.

Berbrich, Joan D. *Fifteen Steps to Better Writing*. New York: AMSCO, 1988.

Blum, Jack, et al. *A Guide to the Whole Writing Process*, 2nd ed. Boston: Houghton Mifflin, 1988.

Brereton, John C. *A Plan for Writing*, 3rd ed. New York: Holt, 1987.

Campbell, Dianna S., and Terry Ryan Meier. *Easy Writer II: Basic Sentence Combining and Comprehensive Skills*. New York: Harper and Row, 1987.

Cavender, Nancy, and Leonard Weiss. *Thinking/Writing*. Belmont, Calif.: Wadsworth, 1987.

Clouse, Barbara Fine. *Process and Structure in Composition*. New York: Macmillian, 1987.

Day, Susan, Elizabeth McMahan, and Robert Funk. *Keeping in Touch: Writing Clearly*. New York: Macmillan, 1987.

De Villez, Randy. *Step by Step: College Writing*, 3rd ed. Dubuque: Kendall/Hunt, 1984. (4th ed., 1989, unavailable for review)

Donald, Robert B., et al. *Writing Clear Paragraphs*, 3rd ed. Englewood Cliffs: Prentice-Hall, 1987.

————. *Writing Clear Sentences*. Englewood Cliffs: Prentice-Hall, 1987.

Emery, Donald W., John M. Kierzek, and Peter Lindblom. *English Fundamentals*, 8th ed. Forms A, B, and C. New York: Macmillan, 1985, 1986, 1987.

Epes, Mary, and Carolyn Kirkpatrick. *Editing Your Writing: The COMP-LAB Exercises, Level 2*. Englewood Cliffs: Prentice-Hall, 1988.

Fawcett, Susan, and Alvin Sandberg. *Evergreen: A Guide to Writing*, 3rd ed. Boston: Houghton Mifflin, 1988.

————. *Grassroots: The Writer's Workbook*, 3rd ed. Boston: Houghton Mifflin, 1987.

Fitzpatrick, Carolyn H., and Marybeth B. Ruscica. *The Complete Paragraph Workout Book*. Lexington, Mass.: Heath, 1989.

————. *The Complete Sentence Workout Book*, 2nd ed. Lexington, Mass.: Heath, 1988.

————. *The Complete Writer's Workout Book*. Lexington, Mass.: Heath, 1988.

Friedmann, Thomas. *Skills in Sequence*. New York: St. Martin's, 1988.

Glazier, Teresa Ferster. *The Least You Should Know about English: Basic Writing Skills*, 3rd ed. Form C. New York: Holt, 1987.

Greenberg, Karen L. *Effective Writing: Choices and Conventions*. New York: St. Martin's, 1988.

Herman, William. *The Basic Writer's Rhetoric*. New York: Holt, 1988.

Immel, Constance, and Florence Sacks. *Sentence Dynamics: An English Skills Workbook*, 2nd ed. Glenview: Scott, Foresman, 1987.

Jacobus, Lee A., and Judith Davis Miller. *The Sentence Book*, 3rd ed. San Diego: Harcourt, 1989.

Kurilich, Frances, and Helen Whitaker. *Re: Writing: Strategies for Student Writers*. New York: Holt, 1988.

Langan, John. *College Writing Skills with Readings*, 2nd ed. New York: McGraw-Hill, 1989.

————. *English Skills*, 4th ed. New York: McGraw-Hill, 1989.

————. *Sentence Skills: A Workbook for Writers*, 3rd ed. Form B. New York: McGraw-Hill, 1987.

Laubheim, Charles S., Joan E. Schnell, and Alvin J. Starr. *Just Writing*, 4th ed. Dubuque: Kendall/Hunt, 1988.

Loewe, Ralph E. *The Writing Clinic: Writing—Grammar—Readings*, 4th ed. Englewood Cliffs: Prentice-Hall, 1988.

McKoski, Martin M., and Lynne C. Hahn. *The Developing Writer: A Guide to Basic Skills*, 3rd ed. Glenview: Scott, Foresman, 1988.

Martin, Marlene. *Review and Revise*. New York: McGraw-Hill, 1989.

Meyers, Alan. *Composing with Confidence*, 2nd ed. Glenview: Scott, Foresman, 1989.

————. *Writing with Confidence*, 3rd ed. Glenview: Scott, Foresman, 1988.

Mihm, Madelyn Timmel. *Sentence by Sentence: A Basic Rhetoric, Reader, and Grammar*. San Diego: Harcourt, 1989.

Neuburger, T. R. *Foundation: Building Sentence Skills*, 3rd ed. Boston: Houghton Mifflin, 1989.

Nordquist, Richard. *Passages: A Writer's Guide*. New York: St. Martin's, 1987.

O'Hearn, Carolyn. *Writing, Grammar, and Usage*. New York: Macmillan, 1989.

Ostrom, John, and William Cook. *Better Paragraphs Plus*, 6th ed. New York: Harper and Row, 1988.

Paznik-Bondarin, Jane, and Milton Baxter. *Write and Write Again: A Worktext with Readings*. New York: Macmillan, 1987.

Ply, Mary Sue, and Donna Haisty Winchell. *Writer, Audience, Subject: Bridging the Communication Gap*. Glenview: Scott, Foresman, 1989.

Rockas, Leo. *A Creative Copybook*. Lexington, Mass.: Heath, 1989.

Roy, Emil, and Sandra Roy. *Prentice-Hall Guide to Basic Writing*. Englewood Cliffs: Prentice-Hall, 1989.

Scarry, Sandra, and John Scarry. *The Writer's Workplace: Building College Writing Skills*. New York: Holt, 1987.

Selby, Norwood. *Essential College English: A Grammar and Punctuation Workbook*, 2nd ed. Boston: Little, Brown, 1987.

Shea, Michael. *Writing for Meaning: A Basic Worktext*. San Diego: Harcourt, 1988.

Spangler, Mary S., and Rita R. Werner. *Strategies and Structures: A Basic Writing Guide*. New York: Holt, 1989.

Sullivan, Kathleen E. *Paragraph Practice: Writing the Paragraph and the Short Composition*, 6th ed. New York: Macmillan, 1989.

Swartz, Richard. *Starting Points: A Guide to Basic Writing Skills*, 2nd ed. Englewood Cliffs: Prentice-Hall, 1987.

Tyner, Thomas E. *College Writing Basics: A Progressive Approach*. Belmont, Calif.: Wadsworth, 1987.

Wiener, Harvey S. *Creating Compositions*, 5th ed. New York: McGraw-Hill, 1987.

Wyrick, Jean. *Steps to Writing Well: A Concise Guide to Composition*, 3rd ed. New York: Holt, 1987.

BASIC WRITING TEXTBOOKS COPYRIGHTED BEFORE 1987

Texts That Focus Only on Grammar

Butler, Eugenia, Mary Ann Hickman, and Lalla Overby. *An Auto-Instructional Text in Correct Writing*, 2nd ed. Form B. Lexington, Mass.: Heath, 1980.

————. *Correct Writing*, 2nd ed. Forms 1, 2, and 3. Lexington, Mass.: Heath, 1976, 1978, 1980.

————. *Correct Writing*, 3rd ed. Lexington, Mass.: Heath, 1983.

Epes, Mary, Carolyn Fitzpatrick, and Michael G. Southwell. *The COMP-LAB Exercises: Self-Teaching Exercises for Basic Writing*, 2nd ed. Englewood Cliffs: Prentice-Hall, 1986.

Faulkner, Claude W. *Writing Good Sentences*, 3rd ed. New York: Macmillan/Scribner's, 1981.

Gonzalez, Roseann Dueñas, MaryCarmen E. Cruz, and Ann Barger Thomson. *Copy, Combine, & Compose: Controlling Composition*. Belmont, Calif.: Wadsworth, 1983.

Gorrell, Donna. *Copy/Write: Basic Writing Through Controlled Composition*. Boston: Little, Brown, 1982.

Levy, Wilbert J. *Sense of Sentences*. New York: AMSCO, 1976.

————. *Sentence Play*. New York: AMSCO, 1984.

Licklider, Patricia. *At Your Command: A Basic English Workbook*, 2nd ed. Boston: Little, Brown, 1983.

Spiegel, Harriet. *Cornerstone: Foundations for Writing*. Lexington, Mass.: Heath, 1986.

Grammar with Some Composition

Eisenberg, Nora, and Harvey S. Wiener. *Stepping Stones: Skills for Basic Writers*. New York: Random House, 1985.

Gorrell, Donna, with the Editors of Little, Brown. *The Little, Brown Workbook*, 3rd ed. Boston: Little, Brown, 1986.

Matthew, Marie-Louise. *Pattern and Practice*. Boston: Little, Brown, 1986.

Reynolds, Audrey L. *Exploring Written English: A Guide for Basic Writers*. Boston: Little, Brown, 1983.

Robey, Cora L., Alice M. Hedrick, and Ethelyn H. Morgan. *New Handbook of Basic Writing Skills*, 2nd ed. San Diego: Harcourt, 1984.

Robey, Cora, et al. *New Workbook of Basic Writing Skills*, 2nd ed. San Diego: Harcourt, 1984.

Skurnick, Blanche. *The Heath Basic Writer: Proofreading and Revision*. Lexington, Mass.: Heath, 1983.

Stith, Joyce. *The Basic Writing Book*. Boston: Little, Brown, 1982.

Equal Treatment of Composition and Grammar: Bifurcated Texts

Coats, Sandra, and Mary Anne Sandel. *Paragraph Writing*. Englewood Cliffs: Prentice-Hall, 1986.

DeVillez, Randy, and Susan R. Schreiber *Theory and Practice: Basic College Writing*. Dubuque: Kendall/Hunt, 1986.

Langan, John. *College Writing Skills*. New York: McGraw-Hill, 1984.

Levy, Wilbert J. *Writing English: Foundations*. New York: AMSCO, 1982.

Rubin, Dorothy. *Writing and Reading: The Vital Arts*, 2nd ed. New York: Macmillan, 1983.

Schor, Sandra, and Judith Summerfield. *The Random House Guide to Writing*, 3rd ed. New York: Random House, 1986.

Schwartz, Mona. *Pattern and Practice: A Guide to Basic Writing*. Englewood Cliffs: Prentice-Hall, 1986.

Equal Treatment of Composition and Grammar: Integrated Texts

Foundations for Learning Language. New York: Foundations for Learning Press and Macmillan, 1982.

O'Donnell, Teresa, and Judith L. Paiva. *Independent Writing*. Boston: Little, Brown, 1986.

Sieben, J. Kenneth, and Lillian Small Anthony. *Composition Five: Skills for Writing*, 2nd ed. Glenview: Scott, Foresman, 1985.

Troyka, Lynn Quitman, and Jerrold Nudelman. *Steps in Composition*, 4th ed. Englewood Cliffs: Prentice-Hall, 1986.

Tyner, Thomas. *Writing Voyage: An Integrated Process Approach to Basic Writing*. Belmont, Calif.: Wadsworth, 1985.

Composition Texts with Some Grammar

Bernhardt, Bill, and Peter Miller. *Becoming a Writer: A Basic Text*. New York: St. Martin's, 1986.

Burhans, Clinton S., Jr., and Michael Steinberg, with Jean Strandness. *The Writer's Way: A Process-to-Product Approach to Writing*, 7th ed. East Lansing: Spring, 1983.

Guilford, Charles. *Beginning College Writing*. Boston: Little, Brown, 1985.

Howard, C. Jeriel, and Richard Francis Tracz. *The Paragraph Book*. Boston: Little, Brown, 1982.

Jones, Alexander E., and Claude W. Faulkner. *Writing Good Prose: A Simple Structural Approach*, 4th ed. New York: Macmillan/Scribner's, 1977.

Levy, Wilbert J. *Composition: Prewriting, Response, Revision*. New York: AMSCO, 1982.

———. *Paragraph Play*. New York: AMSCO, 1985.

Lorch, Sue. *Basic Writing: A Practical Approach*, 2nd ed. Boston: Little, Brown, 1984.

McWhorter, Kathleen T., and Candalene J. McCombs. *Write to Read, Read to Write*. Boston: Little, Brown, 1983.

Masiello, Lea. *Writing in Action: A Collaborative Rhetoric for College Writers*. New York: Macmillan, 1986.

Composition Texts with no Grammar

Canavan, P. Joseph. *Paragraphs and Themes*, 4th ed. Lexington, Mass.: Heath, 1983.

Parks, A. Franklin, James A. Levernier, and Ida Masters Hollowell. *Structuring Paragraphs: A Guide to Effective Writing*, 2nd ed. New York: St. Martin's, 1986.

Paternoster, Lewis M., and Charles Didier. *A Commonsense Approach to Composition*. New York: AMSCO, 1983.

Pelz, Karen L. *Exploratory Writing*. Dubuque: Kendall/Hunt, 1984.

Name Index

Abbot, G. W., 128
Acuna, Dagmar, 122
Adams, Peter D., 225
Adkins, Arthur W. H., 53
Akst, Geoffrey, 154
Alderman, Donald, 166
Allen, Harold B., 77
Almasy, Rudolph, 195
Alton, John, 197
Amastae, Jon, 103
Anderson, Alonzo B., 58
Anderson, Arnold, 56
Anderson, James E., 217
Anson, Chris M., 35
Anthony, Lillian S., 221
Appel, Lola, 166
Apple, Michael W., 60
Applebee, Arthur N., 54
Arapoff, Nancy, 123, 124
Arboleda, Jairo, 57
Arbur, Rosemarie, 194
Argall, Rebecca, 84
Arkin, Marian, 173, 174, 194, 216
Armbrecht, B. G., 84
Arms, Valerie, 173, 180
Armstrong, Bondie, 101
Arnold, Daniel S., 155
Arnove, Robert F., 57

Aronowitz, Stanley, 61
Arthur, Bradford, 132
Auten, Anne, 167
Au-Yeung Lo, Winnie, 119

Bacig, Thomas, 168
Bailey, Edward P., 231
Bailey, Guy, 97
Bailey, Richard W., 108
Baker, Tracey, 198
Ballard, Brigid, 121
Bamberg, Betty, 88, 143
Barnwell, William H., 228
Barritt, Loren S., 31
Bartholomae, David, 6, 7, 8, 22, 24, 26,
    37, 49, 50, 51, 67, 78, 82, 146, 149,
    152, 168, 199
Bataille, Leon, 57, 60
Baum, Joan, 149
Baxter, Milton, 229
Beach, Richard, 28
Bean, John, 21
Beck, Paula, 217
Becker, Alton L., 81
Becker, Henry J., 166
Beers, Susan, 42
Belanoff, Pat, 149
Bennett, Adrian T., 63

Berbich, Joan D., 232
Bereiter, Carl, 170
Berg, Anna, 35, 151
Bernhardt, Stephen A., 176
Berthoff, Ann E., 42, 61, 68
Beserra, Wendy C., 175
Bevan, John, 59
Birnbaum, J., 175
Bizzell, Patricia, 21, 26, 41, 42, 50, 54, 62, 149
Blair, Linda, 122
Blatchford, Charles H., 136
Bloom, Benjamin S., 21
Bloomfield, Leonard, 78, 80
Blum, Jack, 228
Bobson, Sarah, 99
Bommarito, Ellen M., 217
Boruta, Marcia J., 181
Bowles, Samuel, 59, 60
Bracewell, Robert J., 35, 44
Braddock, Richard, 79
Bradford, Annette N., 21
Brandes, Paul, 97
Brandt, Deborah, 64, 66, 88
Brannon, Lil, 215
Brereton, John, 210, 211, 226
Brewer, Jeutonne, 97
Bridgeman, Brent, 131
Bridges, Charles W., 213
Bridwell, Lillian, 165, 168, 171, 174, 175
Bridwell-Bowles, Lillian, 173
Brière, Eugene, 124
Briggs, Olin, 101
Bringuier, Jean-Claude, 32
Brinton, Donna M., 126
Britton, James, 36, 37, 40
Brodkey, Dean, 131
Brooke, Robert, 173, 174, 175
Brostoff, Anita, 195
Brown, Betsy E., 216
Brown, H. Douglas, 122
Brown, Rexford, 147
Bruder, Mary, 107
Bruffee, Kenneth A., 83, 217
Bruner, Jerome, 31
Bryson, M., 176
Buckingham, Thomas, 124

Burke, Kenneth, 27, 67
Burnham, Christopher C., 42, 215
Burns, Hugh L., 165, 170
Burt, Marina K., 120, 129, 130
Butler, Margaret S., 157
Byerly, Gayle, 166, 183
Byrne, Diane F., 39

Campbell, Dianna S., 222
Campbell, Sarah, 32
Cannon, Garland, 106
Cardenal, Fernando, 59
Carkeet, David A., 23, 82
Carlson, Sybil, 131
Carnicelli, Thomas A., 196
Carpenter, Cristin, 126
Carr, Donna H., 126
Carrell, Patricia, 126, 127
Casanave, Christine P., 126
Castro, Fidel, 59
Catano, James V., 174
Cavender, Nancy, 232
Cayer, Roger L., 24
Celce-Murcia, Marianne, 118
Chappel, Virginia, A., 195
Cheek, Madelon, 181
Cherry, Roger, 87
Chomsky, Noam, 78, 81
Christensen, Bonniejean, 85
Christensen, Francis, 85
Christison, Mary Ann, 120
Chun, Judith, 120
Cirello, V. J., 177
Clanchy, Michael, 58
Clark, Irene L., 197
Cohen, David K., 64
Cohen, Michael E., 170
Cohen, Paul, 174, 177
Cole, Michael, 49, 52, 53, 54, 55, 62, 63, 64, 65
Coleman, Gerald, 35, 151
Coles, Nicholas, 20, 152
Coles, William E., 68
Collier, Richard M., 174
Collins, Allan, 181
Collins, J. J., 100
Collins, James L., 24, 172, 198, 214
Comley, Nancy R., 213

Comprone, Joseph, 209, 210, 211, 212
Connor, Ulla, 87, 127
Connors, Robert J., 50, 79, 86
Cook, William, 225
Cook-Gumperz, Jenny, 49
Cooper, Charles R., 87, 146, 154
Cooper, Grace, 104
Copes, Larry, 42
Corbett, Edward P. J., 51
Corder, S. P., 118
Coulter, Catherine A., 178
Criper, C., 118
Croft, Mary K., 194
Cronnell, Bruce, 99, 167
Crosby, Harry, 150
Cross, John A., 178
Cross, K. Patricia, 17, 18, 25, 155
Crowhurst, M., 87
Crymes, Ruth, 127
Crystal, Daisy, 112
Culp, George H., 170
Curey, Bob J., 178
Curtis, Marcia, 180

Daiker, Donald A., 84
Daiute, Colette, 24, 168, 169, 170, 172, 174, 180
D'Angelo, Frank, 35, 55
Daniels, Harvey, 3, 4
Davidson, David M., 127, 131
Davidson, Fred, 130
Davies, Alan, 118
Dawe, Charles W., 196
Day, Susan, 229
de Beaugrande, Robert, 80
Deen, Rosemary, 5, 6
Deese, James, 78
Dehghanpisheh, Elaine, 124
Delattre, Edwin J., 50
D'Eloia, Sarah, 23
Desy, Jeanne, 151
De Villez, Randy, 233
Didier, Charles, 238
Diedrich, Paul B., 154
Dillard, J. L., 106, 111
Dixon, Arthur L., 147, 150
Dobrin, David N., 171
Dodd, William M., 4, 5

Donald, Robert B., 223, 230
Donovan, Richard, 145
Dornan, Edward A., 196
Doughty, Catherine, 126
Dreyfus, Hubert L., 172
Dreyfus, Stuart E., 172
Duin, Ann, 171
Duke, Charles R., 195
Dulay, Heidi, 120
Dulit, Everett, 33, 42
Dunham, Trudy, 173
Dykstra, Gerald, 123

Ede, Lisa, 38
Edwards, Penny, 176
Eisenberg, Nora, 221
Elbow, Peter, 39, 149
Elgin, Suzette H., 81
Elsasser, Nan, 62, 153
Emery, Donald W., 223
Enos, Theresa, 7, 189
Epes, Mary, 24, 102, 109, 111, 150, 192, 222
Erazmus, Edward, 124
Erickson, Fred, 63
Esau, Helmut, 122
Etchison, Craig, 167, 176
Everhart, Robert B., 60

Fagen, Richard R., 59
Faigley, Lester, 84, 86, 127, 155
Fais, Laurie, 173
Falk, Julia S., 122
Fanselow, John F., 134
Farnsworth, Maryruth B., 130
Farr, Marcia, 3, 4
Farrell, Pamela B., 180
Farrell, Thomas J., 10, 24, 54, 55, 108, 151
Fasold, Ralph W., 97, 107
Fawcett, Susan, 222, 226
Feldman, Paula R., 174
Fingeret, Arlene, 58
Finnegan, Ruth, 53, 57
Fiore, Kyle, 153
Firbas, Jan, 86
Fitzpatrick, Carolyn, 224, 227
Flavell, John H., 32, 38

Flower, Linda S., 21, 40, 41, 197
Ford, James E., 149
Foss, Karen, 121
Fossum, Sheldon, 181
Foster, Dan, 88
Foxx, Virginia, 147
Francis, Nelson, 80
Frase, Lawrence T., 169, 171
Fraser, Ian S., 79, 86
Freedman, Sarah W., 148
Freeman, Donald, 82, 85
Freeman, Lawrence D., 106
Freire, Paulo, 60, 61, 62, 67, 68
Friederichs, Jane, 126
Friedman, Morton P., 170
Friedman, Thomas, 223
Friedmann, Thomas, 200
Fries, Charles, 78, 80
Frisbie, D. A., 145
Funkhouser, James, 98, 101

Gaies, Stephen, 132
Gallagher, Brian, 173, 174, 180
Garcia, Ricardo L., 104
Garnes, Sara, 147, 150, 209, 214
Garrison, Roger, 196
Gathercole, Virginia, 118
Gebhard, Ann O., 82
Gebhardt, Richard C., 213, 215, 217
Gee, James P., 122
Gefvert, Constance J., 111, 213
Gentner, Dedre, 181
Gere, Anne Ruggles, 7
Gerrard, Lisa, 165
Ghadessy, Mohsen, 127
Giannasi, Jenefer, 80, 99
Gibson, Walker, 198
Gilles, Philip D., 170
Gilmore, Perry, 63
Gingiss, Peter J., 82
Ginn, Doris O., 109
Gintis, Herbert, 60
Giroux, Henry, 60, 61, 62
Glaser, Robert, 168
Glassman, Susan, 200
Glazier, Teresa F., 111, 223
Goelman, Hillel, 51, 66
Goldberg, Marilyn K., 21, 35, 36

Goldsby, Jackie, 196, 217
Goldstein, Lynn M., 122
Goodin, George, 88
Goody, Jack, 53, 54, 63
Gorrell, Donna, 23, 123, 147
Gould, Christopher, 154
Graff, Harvey, 50, 53, 58, 61, 62, 65
Grant, Mary K., 156
Gray, Barbara Q., 109, 110, 143, 146,
    152, 156
Green, J. F., 129
Greenberg, Karen L., 24, 50, 55, 145,
    148, 152, 233
Greene, Wendy T., 173
Gregg, Joan, 119
Griffin, Jacqueline, 150
Gross, Theodore L., 156
Guralnick, Elissa S., 156

Haas, Christina, 174
Haas, Terri, 199
Hacker, Diana, 111
Hahn, Lynne C., 20, 230
Haisty, Donna B., 42
Hake, Rosemary, 149
Halliday, M.A.K., 86, 88, 127
Halpern, Jeanne W., 181
Hammar, Diane D., 177
Hammons, Myrna A., 100
Harley, Kay, 216
Harman, David, 50, 51, 58
Harris, Jeanette, 174, 180
Harris, Muriel, 7, 181, 192, 194, 199
Harrold, Sally, 8
Hartfiel, V. Faye, 131
Hartnett, Carolyn G., 87
Hartwell, Patrick, 24, 55, 80, 102, 109,
    196, 197
Harwood, John T., 216
Hasan, Ruqaiya, 86, 91, 126
Hashimoto, Irvin, 193, 201, 214
Haswell, Richard, 25, 87
Havelock, Eric A., 53
Hawisher, Gail, 177, 178, 180
Hawkins, Thom, 197, 217
Hayden, Luddy, 107
Hayes, Ira, 85
Hayes, John R., 40, 41, 174

Hays, Janice N., 21, 42, 150
Heath, Shirley Brice, 25, 49, 63, 65
Hecht, Miriam, 154
Hedrick, Alice M., 115
Heffernan, James, 111
Hendrickson, James, 129
Herman, William, 231
Herrmann, Andrea, 175, 180
Heyda, John, 154
Hill, Clifford, 128
Hill, Susan, 126
Himley, Margaret, 55
Hirsch, E. D., 55, 102
Hoddeson, David, 197
Hodgkinson, Harold L., 144
Hodson, Lynda M., 79, 86
Hoeber, Daniel R., 3, 156
Hoey, Michael, 119
Hoffman, Paul, 88
Hoggart, Richard, 63
Holdstein, Deborah, 170
Holland, Robert M., 33
Holzman, Michael, 58, 60
Homburg, Taco Justus, 131
Horn, Vivian, 123, 127
Hornick, Karen, 109
Horning, Alice S., 109, 117, 153
Horowitz, Daniel, 125, 126
Houghton, Diane, 119
Howatt, A.P.R., 118
Hughey, Jane, 131
Hull, Glynda A., 8, 9, 50, 78, 168
Hult, Christine, 171, 180
Humphrey, Mary, 173
Hunt, Doug, 200
Hunt, Kellogg, 84
Hunter, Carmen St. John, 50, 58
Hunter, Judy, 126
Hunter, Linda, 173, 175

Ibrahim, Muhammad H., 128
Inhelder, Bärbell, 32, 38

Jackson, Kathy D., 84
Jacobs, Holly L., 131
Jacobs, Suzanne E., 195
Jacobson, Rodolpho, 107, 110
Jacobus, Lee, 200, 222

James, William, 67
Janopoulos, Michael, 122
Jennings, Edward M., 181
Jensen, George H., 19, 20, 22, 156
Jesperson, Otto, 78
Jester, Valerie, 179
John-Steiner, Vera P., 52, 62, 153
Johns, Ann M., 89, 126, 127
Johnson, Falk S., 80
Johnson, Nancy W., 146
Johnson, Paula, 146, 153
Johnson, Sabina T., 146, 153
Joiner, Charles W., 98
Jolly, Peggy, 34
Jones, David E., 35
Jones, Stephen C., 111
Juettner, Virginia, 177

Kaestle, Carl F., 61
Kagan, Dona M., 23
Kameen, Patrick T., 128, 131
Kaplan, Bernard, 39
Kaplan, Robert B., 119
Karliner, Adela B., 195
Kasden, Lawrence N., 3, 149
Keene, Michael, 122
Keller, Joseph, 104
Kelly, Lou, 191, 192, 196, 202, 214
Kemp, Fred, 168
Kerek, Andrew, 84
Khalil, Aziz, 129
Kiefer, Kathleen E., 149, 150, 169, 171
King, B., 175
Kinkead, Joyce, 169
Kinney, James, 81
Kiparsky, Carol, 130
Kirk, R. Wade, 156
Kirkpatrick, Carolyn, 111, 150, 192, 222
Kirschner, Samuel, 100
Kitzhaber, Albert R., 31
Klassen, Bernard, 127
Kleen, Janice, 201
Kleiman, Glen, 173
Kneupper, Charles W., 81
Kochman, Thomas, 104
Kogen, Myra, 26, 34, 42
Kohlberg, Lawrence, 39
Kolln, Martha, 79

Kozol, Jonathan, 57, 59, 60
Kozulin, Alex, 52, 53
Krahnke, Karl J., 120
Krashen, Stephen D., 83, 120, 121, 122, 152
Krishna, Valerie, 23
Kroll, Barbara, 122
Kroll, Barry M., 21, 24, 31, 37, 38, 199
Kurfiss, Joanne, 42
Kurilich, Frances, 231
Kurth, R. J., 173

Labov, William, 96, 105
Lamb, M. E., 198
Langan, John, 223, 227
Langer, Suzanne K., 67
Lansing, Margaret L., 165, 174, 175
Larkin, Gregory, 149
Larmouth, Donald, 168
Larsen-Freeman, Diane, 131
Lattin, Vernon E., 149
Laubheim, Charles S., 223
Lauer, Janice, 87
Laurence, Patricia, 24, 37, 83
Lave, Jean, 52
LeBlanc, Paul, 180
Lederman, Marie J., 21, 143
Leech, Geoffrey, 78
Lees, Elaine O., 152, 181
Lees, Robert B., 77
Leeson, Lee Ann, 199
Lesgold, Alan, 168
Lester, Mark, 81
Levin, James A., 181
Lewis, Ruby M., 155
Lieber, Paula E., 127
Liggett, Sarah, 181
Lincoln, John, 111
Lindemann, Erika, 8
Linn, Michael, 104
Lintermann-Rygh, Irmgard, 87
Lloyd-Jones, Richard, 79
Lockridge, Kenneth, 58
Loewe, Ralph E., 226
Lorch, Sue, 221
Lorenz, Frederick O., 129
Louth, Richard, 177
Low, Graham, 121

Luchte, Jeanne, 165
Ludwig, Jeanette, 129
Lunsford, Andrea A., 7, 8, 9, 21, 23, 25, 36, 37, 39, 49, 66, 78, 147, 149, 150, 155, 198, 214
Lunsford, Ronald F., 8, 9
Luria, A. R., 52, 53, 55, 56
Lutz, William, 145, 209
Lyons, Chopeta, 201
Lyons, John, 78

McAllister, Carole, 177
McAndrew, Donald A., 194
McArthur, Charles A., 173
McCulley, G. A., 87
McDaniel, Ellen, 170
McDavid, Raven I., 96
McDonald, Susan P., 155
Macgregor, W. B., 167
McKay, Sandra, 124, 125
MacKenzie, Jamieson, 180
Mackie, Robert, 62
McKinnon, Joe W., 33
McKoski, Martin M., 20, 230
MacLennan, Tom, 173
McQuade, Donald A., 210, 212
Maimon, Elaine P., 153, 160
Marchesano, Louis, 167
Marcus, Stephen, 168
Markels, Robin B., 87
Martin, Anne V., 128
Martin, Marlene, 224
Martinez, Joseph G. R., 34, 42
Martinez, Nancy, 34, 42
Martlew, Margaret, 35
Masters, Kathy, 84
Masters, Mitchell, 84
Matalene, Carolyn, 120
Mathesius, Vilem, 86
Matthews, Roberta S., 148
Maxwell, Martha, 143, 155, 157
Meier, Terry R., 222
Mellon, John, 84
Memering, Dean, 79
Menendez, Diane S., 84
Merrill, Celia, 103
Metzger, Elizabeth, 156
Meyer, Daisy E., 129

Meyer, Emily, 7, 194, 200
Meyers, Alan, 224, 227
Mihm, Madelyn T., 229
Miller, Judith D., 222
Miller, Michael A., 155
Miller, Valerie, 59
Mills, Helen, 148, 150
Mito, Yuichi, 120
Moberg, George, 175
Moffett, James, 37, 39
Mohan, Bernard A., 119
Monahan, Brian D., 40
Montessori, Maria, 67
Montgomery, Michael, 97
Moody, K. W., 123
Moore, Wayne, 173
Moore, William, 18, 19
Moran, Charles, 208, 209, 210, 212
Moran, Michael G., 8
Morenberg, Max, 84
Morgan, Ethelyn H., 115
Morrison, Donald M., 121
Morrow, Daniel H., 100
Mosenthal, James H., 87
Mukattash, Lewis, 119, 136
Murray, Donald M., 195, 196
Murray, Richard T., 166
Mussen, Paul H., 46

Nancarrow, Paula R., 165
Nash, James, 174, 180
Nash, Thomas, 192, 197
Nauer, Barbara, 110
Nembhard, Judith P., 109
Nemser, William, 118
Neuberger, T. R., 222
Neuner, Jerome L., 86
Newkirk, Thomas, 68
Newman, Judith M., 179
Nichols, Randall G., 175
Noonan-Wagner, Desley, 104
Nordquist, Richard, 228
Noreen, Robert G., 147
North, Stephen M., 191, 196, 216

Oates, William, 167
Oberg, Antoinette, 51, 66
Obler, Susan S., 144, 148

Odell, Lee, 81, 146
O'Hare, Frank, 200
O'Hearn, Carolyn, 224
Ohmann, Richard, 26
Oliver, Lawrence, 171
Olson, David, 63
Olson, Gary A., 197
Ong, Walter, 54, 55
Orr, Jack, 42
Ostrom, John, 225
Otto, Lee, 167
Overton, Betty J., 155

Palmer, David, 129
Partenheimer, David, 170
Pattison, Robert, 49, 50, 51, 53, 63, 64
Paul, Terri, 167
Paulston, Christina B., 123
Payne, Don, 167, 181
Paznik-Bondarin, Jane, 229
Pech, William C., 124
Pedersen, Bruce, 172
Pederson, Elray, 167, 192
Peirce, C. S., 67
Perdue, Virginia A., 153
Perkins, D. N., 178
Perkins, Kyle, 88, 130, 131
Perl, Sondra, 3, 22, 197
Perry, William G., 40, 41, 42
Petrie, Ann, 150
Petrosky, Anthony, 6, 7, 68, 79, 152
Pfingstag, Nancy, 125
Piaget, Jean, 9, 21, 31, 32, 38, 55, 198
Pianko, Sharon, 197
Pica, Teresa, 126
Piche, Gene, 40
Pierson, Herbert, 126
Pike, Kenneth, 81
Pimsarn, Pratin, 122
Pincas, Anita, 123
Pivarnk, Barbara Anne, 177
Ply, Mary Sue, 230
Polanyi, Michael, 21
Ponsot, Marie, 5, 6, 151, 210, 212
Poris, Marilyn, 176
Posey, E. J., 175
Postman, Neil, 63
Poteet, G. Howard, 100

Powell, Joyce E., 85
Powell, Philip A., 231
Pradl, Gordon, 215
Pritchard, R. T., 86
Puma, Vincent, 35
Purnell, Rosentene B., 145

Raimes, Ann, 120, 124, 125
Ramsey, P. A., 210
Rank, Janice, 156
Rankin, David, 152
Rankin, Dorothy S., 127
Raspa, Richard, 111
Raymond, James C., 54
Reed, Carol E., 90, 109, 110
Reid, Joy, 121, 125
Reigstad, Thomas J., 194, 202
Reitzel, Armeda C., 121
Renner, John W., 33
Renshaw, Betty, 111
Resnick, David P., 49, 51, 63
Resnick, Lauren B., 49, 51, 63
Reynolds, R. C., 156
Reynoso, Wendy D., 111
Ribaudo, Michael, 143, 160
Rich, Adrienne, 153
Richards, Amy, 111
Richards, Jack C., 118, 128
Richert, Carol, 110
Risdon, Kenneth, 168
Rittershofer, John S., 128
Rizzo, Betty, 119
Robb, Kevin, 68
Robb, Thomas, 130
Roberts, Patricia, 217
Roberts, Paul, 77
Robey, Cora L., 111
Robinett, Betty W., 128
Robinson, Jay L., 67
Robinson, William S., 148
Rockas, Leo, 224
Roderick, John, 195
Rodrigues, Dawn, 169, 173, 179, 180
Rodrigues, Raymond, 169
Rodriguez, Richard, 63
Roemer, Charles, 212
Rogoff, Barbara, 52
Rohrer, Josef, 128

Rose, Mike, 7, 21, 22, 25, 26, 32, 34,
    37, 42, 49, 51, 67, 154, 199, 202
Roskelly, Hephzibah, 55, 156
Ross, Donald, 165, 168, 171, 181
Ross, Robert J., 33
Ross, Steven, 130
Roueche, John E., 18, 156
Rouse, John, 27
Roy, Emil, 233
Roy, Sandra, 233
Rubin, Donald L., 4, 5, 40
Rukauskas, William V., 155, 161
Ruscica, Marybeth B., 224, 227
Rush, Shirley A., 82
Ruszkiewicz, John, 210
Ryle, Gilbert, 23
Ryzewic, Susan R., 143, 160

Sacks, Renee K., 24
Sadler, Lynn V., 173
Sadow, Catherine, 125
Sally, Ovaiza, 128
Salvatori, Mariolina, 55
Samuel, Shelly, 201
Samuels, Marilyn S., 152
Sandberg, Alvin, 222, 226
Sapir, Edward, 78
Satre, Kay, 195
Scarcella, Robin C., 127
Scardamalia, Marlene, 170
Scarry, John, 226
Scarry, Sandra, 226
Schachter, Jacquelyn, 118, 121
Schafer, John C., 24, 37, 199
Schane, Sanford, 128
Schoer, Lowell, 79
Schor, Sandra, 207, 210, 212, 215
Schumacher, Gary M., 40
Schumann, John H., 121
Schwartz, Helen J., 165, 169, 180, 181
Schwartz, Lawrence, 174, 180
Schwartz, Mimi, 169
Schwebel, Milton, 33
Scollon, Ron, 50, 63
Scollon, Suzanne B. K., 63
Scott, Jerrie, 103
Scott, Margaret S., 120

Scribner, Sylvia, 49, 52, 53, 54, 55, 62, 63, 64, 65
Seijas, Laura, 217
Selby, Norwood, 222
Selfe, Cynthia, 172, 175, 180
Selinker, Larry, 118, 126
Selman, Robert, 38
Shakespeare, William O., 202
Sharon, Amiel T., 155
Shaughnessy, Mina, 2, 8, 9, 17–20, 23, 24, 27, 37, 77, 78, 82, 101, 144, 151, 155, 199, 207, 210
Shea, Michael, 224
Sheal, P. R., 130
Sherwin, J. Stephen, 79, 80
Shine, Richard A., 151
Shollar, Barbara, 194
Shor, Ira, 60, 62
Shortreed, Ian, 130
Shostak, Robert, 168, 188
Shriner, Delores, 178, 188
Sieben, J. Kenneth, 221
Silber, Patricia, 117
Silver, Marcia, 217
Simmons, Jo An M., 196
Sirc, Geoffrey, 173, 174, 175
Slaughter, Virginia B., 109, 113, 143, 146, 152, 156
Sledd, James, 10, 27, 108
Smith, Charles, 169, 171
Smith, Frank, 51, 54, 66
Smith, Louise Z., 7, 194, 200
Smith, William L., 168
Smitherman, Geneva, 97
Snow, Jerry J., 156
Snow, Marguerite A., 126
Socrates, 27
Sommers, Elizabeth A., 179
Sommers, Nancy, 22
Soppelsa, Betty, 126
Souberman, Ellen, 52
Southwell, Michael G., 111, 150, 167, 192, 236
Spack, Ruth, 125, 126
Spangler, Mary S., 231
Spann, Milton G., 147, 156
Spear, Karen I., 21, 33, 34, 198
Spooner, Michael, 181

Sridhar, S. N., 118
Stafford, Donald G., 33
Stallard, Charles, 35
Stay, Byron, 198
Steinberg, Daniel R., 23
Sternglass, Marilyn S., 23, 100, 200
Stevik, Earl W., 121
Steward, Joyce S., 194
Stewart, Etta M., 145
Stewart, William A., 97, 110
Stokes, Shelley J., 58
Storms, Gilbert, 177
Stotsky, Sandra L., 26, 86
Stratton, R. E., 55
Street, Brian, 49, 51, 57, 60, 66
Strickland, James, 168, 169
Strom, Virginia, 131
Strong, William L., 84, 200
Stull, William, 200
Sudol, Ronald A., 179, 180
Suggs, Lena R., 80
Suhor, Charles, 178
Sullivan, Kathleen E., 233
Summerlin, Charles T., 210
Sutton, Doris G., 155
Swartz, Richard, 225
Szwed, John F., 62

Tate, Gary, 8
Taylor, Barry, 124
Taylor, D. S., 128
Taylor, David, 194
Taylor, Karl K., 35, 151
Taylor, Orlando, 106
Teichman, Milton, 176
Terrebonne, Nancy G., 101
Thomas, Leon L., 147
Thomas-Ruzic, Maria, 120
Thompson-Panos, Karyn, 120
Thoms, John C., 179
Tierney, Robert J., 87
Traub, Valerie, 195
Tricomi, Elizabeth, 83, 109, 122
Trimble, Louis, 126
Troyka, Lynn Q., 7, 19, 20, 22, 24, 221, 229
Tucker, G. Richard, 120
Tucker, Marc S., 166

Turner, Judith A., 166
Tyner, Thomas E. 230

Ullman, Stephen, 78

Vande Kopple, William J., 88
VanDeWeghe, Richard P., 214
van Dijk, Tuen A., 88
Vann, Roberta J., 129
Vasconcellos, Mary T., 181
Veit, Richard C., 200
Villafane, Santiago, 119
Vik, Gretchen N., 145, 157
Vockell, Edward L., 171
Von Blum, Ruth, 170
Vygotsky, Lev S., 21, 36, 52, 53, 55,
    64, 67, 198

Wageman, J., 175
Wagner, Geoffrey, 156
Wahlstrom, Billie J., 172, 180
Waldo, Mark, 168
Walker, Jim, 62
Wall, Susan V., 20, 152, 153
Wanderman, Richard, 173
Wardhaugh, Ronald, 118
Ware, Elaine, 201
Warfel, Harry R., 77
Warnock, John, 55
Waterfall, Clarence M., 84
Watson, Cynthia B., 125
Watson-Gegeo, Karen A., 122
Watt, Ian, 53
Weaver, Constance, 109
Weis, Lois, 60
Weiss, Leonard, 232
Weissberg, Robert C., 127
Weizenbaum, Joseph, 172
Wells, Susan, 53
Werner, Heinz, 39
Werner, Rita, 231

Wertsch, James V., 52
West, Gregory K., 126
Whitaker, Helen, 231
White, Edward M., 147, 148, 149, 155,
    157
Whiteman, Marcia F., 102
Whittaker, Della, 101
Whorf, Benjamin, 78
Widdowson, H. G., 126
Wiener, Harvey S., 3, 145, 150, 152,
    209, 210, 221, 228
Wikborg, Eleanor, 88
Williams, Darnell, 109
Williams, Joseph M., 24, 85, 148
Williamson, Juanita, 97
Williamson, M. N., 24
Willis, Paul, 60
Wilson, Allison, 109, 145, 148
Winchell, Donna H., 230
Winterowd, W. Ross, 78, 80, 85, 122
Witbeck, Michael C., 130
Witte, Stephen P., 25, 86, 127, 132, 155
Wojahn, Patti G., 176
Wolfram, Walter, 96, 97, 107
Womble, Gail G., 174
Wood, Susan, 130
Woodruff, Earl, 171
Wormuth, Deanna, 131
Wresch, William, 170
Wright, Barbara H. W., 100
Wyatt, Victor, 129
Wyrick, Jean, 231

Yelin, Louise, 149, 153
Youdelman, Jeffrey, 154
Young, Richard E., 81
Young, Virginia H., 198

Zamel, Vivian, 124, 128, 130
Zebroski, James Thomas, 53
Zinkgrat, Stephen, 131

Subject Index

Academic: code, 26; English, 96; language, 11, 26; prose, 6; world 6
Academic discourse, 7, 26, 152; analytical thought needed for, 34
Accommodation, 35–37
ACE Newsletter, 165
Acquired language, 120–21
Acquisition theory, application of, 122
Administration, 144; of courses and programs, 156–57
Adult basic writers, socioeconomic patterns of, 20
Adult literacy campaigns, 56, 57–58
Affirmative Action, 1
Africa, 62
Agreement, 147
Algeria, 56
American College Test (ACT), 147
American Indian languages, 119
Analytic: competence, 55; courses, 10, 149–52; scoring, 130–31
Anthropology, 65, 66
Anxiety, 121
Applied linguistics, 2
Aptitude vs. attitude in language learning, 121
Argumentation, 37
Arrangement, 169

Artificial intelligence, 171–72
Assembly on Computers in English (ACE), 165
Assessment, 6; for placement, diagnosis, and proficiency, 145; surveys of, 145
Assignments, 11, 36, 223, 224
Assimilation, 35, 37
Audience, 224, 232–33
Audience awareness, 32, 38–40; cognitive aspects of, 38
Audio-lingual method, 122
Authority, 6
Autotutorial lab, 11, 192

Back to basics, 63
Basic studies seminar, 6
Basic writers, 17–30; attitudes toward, 1; backgrounds of, 18; definition of, 17–20; diversity of, 25; errors made by, 17; maturation of, 21; processes of writing, 196–99; prose of, 23–25; psychological profile of, 21; self-concept of, 21; strategies and processes of, 20–22
Basic writing, anthologies of, 20; book-length studies of, 3–8; courses, 10, 143–63; exercises, 5; history of, 25; programs, 10, 143–63; seminal texts in, 2–8

Beginning teachers, 3
Behaviorism, 31
Bibliographies, 5, 8, 17, 50, 78, 99,
   194, 207
Bidialectalism, 4, 10, 107–8
Black: dialect, 104, 109, 210–11; Eng-
   lish, 96–97; students, 104–5; vs. white
   writing, 100
Black English Vernacular (BEV), 101
Bloom's taxonomy of cognitive skills, 21
Bonehead English, 1
Brainstorming, 197
British examination system, 40
British Schools Counsel Project, 40

Canada, 61
Case studies, 7
CEEB-ECT, 146
Children's development and languages,
   36
Chinese, 101, 119
Class, lower, 19
Cognition and dialect problems, 95
Cognitive: deficiency, 41; immaturity, 34;
   maturity, 67; overload, 197; reduction-
   ism, 42–43; skills, 151
Cognitive development, 9, 198; studies
   of, 33
Cognitive-developmental approach, 32
Cognitive-developmental psychology, 31;
   systematic delineation of, 32
Cognitive psychology, 21, 26; misuse of,
   34
Coherence, 86–89, 126–27, 147, 226; lo-
   cal vs. global, 88
Cohesion, 86, 89, 126–27
Cohesive ties and quality of writing, 87,
   127
Collaboration, 198
College Entrance Examination Board
   (CEEB), 143, 145
Collegiate Microcomputer, 165
Comments on papers, 3
Competence, 110, 120, 210; model, 82
Competence-performance, 9–10
Competency, 148
Composing, 151; process, 22, 31, 35,
   83, 228

Composition: pedagogy, 67; theory, 3
Computer-Assisted Composition Journal,
   165
Computer-assisted instruction (CAI),
   165–66, 167; problems with, 167; textbooks using, 167; writing process and,
   168–71
Computer: laboratories, 179–82; as tutor,
   166–68
Computers, 11, 165–90; case studies
   about, 174–76; controlled studies
   about, 176–78; and instruction, 179–
   82; interactive programs, 11; learning
   disabled students and, 173; research
   on, 170–71; student attitudes toward,
   173–74, 178
Computers and Composition, 165
Conceptual rhetoric, 35
Concrete-operational stage, 33
Conference-centered instruction, 193
Conference methodology, 194–96
Conferences, 3, 7, 194–96; nondirective
   vs. directive, 195; structure of, 194
Conscientization, 62
Content of essays, 20–21
Contrasting paradigms, 110
Contrastive: analysis, 10, 104, 117–18,
   119; rhetoric, 10, 119–20
Controlled vs. free composition, 123–24
Controlled writing, 123–24
Conventions, 4
Coordination, 5
Correction of error, 129. *See also* Errors
Correctness, 7
Course design, 144, 149–54
Courses in: basic writing theory, 213–14;
   composition theory, 213–14
*Creative Word Processing in the Class-
   room*, 165
Credit for basic writing, 156–57
Creolists, 99
Critical reading, 54
Cuba, 58–60
Cultural: factors, 4; heritage, 19; literacy,
   55

Databases, 166
Decentering, 4, 21, 38, 39, 179, 228

Decline in student writing ability, 143
Declining enrollments, 144
Deduction, 36
Deep structure, 82
Descriptive sociolinguistic studies, 96
Developmental levels, 32–35
Developmental models, 21; misuse of, 22; problems with, 22
Developmental psychology, 9, 31–47; problems with, 42; relevance to composition, 32–33
Diagnosis, 10, 130, 144; of essays, 147–48
Dialectic, 6
Dialectical reflection, 62
Dialectical thinkers, 68
Dialect interference, 10, 24, 83, 99, 101, 103
Dialectology, 11
Dialects, 10, 95–116; attitudes toward, 105–6; composition and workbooks and, 111; culture and, 109; definition of, 96; developmental problems of, 99; English as a second language (ESL) and, 110–11; evaluation and, 105; first vs. second, 110; forms of, 95, 98; patterns of, 95–96; pedagogy, 108–12; political issues of, 105–8; positive attitudes toward students' language and culture and, 109; racial prejudice and, 108; self-correction and, 109; significance of, 105; sources of problems of, 99; validity of, 105; variation of, 4, 37; writing features and, 97–98
Diction, 3
Disadvantaged students, 1
Discourse: analysis, 10, 88, 89; community, 9, 41; theory, 85–89; topic, 88
Diversity of basic writers, 19
Drafting, 168–69; revising and, 197
Drills, 6, 110, 200; exercises and, 6
Dualism, 41
Dualistic thinking, 198

Economic development, 58
Edited American English, 96
Edited Written English, 96
Editing, 3, 151, 168–69, 173

Education, 66
Educational Testing Service's Composition Evaluation Scale, 147
Egocentric: speech, 39; stage, 198
Egocentrism, 32, 35, 38
Electronic bulletin board, 181
Elemental skills, 5
Equador, 56
Equilibrium, 32, 34
Error: analysis, 2, 10, 82, 100, 118–19, 199–201; hierarchy, 129; profiles, 23
Errors, 9, 11, 23, 32, 99, 123, 128–30, 192, 210, 221, 223; contextualization of, 24; dialect and, 24; marking of, 130; oral culture and, 24; principles behind, 37; response to, 130; seriousness of, 129
Errors and Expectations, 2
Essays, 151; writing of, 149
Ethiopia, 56
Ethnic dialects, 97
Ethnography, 65
Evaluating: dialect patterns, 105; students, 144–45
Evaluation, 130–32, 144; of courses and programs, 154–56; of student progress, 130; of teaching methods, 130
Exercises, 83, 200; and drills, 6
Exit examinations, 148–49
Experienced teachers, 3
Experimental World Literacy Campaign, 57
Exposition, 5
Extended Teacher Institutes, 208

Fable, 5
Factors affecting second-language learning, 121–22
Faculty, 208
Field dependence-independence, 43
Field theory, 197
First day, 3
Forensic-discussion technique, 5
Formal: courses, 208; operational procedures, 21; operational thought, 34
Formal operational stage, 32, 33, 35; characteristic potentiality of, 33
Fossilization, 118

FREE, 169
Free: composition, 123–24; writing, 169, 170, 224
Functional literacy, 51, 56–57

Generating ideas, 197
Generative rhetoric, 85
Generative-transformational grammar, 9
Geographical dialects, 96
German, 119
Grades, 148
Grammar, 3, 4, 9, 11, 151, 226; basic writing and, 77–84; errors in, 129; exercises in, 223; formal instruction in, 77–80; instruction in, 79–80, 167; mechanics and, 221–22; practice in, 166; as a useful tool, 78; writing and, 81
GRAMMATIK, 169
Graphics processor, 166
Great Divide Theory, 53, 56, 62
Greece, 5

Habit-formation theory, 118
Harvard Bureau of Study Counsel, 41
HBJ Writer, 120
Hemisphericity, 43
Heuristics, 35, 40, 166, 170; software and, 172
Higher education, 25–27
High risk student, 19
Hindi, 119
Hispanic writers, 100–103
History, 66
Holistic: cognitive style, 104; courses, 10, 49, 152–54; evaluation, 146
Holisticism, 157
Holistic scoring, 130–31, 171; reader reliability and, 131
HOLTCOMP, 169
Home dialect, 107
HOMER, 169
Homeric epics, 53
Hunter College Writing Profile and Score Key, 147
Hypercorrection, 98, 100
Hypothetical and deductive reasoning, 36
Hypothetico-deductive reasoning, 36

Idea processors, 171
Ideology, 26, 49, 58, 60
Impromptu speech, 5
Improvements in student writing, 175
Individualized instruction, 179–80
Induction, 5, 36
Inductive approach to spelling errors, 201
Inferential errors, 36
Innate vs. learned cognitive structuring, 54–55
Inquiry, 168–69
Institutes for the Teaching of Writing, 212
Integrated: curriculum, 6; skills model, 156
Intellectual development, 31
Interaction with social context, 153
Interactive computer programs, 170–71
Interference, 118, 122
Interlanguage, 10, 118
Interpreting texts, 88
Invention, 168–69, 231, 232
Iran, 56, 66
Issues, 10

Japanese, 119
Journal of Basic Writing, 2
Journals, 6

Kernal sentence, 6
Korean, 119
Kurzweil Reading Machine, 181

Language acquisition theory, 102, 117, 120–22, 144, 153; vs. learning, 83, 121
Language of the university, 6
Learned languages, 120–21
Lexical errors, 129
Liberal learning, 144
Limits of basic writing courses, 154
Linguistic: behavior, 80, 104; competence, 4; constraints, 101; geographers, 99; issues, 99–105; misconceptions, 2, 3; perspectives, 9–10, 75–139
Linguistics, 3, 65, 66, 77, 210; and basic writing, 98–99; and composition studies, 77

Literacy, 9, 25, 49–74; autonomous model of, 66; biases about, 51; campaigns, 9; causes of, 52–63; cognitive development and, 52–63; critical thought and, 61–62; definition of, 57, 65–67; development of higher thought and, 53–54; economic development and, 57–58; effect of, 56; ideology and, 66; implications of, 54, 63–68; intelligence and, 26; liberation struggles and, 59–60; literature about, 66; misunderstanding about, 50–51; pedagogy and, 63–64; poverty and, 58; reasoning and, 52–53; types of, 66
Literacy theory, 49–74; bibliographies about, 50; definition of, 49–50; not neutral process, 49; not value free, 49
Literary canon, 25
Literature, 53
Litericization, 52
Logic and nature of error, 24
Low road vs. high road transfer, 178

MacProof, 169
Marxist literary theory, 153
Maxims, 5
Measuring writing proficiency, 148
Mechanics, 4, 105, 109
Mentoring, 7
Mexican Americans, 104
Middle-class students, 22
Minorities, 1, 10
Misspelling patterns, 201
Models, 5, 6
Modern grammar, 77–94
Modes of discourse, 150–51, 229, 231, 234
Monitor model for English as a second language (ESL), 120–21
Morals, 5

Narrative and descriptive writing, 37
Narratives, 151
National Assessment of Educational Progress, 88
National Assessment's primary trait scoring, 147

National Council of Teachers of English (NCTE), 165
National Endowment for the Humanities (NEH), 212
Native: language, 4, 117, 118; speaker, 80
Navajo, 101
Negative transference, 118
Nelson-Denny Reading Test, 146
Newsweek, 143
Nicaragua, 58–60; Literacy Crusade of, 59
Noetic operations, 55
Nominal: constructions, 100; vs. verbal style, 172
Nondirective vs. directive conference, 195
Nonliterate people, 51, 54–56
Nonstandard: dialects, 4, 83; English, 10; usage, 100
Nontraditional students, 1, 19; definition of, 19
Normative judgments, 25
Noun clauses, 88

Objective: scoring, 130–31; tests, 144
One-on-one approach, 191
Ontario, 58
Open admissions, 18, 143–44
Oral: communication, 5; language, 101; traditions, 5
Oral-based cultures, 4
Orality, 54
Orality-literacy, 43
Organization of prose, 126–27
ORGANIZE, 169
Overfamiliarity, 35

Parables, 5
Paragraphs, 3, 8, 147, 149, 150, 151, 169, 223, 225–27, 230, 231, 233
Passive competence, 110
Pattern/practice, 110
Pedagogical perspectives, 10, 141–220
Pedagogy, 3, 6, 65, 66; of knowing, 68
Peer: collaboration, 181; questioning activities, 5; review, 229; tutoring, 144; tutors, 7, 11, 196, 198, 208

Perry scheme, 41–42; dualism and, 41; intellectual development and, 21; problems with, 42; relativism and, 41; replication of, 42
Personal: computers, 165; topics, 6; writing, 26–27
Perspective by incongruity, 27
Persuasive writing, 40
Physical act and dialect problems, 99
Piagetian theory, 32, 34–35; accommodation, 34–35; assimilation, 34; egocentrism, 35; equilibrium, 34; stages of development, 32
PLATO, 166–67
Platonic dialogues, 53
Placement, 10, 130, 144, 145–47; definition of, 145; essays, 21; indirect measures or objective tests for, 145–46; multiple-choice examinations for, 146; standardized tests for, 146; tests, 3; writing sample for, 146
Political issues of dialects, 105–8
Postdegree programs, 208
Practicum training program, 214
Prague School of Linguistics, 86
Precollege programs, 1
Preparing: faculty to teach basic writing, 215; part-time faculty to teach basic writing, 216
Preservice and in-service training of teachers, 214
Pretest-posttest research model, 154–56
PREWRITE, 169
Prewriting, 3, 151, 169, 196, 197, 227, 231; computer programs for, 169; conference, 195
Primary: orality, 54; trait scoring, 130, 147
Problem solving, 9, 40–43; audience and, 41; goal setting, 41; inappropriate for basic writers, 41; procedures for, 152
Professional education and training, 208, 211–14
Proficiency, 10, 144
Progymnasmata, 5
Project Jefferson, 181
Proofreading, 181, 201
Prose, 11

Protocol analysis, 40
Psychological problems, 11; of basic writers, 201–2
Psychology, 65, 66; bibliography about, 35; naturalistic vs. philosophical, 53
Punctuation, 7, 8, 151

Qualifications for teachers, 209
Quantitative vs. qualitative evaluation, 154–56
Queens English Project, 212
QUEST, 169
Questioning: process, 195; strategies, 197
Questionnaires, 195–96

Racism, 211
Reader-based prose, 197
Reading, 1, 6, 56, 63, 64, 102, 151, 152–53, 210; level, 143; skills, 153; theory, 11, 102; writing and, 5; and writing as technologies, 50
Reading-writing connection, 6
Reasoning, 67; hypothetical and deductive, 36–37
Reification, 19
Relativism, 41, 43
Remedial composition, 143
Remediation, 26
Research, 8; paper, 151
Researchers, 3, 7
Research in Word Processing Newsletter, 165
Returning papers, 3
Revising, 168–69, 224
Revision, 4, 8, 22, 83, 172, 173, 177, 198; for audience, 40; conference, 195; strategies, 180
Rhetorical: modes, 150, 151; skills, 5; types, 35
Rhetoric and thought, 35
Role-switching activities, 5
Role taking, 38–39
Rules, 2; of English and dialect problems, 99

Schemata, 89
Schema theory, 126

Scholastic Aptitude Test (SAT), 143, 145, 146
Schools and ideology, 60–62
Secondary: education, 1; orality, 54
Second language, 117
Second-language: students, 199; variation, 37
SEER, 2
Self-teaching materials, 192
Seminal texts in basic writing, 2–8
Seminar, 6
Sentence: combining, 10, 83–85, 127–28, 132, 147, 150, 200–201, 222, 230; manipulation, 3; sense, 147
Sentence-level errors, 129
Sentences, 8, 149
Simplified language, 121
Skills, 5, 125–28, 144; programs, 156–57; of teachers, 209–10
Social: contexts, 5, 11, 152; dialects, 96
Social class, 9; and literacy, 58
Socialized speech, 39
Social science perspectives, 8–9, 17–74
Social sciences, 8
Sociolinguists, 99
Sociology, 66
Software, 168, 169
Speech: patterns, 99; and writing, 36, 101
Spelling, 3, 7, 8, 127, 128, 151
Spoken: vs. written forms, 111; vs. written language, 197; word, 2
Spreadsheet, 166
Staffing, 144
Stages of writing, 228
Standard English, 4, 96, 99, 105–6; descriptive vs. prescriptive views of, 96; usage, 199
Static vs. dynamic ties, 87
Structural: grammar, 80–81; linguistics, 9
Structure, 5; of writing conferences, 194
Students' Right to Their Own Language, 27, 99, 106
Subfreshmen, 1
Subordination, 5
Sudan, 57
Synectics, 169
Syntactic: growth, 84; maturity, 84, 100

Syntax, 127, 151
Systematic instruction, 144

Tagmemics, 80–81
Target language, 118
Teacher: preparation, 207–20; training, 3
Teacher-centered classroom, 11
Teachers, 7, 11; as writers, 210
Teaching Assistants (TAs), 214
Teaching English as a Second Language (TESL), 117–39
Tehran, 57
Testing, 3; instruments and measures, 130–31
Text analysis, 23
Text-analysis programs, 171–72
Textbooks, 11, 221–38
Text theory, 86
Theme/rheme, 88
Thesis statement, 221
Thinking, 232
Third World, 61; literacy programs, 58–59
TICCIT, 166–67
Topic: selection, 131; sentences, 6, 221
Topic/comment, 88
Topic-sculpting activities, 85
Traditional grammar, 79–80
Training: teachers, 3, 207–20; tutors, 216–18
Training programs, 11; in basic writing, 211–14
Transformational generative grammar, 81, 118
Transformational grammar, 81–85; limits of, 85
True-concept formation, 36
T-units, 131–32
Tutorials, 7, 194–96, 208
Tutors, 11, 197, 198, 216–18; training, 216–18

UNESCO, 56–57
Unprepared students, 1
Usage, 8, 105, 147

Vai, 64
Vocabulary, 7, 8, 26, 127, 128, 151

WANDAH, 170
West Africa, 64
Word processing, 166, 172–79; advantages of, 172; revision and, 173
Workbooks, 4
Worksheets, 197
Writer-based prose, 21, 197, 198
Writer's Helper, 169
Writer's Workbench, 171

Writing: across the curriculum, 153; anxiety, 202; centers, 3, 11; laboratories, 11, 144, 150, 191–205, 208, 214, 216; portfolio, 149; process, 3, 124–25, 151, 181, 192, 199, 201, 223, 224, 226; process lab, 193; proficiency test, 148; samples, 144, 146; as a second dialect, 110
Written code, 4

About the Contributors

STEPHEN A. BERNHARDT is Associate Professor of English at New Mexico State University where he works closely with the graduate programs in rhetoric and professional communication. He has published articles on scientific and technical writing, computers and composition, and teacher training. His current research involves hypermedia documentation and workplace literacy.

RICHARD A. FILLOY is a teacher and writer living in Eugene, Oregon. He has previously taught at the University of California at Berkeley, the University of Southern California, and the University of Oregon.

MICHAEL D. HOOD is Associate Professor of English at Belmont Abbey College, Belmont, NC, where he directs freshman composition and the great books program. In 1985 he was the first recipient of the Adrian Award for Teaching Excellence at Belmont Abbey College. His teaching and research interests include the classical enthymeme and composition pedagogy, modern rhetorical theory, and medieval literature and Chaucer.

GLYNDA HULL is Visiting Assistant Professor of Education at the University of California at Berkeley, where she teaches courses on literacy and technology and composition theory and research. She was named a National Council of Teachers of English Promising Researcher and received an Outstanding Dissertation Award for Empirical Research from the American Educational Research Association. Her publications include articles and chapters on editing, basic writing, and technology. Her current research focuses on underpreparation in literacy skills and workplace literacy.

MARTIN J. JACOBI is Assistant Professor of English at Clemson University, where he teaches classical and modern rhetoric, business and technical writing, and American literature. He has published articles on rhetorical theory, professional writing, and modern American dramatists. He is currently working on a book on Richard M. Weaver, the twentieth-century American rhetorician.

ANDREA LUNSFORD is Professor of English and Vice Chair of Rhetoric and Composition at The Ohio State University. She has co-authored or co-edited *The St. Martin's Handbook*, *Four Worlds of Writing*, *Preface to Critical Reading*, *Essays on Classical Rhetoric and Modern Discourse*, and *The 1987 English Coalition Conference: Democracy through Language*. A recipient with Lisa Ede of the Richard Braddock Award for the best article published in *College Composition and Communication* (1984) and of the MLA Mina Shaughnessy Award for the best book on the teaching of language and literature, she is co-author of the forthcoming *Singular Texts/Plural Authors: The Theory and Practice of Collaborative Writing* (with Lisa Ede) and editor of the forthcoming *Alexander Bain's English Composition and Rhetoric*.

RONALD F. LUNSFORD is Professor of English and Head at Southwest Missouri State University. Previously, he taught at Clemson University, where he directed the Composition and Rhetoric Program. He is co-editor of *Research in Composition and Rhetoric* (1984) and co-author of *Writing: Discovering Form and Meaning* (1984). His teaching and research interests include composition and linguistics.

MICHAEL MONTGOMERY is Associate Professor of English at the University of South Carolina at Columbia, where he specializes in English linguistics and American dialectology. He has edited *Language Variety in the South: Perspectives in Black and White* and *Annotated Bibliography of Southern American English*. He directed the USC Program in Linguistics from 1982 to 1985 and teaches courses in applied linguistics, sociolinguistics, and other areas.

MICHAEL G. MORAN is Associate Professor of English at the University of Georgia where he directs the freshman English program. He has directed similar programs at Clemson University and the University of Rhode Island. He is the co-editor of *Research in Composition and Rhetoric* (1984) and *Research in Technical Communication* (1985), which won a National Council of Teachers of English award in 1986. His teaching and research interests include eighteenth-century British literature, history of technical communication, and classical and contemporary rhetorical theory and pedagogy.

DONNA BETH NELSON is the Acting Director of the General Studies Writing Program at Bowling Green State University. Previously, she served nine years as Assistant Director of the Writing Laboratory at the University of Wisconsin–